Graves's Studies in the History of Astrology Volume I

TECHNICAL & PLANETARY DEVELOPMENTS IN ASTROLOGY

by

Philip Graves

REVELORE PRESS
Olympia WA, 2025

Technical & Planetary Developments in Astrology
Graves's Studies in the History of Astrology Volume 1

Copyright © 2025 Philip Graves
First edition published in 2025 by
REVELORE PRESS

All rights reserved. No part of this publication may be reproduced or transmitted in any form or by any means, electronic or mechanical, including photocopy, without permission in writing from the publisher. Reviewers may quote brief passages, as may scholars writing astrological journal articles.

Book design by Jenn Zahrt.
Cover design by Alberto Forero.
Cover images selected from (left to right, at bottom) "Dodekatopos" from *L'astrologie grecque*, Auguste Bouché-Leclercq (1899); "Sun with Sword" from *Destructorium vitiorum ex similitudinum creaturarum exemplorum...* Jean Belot (1500); aspect circle from *L'introduction au jugement des astres; avec un Traité des élections propres pour le commencement des choses*, Claude Dariot (1558); (front and back background) *Dess Menschen Circkel* by Leonhardt Thurneysser zum Thurn(1575).

Publisher's Cataloging-in-Publication
(Provided by Cassidy Cataloguing Services, Inc.)

Names: Graves, Philip (Philip Macartney), author.
Title: Technical & planetary developments in astrology / by Philip Graves.
Other titles: Technical and planetary developments in astrology
Description: First edition. | Olympia, WA : Revelore Press, 2025. | Series: Graves, Philip (Philip Macartney). Graves's studies in the history of astrology ; v. 1. | Includes bibliographical references and index.
Identifiers: ISBN: 9781947544796 (paperback)
Subjects: LCSH: Astrology--History. | Planets. | Houses (Astrology) | Aspect (Astrology) | Sun.
Classification: LCC: BF1671 .G73 2025 | DDC: 133.509--dc23

ISBN: 9781947544796
Printed worldwide through Ingram.

Revelore Press
1910 4th AVE E PMB141
Olympia WA 98506
United States
www.revelore.press

Other books in the *Graves's Studies in the History of Astrology* series

Volume II - *Developments in the philosophy and literature of astrology*

Part 1: Modern Developments Since 1890: 1. How have astrology's philosophy and public image evolved since 1890?; 2. Five Myths of Modern Astrology Reviewed; 3. When did modern astrologers first agree that astrology is not a science?; 4. An Exposition of the Scientific Astrology Movement, 1890-1939.

Part 2: Developments from 1500 to 1900: 5. Astrologer to the Pope and the Holy Roman Emperor: Luca Gaurico; 6. Prefatory poems in English Astrology Books, 1647-1697; 7. The Philosophy of Astrology in Nineteenth Century England: a Literary Survey, 1784-1811; 8. A brief overview of the 19th century astrological revival, 1784-1895; 9. True Pioneer of Astrology? The Career of Astrologer Luke Dennis Broughton in Context

Part 3: Primary Sources: Astrologer Profiles in The Mountain Astrologer, 2021-2024; 10. Gerolamo Cardano; 11. Marcus Manilius; 12. Francesco Giuntini; 13. Heinrich Rantzau; 14. Claude Dariot; 15. John Chamber, Christopher Heydon and George Carleton; 16. Claudius Ptolemy; 17. Giovanni Antonio Magini; 18. Tommaso Campanella; 19. William Lilly; 20. Andrea Argoli; 21. William Ramesey; 22. Placido de Titis; 23. Nicholas Culpeper; 24. Jean-Baptiste Morin de Villefranche

Volume III - *The English Astrological Revival and Early Astrological Journals*

Part 1: From Sibly to Zadkiel: Astrologers and Texts of the 19th Century English Astrological Revival: 1. On the Supposed Death of Astrology in the 18th Century; 2. The Sibly Brothers, J. M. Ashmand and John Cooper; 3. George Mensforth, C. Heydon Junior and Henry Lemoine; 4. John Worsdale Senior and Junior, Thomas Orger and P. J. Swift; 5. Thomas White and George Beaumont; 6. James Wilson; 7. Robert Cross Smith, Mr. Dixon and John Varley; 8. Thomas Oxley and Rupertus Stella; 9. R. J. Morrison, and T. H. Moody; 10. Zuriel, J. T. Hacket and Ebn Shemaya; 11. W. J. Simmonite; 12. William Sharp Cross, Christopher Cooke, Colonel Clements and Edward Vaughan Williams; Epilogue: Alfred Pearce; Appendix: Historical and Theological Astrological Enquiry from 1784 to 1863.

Part 2: Early Astrological Journals; 1. A brief history of astrological journals Part 1: 1700-1830; 2. A brief history of astrological journals Part 2: 1831-1859; 3. A brief history of astrological journals Part 3: 1860-1886; 4. A brief history of astrological journals Part 4: 1887-1890; 5. A brief history of astrological journals Part 5: 1891-1904; 6. A brief history of astrological journals Part 6: 1905-1929 (approx. dates); 7. A history of the earliest French-language Astrological Journals 1904-1939; 8. A history of the earliest German-language Astrological Journals, 1910-1941; 9. A history of astrological prophetic almanacs from 1819 to 1940.

Volume IV - *A Concise History of Western Astrology*

1. Ancient Greek and Roman Astrology; 2. Medieval Astrology; 3. Renaissance and 17th-Century Astrology; 4. 18th- and 19th-Century Astrology; 5. 20th-Century Astrology

for all honest seekers after a truthful, accurate and unprejudiced representation of the history of astrology, and in memory of my late friend Maurice McCann, whose enthusiasm for scholarly astrological research from primary sources contributed significantly to the development of mine

Table of Contents

Acknowledgments   xii

Foreword by Nicholas Campion   xiii

Introduction   xv

Part One:
The Evolution of the Astrological Houses and Astrological Aspect Theory

1. From Manilius to Modernity:
A Study of the Evolution of the Meanings of the Astrological Houses   3
- Introduction   3
- The *Oktatropos* or *Oktatopos*   5
    - i. Thrasyllus   5
    - ii. The Michigan Astrological Papyrus   6
    - iii. Antiochus of Athens   8
    - iv. Julius Firmicus Maternus   8
- Lot-Houses   9
- The Evolution of the Meanings of the 12 Houses   10
    1. Marcus Manilius (fl. 1st century CE)   10
    2. Thrasyllus (died 36 CE)   12
    3. Dorotheus of Sidon (c. 75 CE)   14
    4. Ptolemy (c. 100–178 CE)   15
    5. Vettius Valens (c. 120–175 CE)   15
    6. Antiochus of Athens, *The Thesaurus* (summary)   17
    7. Michigan Astrological Papyrus (estd. 2nd century CE)   18
    8. Porphyry (c. 232–304 CE)   19
    9. Julius Firmicus Maternus (c. 280 – c. 360 CE – text ca. 335 CE)   20
    10. Paulus Alexandrinus – (born 330 CE; written 378 CE)   20
    11. Hephaestio of Thebes (born 380 CE; text written ca. 415 CE)   22
    12. Rhetorius the Egyptian (ca. 505 CE)   22
    13. *Liber Hermetis*   24
    14. Masha'Allah (c. 740–815 CE)   24
    15. Omar of Tiberias (died c. 815 CE)   25
    16. Abu 'Ali Al-Khayyat (c. 770–835 CE)   26
    17. Sahl ibn Bishr (fl. 811–825 CE)   27
    18. Abū Ma'Shar al-Balkhî (c. 787–886)   29
    19. Al-Qabîsî (d. 967)   30
    20. Al-Rijāl (Haly Abenragel) (d. ca. 1040)   31
    21. Al-Bîrūnî (973 – ca. 1048)   35
    22. Abraham Ibn Ezra (c. 1089–1164)   36
    23. Guido Bonatti (ca. 1210–1295)   38

24. Leopold of Austria (compilation written c. 1271) — 40
25. Johann Schöner (1477–1547) — 41
26. Claude Dariot (1533–1594) — 42
27. William Lilly (1602–1681) — 44
28. Morin de Villefranche (1583–1656) — 46
29. John Gadbury (1627–1704) — 48
30. Alan Leo (1860–1917) — 50
Conclusion — 55
Endnotes — 55

2. From Kepler to Addey: A Chronology of Developments in Astrological Aspect Theory from 1602 to 1976 — 63

Part One: Traditional Approaches to Astrological Aspects — 63
   i. Which aspects were traditionally recognised? — 63
   ii. How were aspect orbs traditionally calculated? — 64
Part Two: The Aspect Innovations of Johannes Kepler — 66
   i. What changes did Kepler propose to the system of aspects? — 66
   ii. Reception of the harmonic aspects after Kepler, 1647–1913 — 68
      a. William Lilly — 68
      b. James Wilson — 68
      c. Zadkiel — 69
      d. W. H. Chaney — 70
      e. Llewellyn George — 71
Part Three: Astrologers' Departure from Planetary Orbs, 1861–1900 — 72
   i. Richard Morrison (1861) — 72
   ii. W. H. Chaney (1890) — 73
   iii. Alan Leo and Frederick Lacey (1890) — 75
   iv. Robert T. Cross (1891) — 79
   v. H. S. Green (1892) — 80
   vi. Alfred Pearce (1892) — 81
   vii. George Wilde and J. Dodson (1894) — 82
   viii. Alan Leo (1897) — 82
   ix. Sepharial (1898) — 83
Part Four: 20th-Century Developments in Harmonic Aspect Theory — 84
   i. Noviles gaining acceptance?
      The aspect instruction of Karl Brandler-Pracht — 85
   ii. Septiles and Quarti-squares?
      The new aspect innovations of George Wilde — 85
   iii. Neutral 15° Aspects? The ideas of A. Frank Glahn — 87
   iv. Potent 15° Aspects? The Notions of K. W. von Elmensberg — 88
   v. The Numerological Circle Division Factor Theory
      of Charles E. O. Carter — 89
   vi. Consolidation of Harmonic Aspect Theory by Dr. Walter Koch — 91

vii. Wider adoption of quartisextiles –
  the testimony of Thomas Ring					93
viii. Harmonic Theory Revisited:
  the Integrally Harmonic Astrological Philosophy of John Addey	95
Afterword: the Statistical Research of Karl-Ernst Krafft		98
Appendix: Addey's System Moderated:
  The Graves Method of Orb Calculation				98
The Harmonics after Addey – A summary Bibliography, 1977 to 2019	102
Endnotes								104

Part Two:
Astrologers' modern treatments of the Sun,
and integration of the outer planets and Lilith

3. The Rise of the Sun: the Natal Sun Emphasised, 1887–1959		113
  Part 1: A Summary of Sun-sign Writings before 1887			113
  Part 2: Butler's Revolution:
    Solar Biology and the Soli-Lunar Polarities unleashed		117
  Part 3: The Solar Revolution Reverberates: Increased Solar Prominence
    in General Astrological Writings, 1889 to 1952			123
  Part 4: Solely the Sun:
    The Unstoppable Rise of the Sun-sign Primer, 1894 to 1959		124
  Part 5: Law of the Lights:
    Works on the Sun- and Moon-sign Combinations after Butler		131
  Part 6: The signs of the zodiac divided:
    The Draw of the Degrees, 1879–1953				132
  Part 7: Lustre of the Luminaries through the Lens of Leo:
    Alan Leo's teachings around the natal Sun and Moon, 1896–1913	135
  Endnotes								145

4. The Early History of Sun-sign Forecasting and Newspaper Astrology, 1890–1937
  Introduction: What is Sun-sign Forecasting and Why is it so Controversial?	152
  Part 1: Precursors to Sun-sign Forecasting in the late-19th-C. Astrological Press	154
  Part 2: Representation of astrology in United States Newspapers before 1910	155
  Part 3: The first regular newspaper astrology columns			161
  Part 4: Early Solar Degree Area Forecast Columns			164
  Part 5: The first twelve-paragraph Sun-sign forecast columns		167
  Part 6: The first Sun-sign forecasting in the UK press		171
  Part 7: The true role of R. H. Naylor in the history of newspaper astrology	172
  Conclusion								175
  Endnotes								176

5. **The Earliest Astrological Conceptualisations of the Planet Uranus, 1781–1839**
    When was Uranus first discovered? ... 181
    How and when did Uranus come by its name? ... 182
    How did astrologers react to the discovery of Uranus? ... 184
        The Conjuror's Magazine (1791–93) ... 185
        Thomas White (1811) ... 187
        P. J. Swift (1812) ... 187
        The Monthly Correspondent on Physical and Prognostic Astronomy (1814) ... 188
        James Wilson (1819) ... 192
        The Straggling Astrologer ... 194
    Uranus invoked as a contributory cause of major fires ... 195
    Uranus as a cause of death by transit ... 197
    On the question of the essential dignities of Uranus ... 197
        The Spirit of Partridge (1824) ... 198
        Robert Cross Smith (Raphael I) (1828) ... 200
        Thomas Oxley (1830) ... 203
        Rupertus Stella (1832) ... 203
        Richard Morrison (1833) ... 204
        The Horoscope (1834) ... 205
    Uranus in the prediction of weather ... 206
    Uranus in the prediction of Earthquakes ... 206
    Uranus in Mundane Astrology ... 208
    Debates over the influence and essential dignities of Uranus ... 208
    Uranus in nativities and as a cause of critical illness and death ... 210
        David Parkes (1839) ... 212
    Conclusion ... 214
    Endnotes ... 214

6. **When Did Astrologers First Associate Neptune with Pisces?** ... 223
    Introduction: When and how was Neptune discovered? ... 223
    Part One: Why did it take so long for astrologers to incorporate Uranus and Neptune into their practice? ... 224
    Part Two: The first published sources on the question of Neptune's sign rulership ... 227
        1. Alfred Pearce (1880) ... 227
        2. Friend of J. T. Campbell (1888) ... 228
        3. John Ackroyd (1890) ... 228
        4. Nemo (pseud.) (1892) ... 229
        5. Thomas H. Burgoyne (1892) ... 230
        6. "Sagittarius" (1894) ... 230
    Conclusion ... 232
    Endnotes ... 233

7. The First Published Assessments on the Sign Rulership of Pluto — 235
The first published assessments on the sign rulership of Pluto, 1897–1931 — 235
- 1. Fomalhaut: Aries (1897) — 235
- 2. Isabelle Pagan: Scorpio (1907; 1908; 1911) — 236
- 3. A. E. Thierens: Aries (1911 / 1931) — 238
- 4. A. M. Wrey: Scorpio (1913) — 238
- 5. Sepharial: Aries or Scorpio (1918) — 239
- 6. E. Caslant: indeterminate, probably Aries (undated, before 1926) — 239
- 7. Francis Rolt-Wheeler: indeterminate (1930) — 241
- 8. Elizabeth Aldrich: indeterminate (1930) — 241
- 9. L. H. Weston: indeterminate (1930) — 242
- 10. Llewellyn George: Scorpio (1930) — 243
- 11. Frederick Thoresby: Scorpio (1930) — 247
- 12. J. P. Gross: Leo (1930–31) — 247
- 13. Bessie Leo; and 'E. S.': Scorpio (1931) — 248
- 14. Karleen S. Lyon (presumed): Scorpio (tentative) (1931) — 248
- 15. E. H. C. Pagan: Scorpio (1931) — 249
- 16. C.E.O. Carter: indeterminate (connections with Cancer, Scorpio) (1931) — 250
- 17. Mabel Baudot: Scorpio (1931) — 252

Conclusion — 253
Endnotes — 254

8. Lilith in Astrology: Second Moon, Asteroid, or Lunar Apogee? — 255
Part One: Lilith as a Second Moon of the Earth: Speculations, 1898–1918 — 255
- Sepharial's role in the naming of Dark Moon Lilith — 256
- From Two Moons to Three? — 258
- The Influence of Dark Moon Lilith: first judgements — 259
- The Dark Moon Wars: Sepharial clashes with Wilson — 261
- Three More Dark Moons? The mysteries deepen! — 264
- Fading Interest: Alan Leo Marginalises Lilith — 268
- Alfred Pearce on Lilith: Total Disinterest — 269
- Early French sources on Dark Moon Lilith (selection) — 269
- Later American Sources on Dark Moon Lilith (summary) — 270

Part Two: Black Moon Lilith: first conceptualisations, 1935–1943 — 271
- Later treatments of Black Moon Lilith: selected references — 275

Part Three: Lilith as Asteroid – early research, 1980–2000 (summary) — 276
Endnotes — 277

Index — 281

Acknowledgements

My thanks to Smiljana Gavrančić for her encouragement of my work in the history of astrology and for previously publishing six of the eight studies in this volume in *Infinity Astrological Magazine* in 2019 and 2020; to Lucia Bellizia and Filip Filipov for inviting me to contribute the lecture *From Manilius to Modernity* to the Third European Conference of Astrology, 2021; and to Kim Farnell, without whose pioneering research on the history of Sun-sign astrology as published in her 2007 book *Flirting with the Zodiac* the foundation of knowledge that paved the way for my two chapters on modern historical developments relating to the astrological Sun in this volume would have been significantly poorer.

Foreword
by Nicholas Campion

Philip Graves' meticulous and detailed examination of technical issues in the history of astrology marks an original contribution to our understanding of the development and nature of western astrology. Graves has taken eight specific areas of astrological interpretation, all of which are, in their different ways, fundamental to both the practice of astrology and its cultural position. Concerning the practice of astrology, Graves has documented the development of the meaning of the houses, planetary aspect theory from the seventeenth century onwards, and the textual history of the attribution of meaning and rulership to the three principal 'outer planets', Uranus, Neptune and Pluto, as well as discussions concerning the minor, and loosely-defined body, Lilith. As far as astrology's cultural position and mass appeal is concerned, Graves has documented the development of the ascent of the Sun-sign to its central interpretative role, and the early appearance of the so-called Sun-sign column. He both has questioned the widespread argument that the theosophical astrologer Alan Leo was responsible for the importance attributed to the Sun-sign and overthrows what is now known to be the myth that R.H. Naylor originated the modern newspaper astrology column in 1930.

Graves' fascinating account of the development of the meaning of the astrological houses, aspects, and outer planet rulerships, provides insights into how they are both created and change over time. He therefore reinforces the perspective of those modern astrologers (such as Leo's fellow, but later, Theosophist, Dane Rudhyar) for whom the meanings attributed to astrological symbols were culturally relative (even if they were still believed to provide insight into deeper spiritual truths). He also therefore challenges those astrologers for whom such astrological factors represent some kind of fixed objective truth in themselves.

The boom, small though it is in relation to other areas, in the historiography of astrology over the last fifty years, has been almost entirely concerned with its ideas and intellectual constructs, or 'mentalities', and with social history. Only historians of Mesopotamian astrology have seriously considered technical matters. Graves has done us all a favour by opening a way to the study of the history of technical methods, and the basis on which astrologers' interpretations are constructed, from the Hellenistic period onwards. He has provided future students of the history of astrology with a pathway which can no longer be ignored.

Graves' work is therefore entirely in line with the approaches we have developed in teaching the history of astrology in the MA in Cultural Astronomy and Astrology at the University of Wales Trinity Saint David, where we insist that students explore not just what astrologers say about what they do, but what they actually do. That is, astrologers may write one thing about what they think astrology is, but their delineations of sample horoscopes may tell another story. Graves does not look at individual chart delineations, but he examines the development of the fundamental claims which underpin those delineations.

Graves' book is vital documentary history. It should be essential reading both for those historians who wish to understand the development of technical astrology, and for those students of astrology who wish to be better informed about the foundations of their own practice.

Nicholas Campion
University of Wales Trinity Saint David
February 27th 2025

Introduction

This volume is the first to go to print with Revelore Press in a projected series of three main volumes compiling studies in the history of astrology that I have undertaken primarily for the English-speaking astrological press and international astrological conferences since 2014. In addition to the three main volumes, a fourth, slim volume entitled *A Concise History of Western Astrology* is in preparation.

Although I have never pursued higher academic degrees, and some academic reviewers may therefore, perhaps with good reason, initially feel minded to doubt my suitedness to writing such studies, the entire text has been peer-reviewed and approved for publication with only minor amendments by my PhD-qualified colleague Dr. Jenn Zahrt of Revelore Press, for which I am most grateful.

To those unfamiliar with my background, I would wish to state that the attributes that I believe qualify me to write with authority on the history of astrology can be summarised as follows:

Between 1993 and 1997, I was a full-time student on a demanding BA (Hons.) in French at the University of Hull, which at the time was a nationally acknowledged Centre of Excellence for the teaching of French. Besides honing my language skills, the course included many classic works of literature ranging from the middle ages to the 20th century, many of which dealt with complex philosophical concepts. It also required the writing of a 10,000-word originally researched dissertation in French, for which purpose I chose a subject close to my heart, the history and philosophy of the modern environmental movement. Research towards this dissertation as well as the many modules on the course as a whole instilled in me sound academic discipline. Alongside the French syllabus, I was able to study Spanish for one year, political theory for one year, and philosophy for one year, all in the guise of a system known as Extra-Departmental Options.

Perhaps somewhat ironic in view of the degree to which astrology has conventionally been frowned upon within academia is that it was during my studies towards my BA that my serious interest in astrology was first awakened and that I began to learn its methods and techniques from modern books. My long 'year abroad' in France before the final year of my taught degree studies gave me ample free time in which to study astrology; and by the time of my graduation with upper second-class honours in the summer of 1997, I had also incidentally developed a small collection of some sixty modern books on astrology.

For me, there was actually no contradiction between these two simultaneous paths of unlike study. Academically, I had been studying the arts and humanities, and I was deeply interested in philosophy and in the exploration and evaluation of ideas and experiences at the fringes of science, with dream interpretation having already occupied my interest for years before my first investigations of astrology.

Already in the late summer of 1996, my fascination with astrological concepts after a year of intensive astrological studies had led me to develop my own speculative but rationally guided system for calculating the orbs of astrological aspects in a mathematically coherent, systematic fashion. I joined the Astrological Association for the first time around September 1996 in order to have an article presenting this system considered for publication. In the event, it was not published, but a record of the methodology I proposed in that piece and my reasons for proposing it has been retained as an afterword to the study of the historical evolution of published methods for the calculation of astrological aspects that is found in this volume.

Since 2001, I have been actively involved in the astrology community online. It was that December that I was first appointed as assistant-manager by the manager of a fledgling astrology-themed web group on the MSN Groups network, with a view to solidifying my contributions. I responded by developing original educational astrological articles for the group, which by April 2004 extended to an expansive set of instructive material on a host of astrological topics, easily enough to have filled a book of over 200 pages if it had been conventionally typeset and printed. The challenge of preparing this material on the basis of solid research and to an accurate standard also motivated me to rapidly expand my collection of printed source material on astrology during these years, with the result that by the time the last of those articles appeared that Spring, I was in possession of 300 books on astrology.

Among my acquisitions during the intervening years had been assorted traditional and early modern astrology texts as published or reprinted by Ascella, ARHAT, Project Hindsight, Ballantrae Reprint, and Kessinger Publishing, in addition to Lee Lehman's secondary studies of traditional astrological methods as published by Whitford Press. These sources and commentaries had allowed me to present each astrological topic covered in the group from an historical perspective as well as a modern one.

At the same time, I was aware that there were many more historical sources on the subject that were as yet unexplored, and in many cases still unavailable in modern editions or reprints. It was with this in mind that a loftier vision crystallised in my mind: that of developing a more extensive astrological library that would gather as many such sources as possible and enable the development of source lists on all astrological topics, as well as ultimately historical research into their transmission over time. I knew that such a quest would be neither easy nor cheap, but facilitated by some family money inherited during the remaining portion of the 2000s, I was able to pursue it faster than I had at first anticipated.

Already by 2010, I was in possession of 4,000 books and pamphlets on astrology, including an increasing number in French, my second language, my knowledge of which it seemed only fitting to put to full use in this area of research, and a small number in German. During the 2010s, this collection continued to expand; and by the end of 2023, it had reached 10,000 discrete books and pamphlets, as well as 14,000 issues of periodicals.

Having almost constant and direct access to this independently curated collection of printed materials on astrology has allowed me to research numerous historical astrological topics from primary as well as secondary sources. The potential in this direction was already apparent in 2006, when my late friend Maurice McCann, to whom this volume is partly dedicated, consulted me for help with sources towards a dissertation he was undertaking for his MA in Cultural Astronomy and Astrology in connection with the Sophia Centre. He was himself researching modern changes to the history of astrological aspects, but lacked access to some of the 19th-century sources that by then I had collected, and I was able to help him in ways that he found meaningful.

Between 2005 and 2012, I presented various pieces of historical research of my own informally on Deborah Houlding's Skyscript forum, as and when inspired by new findings in recently acquired and inspected sources. Since 2014, however, my historical research has in many cases been presented more formally, in some cases only on the pages of my own website, but more usually in print journals and at astrological conferences.

My privileged ready access to the far-reaching collection of primary sources that I have assembled and shelved in my own home has given me ample research facility; and with it, valid causes to challenge and dispute some received historical narratives regarding the modern history of astrology in particular. Keen-eyed readers will note that I am eager to dispel myths arising from misleading secondary texts on the history of astrology or from other sources of misinformation. This is because I bow to truth and not to the authority of the writers of past accounts. The history of astrology is still being discovered, and many of the existing printed narratives on the early modern and modern periods in particular are woefully inadequate and inaccurate, according to my research, hence the need for these studies informed by the close inspection of primary sources to see the light of day.

This first volume of my collected historical studies is divided into two parts with distinct themes. Part 1 looks at two distinct areas of technical developments in astrology: the evolution of the meanings accorded to the astrological houses from ancient to modern times, and developments in the theory of astrological aspects since Johannes Kepler's day.

The first chapter, *From Manilius to Modernity*, is the complete text of the lecture I was invited to give for the Third European Conference on Astrology held on November 13th, 2021.

Chapter 2, *From Kepler to Addey*, was first published in *Infinity Astrological Magazine*, September/October 2020.

Part 2 investigates six areas in which the celestial bodies have come under new or changed consideration in the modern period. Two of these studies concern the increased use of the Sun in modern astrology, with one of these focusing on its natal uses and the other on its use in forecasting. Three of them explore astrologers' adaptations to the discoveries of what have conventionally been considered the outer planets, Uranus, Neptune and Pluto. The final study seeks to untangle the convoluted history surrounding the different modern astrological concepts termed Lilith.

Chapter 3, *The Rise of the Sun*, was first published in *Infinity Astrological Magazine*, November / December 2020.

Chapter 4, *The Early History of Sun-sign Forecasting and Newspaper Astrology*, was researched and written during 2020 and submitted for publication in *Infinity Astrological Magazine*, January/February 2021. However, the magazine, which had until then regularly featured my work, unexpectedly ceased publishing at the end of 2020, with the result that this piece has not appeared in print before now. In the intervening years, my esteemed friend and colleague Kim Farnell's further independent research into much the same topic has continued, and she has recently graciously shared with me a new source discovery of hers in the light of which amendments to this chapter and the partial revision of its conclusions were required, so perhaps its non-appearance in the discontinued *Infinity Astrological Magazine* almost four years ago (at the time of writing) in its original form may have proven, in the fullness of time, a blessing in disguise. Her own research on the topic remains ongoing, and it is to be hoped that she will publish her findings in full within the next few years, supplementing and extending the account given here.

Chapter 5, *The Earliest Astrological Conceptualisations of the Planet Uranus*, was first published in *Infinity Astrological Magazine*, March/April 2020, with additions made to the coverage of the original discovery of Uranus in December 2021.

Chapter 6, *When Did Astrologers First Associate Neptune with Pisces?* was first published on astrolearn.com in 2014, at which time it was favoured with an editorial link from the website of *The Mountain Astrologer*, but was revised and extended with new material for publication under the interim title of 'When Was Neptune First Associated by Astrologers with Pisces?' in *Infinity Astrological Magazine*, September/October 2019; and an additional reference to the discovery of Neptune was added in December 2021.

Chapter 7, *The First Published Assesssments on the Sign Rulership of Pluto*, was first published on Astrolearn.com in 2016, and republished in *Infinity Astrological Magazine*, March/April 2019. A small number of typographical errors in source quotations have since been corrected, but the text has not otherwise been changed.

Chapter 8, *Lilith in Astrology*, was first published in *Infinity Astrological Magazine*, January/February 2020. In 2024, the treatment of Dark Moon Lilith has been slightly extended in the light of access to a previously unavailable source, but no other changes have been made.

It is my earnest hope that in reading and digesting the eight studies that together comprise the first volume in this collection, any student of astrology and its history will come away with a much clearer and more nuanced view than before of the timelines and astrological voices underpinning the changes witnessed in astrological practice, at least in the specific areas with which these studies are concerned.

Once you have finished studying this book, you should be left with an enhanced understanding of:

- when and in what ways the meanings accorded to the twelve natal astrological topical places or houses evolved between ancient Greek practice and the 20th century;

- when, how and why astrologers' admission of different classes of aspects to their practice took place, and at the same time, when and by whom the system for calculating aspect orbs was overhauled;

- in what circumstances, under whose influences and by what sequence of events the astrological Sun gained preferential attention in both natal astrological writings and forecasting techniques in modernity;

- how and when astrologers collectively responded to the successive discoveries of Uranus, Neptune and Pluto, and in what ways the traditional assignations of domicile dignity to the planets were affected;

- how astrologers further responded to astronomers' expected discoveries of various solar system objects before they were discovered, whether or not they in fact eventually were.

The coverage of each of these topics is quite dense as my abiding aim as a researcher has been to prioritise thoroughness and accuracy. You may therefore find that it pays you to dip in and out of each study, or to read once and then return and reread while following up the source references more closely, in order to get the most out of this book.

If a few modern misconceptions and false simplifications regarding the history of astrology as may have been absorbed from any of a number of recent secondary histories of the subject are shattered by your acquaintance with the unambivalent evidence presented here, then I feel that I shall have succeeded in my aims as a writer presenting my findings before the world.

Wishing you happy reading and fruitful historical explorations,

Philip Graves,
Newport, South Wales,
December 15th 2024

Part One:
The Evolution of the Astrological Houses and Astrological Aspect Theory

Chapter One
From Manilius to Modernity:
A Study of the Evolution of the Meanings
of the Astrological Houses

Abstract

This chapter will consider the evolution of the *meanings* accorded by selected important historical astrologers to the twelve astrological houses or places from the first century CE to the beginning of the 20th, starting with the readings of them given by Marcus Manilius and ending with those of Alan Leo. This survey illustrates the tension between tradition and originality in successive generations of astrological textbooks and seeks to identify the most important changes and when they took root. Detailed examples of the change of meanings in a selection of the twelve houses will be provided. The purpose of the study is not to detail the technical changes in preferred astronomical methods for calculating the positions of the cusps of the houses, a major topic in its own right that has already been exhaustively treated by scholars such as J. D. North. The scope here is limited to the changing astrological interpretations of the houses, however they may have been defined astronomically.

Introduction

Natal astrology is believed to have first been introduced by late ancient Babylonian astrologers about five centuries before Christ, and over ten centuries after the first-recorded introduction of omen astrology. The natal astrology of the late ancient Babylonians incorporated delineations of the Sun, Moon and planets in the signs of the zodiac, and planetary conjunctions with fixed stars. According to the late James Herschel Holden, none of the extant evidence suggests that the local space around the birthplace was routinely defined or interpreted at this stage, so there was no use of the Ascendant or Midheaven, and there were no topical places cast from the Ascendant – a feature essential to the definition of *horoscopic* astrology.

The ancient Egyptians of the Ptolemaic era spanning the last three centuries before Christ delineated destiny or fate from the rising decan, paving the way to the invention of full-fledged horoscopic astrology in Alexandria around the 2nd century BCE. No texts from the first century or two of horoscopic astrology have survived intact, but scholars have been able to infer much of their doctrine from later summaries and citation.

A notable lost ancient Egyptian astrological manual, the *Salmeschoiniaka*, is cited in Hephaestio of Thebes' *Apotelesmatics*, Book 2 Chapter 18,[1] as having divided the zodiac into thirty-six numbered decans starting with the one in which the Ascendant falls. Each of these decans was associated with its own distinct topical theme, and Hephaestio records that the first was associated with birth, the eighth with children, the tenth with death, the seventeenth with marriage and wives, the nineteenth with injury, the 25th with sickness, and the 28th with livelihood.

At some point in the early development of horoscopic astrology, the use of the thirty-six decan-places appears to have yielded to that of twelve whole-sign places, a system known as the *dōdekatropos* or *dōdekatopos*.[2] Thus, the houses of the horoscope were established as twelve places assigned to successive signs of the zodiac beginning with the rising sign – a method known as the whole-sign house system or sign-house system. In this system, as interpreted by the ancient Greek and Roman astrologers, each place or, in the divinatory language of Manilius, 'temple',[3] is typically associated with the governance of a particular department of life (such as life, honours or children) or time of life (such as infancy or old age).

Most of the surviving Hellenistic astrological texts teach the consideration of suitable whole-sign places and their Lords in the judgement of matters centred upon topics with identifiable generic themes corresponding to those assigned to the places in question. In support of these assignations, some of the places are also accorded a governance in general terms by one of the luminaries or planets with like thematic associations, irrespective of which planet may rule each place in a particular chart. Additionally, the places are held by most of the ancient and medieval astrologers to be to varying degrees fortunate or unfortunate.

The use of a variant form of the whole-sign house system, known as the Equal House system, is implicit in some of the ancient Greek astrological texts, notably the *Tetrabiblos* of Claudius Ptolemy. Instead of using whole signs as the basis for counting the places, the Equal House system takes the Ascendant degree as the beginning of the first house, then counts thirty degrees onwards, crossing sign boundaries in the process, to arrive at the beginning, or cusp, of each successive house.

From these simple beginnings of the whole-sign places and equal houses, there were belatedly added to astrological doctrine more precise calculations of *mundane* or *quadrant* houses. The cusps of the twelve mundane houses are derived from different methods for the trisection of each quadrant of the space around the birthplace framed by the four cardinal points: the Ascendant, the Imum Coeli (sometimes called the Stake of the Earth or the Lower Midheaven), the Descendant, and the Midheaven (or Medium Coeli): which themselves are invariably taken as forming the cusps of the 1st, 4th, 7th and 10th houses, respectively.

One of the earliest recorded systems for deriving the intermediate house cusps is called the Porphyry House System, after the ancient Greek astrologer Porphyry. Where they are expressly referred to at all in ancient Greek astrology, however, the mundane houses are most commonly used as indicators of planetary strength or weakness or in calculations of length of life. They only systematically replace the whole-sign houses or Equal House system as the basis for the delineation of selected topics in later medieval astrological literature.[4]

Having established that the derivation of the topical places changed substantially between Hellenistic astrology and medieval and later astrological practice, we need say nothing more on the technicalities of their derivation. The history of systems of house division has been exhaustively addressed by past scholarship, such as the late J. D. North's *Horoscopes and History* (1986). This chapter is concerned with the tradition and evolution of the topical meanings accorded to the twelve astrological places or houses, howsoever they may have been astronomically or symbolically defined at different times in the history of astrology.

The *Oktatropos* or *Oktatopos*

Before we continue, however, one observation that must be added for the historical record is that there is some manuscript evidence for ancient traditions of topical systems using just eight places, instead of twelve. These eight-place systems are often referred to as *oktatropos* or *oktatopos*.[5] Four examples are worthy of mention here.

i. Thrasylllus

The first notable case is found in the surviving summary of Thrasyllus's lost *Pinax* or Tablet to Heracles.[6] This cites Thrasyllus, who died in 36 CE, as apportioning the following assignments to the eight places:

1. Life, and circumstances or activities conducive to business and profit
2. Manner of living[7]
3. Siblings[8]
4. Parents
5. Children
6. Injuries
7. The wife [of the native]
8. Fortune and death.

These associations are mostly recognisable from those made by many Hellenistic and much later astrologers with the correspondingly numbered places in the twelve-place system. Most scholars, including the late A. E. Housman,[9] G. P. Goold,[10] and Holden, agree that they were indeed meant to be assigned to the first eight only of the twelve whole-sign places counted in the normal fashion from the Ascendant. Others, notably Auguste Bouché-Leclercq and Wilhelm Gundel, had previously read them as evidence of a lost eightfold division of the zodiac from the starting point of the Ascendant, a view that the late Patrice Guinard continued very recently to espouse.[11]

Thrasyllus himself separately cites (according to the summary) a twelve-place topical system he attributes to Hermes, who was reputed among the ancient Greek astrologers as being the founder of horoscopic astrology. If this attribution were correct, it would put paid to the conventional scholarly idea espoused by Franz Cumont among others that the eight-place system was an archaic antecedent of the twelve-place one. Instead, it would seem plausible that both systems may have been in parallel use among the ancient Egyptian astrologers for quite a number of decades.

ii. The Michigan Astrological Papyrus

The second noteworthy example is found in the *Michigan Astrological Papyrus*, a brief, fragmentary Egyptian manuscript that was first edited in 1927[12] by Frank Egleston Robbins, and has been estimated to date from the 2nd century CE, although Robbins leaves open the question of whether or not it was a copy of a considerably earlier work.

Two English translations of the papyrus have been published, the first of which, by Robbins himself, appeared nine years after his edition, in 1936.[13]

A second published translation, by amateur astrological historian Rupert Gleadow, was published in *American Astrology Magazine* in 1950.

The papyrus details an eight-place system, the authority for which is named as Asclepius. According to the interpretations of the text by Robbins,[14] Housman,[15] and Gleadow, the houses in this system run clockwise, at variance with those outlined by Thrasyllus and Antiochus[16] (*see below*). The author of the papyrus outlines the following associations for the eight places:[17]

1. Questions of length of life / Life itself
2. Livelihood
3. Brothers
4. Parents
5. Children
6. Injury or suffering / Hurts and sufferings
7. Wife
8. Fortune and death that puts a bound to all / Fortune, and the death with which it ends.

These readings are almost identical to those of Thrasyllus for his eight-place system, strongly indicating a common origin to both, on which basis the notion as read by Robbins, Housman, and Gleadow from the Papyrus that its set of eight places runs in the reverse (clockwise) order from the (anticlockwise) one of the twelve places would appear most likely to be an historical error and not an accurate account of an alternative, parallel tradition. Whether the error was introduced by the scribe of the Papyrus itself or in a lost intermediary source, we can only speculate. Housman, for his part, in his brief review of the Papyrus six months after it was first published by Robbins, signals numerous problems of language suggestive of a confused scribe and / or a corrupted text.[18]

Robbins cites Franz Cumont as suggesting that Petosiris was the true originator of the *oktatopos*, and Robbins himself sees no inconsistency between this account and the author of the papyrus citing Asclepius, who was a God, and thus a mythical figure who could conceivably have been cited as a persona in place of the author's true name.[19]

iii. Antiochus of Athens

The third example is found in the surviving summary of *The Thesaurus*, a lost text by Antiochus of Athens.[20] At verse 25, the summary refers to the historical use of the 'so-called eight-topic' as though it were no longer in use or recommended at the time of writing. The meanings of the eight places are given as:

1. Place of life, from which things concerning life are studied
2. Things attendant upon life
3. Place of siblings
4. Place of parents
5. Place of children
6. Injuries to the body
7. Place of marriage
8. Place of the end of life.

This is again compatible with the readings in Thrasyllus and the Michigan Papyrus, although with differences of emphasis.

iv. Julius Firmicus Maternus

The fourth case worth studying is found within the second book of the *Mathesis* by Julius Firmicus Maternus,[21] in a section headed 'The Eight Houses and the Angles'.[22] The title and contents of this chapter apparently led previous translator Jean Rhys Bram to infer that Firmicus was describing an eightfold division of the celestial sphere,[23] and to her publisher printing a diagram intended to illustrate this.[24] However, the wording by which Firmicus refers to these eight houses in terms of the number of signs each is counted from the Ascendant indicates that his intention was instead to summarise the conventional eight-place system using the first eight of the twelve whole-sign places, although he is less explicit about this than would be ideally helpful.

The meanings accorded by Firmicus to the first eight places in this scheme are as follows:

1. Life
2. Hope; money
3. Brothers
4. Fathers or parents
5. Children
6. Illness or sickness
7. The spouse
8. Death

These are again broadly compatible with the other accounts that have come down to us of the eight-place system, except for the associations of the 2nd place being somewhat distinctive.

In the following chapters, Firmicus refers separately to the four angular places as 'The Angles of the Nativity', and the other eight places as houses, subdivided into the four succedent houses (which he calls 'The Favourable Houses') and the four cadent houses (which he calls 'Dejected Houses'), before interpreting all twelve in some detail, leaving no doubt that his interpretative attention is primarily invested in the *dōdekatropos*.

There is also a brief incidental mention of the *oktatropos* by a later interpolator who contributed a note to the manuscript of Manilius' *Astronomica* Book 2,[25] although Goold takes pains to point out that this has no relevance to the system taught by Manilius himself.

Lot-Houses

A second important preliminary observation is that the ancient astrologers did not exclusively derive meaning from a system of topical places starting with the Ascendant. Some of them, notably Marcus Manilius, Dorotheus of Sidon, and Vettius Valens, also count twelve places starting with the Lot of Fortune, which are often referred to as Lot Houses. For the judgements of certain topics, Dorotheus additionally teaches the use of places counted from the Moon sign. However, the meanings read by some ancient astrologers from the lot houses or lunar places lie outside the scope of the present study, which is focused solely on the meanings invested in the twelve houses counted from the Ascendant.

The Evolution of the Meanings of the 12 Houses

We shall now examine in approximate chronological order the testimonies of thirty astrological authorities spanning 1900 years, from Marcus Manilius to Alan Leo, and summarise the salient points of their interpretations of the twelve houses, both in general and especially in application to natal astrology. Many of the medieval authors and some of the Hellenistic ones also give extensive accounts of what the houses may be taken to signify in particular types of horary and electional astrological questions, but for reasons of consistent focus and overall concision, these have generally been left out of this survey.

Because of the greater importance of the ancient and medieval periods in establishing the tradition, I have selected twelve ancient sources, from Manilius to Rhetorius, twelve medieval ones, from the *Liber Hermetis* to Leopold of Austria, and a sample of six important early modern ones, from Johannes Schöner to Alan Leo, two of which, namely Morin de Villefranche and Alan Leo, are especially notable for their innovations.

Throughout this chapter, I summarise and selectively paraphrase the existing modern translations of texts written in ancient and medieval languages. The aim has been to succinctly list key concepts rather than to faithfully and thoroughly reproduce the text of the individual authors.

1. Marcus Manilius (fl. 1ˢᵗ century CE)

The *Astronomica* of Marcus Manilius,[26] which takes the form of an extended poem, is the oldest textbook teaching astrology to have survived complete, and has been dated to around 15–30 CE. The author's depictions of the meanings of the houses are a mixture of the familiar and the idiosyncratic, with many assignations common to other ancient Greek and later astrologers, but some found only in his poem. Opinions differ on how to understand his seemingly singular interpretations of some of the houses. They could derive from lost earlier manuscripts or orally transmitted teachings that were not maintained far beyond his time; they could be products of his own personal beliefs, representing astrology as only he or perhaps a small group of astrologers with whom he associated had developed and practised it; or they could even derive from poetic licence applied to the art of creating his poem, without recourse to any astrological beliefs or teachings.

Deborah Houlding makes the case that the house meanings conveyed by Manilius were the received norm at the time of his writing.[27] She suggests that most of his meanings were symbolically related to the motion, position, and degree of visibility of the Sun at different times of day.[28]

> 1st: Life; character; the early years; education; the fortunes of children; the prayers of parents; the success of enterprises; profession
>
> 2nd: No topic assigned; unfortunate and will bring a fall without support from the 1st
>
> 3rd: The fortunes and fate of brothers
>
> 4th: Foundations; wealth; the fortunes of fathers; profits from mining; gains from hidden sources; old age
>
> 5th: Changes in health caused by disease; chance; uncertainty
>
> 6th: Bane; ruin
>
> 7th: The consummation of affairs; the conclusion of work and marriages; good faith; constancy of heart; worship of the Gods; leisure; social intercourse; the end of life
>
> 8th: No topic assigned; unfortunate and will bring a fall without support from the 7th
>
> 9th: Planets here are implicated in health
>
> 10th: Pre-eminence; distinction; honours; fame; popular favour; rule or reign; the rule of law; powers of justice; wedlock and marriage ceremonies
>
> 11th: Brave hopes; ambition for prizes; being blessed with happy fortune.
>
> 12th: Bane; ruin

Manilius' associations of the 5th house with changes in health caused by disease and of the ninth with the determination of health are at variance with all later sources.

Houlding argues that his distinctive reading of the planetary joys played a major role in governing his respective readings of the fifth and tenth places, with Venus given to the tenth under his scheme, accounting for the connection he makes between the tenth place and marriage ceremonies, which is at variance with Firmicus Maternus and most medieval and Renaissance astrologers, who associate Venus with the fifth house.[29] This viewpoint is supported by classical scholar Wolfgang Hübner,[30] who suggests that a trace of Manilius' idiosyncratic planetary joy arrangement was found in the system of Hermes as recorded by Thrasyllus. Dorian Greenbaum has found evidence of earlier Egyptian astrological usage calling the tenth place 'the house of the goddess', which may conceivably have informed Manilius' association of the tenth place with Venus.[31] However, Manilius' distinction between the act of marriage (7th house) and the attendant ceremonies (10th) is an interesting early example of the subtlety with which the houses were often distinguished by ancient and medieval authors. We shall later see only Paulus Alexandrinus and Rhetorius link both these houses with marriage in some way. Otherwise, and in keeping with Houlding's thesis, the connection of the 10th with marriage has largely disappeared.

Manilius notably gives no nuanced topical indications for the 2nd, 6th, 8th and 12th houses – all those lacking a conventional (Ptolemaic) aspect to the ascendant. Instead they are generally regarded as ill omens, with the proviso that the misfortune of the 8th and 2nd may be mitigated if they receive suitable support from their neighbouring cardines. Of further note: Manilius does not connect the 8th house with death, contrary to the *oktatropos* scheme of his contemporary Thrasyllus and to the *dōdekatropos* schemes of major later ancient Greek astrologers such as Dorotheus of Sidon, Vettius Valens, and Firmicus Maternus.

2. Thrasyllus (died 36 CE)

We have previously discussed Thrasyllus as a source on the *oktatropos*. Additionally, citing Hermes, Thrasyllus[32] makes the following assignments to the *dōdekatropos*:

1. Fortune; soul; way of life

2. Hopes

3. Actions or activities; siblings or brothers

4. The foundation of happiness and prosperity; paternal circumstances or estate; the possession of slaves

5. Good fortune

6. Misfortune; punishment or vengeance; injury

7. Death; the native's wife

8. Life; livelihood

9. Living or being abroad; foreign things

10. Fortune in life, and livelihood; conception; children; actions; honour and praise; positions of authority, rule or leadership

11. Good spirit

12. Evil spirit; way of life or livelihood; the subordination of slaves

These associations attributed to Hermes overlap to a degree with those taught by Manilius, but each source has its own peculiarities not found elsewhere. The connection of the 5th and 6th houses with good and bad fortune respectively, and of the 11th and 12th with good and bad spirit (or daimon), became standard in the later Hellenistic tradition, although there is no trace of it in Manilius and little in Dorotheus. Greenbaum notes that Manilius instead refers to the 5th house as *daemonie*, speculatively suggesting, among other possibilities, that this may stem from an earlier Egyptian astrological tradition connecting it with the goddess Shepset.[33]

Thrasyllus' connection of the 10th house with children is unusual by modern standards, but was not uncommon among the ancient astrologers, with Dorotheus, Vettius Valens, and (much later) Paulus Alexandrinus and Rhetorius also drawing this relation, although in the cases of Dorotheus and Valens, children were jointly associated with the 5th and the 10th houses, suggesting the straddling of two traditions. By medieval times, the 5th-house association with children would come to predominate, which Houlding again explains in terms of the increasingly firmly entrenched connection of the 5th house with Venus, the Goddess of Fertility.[34]

The several separate houses (1st, 8th, 10th, and 12th) contributing in Thrasyllus' account to the indication of way of life or livelihood are arguably a recipe for confusion, while both the 3rd and the 10th house are linked to actions.

Another point worth noting here is that the 12-place system cited by Thrasyllus connects death to the 7th house, while the 8-place system he used connects it to the 8th. We have already seen Manilius link the 7th to the end of life, whereas most later astrologers have preferred to connect death to the 8th. It can be surmised that in Thrasyllus' time, death was separately associated under different traditions with the seventh and the eighth houses, and while Manilius preferred the 7th-house tradition, later Hellenistic astrologers gravitated to the 8th. This arguably makes for a worthy anthropological case study in a *de facto* evolutionary competition between two mutually inconsistent traditional readings of the attribution of a single theme to a specified house, of which only one would come to dominate in the long run.

3. Dorotheus of Sidon (c. 75 CE)

The *Carmen Astrologicum* of Dorotheus of Sidon[35] is one of the more extensive originally classical Greek astrological texts of which the greater portion survives, although no complete manuscript is conserved, and the text has been pieced together by modern scholars chiefly from fragments cited by later authors.

In addition to assigning meanings to the twelve places, Dorotheus ranks them in the following order from best to worst: First, Tenth, Eleventh, Fifth, Seventh, Fourth, Ninth, Third, Second, Eighth, and, jointly, Sixth and Twelfth. This would appear to be an attempt to systematise the approach to the reading of the houses along coherent lines, and is broadly followed by many of the Arabic-era medieval authors.

Dorotheus assigns these general meanings to the houses, in addition to numerous more specific ones in horary questions:

1. The native; youth; life
2. Assets; livelihood
3. Siblings; brothers and people dear to one; living abroad
4. Old age and the end of the lifespan; the bestowal of death; fathers
5. Children
6. Slaves; chronic illness
7. Wedding & marriage; women; old age
8. Death
9. Living or travelling abroad
10. Children; adolescence and early adulthood; work; actions taken
11. Good fortune
12. Suffering

As previously mentioned, Dorotheus associates children with both the 5th and the 10th house, seemingly bridging two separate traditions, of which the former would ultimately come to dominate. Similarly, he associates both the third and the ninth house with living abroad, but later authors would increasingly favour the ninth. His connection of women with the seventh was ignored by most of the other Hellenistic astrologers but would later commonly be adopted by the medieval ones.

4. Ptolemy (c. 100–178 CE)

Ptolemy's *Apotelesmatika or Tetrabiblos*[36] would become the most famous and widely studied and cited of all the classical astrological texts among the Renaissance and early modern astrologers, but in its time it was an atypical text that does not seem to have belonged to mainstream astrological tradition, as it taught many points of doctrine quite differently from the pre-existing astrological literature; and nor was it slavishly followed or universally preferred as a source by later ancient Greek astrologers or the early medieval ones.

Ptolemy was first and foremost a scientist, and he is most celebrated today for his works on astronomy and geography. It has been argued that his *Tetrabiblos* was an attempt to restate the philosophy of astrology along causal lines compatible with those established for the natural sciences. To this end, he may perhaps have cast aside or at least given relatively scant attention to elements of astrological doctrine that he did not think compatible with this mode of expression.

Greenbaum points out that Ptolemy uses the 11th place for prognosticating on length of life, and the tenth and eleventh jointly for indicators of children.[37] Chris Brennan further observes that Ptolemy associates the sixth place with injuries, the Ascendant with physical appearance, the Midheaven with occupation, and the twelfth place with slaves.[38]

However, at no point in the text of the *Tetrabiblos* does Ptolemy assign topics systematically to the twelve places. He does not seem to regard them as an important element in the reading of the birth chart. Indeed, he hardly even mentions them aside from brief and occasional citations, although it is clear from the few references in Book III Chapter 10 and occasionally elsewhere that he is familiar with at least some of their traditional names, as he refers to the ninth as the House of the God, the 11th as the House of Good Daemon, and the 12th as the House of the Evil Daemon.

Nevertheless, Ptolemy clearly regards the positions of the houses in their respective quadrants as valid indicators of planetary strength, with the angular houses making planets more powerful, the succedent houses giving them middling strength, and planets posited in the cadent houses being weaker and more ineffectual.[39]

5. Vettius Valens (c. 120–175 CE)

Vettius Valens' *Anthology* is one of the most complete and detailed classical Greek expositions of astrological techniques to have survived to the present day. In marked contrast to Ptolemy's text, it appears to represent the work of a dedicated professional practitioner of astrology, which places its teachings at the heart of the mainstream of ancient astrological practice.

Several separate references to the meanings of the houses and / or to planets when found in them are scattered throughout the *Anthology*'s nine books, namely across Book 2 Chapters 5–16,[40] in Book 4 Chapter 12,[41] and in Book 9 Chapter 3.[42] The latter chapter includes several interpretations that owe to the technique of derived houses,[43] which itself has a very long history extending right through to modern astrological practice. Brennan points out that Valens' derived house readings are limited to meanings obtained from the starting point of the first eight topical places, suggesting an intriguing origin of the practice of derived houses in a lost early text centred upon the *oktatropos*.[44]

Here is a succinct summary of Valens' essential associations with the twelve places:

1. The life essence of the native; sustenance; way of living; body; breath; spirit and soul

2. The livelihood; being overshadowed; giving; receiving; joint ownership; servitude; enmity

3. The mother and affairs associated with her; siblings or brothers; living abroad; friends; relatives; strong feelings; slaves; the Queen

4. The parents or the father; children; the native's woman; elderly people; foundations; inventions; hidden things; mystical matters; the city; the home; dwellings; property; changes, especially of place; praise; action; restraint; dangers; death

5. Good fortune or luck; marriage; children; friendship; association; acts of kindness; the freeing of slaves; spurious mixtures

6. Injuries; sickness; pathologies; debility; meanness; enmity; slaves

7. Marriage; union with a woman; the wife of the native; success; friendship; living abroad

8. Death; benefit from the dead; debility; punishment; ineffectuality

9. The father and affairs associated with him; the quality of foreignness; benefit from foreign things; absence from home; a royal quality; kings or sovereigns; God or manifestations of the Gods; prophetic and divinatory powers; astronomy; mystical and hidden matters; friendship and association

10. Life prospects; career destiny; reputation; action; advancement; innovation and change; praise; children; the wife

11. Good spirit; hopes and desires; passions; friends; affiliations; the acquisition of resources; gifts; children; freed former captives

12. Evil spirit; suffering; pathos; enmity; slaves and slavery; foreign women; mean experiences; legal judgements; dangers; injury; sickness, debility; death

Collating all these designations together from variant translations of the three separate books of the *Anthology* in which they are found is something of a recipe for confusion, firstly since such varied significations are associated with some of the houses, and secondly since, as we have witnessed with some earlier writers, some areas of life appear to be jointly signified by several houses, for example children by the 4th, 5th, 10th and 11th; and friends or friendships by the 3rd, 5th, 7th, 9th, and 11th, while marriage is linked to both the 5th and the 7th houses. Even if there may have been method born of hard practical experience in Valens' attributions, it is probably understandable that later astrologers have tended to seek considerably to pare down the number of houses that can signify each area of life.

One of Valens' most unusual assignments is that of the mother to the 3rd house. I have not found this in any other classical or medieval source. The third place was, however, called the place of the Goddess and associated with the Moon by many ancient astrological writers, including Manilius and Valens himself, as well as the author of the Michigan Astrological Papyrus, Antiochus of Athens, Firmicus Maternus, Paulus Alexandrinus and Rhetorius, which might conceivably account for this eccentric attribution.

6. Antiochus of Athens, *The Thesaurus* (summary)

Antiochus of Athens flourished in the second half of 2nd century CE. His text *The Thesaurus*[45] provided detailed definitions of many astrological terms in use by the classical astrologers. Only a summary of it survives, but even this is useful. Alongside his brief treatment of the *oktatropos*, Antiochus gives the following meanings to the *dōdekatropos*:

1. The beginning of the physical life; the soul; personal behaviour; the first age of life

2. Expectations and things expected

3. Friends and similar associates

4. Home; the heart; treasures; lands; nobility of birth

5. Good fortune; increase in livelihood and of things connected from it; acquisitions of animals

6. Troubles; sufferings; enemies

7. The last age of life; death

8. The 'idle image'[46]

9. God; being away from home; travel abroad

10. Reputation; action; technique; middle age or mid-life; the summit of one's position in life; the fortune associated with one's livelihood

11. Good spirit; the future increase of things

12. Bad spirit; happenings during birth; necessity; troubles; sufferings; conducive to business, according to some[47]

7. Michigan Astrological Papyrus (estd. 2nd century CE)

Further to its aforementioned contribution to the accounts of the *oktatropos*, the Michigan Astrological Papyrus gives a brief, mostly conventional interpretation of $^{11}/_{12}$ths of the *dōdekatropos*, as follows:

1. Life; the individuality of the soul

2. Hope

3. Friends; the Goddess

4. Foundations and bases; beginnings

5. Good fortune

6. Blessings and 'acts of God'

7. Death

8. [Is inactive]

9. Decline of fortune;[48] places travelled to

10. The profession

11. Good spirit

No interpretation is given for the 12th place. This may perhaps be a product of the original manuscript having a lacuna, as it is known to have many.

The signification of the sixth house is probably the most idiosyncratic here, since the sixth house is read entirely negatively by other sources, whereas the author of the Michigan Papyrus seems to be more neutrally attributing to it any act of fate, for good or ill, that appears to come from God.

The association of the profession with the tenth house departs from Manilius, who connected it with the first, but is familiar from many later texts.

8. Porphyry (c. 232–304 CE)

In his *Introduction to the Tetrabiblos*, Porphyry limits himself to relating the twelve places to periods of human life grouped around the four angles, without connecting them expressly to topical areas of life. Each angle signifies one of the four key stages of life, including birth and death, while the cadent houses leading to the angles are related to the times immediately before these key moments, and the succedent houses following them are connected to the times after them. This creates a composite picture of three shades of each of four main ages of life. Thus, we find in Chapter 52:[49]

1. Birth and the time immediately following
2. End of the first age of life
3. The time before death
4. Death, and posthumous praise or disparagement
5. The time after death
6. First part of old age
7. Middle part of old age
8. Latter part of old age
9. First part of middle age
10. Central part of middle age
11. Last part of middle age
12. Happenings in the womb while still unborn, including labour pains for the mother

9. Julius Firmicus Maternus (c. 280 – c. 360 CE – text ca. 335 CE)

Further to the previous discussion of Firmicus' contributions to the records on the *oktatropos*, here we shall summarise the meanings he gave to the twelve-place scheme.

1. The life and spirit of men; the framework and substance of the whole nativity

2. Increases in hope; increases in possessions

3. Brothers; friends; travel

4. Parents; foundations; assets; inheritance; movable belongings; hidden and remote sources of wealth

5. Good Fortune; children

6. Bad Fortune; causes of bodily defects

7. Marriages; violent association with matters of the first house

8. Falling down; the quality of death

9. Sects; religions; travels

10. The life and spirit; actions; home; native country; arts and their rewards; association; defects of the mind

11. Good Spirit

12. Bad Spirit; enemies; slaves; bodily defects; illnesses

Here we see three more examples of much the same general qualities seemingly being associated with two distinct houses: in this case, life and spirit with the first and the tenth, travels with the third and ninth, and physical disabilities with the sixth and the twelfth. Note also that Firmicus' reading of the tenth is quite distinctive, including home and the native country, matters more commonly associated with the fourth, as well as other keywords not usually linked to the tenth house, such as association, which Valens connected instead to the fifth and ninth.

10. Paulus Alexandrinus – (born 330 CE; written 378 CE)

Paulus Alexandrinus, in his *Introductory Matters*,[50] gives some quite detailed and specific descriptions of the meanings of the twelve houses in Chapter 24: *On the Tabular Exposition of the Twelve Places*:

1. The origin of life; the foundation of the nativity, through which all circumstances affecting the native are apparent; the time of youth, and what happens in it

2. Mode of living or livelihood; work and actions undertaken; good expectations; the acquisition or squandering of goods, property and inheritance

3. Accumulation of wealth or possessions; brothers; friendship; affection; patronage; a contributing cause to living abroad

4. Old age, the end of life, and what follows death; the house, home and fatherland; household goods; the father; parents; close associations; the acquisition of ships and watery places

5. Good Fortune; children and their fate; childbirth

6. Bad or Evil Fortune; retribution; punishment; injury; plots; rebellions; enmities; service; slaves; female beasts

7. Wedding preparations; long periods spent abroad; old age; the cause and quality of death

8. An idle, dysfunctional, unfortunate place; the event of death

9. Living abroad; Gods; dreams; astronomy

10. Work; action; reputation; worth; privilege; rank; status and standing; the father; the fatherland; permanence; marriage; male children

11. Good Spirit; alliance and standing together; patronage; good expectations; relevant together with the 4th, 5th, and 10th places to the determination of children

12. Evil Spirit; sicknesses; sufferings; childbearing; enemies; male slaves; four-legged animals

We find many house keywords familiar from earlier accounts in this late classical text. Observe that Paulus assigns marriage to the 10th house but another aspect of weddings to the 7th, similarly to but distinctly from Manilius' attributions relating marriage to the same two houses. Also note Paulus' attempt to subdivide affairs connected with death and spread them between the fourth, seventh and eighth houses, all of which have been connected with it by at least one earlier source. His distinction between the acquisition of goods (2nd house) and the accumulation of possessions (3rd house) is not found elsewhere. Possessions are increasingly tightly associated with the 2nd house by the medieval authors. In contrast, we saw earlier that Firmicus Maternus connected them (in the guise of movable belongings) with the 4th house, and only their increase in the second.

11. Hephaestio of Thebes (born 380 CE; text written ca. 415 CE)

Hephaestio's *Three Books of Apotelesmatics*[51] contains no systematic description of the meanings of the houses. Hephaestio uses the cardines extensively in inceptions, but only a few other scattered references are found to any of the other houses. Like Ptolemy, Hephaestio seems relatively uninterested in the scheme of *dōdekatropos*, and when he mentions non-cardinal houses at all, it is only briefly, to relate what other writers such as Apollonarius and the Egyptians have called them or said about them. For the angular houses, however, he admits to the following general meanings:

1. Appearance; the body
4. Parents
7. Marriage; sexual union; associated by Ptolemy with death
10. The quality of one's actions; what one does; the maternal place

Hephaestio is notably the earliest source we have found to connect the tenth house with the mother. The late Robert Schmidt interprets this as an historical misreading by Hephaestio of a statement Ptolemy made about a derivative house scheme using the tenth place taken from either the Moon or Venus. This misreading, according to Schmidt's research, was then carried down from Hephaestio into the medieval tradition, and it has since survived into modern times, although in some twentieth-century texts, the mother has come to be associated with the fourth house.

12. Rhetorius the Egyptian (ca. 505 CE)

In Chapter 57 of his *Astrological Compendium*,[52] Rhetorius the Egyptian briefly summarises the meanings of all twelve houses along mostly conventional lines, as would befit the work of a self-declared compiler, but with a few peculiarities. We find the following:

1. Life and its foundation; breath

2. Livelihood; an idle, ineffective house

3. Foreign matters; friends; brothers; dreams; religious observance; the Queen; an ineffective house

4. The dwelling into which one is born; property; foundations; parents; hidden matters; old age; happenings after death

5. Good Fortune

6. Bad Fortune; injuries; the feet and sicknesses involving them; enemies; slaves; four-footed animals; sometimes signifies actions; an ineffective house

7. Old age; marriage; travel abroad; the fingers, feet, and bladder; sometimes, inheritance; sometimes, injury

8. Death; the turning away of life; an ineffective house

9. God or Gods; religious observance; dreams; astronomy; kings; foreigners; travellers to foreign places

10. Youth; marriage; children; the substance of the parents; action

11. Good Spirit; patronage; precedence in the prime of youth; the third period of life; children; action

12. Bad Spirit; happenings between conception and birth; enemies; slaves; four-legged animals; an ineffective house

Rhetorius' association of children with both the tenth and the eleventh house is shared with Valens and Paulus Alexandrinus before him, although they both additionally referenced the fifth.

The abiding peculiarity of Rhetorius' list of house keywords for his time is his association of certain houses with particular parts of the body, although only the sixth and seventh have been singled out for this treatment, and both of them are connected with the feet. The medieval authors would go on to routinely connect each of the houses with one or more parts of the body.

We can also see that Rhetorius connects both the fourth house and the tenth with parents. Previously, they had been the exclusive preserve of the fourth, unless one counts the then-recent idiosyncratic connection drawn by Hephaestio with the mother.

13. Liber Hermetis

The *Liber Hermetis* survives only in an early medieval Latin translation,[53] but supposedly conserves records of the ancient doctrine of Hermes Trismegistus from either a lost Greek original or (according to the late Robert Zoller, who translated the source text established by Wilhelm Gundel into English) various older Greek manuscripts compiled into a single translation.

The medieval Latin translation has been variously dated to the 5th century CE by Gundel; the 12th century by David Pingree; and the 6th or 7th century by Zoller. The latter argues that the absence of mention of Arabic-era astrological authors, the absence of Arabic astrological techniques, and the earlier style of the Latin, all rule out Pingree's dating, making it untenable. Gundel dates portions of the original manuscripts on which the Latin translation was based to the 2nd century CE, with which Pingree selectively agrees.

Zoller[54] notes Pingree's view that large parts of the *Liber Hermetis* were derived from Rhetorius, Valens, and Firmicus Maternus, while acknowledging that some of the content of the *Liber Hermetis* that resembles that of the *Mathesis* of Firmicus could come from a common ancestor to both.

Brief names for the topical places are found in Chapter XIV of the *Liber Hermetis*.[55] As we saw in Hephaestio, there is no comprehensive description of the topics corresponding to the houses. In fact, topical details are given for the first house only, in Chapter XXVI, entitled 'On the XII Places and the Signification of the Planets When They are Found in Them in Nativities':[56]

> *The giver of life, both of the body and of the spirit; the measure of life; childhood, the first age of life; the first operation of good things.*

There is nothing unusual here.

14. Masha'Allah (c. 740–815 CE)

The celebrated early medieval astrologer Masha'Allah wrote many short books on different astrological topics, and has also been identified as the true author of the lengthier *Liber Aristotilis* (traditionally credited to Hugo of Santalla), to which we refer here,[57] alongside one of his short books, *The Signification of the Planets in their Own Signs and in the Signs of Other Planets*.[58] Compared with those of later medieval astrologers, his comments about the meanings of the astrological houses in general are brief and scattered. We find the following:

1st: No clear signification given

2nd: Wealth acquired or lost; the joint-third-worst house

3rd: The House of Brothers, especially elder brothers; travel

4th: Parents; impediments or lawsuits from higher-ranked people

5th: Children and their begetting

6th: Servile actions; illness; physical infirmities; defects to eyesight; weakness; paralysis; long-lasting suffering and pain; the joint-worst house

7th: The spouse; relationship to women

8th: The cause, kind and place of death; old things; inheritance; the joint-third-worst house

9th: The House of Travel; excelling in knowledge; faith and prayer to God

10th: Greatness and elevation; rulership; profession in general

11th: Faith; victory; many friends; slaves

12th: Friendship; hatred; enemies; rivals; the joint-worst house

While most of these associations are familiar from earlier and later sources, a couple are worthy of particular comment. The association of the 11th house with the enslaved is peculiar, and Benjamin Dykes regards it as a mistake, perhaps of manuscript transcription. Similarly, the linking of friendship to the 12th house is highly irregular and contradicts the later Arabic astrological tradition. Friends have already been connected elsewhere by Masha'Allah with the 11th, one of the several houses to which Valens linked it, so this could conceivably be another distortion in the *Liber Aristotilis*.

15. Omar of Tiberias (died c. 815 CE)

In his *Three Books on Nativities*,[59] Omar of Tiberias gives brief keywords for each of the twelve houses, with those for only a few of them extending to multiple concepts:

1st: [No topical description given]

2nd: Substance

3rd: Siblings

4th: The father

5th: Children; pregnancies

6th: Illnesses; infirmities; accidents

7th: Sexual unions

8th: [No description of this house has survived in the available manuscripts]

9th: Travel; journeys; change; faith

10th: The mother; magistery; kingship

11th: Friends

12th: Enemies

Here we see a division of the parents firmly along gender lines between the 4th and the 10th house for the first time, although the 10th was previously granted to the mother by Hephaestio, who associated the 4th with the parents in general.

16. Abu 'Ali Al-Khayyat (c. 770–835 CE)

Abu 'Ali was a student of Masha'Allah and wrote his own dense treatise *On the Judgments of Nativities*.[60]

This is one of many medieval texts that assign special roles to the triplicity Lords of some of the houses, but as these associations are more specific than the meanings of the houses in general, we have skipped over them here.

We find the following:

1st: The circumstances of the native in general; the 1st and its lord are a partial significator of the causes and occasions of death

2nd: The native's wealth and its sources

3rd: The fortune of the brothers; jointly with the 9th house, signifies the native's religion, faith, personal moral law, and dreams

4th: The fortune of the parents; the 4th and its lord are a partial significator of the causes and occasions of death

5th: Children and their status

6th: The circumstances of subordinates, captives and slaves; the occurrences, causes and kinds of infirmities of the native

7th: Matters relating to marriage

8th: The quality of death

9th: The native's travel and journeys; jointly with the 3rd house, signifies the native's religion, faith, personal moral law, and dreams

10th: The native's dignity, work, power, and acclaim before the king

11th: The condition of friends

12th: Enemies; the luck of the native in relation to cattle and other animals

Most of these designations are widely familiar from modern usage. The 3rd house being given joint signification with the 9th over religion and dreams is peculiar by both ancient and modern standards, but is common to Rhetorius writing just a few centuries earlier.

17. Sahl ibn Bishr (fl. 811–825 CE)

Sahl ibn Bishr, usually referred to in later Latin editions of his work as Zahel, is another major early medieval astrologer to have written in Arabic. For the purposes of this investigation, we shall look at the meanings he accords to the houses in both the Arabic and the Latin versions of his *Introduction*, as translated by Benjamin Dykes,[61] which are collectively quite extensive. We find as follows:

1st: Life and death; the body; all movable and rational things; the beginnings of all matters; the establishment or coming about of every matter

2nd: Substance; property and assets; labour; assistants; the condition of people serving; donations; taking; profiting

3rd: Brothers; sisters; relatives; close companions; counsels; faith and religion; travel (especially foreign); dreams; contentions

4th: Fathers; family relationships; prisons; lands; the countryside; cities; villas; houses; all buildings; covered and concealed things, especially if under the earth; hidden treasures; death and what happens to the dead person; outcomes

5th: Love; children; trust; honour; donations; legates; the fruits of property; friends, especially the seeking of friendships with women; cities and citizens

6th: An evil or malign place; slaves; injustices; infirmities and their causes; movement from place to place

7th: Marriages; women; battles and wars; contentions and lawsuits; contrarieties; unions of two people; lost things and the causes of their losses; seekers and sought people; transactions between two people

8th: Death; murder; lethal poisons; destruction; evil in general; inheritances; everything that perishes or has perished; things consigned for preservation; dread; sorrow; grieving; wars; contentions; labour; farmers; things demanded back; sluggishness; tricky mental characteristics

9th: Foreign travels and journeys; places of religious worship; the culture of deity; divine wisdom; sanctity; piety; religion; philosophy; foresight; divination; dreams; matters of the future world; knowledge of the hereafter; the wisdom of the stars; invisible things; distant things; letters; legates and legations; rumours; past and receding things; outcomes that have already transpired; withdrawal

10th: The king or kingdom; princes; rulers; magistrates; empire; glory; exaltation; the voice of praise; mothers; the authorities presiding over works; profession or vocation; mastery; items lost or stolen

11th: Good fortune; friends; trust; hopes; orations; children

12th: Enemies; jealousies; craftiness; evil wills and malice; whisperings; distresses, lamentations and sorrows; downfalls; labours; travels (especially foreign); beasts; riding animals; prisons

These phrases include many nuances not expressly covered by the classical authors, although the general thrust of most of the key significations is in keeping with previous tradition.

Sahl is the first author we have found to explicitly associate the 5th house with love, a common association in modern astrology. His joint assignation of friendship to the 5th and 11th houses has echoes of Valens. Most of the ancient horoscopic astrologers linked friendship primarily or solely to the 3rd house, but this pattern had been broken by medieval times, with the 11th coming to dominate. Additionally, Sahl is the first astrologer we have seen to associate the 6th house with frequent travel or migration. This tradition continued through several later major medieval astrologers, including Abū Ma'Shar, al-Rijal, and Bonatti, as well as Leopold of Austria and Dariot (*see below*), but disappeared without a trace in the 17th century and has not been renewed in modernity. Note also that Sahl jointly associates the 3rd, 7th, and 8th houses with contentions; and that he assigns honour to the 5th, whereas Thrasyllus associated it with the 10th.

Sahl's teachings were not limited to natal astrology; and many of his keywords shown here might be expected more commonly to be encountered in horary and electional readings.

18. Abū Ma'Shar al-Balkhî (c. 787–886)

Ja'far ibn Muḥammad Abū Ma'Shar al-Balkhî was one of the foremost Arabic astrologers in terms of both his written output and his repute. His main general treatise of astrology is called *The Great Introduction*. It was twice translated into Latin in the Middle Ages, by John of Seville and by Hermann of Carinthia, of which only the latter translation was published in the Renaissance, although that of John of Seville was finally edited by the late scholar Richard Lemay and published thus in 1996. In the Latin textual tradition, Abū Ma'Shar is usually referred to as Albumasar.

Two English translations of the *Great Introduction* have appeared since 2019, rendered by Charles Burnett and Benjamin Dykes, respectively. We refer to Dykes's translation here.[62] Details of the essential meaning of the twelve houses, as well as names for them, are given by Abū Ma'Shar in Book VI, verses 8–19:

1st: the Ascendant - life; bodies; the conditions of every inception and motion

2nd: the House of Assets - the collecting and amassing of assets; food; the causes of one's means of subsistence; taking; giving

3rd: the House of Siblings – brothers, sisters, relatives, in-laws, religion; religious contentions; musing and reflection; opinions; understanding; books; reports; messengers; dreams; travel; women; virtue associated with withdrawal

4th: the House of Fathers – fathers; roots / personal origins; race; lands; cities; villages; building; waters; everything concealed, hidden or under the earth; buried treasure; movable property in general; outcomes; death and what follows it

5th: the House of Children – children; women; the seeking of women; friends; the formation of friendships; messengers; charitable giving; hope; delight; sexual intercourse; entertainment; cities and the conditions of their people; the produce of the land

6th: the House of Illness – illnesses including chronic illness; ailing; suffering; oppression; slavery; slaves; servant-girls; price reductions; migration; sometimes, riding animals

7th: the House of Women – women; marriage and its causes; making friends; demanding or seeking things from people; contentions; antitheses; destruction and its cause; travel

8th: the House of Death – death; killing; lethal poisons; inheritances; things entrusted for safekeeping; ancient things; distresses; anxieties; fears relating to things lost or destroyed; confusion; loss of the faculty of reason; idleness; negligence

9th: the House of Travel – travels; roads; absence from the homeland; divinity; religion; houses of worship; piety; virtue; charitable actions; prophethood; foreknowledge; visions; soothsaying; the science of the stars; philosophy; books; messengers; reports; migrations

10th: the House of Authority – the king; government; rulers; the nobility; judges; high rank; leadership; the seeking of authority; might; subjugation; fighting; wars; fame; reputation; trade professions; works; mothers

11th: the House of Good Fortune – hope; good fortune; splendour; praiseworthy actions; commendation; friends; helpers; children

12th: the House of Enemies – enemies; envy; slander; cunning; stratagems; suffering; distresses; sorrow; toil; trouble; riding animals; sometimes, illness

Among the noteworthy inclusions here are the relatively extensive keywords related to mental attributes and to behaviour arising from qualities of the personality, which is particularly noticeable in the portrayal of the 8th house. It is also notable that Abū Ma'Shar severally links women to the 3rd, 5th, and 7th houses; messengers to the 3rd, 5th, and 9th; friends to the 5th, 7th, and 11th; children to the 5th and the 11th; and both riding animals and illness to the 6th and the 12th. We further see that the 5th house is now shaping up as a catch-all for the experience of pleasure.

19. Al-Qabîsî (d. 967)

Abū al-Ṣaqr al-Qabîsî 'Abd al-'Azîz ibn 'Uthmān, better known in the later Latin tradition as Alchabitius, was another important medieval astrologer writing in Arabic. His *Introduction to the Art of the Judgments of the Stars* was later translated into Latin by John of Seville and was widely printed in the Renaissance. It was translated into English in 2004 by Charles Burnett, Keiji Yamamoto and Michio Yano;[63] and it is to this translation that we refer here. The following associations are spelt out in Chapter 1, verses 57–68:

1st: Soul; life; bodies; the beginning of life; beginnings of activities; the subject matter of questions; logic; speech; eloquence; rumours

2nd: Property; livelihood; helpers; the latter years of youth

3rd: Brothers; sisters; relatives; in-laws; love; religion; jurisprudence; messages; messengers; moving; short journeys; journeys by water; the condition before death

4th: Fathers; landed properties; outcomes; treasures; matters hidden or covered over; the kind of death

5th: Children; joy; eating and drinking; gifts; messengers; reputation after death

6th: Illness; slaves; slave-girls; the years before old age

7th: Women; marriage; partners; opponents; disputants; controversies; the middle years of old age

8th: Death and inheritance and their causes; fear; theft; poisons; the possessions of women; conditions of opponents; the last years of life

9th: Journeys; roads; absence; religion; religious observance; philosophy; visions; sciences; messengers; books; the early years of mid-life

10th: Authority; governorship; kingship; high rank; renown; fame; professions; the job of the native; mothers; the middle years of life

11th: Hope; good fortune; praise; recompense; friends; helpers; affection; love; joy; dignity; garments; scents; late middle-age

12th: Enemies; envy; slander; cunning; strategem; misfortune; sadness; grief; riding animals; the embryonic life before birth

Among the more interesting observations here is the according of logic, speech, and eloquence to the first house, which we have not found with any earlier writer. Al-Qabîsî also jointly ascribes helpers to the 2nd and 11th houses; joy to the 5th and 11th; and religion to the 3rd and 9th. His joint assignation of love to the 3rd and 11th is unorthodox by modern standards, and contradicts that of Sahl, who accorded it to the 5th, but has partial echoes in Paulus Alexandrinus, who associated the 3rd with affection, which Al-Qabîsî expressly links to the 11th alongside love.

20. Al-Rijāl (Haly Abenragel) (d. ca. 1040)

'Alî ibn abî al-Rijāl, Abū'l-Ḥasan, known in the Latin and later English textual tradition as Haly Abenragel, or often just Haly for short, was one of the most widely studied and cited astrologers from late medieval times through to the early modern period. He wrote a major textbook on astrology called *The Complete Book on the Judgements of the Stars*. The Arabic original is lost, but it mostly survives in a 13th-century medieval Castilian translation, of which Books 1–5 were edited in 1954.[64] At the time of that edition, Books 6, 7 and 8 of the Castilian translation were all thought to be lost. However, Books 6 and 8 were rediscovered in manuscript form in the 1960s, and were edited as recently as 2005, together with a modern transcription of an early literal rendering into Judaeo-Portugese of Book 7, which does not survive in the medieval Castilian.[65] A secondary Medieval Latin translation was also produced from the Castilian; and in 1997, a modern Spanish translation of Books 1–5 only appeared.[66] Al-Rijāl's work has yet to be translated into English, so for present purposes I have worked from the Spanish translation.

Extensive references to the essential meanings and judgements of topics related to the houses are scattered across the first five books. We find:

1st: Bodily form

2nd: The house of assets – highly valued things that are kept; money; earnings; possessions; daily sustenance; things given or received; the dignity and lordship of the native; inheritances from women; shared property; bailiffs; executioners and agents of authority; the making of wills; future events; the distribution of things; high-priority issues; requests for advances; fidelity; betrayal and envy of friends; coffers, wardrobes, and other furniture used for storage; keys; the tasks of children; taxes; benefit from properties and farms; the fortune in the native's property; notices sent by authorities; entrances to cities; the time in which the native will have luck, and the cause of that luck; the loss of luck; losses consequent upon adversity

3rd: The house of siblings – signifies brothers; sisters; brothers-in-law; relatives; friends; short journeys; the deterioration of houses; laws and their knowledge; dreams; the essences of things; wet-nurses; governesses; house moves; thought; the intellect; obedience and service to God; synagogues; the expansion of the Christians and their Churches

4th: The house of parents – governs above all parents and their fortunes, difficulties, health and illness; also, relatives related via the father, mother or grandparents; stepparents; the end of things; happenings after death; inheritance from parents; sowings; hidden things; treasures; precious stones; the elements and roots of things; the past; the form of the house where the native was born; castles; houses; the works and structures of buildings;

schools; prisons; various places; good and bad happenings in the world; the viscera of the body; the character of women

5th: The house of children – signifies children; pregnancy; interchange, friendship and love with women; close friendships in general; the courting of women; income from taxes; property taxes; inheritance taxes; gifts, especially the gifts one receives for helping others; inheriting from good wives; the assets of the ancestors; enjoyment of the heritage of the parents; joys; dinner parties and drinks parties; messengers; what happens after death; what will be left to inherit; bread and its scarcity in built-up areas; the status of citizens from year to year; cosmetics; perfumes

6th: Diseases and their causes; injuries to limbs; bodily blemishes; thin and weak bodies; enemies; betrayals; curses; captives and their redemption; the means of discovering fears and affronts; suspicion of women; servants; movements from one place to another; farmers; animals, especially fled beasts; banished men; lost, vile or low-priced things; everything that has little chance of being achieved; changes in the affection of friends; lies; false testimonies; envious words and deeds; the worship of devils; those enchanted by necromancy; the first part of life

7th: The house of women – signifies women; weddings; marriages; lying down with women; grandparents; adversaries; lawyers; lawsuits; old age; lost items; thefts; the location of thieves; buying; selling; hunting; the desired destination of travellers; absent or foreign men; things lost, hidden and denied; the loss of social class; arrests; repressions; pauses; killings

8th: Death, especially the death of the native, how it will occur, and its cause; death by fire; murder; drowning; deadly poisons; poisoning by spices; disease; tiredness; poverty or abundance; great losses; all that is lost or destroyed; fears; people who are unfortunate in this world, such as the blind, the one-armed, the disabled and the chronically ill; empty places; terrifying places; things that frighten because of their ugliness; devils; what happens to a person before death; reasoning about old things, false things and inheritances; earnings from travel and outside the place of birth

9th: the House of Travels – signifies journeys; movements from one place to another; changes of locality; foreigners; things of God; religious men; hermits; houses of prayer; incantations; philosophy; predictions; divination; astrology; astronomy; alchemy; dreams and their interpretation; the wisdom attributed to someone, whether rightly or wrongly; books; memories of past things; keeping secrets; narratives; prisoners and captives; exiles; serving the kings; tricksters; deception; those who gather people around them and tell them jokes for personal gain; the middle part of life

10th: the House of the King – signifies the king and his actions towards his people; the kingdom; wives of kings; lordship; high dignities; the nobility; noblewomen; the mayoralty; the father's wives; renown and lasting good reputation; high esteem; profession or mastery; good manners; right behaviour; correct thoughts; honour; thanks; things that are manifest; a good memory; mid-life

11th: the House of Friends – signifies hopes; adventures; thanks; good reputation; rewards; children; protectors; receiving protection from women; the friendship of and privileges bestowed by powerful men; the help of mayors and lawyers; goods; profitable things; absent people; populations; high and select lineages; the number of enemies; the end of life and what happens at that time

12th: enemies; envies; great resentments; contempt; deceptions; the evil arts; evil deeds; vile and despicable men; evildoers; boastful people; spiteful people; ruthless people; those disobedient to their bosses; discoveries of secrets; misfortunes; sadness; mourning; fatigues; efforts; stumbles; wounds in the limbs; economic losses; the money of thieves; prisons, confinements; servants; pawns of the bailiff; men outside their homes; men who wish to live in solitude; what happened to the native in the womb; the quality of the native's birth; all four-legged land animals

This is the most expansive list of essential significations of the houses we have encountered in any source so far, and it tends to indicate that al-Rijāl was writing from extensive personal experience of the many ways in which he interpreted the meanings of the houses in different types of astrological judgements, including those from horary figures. Additionally, a number of meanings of derived houses are included in the text, which was a common practice among the medieval and Renaissance astrologers, although the technique had been taught long ago by Valens; to restrict the length of the list, these derived significations are omitted here.

Unusually, we see al-Rijāl straddling the modal classical view and the usual medieval one in his joint assignation of friendship to the 3rd and 11th houses. Even more peculiarly, we see him connect the 11th house to enemies to a lesser degree, alongside the 12th – a lead that would be followed by Al-Bîrûnî.

From time to time, al-Rijāl also cites the opinion of Ptolemy regarding the procedure for judging a particular question (such as the state of the children), where it is at variance with the house association-based rules that al-Rijāl himself has set down. This suggests that by the 11th century, Ptolemy had come to be considered one of the foremost ancient authorities on astrology.

21. Al-Bîrūnî (973 – ca. 1048)

Muḥammad ibn Aḥmad al-Bîrūnî, a native of modern-day Uzbekistan who also spent several years in India, was a polymath much like Ptolemy and had a particular interest in astronomy and astrology. In addition to a short treatise on transits, he wrote a compendious introductory textbook on astrology, astronomy, and mathematics, entitled the *Book of Instruction in the Elements of the Art of Astrology*. This was written in Arabic and was never translated into Latin, but a modern edition of the Arabic with a full facing English translation was published in 1934,[67] making it the first complete Arabic medieval astrological text to be favoured with translation into English.

In his *Book of Instruction*, al-Bîrūnî makes space for succinct and separate lists of house keywords pertaining to nativities and to horary questions. For present purposes, we shall consider only those relating to nativities. He also perpetuates the tradition of linking the houses to ages of life, and gives the first fully-formed list we have seen of keywords tying each house to a particular part of the body, crystallising the genesis of a tradition that would run through many later medieval and early modern works.

1st: Soul; life; length of life; education; native land; infancy; the head

2nd: Suckling; nutriment; disaster to the eyes if unlucky; the livelihood; household requisites; assistants; work of children; the remainder of childhood; the neck

3rd: Brothers; sisters; relations; in-laws; friends; jewels; short journeys; migration; knowledge; intelligence; expertise in religious law; the arms and hands

4th: Parents; grandparents; descendants; knowledge of genealogy; property; houses; fields; the water supply; old age; death; what follows death and what happens to the dead; the sides of the body

5th: Children; friends; clothes; pleasure; joy; the accumulated wealth of the father; what was said of the father at his funeral; the heart

6th: Sickness; disease of internal organs; defects of the body; accidents to the legs, if unfortunate; overwork; loss of property; slaves; maids; cattle; the abdomen or belly

7th: Concubines; women; marriage-feasts; giving in marriage; partnership; contentions; losses; lawsuits; the prime of life; the back and hips

8th: Death and its causes; murder; poisoning; the deleterious effects of drugs on the body; the feigning of death; inheritance; the wife's property; expenditure; poverty and extreme deprivation; the sexual organs

9th: Travel; religion; piety; philosophy; the attainment of knowledge from the stars and from divination; the interpretation of visions and dreams; fate; seriousness; sharp discernment; surveying; trustworthiness; the beginning of youth; the thighs

10th: The rule of the Sultan; government by a council of nobles; absolute authority; success in business; commerce; professions; well-behaved children; liberality; the middle part of youth; the knees

11th: Happiness; friends; enemies; prayer; concern for the afterlife; praise; the friendship of women; love; commerce; ornaments; dress; perfume; longevity; the latter part of youth; the calves

12th: Enemies; adversity; misery; anxieties; fear; disease; tumults; debt; fines; prison; bail; slaves; servants; armies; cattle; exile; harbours; the prenatal fancies of the mother; the feet

Among the more novel readings by al-Bîrûnî in his day is his assignation of fear to the 12th house instead of the 8th, as was then traditional. When we come to Abraham Ibn Ezra, we shall witness him associating both these houses with fear.

22. Abraham Ibn Ezra (c. 1089–1164)

Abraham Ibn Ezra was a Jewish scholar famed for his Bible commentaries. He also wrote numerous works on astrology, the surviving Hebrew manuscripts of which have recently been edited and translated into English by Shlomo Sela. For the purposes of this study, however, we shall refer to Meira Epstein's earlier translations of the two volumes of greatest relevance, which are the *Beginning of Wisdom*,[68] and the *Book of Nativities and Revolutions*.[69] It is chiefly in the *Beginning of Wisdom*, Chapter 3, that Ibn Ezra sets out the essential meanings of the houses, as part of his exposition of the general principles of astrology.

1st: The life of the person; the body; the mind; intelligence; the thoughts on one's mind; the soul; faith; speech; fruitfulness or fertility; the beginnings of all actions; the beginning of life

2nd: Money; possessions; treasures; trading; food; one's assistants; those who obey one's command; witnesses; keys

3rd: Brothers; sisters; relatives; in-laws; knowledge in general and of the Torah and the prevailing laws; faith; dreams; modesty; counsel; rumours; letters; short-distance travel

4th: The father; land; houses; fields; building; regions; hidden treasures; all hidden things; the end of any matter

5th: The son or children; food; drink; pleasure; gambling; gifts; clothing; emissaries; the crops and treasures of the father

6th: Chronic illness; lies; slander; prison; slaves; maids; small animals

7th: Women; intercourse; partnership; partners; standing trial; dispute; fighting; war(s); robbers

8th: Death; grief; separation; loss; fear; inheritance; loans

9th: Travel; distant roads; emissaries; philosophy; religion and the worship of God; oaths; dreams; divination; laws; judgement; the sciences; rumours; anyone removed from high position

10th: The mother; government or authority; kingdom; dominion; reputation; honour; all professions

11th: Honour; grace; good name; friends; companions; hope; the king's ministers, treasurers and wardrobe stewards

12th: Grief; poverty; affliction; disgrace; fear; jealousy; hatred; prison; captivity; fraud; vigilance; animals used for riding

It is notable that Ibn Ezra associates faith with the 1st and 3rd houses, in contrast to Masha'Allah, who associated it with the 9th and 11th, and Manilius, who associated it with the 7th. The 1s house connection is altogether novel, although several of the Arabic astrologers had linked faith to the 3rd. Ibn Ezra's joint indication of the 11th house (together with the 10th) in matters of honour is also without known precedent. Additionally, he is the first source we have found to link the 5th house specifically to gambling, although it was earlier connected with entertainment by Abū Ma'Shar.

23. Guido Bonatti (ca. 1210–1295)

The 13th-century Italian astrologer Guido Bonatti wrote one of the longest textbooks of astrology of the Middle Ages in the form of his *Liber introductorius ad iudicia stellarum*, or *Book of Introduction to the Judgements of the Stars*, which compendiously draws on his reading of many earlier medieval and ancient authorities, including numerous texts that have been lost to history. When Bonatti's work was finally printed in 1491, the publisher confusingly labelled it *Decem Continens Tractatus Astronomie*, meaning 'Containing Ten Treatises on Astronomy'. While it does indeed contain ten treatises, they are all on astrology. The entire work was first translated into English by Dykes in 2007,[70] and it is to his translation that we refer here.

As could reasonably be expected from a volume that spans over 800 pages of dense Latin text, the book contains plenty of references to the meanings of the twelve houses, found chiefly in Treatise 2: Signs of Houses, Chapter 5. Many of these meanings are ascribed to named authorities such as Al-Qabisi and a favourite of Bonatti's who is little known today, ad-Dawla. This summary presents Bonatti's house meaning readings together without individual attributions:

1st: The life and body of the native; the beginning of life; the beginning of any work; the shortest journeys

2nd: Substance; acquisition; the aggregation of possessions and money; receiving and donations; assistants; allies; letters; the end of youth

3rd: Brothers; sisters; relatives in general, especially younger ones; those who have fewer riches or less wisdom or power than the native and seek advice and help from him in the handling of their own affairs accordingly; close friendships; loves; faith; religion; contracts; legates; changes of place or dwelling; short journeys; patience; endurance; sects; contention in sects; heretics; dreams; letters; life just before death

4th: Fathers; grandfathers; direct ancestors in the male lineage of either the native or the spouse; houses; lands; inheritances other than from the dead; all immovable things, including roofed dwellings, buildings, towers, castles and cities; anything buried, underground, or put in the ground; hidden treasures; secret things or those kept in a secret place; the act of capturing prisoners; what happens to the corpse after death; the end of matters

5th: Children; games; delights; joy; legates; donations; clothing; what is said about a man after his death; papers; books; short stories; anything in which trust is invested, including honour, petitions, friendship, a woman, the condition of the citizens, and the fruits of inheritance

6th: Illnesses; infirmities; justices; vassals; slaves; servants; beasts that are not ridden, including chickens, geese, ducks, hawks and bees; movement from place to place; the period before old age

7th: Women; wives; weddings; marriages and matters of marriage; participation; partners; very pleasing things; contentions and contrarieties between people; battles; hostile things; people overthrown by their burdens or work; opposition; opposites; buying and selling; thieves; robbers; fugitives; road cutters; medium to long journeys; pilgrimages; exiles; the loss of things and their purposes; lost items; the simplest, pure culture of the deity; religion; divine wisdom; faith; foreknowledge; the science of the stars; the diviner; dreams; health; rumours; letters; legates; the middle of the latter part of life

8th: Fear; sorrow; death; killing; lethal poisons; all that is inherited from the dead; women's dowries; all that perishes; labour; skills; wars; bellicose people; spiteful people; cunning; the act of incarceration; things deposited for safekeeping; estate management; interest on loans (according to certain people); the final years of life after old age

9th: Philosophy; faith; religion; places of worship; wisdom; the culture of the deity; vision; foreknowledge; dreams; long journeys; writing; books; letters; legates; reputation; the middle of life

10th: The king; empire; kingdom; glory; dignities; honours; the reputation of one's worth; offices; positions; professions; mastered arts; divine things; mothers; grandmothers; mothers-in-law; female ancestors; judges; overseers of works; stolen items; mid-life

11th: Fortune; trust; hope; praises; children; ministers; the end part of the middle years of life

12th: Hidden enemies; deceivers; the envious; whisperings; slanders; evil wills; evil thoughts; bad characters; cunning; griefs; sorrows; wailing; weeping; lamentations; prisons (as places); prisoners; cows; horses; donkeys; camels; animals ridden; labours; what happens to women from conception of a child and from giving birth; the end of life.

Because Bonatti cites so many sources that they sometimes contradict each other, he leaves us with a somewhat confused picture of the scope of the meaning of a few of the houses, for example with religion, faith, and dreams all connected with the 3rd, 7th, and 9th; and books with the 5th and 9th. He also adds in his own notions, such as connecting reputation to the 9th house, as well as to the

10th. On the whole, however, he merely repeats what has been written by earlier authorities. Bonatti, like Valens before him, illustrates the dangers of trying to cover too many opinions and possibilities on the essential interpretation of any astrological feature at once, leaving a sense of disorder, with no clearly stated guidance or general rule to follow.

24. Leopold of Austria (compilation written c. 1271)

Leopold of Austria was a 13th-century Austrian astrologer who wrote a manuscript compendium of astrology entitled *Compilatio... de Astrorum Scientia Decem Continens Tractatus* ('Compilation about the Science of the Stars, containing Ten Treatises'). It was eventually printed in 1489, and again in 1520. Dykes recently undertook the first English translation, which he published in 2015.[71]

In Treatise IV, *De Introductoriis Iudiciorum*, verses 77–93, Leopold gives a brief account of the essential significations of the twelve houses as follows:[72]

1st: Life and its weakness; the illumination and revelation of things previously concealed

2nd: Assets and their acquisition and storage; the reason for one's means of earning a living

3rd: Brothers, sisters, and older relatives

4th: Fathers; buildings; lands; hidden things; prison; storehouses; death and its aftermath

5th: Children; delights; legates

6th: Infirmity; slaves; movement from place to place

7th: Women; contentions; contrarieties

8th: Deaths; killings; the assets and wills of the dead

9th: Travels abroad; religions; dreams; divination

10th: Rulership; boldness; loftiness; glory; mastery; works; judges; the nobility; mothers

11th: Trust; praise; the fortune of friends; ministers

12th: Productive labours; limitation; enemies; animals

Most of these assignations are familiar from those previously compiled by Bonatti, and it seems reasonable to take Leopold at his word that his book is only a compilation of existing lore.

25. Johann Schöner (1477–1547)

Johann Schöner was a German mathematician and astronomer who also took an active interest in astrology and wrote two astrological textbooks that were published within his lifetime. The first of these, *Opusculum Astrologicum* (1539), was a brief work by design. It was eventually translated into English by Robert Hand for Project Hindsight and first published thus in 1994.[73] Schöner's major astrological work, however, was his second, *De iudiciis nativitatum libri tres* ('Three Books on the Judgements of Nativities') (1545). The first component 'book' of its three internal books has also been rendered into English by Hand, and was published thus by ARHAT in 2001.[74] The second and third books remain untranslated.

For present purposes, we refer to the available English translation of *Opusculum Astrologicum*, which deals with the fundaments of the house meanings in Canon V of its Second Part. Book 1 of *De iudiciis nativitatum libri tres* was inspected too but was found not to cover this ground.

1st: Human life; spirit; the constitution of and incidents to the body; the head; the eyes; the ears; the nose; the mouth; polyps

2nd: Wealth; property; household furnishings; the neck; the throat; the glands

3rd: Brothers; sisters; relatives; in-laws; neighbours; hospitality; relatively short journeys; the hands; the arms; the shoulders

4th: Buildings; foundations; immovable property; treasures; hidden things; agriculture; the oesophagus; the chest; the lungs; the spleen

5th: Children; gifts; favours; clothes; the heart; the liver; the stomach; the sides; the back

6th: Illnesses; injuries; servants; small animals; the lower abdomen including the intestines

7th: The state of marriage; dowries; contentions, disputes, and damages arising from them; the kidneys; the loins; the groin

8th: The quality of death; inheritances; occult faculties; sadness; great fears; lethal poisons; strangulation; stones;[75] constipation; colic; haemorrhoids; the spine; the bladder; the genitals; pubic hair

9th: Truth; piety; sects of faith; philosophy; wisdom; divination; dream interpretation; long journeys; the liver; chyme; the hips and buttocks

10th: Dominion; office; honours; magistery; nationhood; studies; liberal arts; the mother; the upper legs; the knees

11th: Friends; counsellors; supporters; favours; hope; the lower legs and ankles

12th: Sadness; hardship; enemies; servants; prison; large animals; gout; the feet

Schöner gives more space to the rulership of parts of the body than any previous author we have seen, building on the readings of Al-Bîrûnî to specifically refer to a greater number of organs and regions, these collectively amounting to about half his overall coverage of each house. His notes on the general significations of the houses are otherwise relatively brief and conventional.

26. Claude Dariot (1533–1594)

French astrologer Claude Dariot wrote an important 16th-century Latin astrological work entitled *Ad astrorum iudicia facilis introductio* ('Easy introduction to the judgements of the stars'), which served chiefly as an introduction to the principles of astrology and a guide to horary and electional judgements. In the original Latin edition, it was bound with a separate treatise by Dariot on medical astrology, although that has never been translated into modern languages. A translation of the rest of the book into French appeared the following year, and a rendering of it into English by Fabian Withers was published in 1583 and reprinted in 1598 and 1653. It is to the 1598 edition of the Withers translation that we refer here.[76] The significations of the houses in general are covered in Chapter XII:

> 1st – called Life – signifies the life and body of the native or querent; the beginning of all things; health; complexion; spirit; sickness; accidents of the body; the first age of life; the head; the colour white
>
> 2nd – called Hope – signifies substance; riches; gain by labour; household things; servants; the neck; the colour green
>
> 3rd – called the Goddess or the House of Brethren – signifies brothers, sisters, cousins and kindred; changes; short journeys; faith; religion; the shoulders, arms and hands; the colour croceal[77]
>
> 4th – called the House of Parents – signifies fathers; houses; lands; ancient heritages; gardens; waters; woods; pastures; immoveable things; happenings after death; hidden treasures; things hidden in the earth; the end of all things; the chest, lungs and spleen; the colour red

5th – called the House of Children – signifies children; ambassadors and messengers; playing; gifts; loves; banquets; clothes; the stomach, liver, heart, sinews, sides and back; honey colour

6th – called the House of Health, or Sickness – signifies infirmities and sickness; servants and maids;[78] happenings before old age; moving from place to place; all small beasts and cattle; the lower part of the abdomen; the colour black

7th – called Marriage and Wife – signifies marriage; women; contentions; wars; public enemies; banishments; robberies; the end of middle age; buying and selling; runaways; thefts; rapines; all wickedness; death; parts of the body beneath the navel, and the thighs and haunches; the colour black

8th – called the House of Death – signifies death; labours; sadness; heaviness; inheritance from the dead; the end of the life; hidden treasures; deadly poisons; fears; strangury, colic, stones and haemorrhoids; the womb and bladder; the colour white

9th – called the house of Religion, or God – signifies religion and faith; visions; wisdom; the deity; ecclesiastical dignities; worship; rumours and tales; dreams; predictions; ambassadors; long journeys; early mid-life; arts; the fundament, buttocks and hips; the colour black

10th – called the Middle of the Heaven – signifies empire; rule; dignities; offices; arts, especially the art that a man is inclined to; mothers; things stolen; mid-life; the knees and hams; the colour red

11th – called the Good Spirit – signifies hope; trust; confidence; footmen; assistants to and favourites of the king; praise and commendation; familiar friends; the legs to the ankles; the colour croceal

12th – called the Evil Spirit – signifies private and secret enemies; deceivers; envious persons; imprisonments; evil thoughts; whisperings; large beasts and cattle; events attending the travel of women; sex workers;[79] hatred; dissentions; certain diseases and sicknesses; gout; the feet; the colour green

Dariot appears to have compiled a wide variety of the medieval and earlier tradition here, while simultaneously including some of the extended anatomical associations found in the *Compilation* of Leopold of Austria. Additionally, Dariot is the first source we have encountered to give prominence to colours in connection with the houses. A practically problematic feature of his text as translated by Withers is the use of three different houses to signify the colour black, and two each to signify croceal, white, red, and green; leaving just one to signify honey-coloured and none to signify any other colours. We may reasonably infer that the doctrine was perhaps at an experimental stage and had tentatively been used in horary judgements.

27. William Lilly (1602–1681)

William Lilly was at the vanguard of the succession of English astrologers who flourished in the mid-17th century. His most important book, *Christian Astrology Modestly Treated of in Three Books* (1647),[80] was a compendious reference work on the principles of astrology (Book 1) and both horary (Book 2) and natal (Book 3) astrological methods. It is in Book 1 Chapter VII that we find Lilly's main account of the essential significations of the houses. There are some further hints in chapter titles to Book 3, as well as in a brief chapter within Book 3 headed 'The nature of the HOUSES'.

For the sake of consistency in our coverage of the views of different authors, Lilly's separate readings of the houses in mundane astrological contexts have been excluded here. We find:

1st: The life of man; the stature, colour, complexion, form and shape of the querent or native; the head and face; the colour white

2nd: Riches; the goods of fortune; the estate, fortune, wealth, or poverty of the querent; moveable goods; money lent; profit or loss; friends or assistants in lawsuits or in private duels; in nativities, the wealth and substance necessary to support life; household goods; gain procured by the native's labour; the neck; the colour green

3rd: Brothers, sisters, cousins and kindred; near neighbours; short or inland journeys; frequent moves between places; hospitality; epistles; letters; messengers; rumours; sudden news; novelties; the shoulders, arms, hands and fingers; the colours red, yellow and croceal

4th: Fathers in general and the father of the native or querent in particular; the patrimony; lands; buildings, houses and tenements; immovable goods; inheritances; tillage of the earth; hidden treasures; mines and profit from the earth; the outcome or end of anything; towns, cities and villages; castles; ancient dwellings; gardens; fields; pastures; orchards; grounds and the quality of their soil; farming and land management; the chest and lungs; the colour red

5th: Children and their health or sickness; ambassadors; pregnant women; banquets; ale-houses; taverns; plays; messengers or agents for republics; the ammunition of a town under siege; pleasure, delight and merriment; gifts; curious clothing; all pleasant things; the stomach, liver, heart, sides and back; the colours black, white, and honey-colour

6th: Infirmities and diseases; sickness and its cause and prognosis; hurts of the body or limbs; medicine; uncles and aunts on the father's side of the family; servants; galley slaves; day-labourers; farmers; shepherds; hogherds; cattle herders; gamekeepers; pigs; sheep; goats; hares; conies;[81] small cattle; bees; doves; geese; hens; causes of sorrow or cares; the lower abdomen and intestines; the colour black

7th: Marriages; love questions; women; wives and sweethearts; lawsuits and the defendant in them; quarrels; duels; wars and the enemy in them; foreign affairs; thieves and thefts; rapines; public enemies; seditions;[82] fugitives, runaways, exiles and outlaws; the haunches and navel to the buttocks; a dark black colour

8th: Death and its quality and kind; the wills, legacies, estates and heirs of the deceased; unexpected inheritances; dowries; the estate of women; the portion[83] of maids; fears; mental anguish; in lawsuits, friends of the defendant; haemorrhoids; stones; strangury; poisons; the bladder and privy-parts; the colours green and black

9th: Journeys, especially long journeys and voyages over sea; religions and their sects; clergy and ministers of religion; livings from church appointments; godliness; all things pertaining to the Church; wisdom; dreams; visions; foreign countries; books; learning; epistles; scholarship; the work or messages of ambassadors; the fundament, hips and thighs; the colours green and white

10th: Honour; preferment; dignities; office; power; command; profession, trade or vocation; esteem; kings and kingdoms; princes and principalities; dukes and dukedoms; empires; counties; earls; judges; lawyers; senior military officers and local government officials; public administrations in the Commonwealth; magistracy and public magistrates; mothers; the knees and hams; the colours red and white

11th: Friends and friendship; hope; trust; confidence; praise or disapproval; preferment; promotion by the commendation of friends; the counsellors, servants, allies, associates and favourites of kings; courtiers; the advisors of governors; the happy conclusion of any business; the legs to the ankles; the colours saffron and yellow

12th: Enemies, especially private enemies; witches; large animals including horses, oxen, cows, and elephants; tribulation; sad events; sorrow; mental anguish; affliction; poverty; self-undoing; imprisonment; those who maliciously undermine or secretly inform against their neighbours; labour; impostors; sex workers; the feet; the colour green.

Lilly's significations of the twelve houses are broadly compatible with those of Dariot as translated by Withers; however, he drops Dariot's association of the 6th house with movement from place to place and selectively overhauls his scheme of colour significations, replacing white with green and black for the 8th house, adding black and white to the 5th house, and replacing black with green and white for the 9th house. The result is that under Lilly's scheme, the 5th, 6th, 7th, and 8th houses can all signify black, whereas under Dariot's, only the 6th, 7th, and 9th could. Lilly's association of certain colours with multiple houses is arguably no less confusing than Dariot's.

28. Morin de Villefranche (1583–1656)

Jean-Baptiste Morin wrote a vast Latin manuscript in 26 books called *Astrologia Gallica*, by which he sought to redefine the philosophy of astrology while also setting out its most practically valuable methods and techniques. Although he did not live to see it in print, it was published five years after his death, in 1661, thanks to the support of Queen Marie Louise of Poland (1611–1667), who had been one of his clients. Book 17 of Morin's masterwork is dedicated to the astrological houses, and it was published in a modern English translation by the late James Herschel Holden. Additionally, Morin wrote a much briefer treatise outlining his philosophy for the astrological houses, entitled *The Cabal of the Twelve Houses Astrological* – as translated by George Wharton and published thus in 1659.[84] This generally agrees with Book 17 of *Astrologia Gallica* but has much less to say about the essential meanings of the houses, tending to be limited to a single keyword on each, so we shall primarily refer here to Holden's translation.

1st: Life; health; the constitution of the body; temperament; intelligence; habits; an accidental significator of marriages

2nd: Riches; acquisitions; immobile goods acquired by the native's own labour; gold; silver; estate; furniture; equipment; inanimate material things in general

3rd: Brothers; relatives; connection by blood

4th: The parents and their status during the life of the native; successions; suffering occasioned to the body and imprinted in the mind from the beginning of life by the parents; the expectations and hopes of the parents for the native

5th: Children; bodily pleasures

6th: 'Animate material things'[85] such as servants, subordinates and domestic animals; a secondary or accidental significator of illnesses, imprisonment, and secret enemies

7th: Matrimony and marriage; open enemies; lawsuits; a significator of illnesses and death because of its opposition to the first

8th: Death

9th: Religion; the life in God as understood by man through the mind or reason; travel

10th: Magistracy; dignity; nobility; fame; profession; action; immaterial profit or worldly good emerging from one's own actions, such as honours awarded

11th: Friends; simple benevolence that engenders friendship

12th: Enemies, especially secret enemies; illnesses; troubles; miseries; servitude; prisons and imprisonment; exiles; an accidental significator of servants and animals

Morin reasons that there are close ties between opposite houses, and that by dint of the opposition between each pair, each house can impart a secondary hue of its own meaning upon the facing house, thus imbuing its counterpart with accidental significations along the lines of its own essential meaning.[86] This is how he justifies the attribution of illnesses, imprisonment, and secret enemies to the sixth house, and servants and animals to the twelfth, for example.

It cannot have escaped Morin's notice that many earlier sources going back to the Middle Ages have given closely related meanings to some pairs of opposite houses, and it would seem that he has determined to elucidate a coherent rational justification for this traditional practice. For example, we have seen the 6th house preferred for sickness or illness by multiple ancient and medieval authorities, including Firmicus Maternus, Valens (who also linked them to the 12th), al-Rijāl (who also connected them to the 8th) and al-Bîrûnî; and we have seen the 12th also linked to servants by both al-Rijāl and al-Bîrûnî, and to slaves by Thrasyllus, Valens, Firmicus Maternus, Paulus Alexandrinus and Rhetorius. In Morin's view, these significations are only accidental ones arising by virtue of the oppositions cast from the 12th (in the case of sickness) or 6th (in the case of servants) houses.

In addition to drawing connections between opposing pairs of houses, Morin is eager to divide the houses into four triplicities grouped akin to the elements of the signs, with houses 1, 9, and 5 comprising the first triplicity, governed by the Ascendant; houses 10, 6, and 2 comprising the second, presided over by the Midheaven; houses 7, 3, and 11 comprising the third, ruled by the Descendent; and houses 4, 12, and 8 comprising the fourth, ruled by the Imum Coeli. This grouping is first set out in his *Cabal of the Twelve Houses Astrological*, and is then reiterated in the *Astrologia Gallica*. Morin seeks to demonstrate a fundamental relatedness of the three houses in each triplicity.

The first triplicity, he says, pertains to childhood, and is called the triplicity of life and being; the second pertains to youth and is called the triplicity of action; the third pertains to virility and is called the triplicity of marriage or love; and the fourth pertains to old age and is called the triplicity of suffering.

It is beyond our present purposes to seek to deconstruct or critically review Morin's rationale for this grouping. Historically, however, it stands as a noteworthy example of an attempt by an early modern astrologer to systematise, or instil a coherent reason to, a set of traditional astrological doctrine received from the ancients.

29. John Gadbury (1627–1704)

Several of the later 17th-century English astrologers, notably including Henry Coley and John Partridge, wrote their own astrological textbooks after that of Lilly, but on inspection there appear to be only minor variations between most of their interpretations of the essential significations of the houses, so we shall consider just one other famous example here, the prolific astrological writer John Gadbury.

Gadbury wrote several substantial astrological books, but his main work setting out the principles of astrology was *Genethlialogia, or the Doctrine of Nativities* (1658),[87] to which we refer here. His readings of the houses are found in Chapter VI: 'Shewing the Significations of the Twelve Coelestial Houses, and of the Planets posited therein'.

> 1st: The life of the native; his stature, form, and shape; the temperature and accidents of the body; the qualities of the mind; the face, its shape and colour
>
> 2nd: The estate, fortune, and riches of the native; all things necessary to life; moveable goods; the neck

3rd: Called the Goddess, signifying happiness or felicity; signifies the brothers and sisters, kindred, and neighbours of the native; changes of address;[88] short or inland journeys; epistles; letters; the arms and shoulders

4th: The dwelling-place, houses and tenements, lands, inheritances, and patrimony of the native; the father and his quality and condition; the conclusion or end of things; the chest and stomach

5th: The native's children; the native's pleasure and delight; joy; plays, banquets, revelries, merriments; taverns and inns;[89] gaming; the heart and back

6th: The sickness and diseases of the native, and their quality, cause and prognosis; uncles and aunts; servants; small beasts, including sheep, pigs, hares and dogs

7th: Marriage; the kind of person the native will marry; public enemies; lawsuits, contests and controversies; partners and trading associates; the kidneys and loins

8th: The death of the native; the goods of the deceased; legacies; wills; administrations; deeds; dowries of wives; an unfortunate, cruel and malicious house that portends evil unto the native; the genitalia[90]

9th: Fear; doubt; the House of religion; churchmen; lawyers; dreams and visions of the native; voyages or long journeys; knowledge in all sciences; the thighs and hips

10th: The House of sovereignty, kingship, and dignity; signifies the preferment, honour, renown, magistery and profession of the native; the mother; and the knees and hams

11th: Called of the Greeks... the good Daemon, Angel, or Spirit, from [its signification of] favour, friendship and benignity; signifies the native's friends, confidence and hopes; the favourites, counsellors and servants of a king; the legs and ankles

12th: Called in Greek... the evil Angel or Spirit; represents the imprisonments, captivities, banishments and private enemies of the native; large beasts, such as oxen, horses and cows; the feet.

Notably Gadbury includes references to the ancient Greek names for the houses, which appear in Greek characters without being translated into English (with occasional exceptions, such as the examples included above for the 11th and 12th houses). He nonetheless usually adds an aside aiming to rationally account for the earlier Greek choice of names. This would suggest that more than most of his 17th-century English astrological contemporaries, he was thinking as a scholar and also presuming a significant level of education in classical languages among his readership.

Otherwise, Gadbury is briefer than Dariot and Lilly, but covers most of the same ground, although while Gadbury keeps up the relatively recent tradition of relating the houses to parts of the body, he does not have anything to say in this chapter to link them to colours. Could it be that he was privately dismissive of this doctrine and felt cause to exclude it?

30. Alan Leo (1860–1917)

Alan Leo, born William Frederick Allan, was the leader of the theosophical astrology movement in the United Kingdom from 1890 until his death in 1917. He was not the only significantly influential astrologer active in the UK during those years, nor was he the only influential theosophical or esoteric astrologer on the world stage. But by tapping into the popularity of Theosophy in his day and by creatively adapting astrology in accordance with esoteric spiritual principles aligned with those espoused by Theosophy, he contributed significantly to the modernisation of astrological practice as well as to its revitalisation among the British public in his time.

In his first decade of involvement in astrological publishing, spanning 1890 to 1900, Leo was active chiefly as co-editor or editor of a succession of two popular monthly astrological magazines and as an organiser of the astrological community in London proper and England as a whole. However, in 1899, he began to serialise in the pages of his second magazine, *Modern Astrology*, the first of what would ultimately become a series of seven substantial self-penned textbooks on astrology aiming to provide the enthusiastic novice with a complete course of instruction in the principles and practice of natal astrology from a primarily spiritual perspective.

While Leo's books are technically quite simple compared with the astrological tradition, the esoteric spiritual language and concepts that run through them make them demanding to read for the theosophically uninitiated or anyone more accustomed to traditional astrology.

He is sometimes miscast as the arch-populariser of Sun sign astrology by 21st-century historians relying on unreliable secondary sources, which is a travesty of the truth. He was in fact a subtle esoteric thinker who used most of the elements of astrology handed down in the early modern English texts in interpretation, even if he was oblivious, like most of his contemporaries, to many of the techniques found in the ancient and medieval source texts that had yet to be translated into any modern language in his time.

Thus, he had plenty to say about the twelve astrological houses. The first two volumes in his series of textbooks, *Astrology for All* (copyrighted 1899; published 1900) and *Casting the Horoscope* (1901), were kept deliberately simple, the former dealing with the 144 soli-lunar sign combinations and the interpretation of the planets in the signs, and the latter serving as a step-by-step guide to the manual calculation of the nativity. His most detailed accounts of astrological interpretation were reserved for Volumes 3 and 4, *How to Judge a Nativity* Parts 1 and 2 (1903 and 1904), and his final exposition of astrology from a theosophical conceptual perspective was saved for Volume 7, *Esoteric Astrology* (1913).[91] There are advance summaries of the meanings of the first, fifth, and ninth houses in *Casting the Horoscope*.[92] Otherwise, it is in *How to Judge a Nativity Part 1*[93] that we find his most thorough accounts of the essential topical significations of the twelve astrological houses. These are unfortunately scattered across several distinct parts of the book, and demonstrate some repetition. Here we summarise the salient wordings for each house:

1st: The personality in all its expressions, such as heredity, environment, temperament, disposition, physical conditions, health conditions, sensations, emotions, and mental impressions;[94] the quality of the life forces; the desires; natural disposition; worldly outlook; physical experiences obtained through the senses; the head and face;[95] the personal appearance, health, and mind;[96] the physical body as a whole[97]

2nd: The outcome of the labour or profession in financial advantage, remuneration and monetary condition; hereditary honour; fame; worldly position; finance; service;[98] monetary prospects; moral growth; throat and ears;[99] the emotional and desire nature[100]

3rd: Relatives and in-laws; the expression through the brain of union with the subjective and objective mind; somewhat related to short journeys because of its connection to the concrete mind;[101] travelling; intellect derived from education and study; minor impressions made upon the physical brain; the neck, arms, shoulders and lungs;[102] has a definite influence over the mind, ruling mental tendencies and all affairs that seriously affect the mind; all that relates to movement, transition, and change;[103] the smaller and slower mind which has its range in the physical world only; travel by land; education and studies of the minor and more conventional order; perception[104]

4th: The psychic conditions; that which has to do with the end of life; death; withdrawal from the material world;[105] the environment; the life of the householder; the hidden and secret affairs connected with parentage or domestic affairs; the conditions at the close of life;[106] hereditary tendencies; home and domestic life; parentage; the breasts, stomach and digestive organs;[107] the grave; the conditions and affairs of the parents;[108] sometimes only one parent is indicated, usually the father[109]

5th: The outgoing sensational, emotional energy of the personality; physical generation; worldly pleasure of a more or less concrete nature; children; speculation; bodily activities;[110] the generative fire;[111] offspring; enterprise; emotional impulses;[112] generative powers; sensations; pleasurable emotions arising from the senses, worldly enterprise and energy; the loins, heart and back;[113] society and social inclinations; the emotions and feelings; the worldly fulfilment of hopes and wishes; the native's love affairs, courtships, and the affections which spring from the feeling and emotional side of the nature; the seat of the physical and magnetic attractions between the sexes; speculative affairs; all matters of enterprise and activity prompted by the desire nature; the internal nature of the desires, hopes and wishes;[114] an index to the state of the lower feelings, sensations and passional tendencies; the inner feelings; all out-of-sight matters[115]

6th: The service required; all matters connected with servants, helpers, and inferiors according to the social standard;[116] service and attachments arising from the expression of the tenth house, therefore servants and inferiors in social rank; sickness arising from worry and anxiety; phenomenal magic; the bowels and the plexus;[117] employees; situations, positions, or spheres of activity in which money may be earned;[118] relates to work; sickness; the condition of the physical body;[119] food and nourishment; ill-health through inattention to suitable diet;[120] a psychic house indicating the psychic tendencies of the native; all forms and ceremonies in which the native is interested; a latent, unexpressed house[121]

7th: Unity, such as marriage and partnership, brethren and kindred, friends and acquaintances;[122] union; all partnerships and unions of every kind; the house of marriage and of the individuality;[123] individual character and humane tendencies; the reins and kidneys;[124] represents the unifying of all that is separate or isolated in the ascendant; the complement of the first house; signifies the transmutation of the passions into pure love; the exchange of intellect for wisdom; the perfect individualisation of the conscious Self; if a planet is found in the 7th, it will describe the partner and any union;[125] also governs legal affairs; opponents; partners and co-workers; the individuality during the period of manifestation as contrasted with the personality[126]

8th: Death, and associated affairs and legacies; an occult house; denotes the sexual organs and generative system;[127] money inherited or coming to the native through other people (chiefly the business or marriage partner;[128] has bearing upon the goods of the dead; occupations connected with death; executorships; coroners; surgeons; medical officers; sanitary officers or inspectors; slaughter-houses and butchers; related to practical, executive forms of mediumship and occultism;[129]

9th: The aspirations; religion and religious tendencies; philosophy and philosophical scope; metaphysics; science; the higher mind generally;[130] the mental or spiritual fire;[131] the highest thought the mind is capable of; from the idea of the mind being able to transmit itself away from the brain limitation, associated with travel, dreams, and thought-transference;[132] long journeys; the power of imagination; the thighs;[133] the scientific and religious attitude of the native; the subjective and abstract mind, wider and less limited than the concrete brain mind represented by the third house; voyages; rapid transit; foreign travel; deep thinking; reason; legal matters; many conditions outside the native's immediate environment; the future; visions; prophecy; intuition;[134] the metaphysical and occult mind in which the subconscious state is concerned, wherein is denoted all that pertains to the intangible, the subjective, and the idealistic side of life; the unfolding of future possibility; the inexpressible; the motive behind the act; the thought behind the speech; the gift of prophecy; the power to become clairvoyant[135]

10th: Hereditary or general honour; fame; worldly position; finance; service;[136] worldly status; parentage and hereditary tendencies; profession; business employment; occupation;[137] business ability; material or general reputation; all worldly activities and moral responsibilities; the knees;[138] work; business; public standing; honour or dishonour according to the good or evil expressed;[139] a partial indicator of the native's employment or trade, considered alongside the houses and signs containing the majority of the planets[140]

11th: Friends and acquaintances; hopes and wishes;[141] aspirations; the ankles;[142] a partial indicator alongside the seventh in questions of marriage;[143] as the fifth house of the marriage partner, relevant to questions concerning children; a benefic house tending towards good fortune, pleasure, happiness and prosperity; often found containing strong or fortunate planets in the horoscopes of persons who are prominent in politics, municipal affairs, or business matters concerned with the many rather than the few; in some cases the lover or marriage partner is more accurately described by the eleventh than the seventh as it stands for friendships that may end in marriage[144]

12th: The house of confinement or matters that spring out of parentage, inheritance and unseen affairs connected with the inner or psychic life; therefore often called the house of occultism and physical self-undoing;[145] occult tendencies; the psychic inheritance from the past resulting in joy or sorrow; the feet;[146] sorrow; misfortune; enemies; imprisonment;[147] related to the psychic mind in which receptivity or mental sensitiveness to the unseen worlds is awakened, which may tend to induce sorrow in matters of an external or purely physical type; trouble and difficulty in matters of an emotional character; annoyance, worry and anxiety in intellectual or mental matters, but in this relation it may also bring joy or peace; the voluntary recluse; the prisoner; the pauper; the invalid; enemies, or may show the native to be his own worst enemy[148]

The detailed way Leo relates the houses to the mental or spiritual nature of the individual departs form earlier approaches that link the houses purely factually to departments of life, circumstances, or concepts in isolation. Yet it is also apparent that Leo largely still follows tradition in connecting the houses with key themes. He has not completely reinvented the wheel of house meanings, but he has sought to account for them according to a coherent intellectual perspective.

Like Morin before him, Leo also attempts to systematise the understanding of the essential meanings of the houses by linking them together in groups. Unlike Morin, he draws particular attention to the quadruplicities of the cardinal, succedent and cadent houses. He associates the angles with the body, actions, and outward expression; the succedent houses with the soul, speech, and feelings and emotions undergoing maturation for future development; and the cadent houses with thought, spirit, matters latent in the mind, and affairs brought over from past lives that are not yet ready for expression in the physical world.[149]

In *Esoteric Astrology* Chapter V, *The Houses and their Importance*, Leo states that the twelve houses have a more direct bearing upon fate and fortune in the outer world, or the Karma of the current life, than either the zodiacal signs or the planets do. In linking the houses to karma, he connects them with his theosophically inspired belief in reincarnation, and foreshadows the later 20th-century development of karmic astrology.

Conclusion

In this study, we have closely examined the evolution of house meanings among the ancient and medieval astrologers, and have seen an intriguing combination of continuity and change in those meanings during the period spanning from the early 1st century CE to the mid-thirteenth. The changes witnessed can be understood primarily in terms of the ongoing experimentation and practical experience of astrologers practising and writing at different points in time, and secondarily in terms of astrologers' selective access to past sources and partial preferences for certain astrological authorities over others.

We have also sampled six early modern sources ranging in date from the mid-16th to the early 20th century, and among these, investigated two early modern attempts to intellectually systematise these meanings by grouping the houses together based on their natural astronomical relationships to each other and by connecting them to fundamental concepts of human psychology and its inward and outward manifestations.

The house meanings are but one case of an area of astrological tradition that has evolved for two thousand years while retaining a core of continuity, and we know that some astrological techniques and ideas in use in ancient times fell into almost total disuse until the recent revival of traditional astrology and related historical scholarship. Every case is different, and every element of a tradition such as astrology is subject to different evolutionary pressures from both within and outside the circle of its professional and serious amateur practitioners.

Endnotes

[1] Hephaistio of Thebes, tr. Robert H. Schmidt, *Project Hindsight Greek Track Volume XV: Apotelesmatics Book II* (Berkeley Springs, WV: Golden Hind Press, 1998), p. 66.

[2] Manuscript sources vary between the two forms. Chris Brennan notes that either would make sense. See Chris Brennan, *Hellenistic Astrology: The Study of Fate and Fortune* (Denver, CO: Amor Fati, 2017), p. 340.

[3] See Dorian Gieseler Greenbaum, *The Daimon in Hellenistic Astrology: Origins and Influence* (Leiden: Brill, 2016), pp. 56–57.

[4] See Brennan, *op. cit.*, p. 370.

[5] Meaning 'eight-turning' and 'eight-place' [system], respectively.

[6] See Robert Schmidt (tr.); Robert Hand (ed.), *The Astrological Record of the Early Sages in Greek [Project Hindsight Greek Track Volume X]* (Berkeley Springs, WV: Golden Hind Press, 1995), p. 59; and James Herschel Holden, *A History of Horoscopic Astrology*

from the Babylonian Period to the Modern Age (Tempe, AZ: AFA, 1996).
7. As translated by Schmidt; Holden instead gives 'livelihood'.
8. As rendered by Schmidt; Holden instead gives 'brothers'.
9. See footnote 54 in Brennan, *op. cit.*, pp. 342–43.
10. See the Loeb Classical Library edition of Manilius's *Astronomica*, as edited by Goold, p. lxii.
11. See his article *Dominion, or the System of 8 Houses* at http://cura.free.fr/11domi2e.html
12. In *Classical Philology*, Volume XXII, Number 1 (January, 1927).
13. In John Garrett Winter, ed., *Michigan Papyri Vol. III: Papyri in the University of Michigan Collection* (Ann Arbor: University of Michigan Press, 1936), pp. 107–17.
14. Winter, *op. cit.*, p. 100, citing the text on column ix, line 22 of the Papyrus.
15. A. E. Housman, 'The Michigan Astrological Papyrus', *Classical Philology*, Vol. XXII, No. 3 (July 1927): pp. 259–60.
16. *Ibid.*
17. Here, I have given the readings of Robbins first, from Winter, *op. cit.*, pp. 112–13, with those of Gleadow added after the / in each line only where they differ from those of Robbins (*see below*).
18. Housman, 'The Michigan Astrological Papyrus', pp. 257–63.
19. Frank Eggleston Robbins, ed., *A New Astrological Treatise: Michigan Papyrus No. 1*, pp. 36–37.
20. See Antiochus of Athens; tr. Robert Schmidt; ed. Robert Hand, *The Thesaurus [Project Hindsight Greek Track Volume II-B]* (Berkeley Springs, WV: Golden Hind Press, 1993).
21. See Julius Firmicus Maternus; ed. / tr. James Herschel Holden, *Mathesis* (Tempe, AZ: AFA, 2011), and Firmicus Maternus, tr. Jean Rhys Bram, '[Noyes Classical Studies :] Ancient Astrology Theory and Practice: Matheseos Libri VIII' (Noyes Press, 1975).
22. Holden tr., Book II, Ch. 18; Bram tr. (as 'The Eight Houses'), Book II, Ch. XIV.
23. See Bram tr., p. 308, fn 36,
24. Bram tr., Book II Ch. XIV, p. 45,
25. See Loeb Classical Library edition, Book 2, lines 968–70, pp. 158–59.
26. See Manilius; ed. / tr. G. P. Goold, *[The Loeb Classical Library, LCL 469:] Astronomica.* Revised edition, reprinted with corrections (Harvard University Press, 1997).
27. See Deborah Houlding, *Houses: Temples of the Sky* (Ascella, 1998), p. 16; pp. 37–38.
28. See, for example, *ibid.*, pp. 23–24.
29. *Ibid.*, p. 36; pp. 41–42.
30. Wolfgang Hübner, *Die Dodekatropos des Manilius* (Franz Steiner Verlag, 1995), diag. p. 33; pp. 62–65.
31. Greenbaum, *op. cit.*, p. 57; pp. 57–58, fn 54.
32. See Schmidt and Hand, *The Astrological Record of the Early Sages in Greek*, p. 60; and Holden, *A History of Horoscopic Astrology*, pp. 27–28.
33. Greenbaum, *op. cit.*, pp. 60–61.

34 Houlding, *op. cit.*, p. 42.
35 See Dorotheus of Sidon; tr. / ed. Benjamin N. Dykes, *Carmen Astrologicum: The 'Umar al-Tabari Translation* (Minneapolis, MN: Cazimi Press, 2017); and Dorotheus Sidonius; ed. / tr. David Pingree, *Dorothei Sidonii Carmen Astrologicum – Interpretationem Arabicam in Linguam Anglicam Versam una cum Dorothei Fragmentis et Graecis et Latinis* (Leipzig: BSB B. G. Teubner, 1976).
36 See Ptolemy; tr. F. E. Robbins, *[The Loeb Classical Library, LCL 435:] Tetrabiblos* (Cambridge, MA/London: Harvard University Press, undated reprint of 1940 edition).
37 Greenbaum, *op. cit.*, pp. 65–66.
38 Brennan, *op. cit.*, p. 384.
39 See Ptolemy, *op. cit.*, p. 239.
40 See Vettius Valens; tr. Andrea L. Gehrz, *2.1* (Portland, OR: Moira Press, 2016); and Vettius Valens; tr. Robert Schmidt; ed. Robert Hand, *The Anthology Book II, Part 1 [Project Hindsight Greek Track Volume VII]* (Berkeley Springs, WV: Golden Hind Press, 1994).
41 See Vettius Valens of Antioch; tr. Andrea L. Gehrz, *4.1* (Portland, OR: Moira Press, 2017); and Vettius Valens; tr. Robert Schmidt; ed. Robert Hand, *The Anthology Book IV [Project Hindsight Greek Track Volume XI]* (Berkeley Springs, WV: Golden Hind Press, 1996).
42 See Vettius Valens of Antioch; tr. Andrea L. Gehrz, *9.1* (Portland, OR: Moira Press, 2017).
43 *Ibid.*, [Ch. 3:] *On the 12 Tropes in the Practical and Impractical Places* [unpaginated].
44 Brennan, *op. cit.*, p. 351.
45 See Antiochus of Athens; tr. Schmidt; ed. Hand, *The Thesaurus, op. cit.*
46 It is not immediately clear if this means that it begets an idle quality in the planets found in or ruling over the house, or if the house itself is regarded by Antiochus as not governing anything in particular, and therefore 'idle', but it seems likely that its perceived idleness is a product of the lack of a conventional (Ptolemaic) aspect from the Ascendant to the Eighth.
47 The summary of Antiochus would appear to be citing an unnamed authority for this outlying opinion.
48 Gleadow gives the unusual expression 'declension of fortune', where 'declension' is an archaic word for deterioration or decay.
49 See Porphyry the Philosopher; tr. James Herschel Holden, *Introduction to the Tetrabiblos* (Tempe, AZ: AFA, 2009), pp. 46–47.
50 See Paulus Alexandrinus; tr. Robert Schmidt; ed. Robert Hand, *Introductory Matters [Project Hindsight Greek Track Volume I]*. Third Edition, Revised (Berkeley Springs, WV: Golden Hind Press, Feb. 1995); and Paul of Alexandria; tr. James Herschel Holden, *Introduction to Astrology*. Stated Third Edition. (Tempe, AZ: AFA, 2012).

51. See especially Hephaistio of Thebes; tr. / ed. Robert H. Schmidt, *Apotelesmatics Book II [Project Hindsight Greek Track Volume XV]* (Cumberland, MD: Golden Hind Press, 1998); and Hephaistion of Thebes; tr. Eduardo J. Gramaglia; ed. Benjamin N. Dykes, *Apotelesmatics Book III: On Inceptions* (Minneapolis, MN: Cazimi Press, 2013).
52. See Rhetorius the Egyptian; tr. James H. Holden, *Astrological Compendium, Containing his Explanation and Narration of the Whole Art of Astrology*. First Published Edition. (Tempe, AZ: AFA, 2009).
53. First edited by Wilhelm Gundel in 1936 as *Neue Astrologische Texte des Hermes Trismegistos: Funde und Forschungen auf dem Gebiet der antiken Astronomie und Astrologie* – with a reprint edited by Hans-Georg Gundel published by Gerstenberg Verlag, Hildesheim, in 1978.
54. See [Hermes, attrib.]; tr. Robert Zoller; ed. Robert Hand, *Liber Hermetis Part I [Project Hindsight Latin Track Volume II]* (Berkeley Springs, WV: The Golden Hind Press, 1993), pp. xvii–xviii.
55. *Ibid.*, p. 37.
56. [Hermes, attrib.]; tr. Robert Zoller; ed. Robert Hand, *Liber Hermetis Part II [Project Hindsight Latin Track Volume III]* (Berkeley Springs, WV: The Golden Hind Press, 1993), pp. 39–40.
57. See Hugo of Santalla; eds. Charles Burnett and David Pingree, *[Warburg Institute Surveys and Texts 26:] The Liber Aristotilis of Hugo of Santalla* (London: The Warburg Institute, 1997); and *Liber Aristotilis* Ch. II.7 and Ch. III, in Benjamin N. Dykes, tr. / ed., *Persian Nativities Volume I: Masha'Allah & Abu' Ali* (Minneapolis, MN: Cazimi Press, 2009).
58. Part of *The Book on the Significations of Planets in Nativities* in Masha'allah; ed. / tr. James Herschel Holden, *Six Astrological Treatises* (Tempe, AZ: AFA, 2009), pp. 16–17.
59. See Omar of Tiberias; tr. Robert Hand; ed. Robert Schmidt, *Three Books on Nativities [Project Hindsight Latin Track Volume XIV]* (Berkeley Springs, WV: Golden Hind Press, 1997); and Benjamin N. Dykes, tr. / ed., *Persian Nativities Volume II: Umar Al-Tabari & Abu Bakr* (Minneapolis, MN: Cazimi Press, 2010).
60. See Abu 'Ali Al-Khayat; tr. James H. Holden, *The Judgments of Nativities, Translated from the Latin Version of John of Seville* (Tempe, AZ: AFA, 1988); and Benjamin N. Dykes, tr. / ed., *Persian Nativities Volume I: Masha'Allah & Abu' Ali* (Minneapolis, MN: Cazimi Press, 2009).
61. See [Sahl bin Bishr and Masha'allah bin Athari]; tr. Benjamin N. Dykes, *Works of Sahl & Masha'Allah* (Minneapolis, MN: Cazimi Press, 2008); and Sahl, ed. / tr. Benjamin N. Dykes, *The Astrology of Sahl B. Bishr Volume I: Principles, Elections, Questions, Nativities* (Minneapolis, MN: Cazimi Press, 2019).
62. Abū Ma'Shar; tr. / ed. Benjamin N. Dykes, *The Great Introduction to the Science of the Judgments of the Stars* (Minneapolis, MN: Cazimi Press, 2020).
63. Al-Qabisi (Alchabitius); ed. / tr. Charles Burnett, Keiji Yamamoto, and Michio Yano,

[Warburg Institute Studies and Texts 2:] *The Introduction to Astrology: Editions of the Arabic and Latin Texts and an English Translation* (London: Warburg Institute / Torino: Nino Aragno Editore, 2004).

64 Aly Aben Ragel, ed. Gerold Hilty, *El libro Conplido en los Iudizios de las Estrellas. Traducción hecha en la corte de Alfonso el Sabio* (Madrid: Real Academia Española, 1954).

65 Aly Aben Ragel; ed. / intr. Gerold Hilty, con la colaboracion de Luis Miguel Vicente Garcia, *[Serie Estudios Arabes e Islamicos:] El libro Conplido en los Iudizios de las Estrellas. Partes 6 a 8: Traducción hecha en la corte de Alfonso el Sabio* (Zaragoza: Instituto de Estudios Islamicos y del Oriente Proximo, 2005).

66 Ali Ben Ragel; tr. Escuela de Traductores de Sirventa, *El Libro Conplido en los Iudizios de Las Estrellas* (Barcelona: Ediciones Indigo, S.A., 1997).

67 Abu'L-Rayhan Muḥammad Ibn Aḥmad Al-Bîrūnî; tr. R. Ramsay Wright, *The Book of Instruction in the Elements of the Art of Astrology, reproduced from Brit. Mus. MS. Or. 8349* (London: Luzac & Co., 1934).

68 Avraham Ibn Ezra; tr. Meira B. Epstein; ed. Meira B. Epstein and Robert Hand, *The Beginning of Wisdom* (ARHAT, 1998).

69 Rabbi Avraham Ibn Ezra; tr. Meira B. Epstein; ed. Meira B. Epstein and Robert Hand, *The Book of Nativities and Revolutions by Rabbi Avraham Ibn Ezra* (ARHAT, 2008).

70 Guido Bonatti, *Book of Astronomy* (2 vols.), tr. Benjamin N. Dykes (Golden Valley, MN: Cazimi Press, 2007).

71 Leopold of Austria; tr. / ed. Benjamin N. Dykes, *A Compilation on the Science of the Stars* (Minneapolis, MN: Cazimi Press, 2015).

72 These readings are condensed and selectively paraphrased from the translation by Dr. Benjamin Dykes as *A Compilation on the Science of the Stars* (Minneapolis, MN: Cazimi Press, 2015).

73 See Johannes Schoener; tr. / ed. Robert Hand, *Opusculum Astrologicum [Project Hindsight Latin Track Volume IV]*. Second Edition, Revised and Corrected (Berkeley Springs, WV: Golden Hind Press, 1996 [after original ed. of 1994]).

74 Johannes Schoener; intr. Philip Melanchthon; tr. Robert Hand, *On the Judgments of Nativities, Three Books. Book 1* (Reston, VA: ARHAT, 2001).

75 In this context, this is likely to mean kidney stones and / or gallstones

76 Claude Dariot; tr. F. W. [= Fabian Withers], *A Brief and most easie Introduction to the Astrological Iudgement of the Starres. Whereby the diligent Reader with easie laboure may give a certen, true, and determinate Iudgement to any Question demanded, upon the naturall causes thereof. Written by the most famous Phisition Claudius Dariot: and translated by F. W. gent. And lately renued, and in some places augmented and amended by G. C. Gentl. Whereunto is annexed a most necessarie Table for the finding out of the Planetarie and unequall houre, under the Latitude of 52 Gr. 30 Mi. exactly calculated by the sayde F. W..* (London: Printed by Thomas Purfoot, 1598).

77 An orange-yellow colour, like that of the stamens of the Autumn crocus or meadow saffron.
78 The Withers translation is confusingly worded here, starting 'The sixt house doth signifie infirmities & Sicknesse, chiefly afflicting these, servants & maydes', with the result that it is not clear whether servants and maids are inherently signified by the sixth (as I have read) or only their illnesses are (in which case it would seem to be implying that illnesses of anyone other than servants and maids are not especially signified by the sixth house, which seems illogical and out of keeping with tradition).
79 Withers and in his turn Lilly (see below) both use the antiquated term 'harlots', which I have here rendered into 21st-century English.
80 William Lilly, 'Student in Astrology', *Christian Astrology Modestly Treated of in three Books*. Printed for Tho. Brudenell for John Partridge and Humph. Blunden, in Blackfriers at the Gate going into Carter-lane, and in Corhil, London, 1647.
81 Spelt *connies* by Lilly; an old word for rabbits, from the Latin noun *cuniculus*.
82 Incitations to rebel against the prevailing state authorities.
83 A sum of money; the meaning is less than clear without further research into the mores of the times, but if, as it appears, Lilly is indeed referring to maidservants, who would not reasonably have been expected to contribute financially to the households in which they were employed, then it is presumed that he is referring to circumstances in which maids are pensioned off with a 'portion' of money to support them, such as when their employers die. Maids also has an archaic meaning of unmarried young women, but it seems unlikely that this was Lilly's meaning here, as those same maids' portions would then have become their dowries upon marriage, making the separate reference to each superfluous.
84 It was reissued as part of George Wharton; John Gadbury, ed., *The Works of that Late Most Excellent Philosopher and Astronomer, Sir George Wharton, Bar. – Collected into one Entire Volume*. Printed by H. H. for John Leigh, at Stationers Hall, London, 1683.
85 This expression seemingly refers to living beings that are incarnate and in that sense, material, although it is not modern custom to refer to people or animals as 'things'
86 See Morin's note on this point of principle in *Astrologica Gallica*, Book XVII, Ch. 6.
87 John Gadbury, *Genethlialogia, or, the Doctrine of Nativities, Containing the Whole Art of Directions, and Annual Revolutions: Whereby, any man (even of an Ordinary Capacity) may be enabled to discover the most Remarkable and Occult Accidents of his Life, as they shall occur unto him in the whole Course thereof, either for Good or Evil*. Printed by Ja: Cottrel, for Giles Calvert, at the black Spread-Eagle neer the West-end of Pauls; William Larner, at the Blackmoor neer Fleet-bridge, and Daniel White, at the seven Stars in S. Paul's Church-yard, 1658.
88 Gadbury uses the archaic term 'his removals'.
89 Gadbury uses the archaic term 'victualing houses', for which I have substituted 'inns'
90 Gadbury uses the archaic term 'the secrets', which to avoid confusion as to its possible

meaning, I have translated into modern English.

91 Alan Leo, [Astrology for All Series – Vol. VII.] *Esoteric Astrology: A Study in Human Nature*. Published at *Modern Astrology* Office, Imperial Buildings, Ludgate Circus, London, EC, 1913 / The Trade Supplied by N. Fowler & Co., 7, Imperial Arcade, London, EC.

92 Alan Leo, [Astrology for All Series:] *Casting the Horoscope*. Published at 7 Imperial Arcade, Ludgate Circus, EC, and 9, Lyncroft Gardens, West Hampstead, London, NW, 1901.

93 Alan Leo, *How to Judge a Nativity: 'Astrology for All'* Series. Published at 7, Imperial Arcade, Ludgate Circus, EC, and 9, Lyncroft Gardens, West Hampstead, London NW, 1903.

94 *Casting the Horoscope* (1901), p. 48

95 *How to Judge a Nativity Part 1* (1903), pp. 11 and 13.

96 *H.J.N. Part 1* (1903), p. 64.

97 *H.J.N. Part 1* (1903), p. 109.

98 *H.J.N. Part 1* (1903), p. 12.

99 *H.J.N. Part 1* (1903), p. 13.

100 *H.J.N. Part 1* (1903), p. 109.

101 *H.J.N. Part 1* (1903), p. 12.

102 *H.J.N. Part 1* (1903), p. 13.

103 *H.J.N. Part 1* (1903), p. 109.

104 *H.J.N. Part 1* (1903), p. 148.

105 *H.J.N. Part 1* (1903), p. 9.

106 *H.J.N. Part 1* (1903), p. 12.

107 *H.J.N. Part 1* (1903), p. 13.

108 *H.J.N. Part 1* (1903), p. 116.

109 *H.J.N. Part 1* (1903), p. 120.

110 *Casting the Horoscope* (1901), p. 48.

111 *H.J.N. Part 1* (1903), p. 7.

112 *H.J.N. Part 1* (1903), pp. 11–12.

113 *H.J.N. Part 1* (1903), p. 13.

114 *H.J.N. Part 1* (1903), p. 122.

115 *H.J.N. Part 1* (1903), p. 126.

116 *H.J.N. Part 1* (1903), p. 12.

117 *H.J.N. Part 1* (1903), p. 13.

118 *H.J.N. Part 1* (1903), p. 102.

119 *H.J.N. Part 1* (1903), p. 127.

120 *H.J.N. Part 1* (1903), p. 131.

121 *H.J.N. Part 1* (1903), p. 132.

122 *H.J.N. Part 1* (1903), p. 8.

[123] *H.J.N. Part 1* (1903), p. 12.
[124] *H.J.N. Part 1* (1903), p. 14.
[125] *H.J.N. Part 1* (1903), pp. 133–34.
[126] *H.J.N. Part 1* (1903), p. 138.
[127] *H.J.N. Part 1* (1903), p. 14.
[128] *H.J.N. Part 1* (1903), p. 102.
[129] *H.J.N. Part 1* (1903), p. 142.
[130] *Casting the Horoscope* (1901), p. 48.
[131] *H.J.N. Part 1* (1903), p. 7.
[132] *H.J.N. Part 1* (1903), p. 12.
[133] *H.J.N. Part 1* (1903), p. 14.
[134] *H.J.N. Part 1* (1903), p. 148.
[135] *H.J.N. Part 1* (1903), p. 152.
[136] *H.J.N. Part 1* (1903), p. 8.
[137] *H.J.N. Part 1* (1903), p. 12.
[138] *H.J.N. Part 1* (1903), p. 14.
[139] *H.J.N. Part 1* (1903), p. 153.
[140] *H.J.N. Part 1* (1903), pp. 158–59.
[141] *H.J.N. Part 1* (1903), p. 12.
[142] *H.J.N. Part 1* (1903), p. 14.
[143] *H.J.N. Part 1* (1903), p. 141.
[144] *H.J.N. Part 1* (1903), p. 164.
[145] *H.J.N. Part 1* (1903), p. 12.
[146] *H.J.N. Part 1* (1903), p. 14.
[147] *H.J.N. Part 1* (1903), p. 171.
[148] *H.J.N. Part 1* (1903), p. 172.
[149] *H.J.N. Part 1* (1903), p. 13.

Chapter Two
From Kepler to Addey:
A Chronology of Developments in Astrological Aspect Theory from 1602 to 1976

The purpose of this primarily historically-focused chapter is to catalogue and date the main notable changes to the traditional system of inter-planetary aspects in astrology from the early 17th century through to the beginning of the fourth quarter of the 20th, with reference to a selection of key source texts.

The following text presupposes a pre-existing elementary understanding by its readership of the meaning of the term *aspects* in astrological theory and practice[1] and of the definitions of related terms such as *partile* and *platic*, and its purpose is neither to introduce the concept to beginners, nor to comprehensively survey the traditional use of aspects by ancient, medieval, or Renaissance astrologers, but rather to look closely at the way the theory has evolved as presented within the astrological text books of the past 400 years, which is to say since the last identified major writings of the notable German astronomer and amateur astrologer Johannes Kepler on the subject in 1619.

We must, however, begin with a summary of how aspects were generally calculated in the prevailing astrological practice before this period, in order to identify what has changed since then, before looking at the changes to this system proposed by Kepler at the very start of the 17th century.

Part One: Traditional Approaches to Astrological Aspects

i. Which aspects were traditionally recognised?

In traditional astrological practice as taught by Claudius Ptolemy in his *Tetrabiblos*, the most abidingly influential ancient Greek astrological text-book still being routinely cited by the 17th-century English astrologers, only the sextile (60°), quartile (90°), trine (120°) and opposition (180°) were recognised as true aspects as calculated by degrees of longitude in the zodiac. The conjunction (0°) was nominally seen as a *configuration* or *position*, but was nonetheless regarded as very important, so it could be reasonably argued that despite the different use of terminology to classify it, to all practical intents and purposes the conjunction was treated as being as powerful an aspect as it has been considered in modern practice.

However, it is notable that the semi-sextile (30°) and quincunx (150°) as we know them today were not recognised as being aspects at all. Nonetheless, according to Ptolemy and subsequent authors through to the late Renaissance including William Lilly, planets in signs separated from each other by these distances were considered related by *antiscia* or *contra-antiscia* if the signs involved were in antiscial or contra-antiscial relationship to each other.[2] Signs related by antiscia were known as *signs beholding* or *signs of equal power*, while those related by contra-antiscia were known as *signs commanding and obeying*.[3] Aside from a close parallel of declination (if found), the presence of a whole-sign antiscial or contra-antiscial relationship was the closest thing to being considered in aspect for planets separated by distances of 30° or 150°.

We find that Aries in relation to Virgo, Gemini to Cancer, Libra to Pisces and Sagittarius to Capricorn are the only sign-pairings separated by either 30° or 150° and in antiscial relationship, while Pisces in relation to Aries, Capricorn to Gemini, Cancer to Sagittarius and Virgo to Libra are the only sign-pairings separated by either 30° or 150° and in contra-antiscial relationship.[4]

On the other hand, none of the other sign-pairs separated by 30° or 150° are in any such relationship, and they were all considered after the writing of Ptolemy to be pairings of 'signs inconjunct' (Robbins translation) or 'disjunct signs' (Ashmand translation) accordingly, the word *inconjunct* meaning mutually 'disconnected' or 'not in aspect'.

Thus, for example, a planet in Taurus would be considered inconjunct one in Aries, Gemini, Libra, or Sagittarius, because these sign pairings are not related by either antiscia or contra-antiscia although they are separated by either 30° or 150°. This is shown in William Lilly's table headed 'Signes not beholding one another' in his *Christian Astrology* (1647).[5]

ii. How were aspect orbs traditionally calculated?

It is widely held that in the prevailing ancient practice, aspects were calculated based on whole sign separation only. However, at a certain point in time, narrower aspects calculated by degrees according to the planets involved in each aspect came into use, and this system of variable planet-based orbs was widely taught by the early medieval Arabic astrologers and remained in consistent use thereafter right through to the mid-19th century. Under this system, the allowable orb for any aspect was based on the *moiety* (or half-sum) of the orbs granted to each planet, and was thus determined by adding these variable orbs together for the two planets involved in the aspect under consideration and dividing the result by two.

In his seminal secondary text *The Sun and the Aspects*,[6] the late Maurice McCann places in strong relief this traditional system of variable planet-based orbs, and contrasts it with the modern system of uniform aspect-based orbs, strongly criticising the change in practice that he at that time saw as having occurred at the end of the 19th century. As we shall go on to show, it in fact began to develop a little earlier than that, with the first clear evidence of a shift in practice found in a major text-book of the early 1860s.

With reference to the modern English translations of astrological texts that were available at the time of his writing, McCann identifies Al-Bîrûnî's *Book of Instruction in the Elements of the Art of Astrology* as the earliest medieval astrological source text to specify variable orbs for each of the planets,[7] according to which the orb of the Sun was 15°, that of the Moon was 12°30', those of both Jupiter and Saturn were 9°, that of Mars was 8°, and those of both Mercury and Venus were 7°.

Based on Al-Bîrûnî's values, a sextile, quartile, trine, or opposition between the Sun and Mars would be allowed an orb of $[(15° + 8°)/2] = 11°30'$. It can be seen that this is a much wider orb than would be allowed for any of the same aspects between this planetary pairing in typical modern practice among all other than traditional astrologers, but more particularly so for the sextile, which in the teachings of 20th-century textbooks has usually been limited to somewhere between 3° and 6° irrespective of the planets involved.

By the mid-17th century, when William Lilly's *Christian Astrology* was first published, the system of planetary orbs had been adjusted somewhat, with Lilly sitting on the fence between slightly wider and narrower orbs proposed by earlier authorities for most of the planets. He accordingly assigns between 15° and 17° to the Sun, between 12° and 12°30' to the Moon, between 9° and 12° to Jupiter, between 9° and 10° to Saturn, between 7° and 8° to Venus, between 7° and 7°30' to Mars, and invariably 7° to Mercury.[8] So the Sun, Jupiter, Saturn, and Venus had all gained in orb allowance according to some authorities since Al-Bîrûnî's time, while Mars had lost a little according to all authorities consulted by Lilly, and the Moon had lost a fraction of a degree according to some but was unchanged according to others.

In his book *Astrological Essays* (2003), McCann further sets out in a table headed 'The Orbs of the Planets according to various other authorities' the orbs he records as having been assigned by Guido Bonatti, Claude Dariot, William Lilly, W. J. Simmonite, and W. H. Chaney.[9] We have already covered Lilly above. Of the rest, according to McCann's record, both Bonatti and Dariot directly take after Al-Bîrûnî without any change; while Simmonite mostly follows Al-Bîrûnî but extends the orb for the Moon to 15° and reduces that for Mars to 7°.[10]

It is beyond the purposes of this chapter to inspect every variation on these themes, but McCann's table by itself is sufficiently suggestive of the existence of more variation from the doctrine as taught by Al-Bîrûnî from the 17th century (Lilly's day) through to the mid-19th (that of Simmonite) than was to be found up to and including the 16th (Dariot's lifetime).

Part Two: The Aspect Innovations of Johannes Kepler

i. What changes did Kepler propose to the system of aspects?

In a short Latin tract entitled *De Fundamentis Astrologiae Certioribus*, first published in 1602, and since translated into English by multiple 20th-century translators,[11] Kepler briefly sets out three proposed new types of astrological aspect: the quintile (72°), biquintile (144°), and sesquiquartile[12] (135°). These are mentioned in the paragraph labelled Thesis 38:

> To be sure, the ancients did not, indeed, admit more than five (aspects, as they are generally called): conjunction, opposition, square, trine, sextile. Yet my mind told me first to add three: quintile, biquintile, sesquiquartile, which have subsequently been confirmed by manifold experience.[13]

Kepler's new aspects have been termed the *harmonic aspects* because, together with the Ptolemaic aspects he accepts, they correspond to a variety of intervals within a musical scale that, when both notes are played together, generate harmonic chords. To wit, the opposition corresponds to an *octave*, the trine to a musical *fifth*, the quartile to a *fourth*, the sextile to a *minor third*, the quintile to a *major third*, the biquintile to a *major sixth* and the sesquiquadrate to a *minor sixth*.[14]

It is notable that Kepler does not at this early stage propose the semi-quartile or semi-square (45°) that in modern practice is widely used as an aspect together with the sesquiquartile and regarded as its natural counterpart on the basis of the division of the 360° zodiacal circle by eight.

Seventeen years later, however, in his major work *Harmonices Mundi* (1619),[15] Book IV, Chapters V–VI, Kepler expounds his views on astrological aspects in much more detail[16] and introduces five further new aspects he had not allowed in 1602:[17] the semi-sextile (30°), the quincunx (150°), the octile or semi-quartile[18] (45°), the tridecile (108°), and the decile (36°).[19] This takes the total number of types of aspect by longitude that he admits to thirteen (including the original five Ptolemaic aspects and his eight additions).

He goes on to rank all these aspects by 'degrees of influentiality', stating that the strongest degree of influence comes from the conjunction and opposition, the next strongest from the quartile, the third strongest from the trine, sextile, and semi-sextile, the fourth from the quintile, biquintile, and quincunx, and the fifth from the decile, tridecile, octile, and trioctile.[20]

Finally, Kepler states that there are two additional configurations that are 'on the borderline between influential and non-influential', specifying these as the arcs of 24° (the quindecile) and 18° (the vigintile).[21] He further notes that the 24° arc corresponds to a fifteen-sided figure whose sides also produce angles of 48°, 96°, and 168°, while the 18° arc corresponds to a 20-sided one whose sides also produce angles of 54°, 126°, and 162°.[22] These eight additional 'borderline' aspects, if admitted, would take the total number of harmonic aspect types added by Kepler up from eight to 16 and raise the total number of aspect types allowed by him from 13 to 21.

In proposing so many new aspects and 'borderline' aspects at a stroke, Kepler set the stage in the early 17th century for the much later development of harmonic aspect theory, speculation, and experimentation in the 20th century.

Kepler subsequently acknowledges and attempts at some length to account for his change of opinion regarding the number of valid aspects since his earlier publication of *De Fundamentis Astrologiae Certioribus*, asserting that 'there are not the same number of aspects as there are harmonic divisions in music, as I had believed up to 1608',[23] and explaining the aspects instead in terms of geometry within a circle.[24]

So even in Kepler's lifetime and within the body of his work, it can be seen that the so-called 'harmonic' theory of aspects had already deviated from its original theoretical underpinning in musical harmonics. And yet, it retained its name.

However, he acknowledges that decoupling his theory of aspects from musical harmonics has generated a new theoretical problem of determining on what basis to limit the number of aspects,[25] a theme that would find frequent discussion by the later 20th-century authors working on the harmonic theory of aspects.

In his important secondary text on Kepler's aspect teachings, however, Dr. Walter Koch links even one of Kepler's 'borderline' aspects as proposed in his *Harmonices Mundi* to a musical interval, correlating the 24° aspect (i.e., the quindecile, although he does not give it a verbal name) to a minor second.[26]

ii. Reception of the harmonic aspects after Kepler, 1647–1913

During the remainder of the 17th century and throughout the 19th century, most astrologers writing new textbooks in English included in them evidence that they were aware of Kepler's proposed new aspects, and noted at least some (though not consistently all) of his new aspects and in some cases even his 'borderline' aspects in their own texts, though according varying degrees of credulity to them. To characterise their reception in every text of this period would take far more space than is available for the purposes of this chapter, so we shall explore just a small but broadly representative selection of influential general astrological textbooks below.

a. William Lilly

Less than thirty years after Kepler's *Harmonices Mundi* was published, William Lilly's magnum opus *Christian Astrology* became the first major general astrological text-book originally written and published in the English language. It makes welcoming references to eight of Kepler's so-called 'new aspects', albeit using eccentric orthography and some outdated names by modern standards: the *Semisextill* (30°), the *Semiquintill* (36°), the *Semiquadrate* (45°), the *Quintill* (72°), the *Sesquiquintill* or *Tredecile* (108°), the *Sesquiquadrate* (135°), the *Byquintill* or *Biquintill*[27] (144°) and the *Quincunx* (150°).[28] These are notably the very same eight new aspects that Kepler had advocated with a greater degree of certainty in his *Harmonices Mundi*, and exclude all his 'borderline' aspects.

b. James Wilson

In his *Dictionary of Astrology* (1819), a substantial and influential early 19th-century astrological reference work that continued to be periodically reprinted for more than 150 years through to the 1970s, James Wilson lists from among Kepler's new aspects the quintile, biquintile, and sesquiquadrate as being 'the only aspects approved of by Placidus' and gives examples of directional calculations using them,[29] but adds passing references to the Vigintile (18°), Quindecile (24°), Semi-sextile (30°), Semiquintile (or Decile) (36°),

Semiquadrate (45°), Sesquiquintile (108°), and what he eccentrically calls the Quadrasextile[30] (meaning the quincunx, 150°).[31]

So like Lilly, Wilson has covered all eight of Kepler's approved new aspects, but unlike Lilly, he has also added in mentions of the base aspects of both the series Kepler declared borderline cases (the vigintile and quindecile).

However, Wilson declares his own opinion in less than glowing terms:

As to the new aspects invented by Kepler, I own, I have not so much confidence in their efficacy as that astronomer had, but experience alone can decide this question.[32]

He later adds in relation to Kepler's consideration of the semi-sextile and quincunx as aspects:

How far their effects correspond with the opinion of Kepler, repeated trials and long practice alone can determine, but my opinion of Kepler is, that he relied more upon the imaginary charm of numbers, than upon the conviction arising from experiment.[33]

This is vintage Wilson rhetoric. His *Dictionary* is notable for taking no prisoners even among the most famous astrological authorities in history such as Ptolemy and Kepler, and for its direct though eloquent criticism of every perceived historical error by whomsoever may have made it. This particular comment also exemplifies the empirical approach to astrology that was abidingly popular with 19th-century modernisers.

c. Zadkiel

In his *Grammar of Astrology* (1833), the original astrological author using the pen-name of *Zadkiel*, Richard Morrison, who would be the long-serving editor of the prophetic astrological annual *Zadkiel's Almanac*[34] for more than forty years starting in 1830, includes the semi-sextile, the semi-quartile, the quintile, the sesquiquadrate and the biquintile, but unlike Lilly and Wilson, he does not mention the decile (36°), the tridecile (108°), or the quincunx (150°).

Perhaps taking inspiration from Kepler's theories, Zadkiel presents his own theory of the geometric derivation of valid aspects, opining that 'every astrological aspect forms an exact angle, or supplemental angle, of a regular polygon, which may be inscribed in a circle', adding in effect that the number of degrees resulting from such an angle must be a mathematical integer that divides equally into 360° for the aspect to be valid. On this basis, he argues that circle division factors of 3, 4, 5, 6, 8, 9, 10, and 12 all produce valid aspects, but 7 and 11 do not,[35] and notes that a hypothetical aspect of 40 degrees[36] should also therefore be considered, although previous writers (implicitly including Kepler) have not accorded it any legitimacy.[37]

d. W. H. Chaney

In his *Primer of Astrology and American Urania*, which was originally issued serially by subscription in monthly parts during the year 1890, American astrologer W. H. Chaney has plenty to say about the new aspects, but none of it complimentary. In the first instalment, he lists in a table of aspects six of Kepler's new aspects together with the traditional Ptolemaic aspects. The new aspects he includes here, as named by him, are the *Semi-sextile* (30°), *Semi-quartile* (36°),[38] *Quintile* (72°), *Sesqui-quartile* (135°), *Biquintile* (144°), and *Quincunx* (150°).[39] It is notable that he omits both the true Semi-quartile or Semi-square (45°)[40] and the Tridecile (108°) among the eight aspects Kepler specified as being assuredly worthy of use.

In the second issue of his *Primer*, Chaney features a lengthy discussion in *Chapter V: Explanations of the Aspects with Comments and Criticisms*, asserting a decidedly sceptical position with regard to the new aspects, aided by the use of satirical humour:

> *In PART 1 I have given a long list of aspects, but must caution the reader against placing much reliance upon any except the* Conjunction, Sextile, Quartile, Trine *and* Opposition.... *It is recorded that Kepler "discovered" some new aspects, such as the* Semi-sextile, Semi-quartile, Quintile, Sesqui-quartile, Biquintile, *etc.. The door of discovery being thus thrown open, every* fakir *in the science has sought distinction by discovering other aspects. But why some smart Aleck has not discovered a* Semi-quincunx[41] *before this time is very strange, for it would be as scientific as its name is poetical. The reason assigned for a quartile, trine, etc., is that it is the quotient, leaving no remainder, after dividing the circle by a given* whole *number. But to obtain* Quincunx *the circle must be divided by a mixed number, namely, two and two-fifths. Where did Kepler find his two and two-fifths? If we are to have a Biquintile, by all means let us have a Biquincunx, or 300°.... But when old fogy England sets up the Biquincunx aspect, depend upon it some enterprising Yankee will move backward in the Zodiac, or converse, and discover that it is exactly a sextile....*[42]

In his above show of mockery, Chaney unfortunately displays his own confusion regarding the derivation of the quincunx, which he does not seem to appreciate as being a counterpart of the semi-sextile, based on the division of the zodiacal circle by twelve and the multiplication of the result by five. He adds:

> But I will not waste time combating with hypotheses, and have referred to these 'new aspects' only that I might expose the quackery which has sprung up in consequence. It is in no way a personal matter, but if men calling themselves astrologers feel that the coat fits them, they are welcome to it. I cannot do justices to truth without exposing error.[43]

Chaney's contribution is notable for its staunch traditionalism and disinclination to admit the new aspects over 270 years after Kepler proposed them, in marked contrast to the relatively welcoming attitude of Lilly much closer to Kepler's time. Perhaps not all of today's traditional astrologers tending to regard Lilly and his text as a bastion of earlier astrological tradition have encountered the writings of Chaney – on this one point, at least.

e. Llewellyn George

Our final sample source on the early modern reception of Kepler's aspects is Llewellyn George's *A-Z Horoscope Delineator*, a strongly influential best-selling American primer of natal astrology that went through numerous editions[44] authored by George himself and reprints thereof from 1910 through to the 1970s, before being reduced in scope and revised by other authors working for the publishing company that bears George's forename to this day, Llewellyn, from the early 1980s onwards.

The earliest edition of George's primer to hand is the 2nd, which dates from 1913. In this edition, the author lists in a table under the heading *The Minor Aspects* six of Kepler's new aspects: the Semi-sextile, Semi-square, Quintile, Sesquiquadrate, Bi-quintile, and Quincunx.[45] He therefore omits from this table only the decile and tridecile from among the eight aspects assuredly proposed by Kepler.

Yet paradoxically, in an appendix to the book headed *Explanation of Astrological Terms*, he includes them, calling the decile a *Semi-quintile* (p. 36) and the tridecile a *Tredecile* or *Trecile* (p. 37). Additionally, he here includes the base aspects of both Kepler's 'borderline' series: the *Quindecile* (24°), which he refers to as 'Another of Kepler's aspects',[46] and the *Vigintile* (18°), which he calls 'One of Kepler's aspects; slightly good'.[47]

71

The fact that George lists not only all eight of the minor aspects proposed by Kepler but also the most basic aspects from each of his series of borderline aspects shows that awareness of these new aspects had remained in circulation within the more well-read portions of the astrological community at least since the time of Wilson's *Dictionary*, which had been reprinted in the United States in 1885 and could conceivably have been George's source for this information.

Yet George's omission of the decile series (including the tridecile), the vigintile, and the quindecile from his main table of minor aspects would appear to indicate that he was relatively unsure of their effectiveness as compared with all the others.

They are also omitted from his separate tables headed *Lunar Aspects* and *Mutual Aspects* (p. 46), which indicate the boundaries in terms of degrees of separation within which he believes the aspects of each type to be effective. In contrast, the Semi-sextile, Semi-square, Quintile, Sesquiquadrate, Bi-quintile, and Quincunx are fully integrated into these schemes.

Part Three: Astrologers' Departure from Planetary Orbs, 1861–1900

During the mid-to-late 19th century, the first signs of deviation in astrological teaching from the received variable planet-based orbs come to light. In chronological order, we shall examine the pivotal views of many of the leading astrologers of the period on how orbs should be calculated, as encapsulated in a selection of nine important sources, here numbered from i. to ix.

i. Richard Morrison (1861)

Veteran mid-19th century British astrologer Richard Morrison (aka Zadkiel), writing in the first volume of his definitive two-volume astrological text-book *The Hand-Book of Astrology* (1861), declares simply regarding the orbs to be allowed for aspects:

> *The perfect aspects are the most powerful; but they are found to operate generally when within about 5° to 7°; and, as regards the Sun or Moon, when within 10°.*[48]

This appears to be a major step towards simplification of the traditional system of planet-based orbs. Instead of a complex calculation based on the half-sums of the individual orbs for each planet, Morrison is advocating uniform orbs of 5 to 7 degrees for all aspects between all planets except those involving one of the luminaries, and in the case of aspects involving at least one luminary, a uniform orb of 10 degrees. It is interesting to note here the language within which Morrison's declaration is framed, which is the language of empiricism: 'they are *found to* operate generally'. This suggests that his simplification of the system of planetary orbs is based on his long experience as a practising professional astrologer, and that he values the wisdom of experience above the tradition of a table.

Nonetheless, the Astrological Lexicon at the back of the book defines a platic conjunction along traditional lines as occurring when two planets 'are within the amount of half their mutual orbs';[49] and defines 'orb of a planet' using very similar values to those proposed by Lilly.[50] This may suggest that the purpose of this lexicon is simply to inform readers of the traditional doctrine related to orbs that they may come across, without the author advocating adhering to these methods closely in practice.

ii. W. H. Chaney (1890)

In 1890, writing in the second instalment of his aforementioned *Primer*, W. H. Chaney addresses the problems that may arise from the use of traditional planetary orbs with the new aspects he holds in such disdain, taking the example of a separation of 81° between the Sun and Saturn in a nativity as being 9 degrees from both a partile trine (90°) and a partile quintile (72°), both of which distances are well within the traditional moiety (half-sum) of 13° for this planetary combination. Chaney seeks thus to point out that the use of the new aspects is practically incompatible with that of the traditional planetary orbs:

> *Here, then, is an aspect that can be read both ways, for good or evil, according to circumstances. If the fakir has some bad luck to account for, he reads it as a quartile but keeps mum about the quintile. On the other hand, if there is good fortune to be accounted for, he reads it as a quintile and is as silent as the grave about the quartile. I might cite scores of similar aspects that can be read either way by adopting the orb theory, and "new aspects," but I deem it a waste of time. With such extended orbs, and aspects so close together, even a tyro can see that they will overlap each other throughout the entire Zodiac, and the fakir will never be at a loss for an aspect to account for any kind of an event. If his client has had a conflicting time, that is, a mixture of good and evil, then the fakir reads the aspect both ways and shows how correctly astrology always points out the event.*[51]

Later in the same chapter, Chaney hints at a possible preference for a universal orb allowance of 5° for all the Ptolemaic aspects, which is at the narrow end of the range Morrison allowed in 1861:

> *I require [my students] to memorize 'The Different Kinds of Signs', as arranged on page 28, PART 1, and having learned that Aries, Cancer, Libra, and Capricornus are 'movable signs', they readily perceive that two planets, one in each of any two of the movable signs, will be either in quartile or opposition, provided the orb does not exceed 5°. The same is true of the fixed signs and common signs. This lesson once well learned, the student can tell at a glance... when two planets are in quartile or opposition.*[52]

This, however, is difficult to definitively interpret because the context is a discussion of the reading of an almanac, and Chaney might merely be saying here that when planets are shown in its integral ephemerides as being within five degrees of a partile quartile or opposition, they are certain to be within orb, without excluding the possibility that they might be at a greater distance, depending on the planets involved. Nonetheless, Chaney's reading appears similar to that of Morrison, and he goes on to affirm that among the good habits he expects of his students:

> *...as my disciple, he must not have the 'new aspects', nor wide orbs, nor dragon's head or tail, nor part of fortune, as scape goats for his mistakes.*[53]

Chaney's objection to the use of the traditional wide platic orbs is further set out in Part 5 of the *Primer*, although here in the context only of the use of the new aspects:

> *Another avenue for the introduction of errors and discrepancies may be traced to the speculations of men whose practice was very limited. Kepler affords a good example. He suggested 'new aspects' merely as hypotheses, but others put them forth as scientific facts, and the worst of it was, were able to prove them to be facts on account of the indiarubber tenacity of the platic orbs. This loose method of reasoning was entirely overlooked for centuries, and even now I expect to be abused for presuming to criticise so great a man as Kepler.*[54]

In the following Part of his *Primer*, Chaney again advocates an orb of 5°, but this time specifically in the context of a *transiting* planet in conjunction, sextile, or trine to the natal Sun or Moon:

> When Jupiter or Venus transit the radices of sun and moon, or in sextile or trine of same, good events are indicated, subject to the orb of 5°.[55]

This is a similar context to that of the reading of an almanac in which the first mention of the 5° orb occurred. Thus, we still do not know for sure what exactly his views were on the allowable orb for natal aspects. He subsequently concedes, even in relation to the practice of predictions from transits:

> Although I speak so definitively of the '5° orb', I am satisfied that the indications may extend much beyond, at times, but have not found them sufficiently reliable to risk predictions beyond the 5°, which I denominate 'powerful orb'.

These closing remarks place Chaney's astrological philosophy when it comes to the handling of aspects in a similar empiricist camp to those of Wilson and Morrison, as we have seen in their respective arguments.

iii. Alan Leo and Frederick Lacey (1890)

Later the same year, in the very first issue of the new British astrological monthly *The Astrologer's Magazine* (August, 1890) that would eventually spawn the more famous title *Modern Astrology*, the editors, Alan Leo and Frederick Lacey, list under the heading *The Orbs of the Planets* the following planetary orbs: for the Sun, 17°; for the Moon, 12°; for Jupiter, 10°; and for Mercury, Venus, Mars, Saturn, and Uranus, invariably, 8°.

This is already noteworthy on account of the partial harmonisation of the system of orbs for the planets in evidence since Lilly's time, with only the Sun, Moon, and Jupiter being singled out for larger orbs than the rest of the planetary stock, all of whose members are treated alike. Yet it is not Leo and Lacey who are responsible for this change, as we find the same orbs used at least 13 years previously in 1877 by Robert Thomas Cross, the sixth 19th-century astrologer to edit *Raphael's Almanac* and to adopt the pen-name Raphael for all his astrological work accordingly, on p. 5 of the very first edition of his *Raphael's Guide to Astrology, Volume I*.[56]

However, even then, the editors of *The Astrologer's Magazine* express reservations, defining the orbs as 'the number of degrees in which a planet is supposed to operate on or with another', with *supposed* being the operative word that indicates their hesitancy to endorse the view expressed. They then add beneath, using bold as shown:

We do not agree with this; we limit the orbs to 5. (See Editor's notes in September number as to this).

Leo and Lacey's proposed limiting of orbs to five degrees closely follows from Morrison's position expressed 29 years earlier, although he had allowed between five and seven degrees for all aspects except those involving the luminaries, so the preference of the editors of *The Astrologer's Magazine* is evidently for the tighter end of his scale. They add on p. 21:

Another vexed question is the planetary orbs, some say that it is absurd to give 17° as the orb of the Sun, 12° the Moon's orb and so on. We hope in our next issue to take this 'orb question' in hand and thoroughly thrash it out and say what we find about it, and, as we before remarked, we shall be glad to hear what our fellow-students have found out as to the number of degrees to which their power is limited....

They thus acknowledge their awareness of existing dissent among astrologers on the traditional orbs before they give their own view, and yet they recognise themselves at this early stage in Alan Leo's astrological career as being mere students among others, and are openly inviting their peers to supply empirical evidence. As was apparent in Zadkiel's *Hand-Book of Astrology Vol. I* in 1861, the emphasis in addressing aspect orbs is upon looking for practical evidence and not blindly following tradition. This was a very modern approach and typical of attitudes among astrologers of the late 19th century.

In the following issue, in another article also headed 'The Orbs of the Planets', Leo and Lacey duly reiterate (p. 44):

According to promise, we now take the 'orb' theory in hand, and hope to be able to give satisfactory reasons why we consider these long orbs should be discontinued. It is true they have been handed down to us for ages, but that is no reason why they should be right or wrong, other vagaries have been transmitted in various departments of life, which upon being subjected to a searching examination have had to be set aside either as useless, or unreliable. All the writers on Astrology have copied one another, more or less; but one and all give an orb of five degrees to the cusp of each house. Lilly, who was one of the best Astrologers, more especially in Horary Astrology..., has copied his predecessors in these long orbs, and yet we have carefully gone through the various maps in his 'Magnum Opus', viz., Christian Astrology, and yet out of the hosts of aspects formed between the heavenly bodies in the numerous examples he has given, we think we are correct in saying that very few of the aspects exceed the orb of five degrees.

This statement of position is important on two accounts: first, in that it is arguing for an aspect orb of five degrees by analogy with or in the quest of harmonisation with the traditional orb assigned to house cusps; and second, in that it is partly basing the proposed orb on the examination of the practical chart delineations featured by none other than William Lilly himself in his greatest work. So it can be said that, far from seeing themselves as rash innovators ready to depart from 17th-century astrological tradition, Leo and Lacey are taking the view that they are adhering more closely to the practice of the most celebrated English exponent of astrology from that era than the references to traditional planetary orbs printed within it did in themselves.

At this point, they argue with reference to the risk of overlapping aspects if traditional orbs are allowed for aspects including the new ones added by Kepler (pp. 44–46):

*Let us take a suppositious example: [Mars] retrograde in the fifth degree of [Aries], and [Venus], also retrograde, in the 28th degree of [Taurus]. These planets are 53 degrees apart. Now according to the authorities, some would say that these planets were in sextile, and others would say they were in semisquare.... According to the wise ones this is both [sextile] and [semi-square] or either. Now which is it? ... Many of our astral friends only use the old aspects, viz., [sextile], [quartile], [trine], [opposition], [conjunction], and [parallel of declination]: by their method they would treat the aspect as [sextile], whilst those who use both old and new aspects ([semi-sextile] [semi-square] and [sesquiquadrate] new) would considerably differ as to what the aspect was. Whenever an aspect similar to the example given occurs, it will generally be found between [semi-sextile] [semi-square] and [sextile] or between [trine] and [sesquiquadrate]. Now the wider the aspect is, the weaker the effect will be. We take the orb of **five degrees** all round, the same as that allowed by the old authors as the distance a planet operates on the cusp of any house.... Don't forget this – **The closer the aspect, the stronger the effect.** Now don't take this for granted, because we say so, apply the rules in any and every nativity you have that you can test; think it well out and let your own experience be your chief guide, do not come hastily to a conclusion, for what is worth doing at all should be well and thoroughly done, for nothing*

> is without labour, application, and research, and we are very confident that upon investigation five degrees will be found quite enough to be allowed as to the space within which one planet can act upon or with another. This we think is further borne out if one takes into consideration the **other** aspects, said to be invented by Kepler, although **we disregard every one of them.**

They go on here to list in this category the *Vigintile, Quindecile, Semi-sextile, Decile, Quintile, Tredecile*[57] [sic], *Bi-quintile* [sic], and *Quincunx*, thus including the base aspects of both Kepler's 'borderline' series as well as all his other proposed aspects except for the semi-square and sesquiquadrate. It is implicit from their inclusion of both the latter pair in their prior shortlist of aspects at risk of overlapping orbs that among all the new aspects introduced by Kepler, Leo and Lacey recognised only those derived from the eight-fold division of the zodiacal circle (the octile series) as being valid.

What is most notable from their argumentation quoted above is that the editors' reduction of the allowed planetary orbs was significantly motivated by avoiding the absurdity of overlapping orbs introduced by the addition of even as few as two of Kepler's new aspects, just as it was for Chaney writing earlier in the same year.

Yet Leo and Lacey remained true to a part of the tradition of aspects in the sense that they did not go as far as to assign variable orbs to the different types of aspects according to how minor or major they felt the aspect types themselves to be, a consequence that astrologers adopting increasing numbers of harmonic aspects in the remaining years of the 19th century and throughout the 20th would find to be logical and even inevitable. This innovation, as we shall see below, fell to their contemporaries R. T. Cross and H. S. Green.

McCann (2002) speculates that Chaney may have directly influenced Leo with his proposal of a five-degree orb, pointing out that Leo's magazine had reviewed Chaney's *Primer*.[58] However, the review in question does not appear before the January, 1891 issue, and here the editors of *A.M.* note:

> The first four numbers of this little work have been sent us for review by a London friend.... The author's experience as to 'long orbs', the Dragon's Head and Tail, and the 'Part of Fortune' are the same as our own.[59]

Both the timeline, with the review appearing five months after the editors' first declaration that a five-degree orb is the appropriate limit, and the commentary to the effect of Chaney's experience being the same as theirs, strongly suggest that the editors' declarations regarding orbs had been made independently of those of Chaney and before they had read the latter. I therefore find no evidence to support my late friend Maurice McCann's tentative suggestion that Chaney may have influenced Leo on this point, although Chaney's writing upon it ostensibly appeared first by a margin of just months. Thus we instead find a confluence of practical opinion in the same year among astrologers on different sides of the Atlantic without prior awareness of each other's views, albeit both writing 29 years after Zadkiel's first intimation that orbs should be limited to 5–7 degrees except for aspects involving the luminaries.

McCann further draws attention to the potential problem of overlapping aspects when using the traditional variable planet-based orbs for calculating the minor aspects added by Kepler. McCann's own proposed solution, at variance with that of Leo and Lacey, is to stick to the traditional aspect orbs but always to prioritise the Ptolemaic aspects and ignore the Keplerian ones when they are found to overlap with each other.[60]

iv. Robert T. Cross (1891)

In 1891, Raphael VI (R. T. Cross) had published another short student-oriented astrological guidebook called *Raphael's Key to Astrology*. Here we find evidence that he has been brought round part-way to the reforms proposed successively by Morrison and the team of Lacey and Leo. He devises his own unique system that is perhaps best described as an idiosyncratic variation on a hybrid between the traditional planetary orbs and what would become the modern 20th-century system of aspect-based orbs (p. 11):

> *The orbs of Uranus, Saturn, Jupiter, Mars, Venus, and Mercury, when applying, are about 6°, and when separating from an aspect, they may be reckoned as 8°.... The Sun and Moon have larger orbs. You may reckon the Sun when applying as 12°, and when separating as 17°; and the Moon, 8° when applying, and 12° when separating from an aspect. These orbs apply only to the following aspects, viz., the conjunction, sextile, quartile, trine, and opposition. The minor aspects, viz., the semi-sextile, quintile and biquintile, I consider them only when the planets are within 2° applying, and 3° separating. The semi-square and sesquiquadrate are to be reckoned 3° when applying, and 4° when separating, that is, with the planets; the Sun and Moon may be allowed an extra 1°.*

Cross's system is traditional in that it allows the greatest orb to the Sun and the second-greatest to the Moon; modern both in the sense that it harmonises the orbs for all the other planets and in that it proposes reduced orbs for the non-Ptolemaic aspects introduced by Kepler; and idiosyncratic in that it proposes differential orbs according to whether the aspect is applying or separating. It is thus a remarkably complex system, and perhaps surprisingly so in view of the author's well-earned reputation as an accessible teacher of elementary astrology to beginner students through the medium of his books such as the *Key*.

For all the complexity of his system, however, Cross's key innovation of allowing drastically reduced orbs for Kepler's new aspects cannot be understated in its historical importance in the development of aspect theory. Perhaps it is after the view of Leo and Lacey, with regard to their relative degrees of importance or lack thereof, that he has further divided those of Kepler's aspects that he has considered at all (which are only six of them) into two classes, allowing greater orbs to the octile series (which alone Leo and Lacey felt to be important) than to the quintile series and the semi-sextile.

v. H. S. Green (1892)

By March 1892, H. S. Green, writing in *The Astrologer's Magazine* under his regular pen-name *Leo*,[61] reports, under the heading *Orbs*, the traditional orbs of the planets according to Alfred Pearce's 1881 book *The Science of the Stars*, as follows:

> [Sun] 17°, [Moon] 12°, [Mercury] 7°, [Venus] 8°, [Mars] 7°, [Jupiter] 12°, [Saturn] 9°, [Uranus] 5°, [Neptune] probably about 5°.[62]

It is remarkable that all these orbs, except for those assigned to the planets newly discovered since his lifetime, are within the ranges proposed by William Lilly in 1647, and therefore much closer to tradition than the orbs suggested by R. T. Cross four years before Pearce was writing. This shows that in the late 19th century there was already a diverse range of sets of received variable planetary orbs in use by the most influential astrologers.

However, Green's own view is that a more radical reform of the system of orbs is now needed:

> *There are many astrologers who express themselves as dissatisfied with these orbs, and advocate a uniform distance of about five degrees for each planet. I do not profess to know for certain where the truth lies, but my opinion is*

that the orbs vary considerably for each aspect. The strongest aspects are undoubtedly the conjunction and opposition, and here, I think, the orbs which are given above are not much too large; but the margin of distance must be diminished for all the other aspects according to their strength. For the square and trine, I would allow about three-quarters of the usual orb. For the sextile, semi-square, and sesquiquadrate, I would allow from one-half to two-thirds the orb. The remaining aspects, semi-sextile, quintile, bi-quintile, and those others which are doubtful, I think, have no influence unless they are within one degree of being exact. Some such arrangement as this appears to be more in accordance with reason than the rule of allowing a fixed orb, long or short, for every aspect, whether strong or weak, indifferently.[63]

Green is thus going much further than either Morrison or Leo and Lacey, and building on the lead of R. T. Cross, by explicitly varying the orbs allowed according to the type of aspect in multiple gradations. It is not enough for him to single out Kepler's new aspects for reduced orbs. He is the first astrologer on record in the modern astrological corpus to assign differential orbs even among the traditional Ptolemaic aspects, regarding the conjunction and opposition as more major than the square and trine. This is manifestly because he is viewing all aspects both old and new as part of a rationally coherent system characterised by variable degrees of aspect strength, and reasoning that there are therefore degrees of major and minor to all types of aspect within that system rather than there existing any kind of a natural duality between the traditional [Ptolemaic] aspects and the [Keplerian] new aspects to justify a sudden reduction in orb uniquely between one collective group and the other.

vi. Alfred Pearce (1892)

Later the same year (1892), Morrison's view of 1861 is echoed quite closely by his long-term successor as editor of *Zadkiel's Almanac*, Alfred Pearce, who had previously had nothing new to say on the topic of orbs at all, at least in his textbooks. Pearce, writing in his short-lived monthly astrological journal *The Future*, under the heading *Lessons in Astrology – No. 5: The Aspects, or Configurations*, bypasses the complexity of Cross's and Green's novel suggestions, but adds detail to the system of Morrison, opining:

The ancients considered that when an aspect was within half the distance of the orbs of the configurated planets added together, it was a platic *aspect. We should not consider any aspect platic even, unless it was within 5°, if a major* one, and within 2° if a minor aspect, except in the case of mutual aspects between the Sun and Moon, which are operative when within 10° in the case of a major, and within 5° if a minor aspect.[64]

The allowance of reduced orbs for minor aspects is the chief difference in Pearce's opinion from that of Morrison. It is implicit from the context of his discussion following a listing of the new aspects 'added by' Kepler that he is referring collectively to all of these aspects as the 'minor' aspects.

vii. George Wilde and J. Dodson (1894)

In their text-book *A Treatise of Natal Astrology* (1894), George Wilde and his otherwise little-known co-author J. Dodson adopt something of a mixed approach that veers more towards the traditional than those of their contemporaries. At first they give the traditional planetary orbs, but with those for all planets other than the luminaries and Jupiter fixed on 8°,[65] which is the same scheme as that put forward previously by R. T. Cross and by the editors of *The Astrologer's Magazine* in its first issue. To this they add their practical opinion:

> We have usually found the major aspects, [sextile], [quartile], [trine], and [opposition], operate when within 10°. The closer the aspect the more powerful it becomes.[66]

This rule-of-thumb allowance of ten degrees is twice as much as we have found most of their leading contemporaries to be advocating in previous years, and gives primary evidence of continuing dissent over the then recently much-fancied 'five-degree rule'.

viii. Alan Leo (1897)

Alan Leo's first full-length printed book, *Practical Astrology* (1897), sets out his mature position on aspect orbs seven years after the tentative initial discussions in *The Astrologer's Magazine*. The book is meant as a teaching guide for the student of astrology, and Leo chooses to include just four of Kepler's aspects: the Semi-sextile, Semi-square, Sesquiquadrate, and Quincunx (which he mistakenly terms the *Inconjunct*,[67] an error carried forward to many 20th-century texts before the record was set straight by Dr. J. Lee Lehman).[68]

With regard to orbs, Leo declares herein:

The orbs, or distances, within which the planets act upon each other, are from 5° to 7° either side of the aspect.... It is not wise to allow more than 7° as the sphere of influence in which a sextile, square, trine or opposition will act. The conjunction will also act within seven degrees either side, becoming more complete as the planets approach the body of each other. In dealing with the semi-square or sesqui-quadrate not more than 3° should be allowed for the sphere of influence.[69]

Leo's position at this stage in terms of orbs for the major aspects is intriguingly almost identical to that of Morrison back in 1861, although varied to specify that the orb for the octile series should be cut to 3° – a position similar to those of Cross and Pearce (*see above*) in the early 1890s. We may reasonably speculate that Leo had taken on board the ideas of all his contemporaries by this stage but that his own practical experience was the ultimate arbiter for him. In any case, the traditional orbs of the planets are not even mentioned by him in the book.

However, it is also notable that he has not adopted the further reforms towards multi-stepped differential orbs depending on the type of aspect that had been proposed by Cross and Green in the early 1890s.

In the Glossary at the back, under the heading *Orb*, he adds:

Some authorities allow as many as 10° and 12° to solar aspects, but this is not safe. Seven degrees is the widest orb that can safely be used.[70]

ix. Sepharial (1898)

In the first edition of his *New Manual of Astrology* (1898), another leading British astrologer of the late 19th and early 20th centuries, Walter Gorn Old,[71] who is better known by his pen-name of Sepharial, opts to list in his table of *The Aspects* only what he calls 'the chief aspects', which comprise mainly the Ptolemaic aspects (including the Conjunction), with the addition of just the semi-square and sesquiquadrate from among Kepler's new aspects.[72] He does, however, make passing reference to the semi-sextile on the following page, stating that it produces benefic results 'in a very minor degree'.[73]

Concerning orbs, however, Sepharial sides squarely with the modernists. He does not declare the traditional planetary orbs or half-sum-based calculation method at all and simply states:

Planets are called 'in aspect' to one another when, at birth, they are found to be within 5° of any of the distances indicated in the list of aspects. The Parallel, however, is limited to a distance of 1°.[74]

It is remarkable that Old, unlike Leo the previous year, makes no attempt to differentiate the orb according to the type of aspect, and prefers simply to exclude from consideration most of the minor aspects introduced by Kepler altogether. Sepharial's position is distinctive in that previous writers arguing for all-round five-degree orbs tended to be significantly motivated by their wish to avoid overlapping aspects between the minor aspects and the Ptolemaic ones. His position does not appear to have their pragmatic rationale, since he doesn't count the quintile series or most of the minor aspects at all, although he does allow the semi-square and sesquiquadrate, and in that respect, keeping the allowable orb down beneath 7½ degrees would appear essential to avoiding overlapping orbs without the need to adopt differential orbs for major and minor aspects. Yet by itself, such a rationale cannot account for reducing them as far as 5 degrees, so we must instead suppose it to be his preference on empirical grounds only to interpret aspects within such an orb, in order to be sure that they are sufficiently strong to produce meaningful readings in practice.

Part Four: 20th-Century Developments in Harmonic Aspect Theory

This last part of our chapter highlights seven important individual contributions that arguably served as partial bridges between the state of the astrological treatment of aspects at the turn of the 20th century and the full-fledged modern harmonic theory presented by John Addey in 1976, before summarising Addey's approach in itself.

It should be noted that this account encompasses a representative selection of important sources and makes no pretence at being a comprehensive survey. Within the time-frame available for research towards this chapter, it has not been possible for me to leaf through every available early-to-mid-20th-century source text of possible relevance, or any 20th-century magazine articles at all. However, many books were considered, inspected, and then cast aside after close inspection showed them to add nothing of pivotal importance to the doctrine, en route to the final selection of the seven intermediary sources discussed here.

One source not selected for detailed discussion here chiefly on account of its relatively late appearance in the record as published, but worthy of further reading thanks to its consideration of a significant number of minor harmonic aspects, is Johannes Vehlow's *Lehrkursus der Wissenschaftlichen Geburts-Astrologie Band VIII: Die Konstellationenlehre: Mass, Zahl und Magische Quadrate*[75] (1955).

i. Noviles gaining acceptance? The aspect instruction of Karl Brandler-Pracht

In his 1910 book *Astrologische Bibliothek Band I: Kleines Astrologisches Lehrbuch*, one of the foremost German astrologers of the early 20th century, Karl Brandler-Pracht, who was a prolific writer at a very early stage in the modern revival of German-speaking astrology, presents the five Ptolemaic aspects as the major aspects, and follows them with the Parallel before adding eight further aspects, seven of which are seven of the eight affirmed by Kepler, excluding only the Decile.

The other aspect cited by Brandler-Pracht is the Novile, which until the end of the 19th century we had seen only tentatively proposed on theoretical grounds by Richard Morrison in 1833, and cautiously adopted by William Joseph Simmonite, who named it the nonagon,[76] in the 1840s. Brandler-Pracht retains Simmonite's proposed name for the aspect.[77] He adds regarding its interpretation:

Nonagon. Nicht ungünstig aber von sehr schwacher Wirkung. Unwichtig.[78]

This translates as: 'Nonagon. Not unfavourable but of very weak effect. Unimportant'. So he sees the novile as a very weak benefic aspect.

It is curious to note that Brandler-Pracht elects to include the tridecile (108°) but not the decile (36°) from among Kepler's new aspects.

With regard to orbs, Brandler-Pracht teaches the traditional half-sum method but only in application to the five Ptolemaic aspects (including the conjunction). For all the minor aspects, he advocates a uniform orb of 3° irrespective of the planet.[79] This seems a pragmatic approach that holds to a vestige of orb-related tradition long after this has been abandoned by most British astrologers, but departs from it where it does not seem to work because the aspects are too minor.

ii. Septiles and Quarti-squares? The new aspect innovations of George Wilde

Until the end of the 19th century, while we have seen plenty of welcome for Kepler's new aspects among astrologers, with the sole exception of Morrison's aforementioned proposal for the introduction of the novile (40°) we saw no serious proposals to move beyond the tramlines of the new aspects introduced by Kepler and develop harmonic theory to a further degree.

One of the first astrologers to move beyond Kepler in the early 20th century was George Wilde. We earlier saw him adopting a more conventional position than his contemporaries with regard to aspect orbs when teamed with his erstwhile co-writer J. Dodson in 1894. But Wilde's career was a long one, and during the 1900s and 1910s he became much more interested in the minor aspects. By the time of the appearance of the third edition of his *Primer of Astrology* in 1911,[80] he was proposing a host of new aspects that Kepler had not.[81] These comprise, using his preferred names but, in all cases where square brackets are shown below, my calculated exact separations to two decimal points, since he gives only an approximate range that is often ill-centred on these:

Semi-demi-quartile[82] ([22.5°])

Septile ([51.43°])

[Unnamed][83] (54°)*

[Unnamed][84] (67.5°)*

Bi-Septile ([102.86°])

[Unnamed][85] ([112.5°])*

Tri-Septile ([154.29°])[86]

[Unnamed][87] (157.5°)*

Those listed above that are marked with an asterisk are acknowledged by Wilde as having been proposed by one of his students, a Mr. W. Kruse, showing that Wilde was not working alone on the development of new astrological aspects beyond those proposed by Kepler at this time.

From among Kepler's 'borderline' aspects, Wilde also adopts the following:

Semi-demi-quintile[88] (18°)

[Unnamed][89] (126°)

[Unnamed][90] (162°)

It is interesting, however, that Wilde does not adopt the Quindecile (24°) or its multiples. He also seems to be extremely vague about the rationale for the harmonic aspects, writing in terms of noticing their efficacy in practice, but without demonstrating how they are derived geometrically, which may explain his confusion as to the exact degrees of separation involved in a number of cases.

Wilde classes the quintile, biquintile, decile, tredecile, vigintile and its multiples, and semi-sextile, all as 'good' aspects, and the 22.5° and 157.5°

aspects as 'bad' aspects. This is broadly in keeping with the later 20th-century development of harmonic theory according to which zodiacal circle division factors comprising solely multiples of the prime number '2' make for harsh aspects while those involving significant measures of '3' and '5' make for softer ones, although no such rationale is presented by Wilde in this text.

Wilde is the first astrologer I have thus far found in print either to give any attention to or to name the Septile and its multiples, and also the first to adopt the series of aspects stemming from the division of the circle into sixteen parts. Kepler did neither, at least in his texts that I have been able to examine in English translation. Wilde's innovations in collaboration with his eager student Mr. Kruse therefore appear in the modern historical record as a pivotal bridge between Kepler's work and the more comprehensive and (some might say) increasingly extreme catalogues of harmonic aspects developed in the second half of the 20th century.

iii. Neutral 15° Aspects? The ideas of A. Frank Glahn

In the second edition to hand (1925) of his main astrological textbook *Erklärung und systematische Deutung des Geburtshoroskopes*, A. Frank Glahn, who was one of the more prolific German-speaking astrological writers of the 1920s and 1930s, opines that all aspects in multiples of 15 degrees are effective, but regards those multiples that do not also constitute more major aspects as 'neutral':

> *Es gibt außerdem noch neutrale Aspekte, denn sicherlich sind alle 15 Gradaspekte wirksam, und nicht unrecht haben diejenigen Astrologen, welche die Bestrahlung mit 15° Orbis annehmen, so daß alle Planeten untereinander in Beziehungen stehen. Praktisch verwende ich alle Aspekte, auch diese neutralen, bei Direktionen, z. B. bei der Bestimmung der Geburtsminute. Für die Prognose haben sie aber keine Bedeutung, weshalb deren Beschreibung in diesem Buche sich erübrigt.*[91]

He further suggests in the above extract that all planets are related to each other in some way, and considering all aspects in multiples of 15 degrees and then with 15-degree orbs can identify their essential relationships, adding that he uses them in directions, for example when rectifying the time of birth.

It is worth pointing out that in Glahn's scheme, all aspects of the quintile, septile, novile, and other minor harmonic series would overlap with at least one fifteen-degree-multiple aspect. I could find no reference to quintile-series aspects in Glahn's book, and it would appear from the evidence that he regarded them as of no value at all at this point in time, although the further investigation of later editions and of his numerous magazine articles could prove illuminating.

The 15-degree aspects he advocates are based on the division of the circle by 24 (2*2*2*3). This 24-fold division of the circle and the aspects that could be seen to result from it had not previously been explored in the known English-language literature, and to this day there is no generally agreed term for them, but astrologers collectively could do worse than to choose between a formulation like *vigintiquartile* (twenty-fourth) or *quartisextile* (quarter of a sixth) for the base aspect, and then prefix whichever is decided upon with *Quinta-* (75°), *Septa-* (105°), or *Undeca-* (165°)[92] for the three multiples (corresponding to 5 times, 7 times and 11 times 15°, respectively) that do not coincide with already established aspects resulting from simpler circle division factors.

Glahn is recorded as having been a student of Alfred Witte, the pioneer of the Hamburg School of Astrology. It is perhaps of relevance here that one of Witte's other influential associates, Friedrich Sieggrün, penned a paper[93] featured in a short book entitled *Die Hamburger Astrologenschule* that was published in the same year as the second edition of Glahn's main textbook (1925), in which there appears a table of aspects including glyphs but no names for aspects of 15°, 75°, 105°, and 165°, and, without either glyphs or names, a further range of aspects in even smaller multiples of 7½ degrees. However, the accompanying text to Sieggrün's paper indicates his belief that all such minor aspects were only of relevance to directions and not to natal character delineation. The likelihood that Glahn and Sieggrün knew each other through their common connection to Witte at this time and were familiar with each other's ideas seems strong.

The first edition of Glahn's book was published about a year earlier, in 1924, and gives the same glyphs as Sieggrün does in 1925 for the aspects of 75° and 105°. Although the glyph Sieggrün gives for that of 15° matches the one Glahn gives for 165°, and the one Glahn gives for 15° is unique to his table, the common root of their thinking on these aspects is clear from the exact confluence of two of their four respective glyphs for these new aspects. In his accompanying text to the table within the 1924 edition, Glahn expressly attributes the origin of the symbols to Witte himself.[94]

iv. Potent 15° Aspects? The Notions of K. W. von Elmensberg

In 1930, a relatively obscure figure in inter-war German astrology, K. W. von Elmensberg, had published the first two volumes of her continuously paginated three-volume work on astrological theory that was collectively entitled *Astrognostica Rediviva: Alte Tempelweisheit in neuer Fassung.*

The second volume contains a dense introductory discussion of the astrological aspects in the chapter *Grundlagen der Aspekte* (pp. 127–33); and this is followed by a dedicated chapter on the 15° series of aspects headed *T oder TAO Aspekt und sein Gegenpart der TRILIN*.[95]

Here, von Elmensberg names the 165° aspect the *Taoaspekt* (Tao aspect) and the 75° the *Trilin*. She describes the effect of the Tao as follows:

> *Der Taoaspekt ist fast rein seelisch-geistiger Wirkung und macht sich uns fühlbar in allen tief einschneidenden Gemütserregungen, oder hart ins Leben eingreifenden Erschütterungen – oder unbreschreiblichen inneren Erlebnisfreuden.*[96]

This translates approximately as the Tao aspect working almost solely on the spiritual level and making itself felt in deeply incisive emotions, shocks that affect life hard, or indescribable inner joys. She adds that its orb is at most five degrees and that it has a much stronger effect when applying than when separating.

The Trilin (75°) is linked by von Elmensberg to tensions or vibrations with a vehement triggering effect.[97] In the following chapter, *Die Dreiheit der strahlenden Aspektwellen*, von Elmensberg summarises the esoteric meaning of the Trilin as '*Naturkampfgesetz*' ('the law of natural struggle') and that of the Tao as '*schwingendes Fluidalgesetz, das atmende "Tat"*' ('the law of vibrating fluid, the breathing "deed"').[98]

Evidently, she regards the quartisextile aspect series as much more powerful and important than did Glahn in his writing just six years earlier.

v. The Numerological Circle Division Factor Theory of Charles E. O. Carter

In his practical guide to the delineation of natal interplanetary aspects, *The Astrological Aspects* (1930), the prominent British astrologer Charles E. O. Carter also sets out a modern theory for understanding why some types of aspects are experienced as stressful and others as harmonious, expressed partly in terms of certain esoteric numerological associations of the prime numbers by which the zodiacal circle is divided to reach them:

> The Harmonious Aspects are the trine, sextile, and semi-sextile, obtained by dividing the circle of 360° by 3, 6, and 12. Three, it need hardly be said, is the number of Ideal Form; hence it is harmonious, ideal, and concordant. These aspects, therefore, tend to happiness. The Conjunction... is analogous to the number One.... It is potentially either harmonious or inharmonious, and actually it derives its character, in particular cases, from the planets composing it, and from other horoscopic conditions. The Inharmonious Aspects are the opposition, the square, and the minor aspects called the quincunx, semi-square, and sesquiquadrate. These, except the quincunx, are derived from the numbers Two and Four, of which the former is a number of Passivity and Receptivity, and the latter is the number of objective manifestation. It follows that the opposition may be unfortunate by reason of its negativity in relation to opposing forces, and the square may have an inharmonious value, because manifestation necessarily implies limitation and circumscription. The aspects derived from Five, which are the quintile and its cognates, are considered to be weakly benefic. I am not sure that their value is not greater than is generally supposed, although they may not be very obvious in their effects. Five symbolises man as the potential master of Nature and natural forces. Hence their value would be intellectual. No known aspects are derived from Seven or Nine, though I should be very loth to say that none exist.[99]

In a footnote to his latter remark, Carter adds that:

> ... it seems to me by no means improbable that 40°, which is a third of the trine and a ninth of the circle, may be a potent benefic influence, at least as strong as the sextile.[100]

This is a significantly stronger statement of the potential value of the novile than both the late Commander Morrison's view expressed 97 years previously in 1833 and that of Brandler-Pracht just 20 years previously in 1910.

So influential was Carter's work during his long career, especially among British astrologers, for whom his voice was a leading authority from the early 1920s until well beyond his death in 1968, that it is difficult not to judge that simple statements like this probably prompted further harmonic research by others in the later 20th century.

In the Revised and Enlarged 1951 edition of his book, which has been reprinted many times since, Carter modifies this important footnote to remove express reference to the novile and instead argues:

I am personally convinced that all exact 10-degree angles constitute aspects, probably of a neutral character but in this respect varying much with the essential natures and radical conditions of the bodies concerned. In these cases, an orb of only 1° may be allowed.[101]

In this later statement, Carter has implied the validity of a thirty-sixfold division of the circle as a basis for deriving a host of additional aspects that had not previously been proposed by any other known astrologer. We might perhaps call the resulting 10° base aspect a *sexti-sextile* (sixth of a sixth) or a *trigintasextile* (thirty-sixth). In the prime number harmonic terms to which Carter subscribes, the division of the circle by 36 is comprised of its division by 2, 2, 3, and 3 again, giving its prime number derivation an even balance of 2 and 3 and conceivably accounting for his belief that it is 'of a neutral character'.

vi. Consolidation of Harmonic Aspect Theory by Dr. Walter Koch

We earlier briefly encountered in the discussion of Kepler's new aspects Dr. Walter Koch's secondary text *Aspekt-Lehre nach Johannes Kepler*, first published in 1950. Aside from giving a thorough account of Kepler's work on the aspects, Koch adds his own extensive commentary and theory, and this is probably the most significant contribution to modern harmonic aspect theory before that of John Addey *(see below)*.

Among the many themes explored by Koch in his book are the division of the aspects into 'hard' and 'soft', a terminology familiar to practically every astrologer raised on the aspect teachings of the late 20th century. Koch attempts to correlate the hardness and softness of aspects with the equivalent musical tones.[102]

Additionally, Koch proposes an innovative system of orb calculation that combines the traditional idea of differential planetary orbs with the modern one of differential orbs according to aspect type.[103]

Koch's orb calculation system works on the basis of initially ranking the importance of the aspect types and giving them differential basic orb values accordingly, as follows:

Conjunction – 5°
Opposition – 4°
Quartile; Trine – 3°
Sextile – 2°
Semi-sextile, Semi-square, quintile, sesquiquadrate, biquintile, quincunx – 1°

These values must then be *multiplied* by a figure of between 1½ and 3 depending on the perceived importance of the planets involved, as shown:

Sun; Moon – 3

Saturn; Mars – 2½

Jupiter; Venus; Mercury; Uranus – 2

Neptune; Pluto – 1½

It is not immediately clear whether Dr. Koch proposes to average the multiplication values of the two planets involved in a given aspect or to use only the stronger of the two, in determining the final orb.[104] But we can see that his system would produce a maximum orb of 15° for a conjunction involving one or both of the luminaries.

Koch adds in respect of the decile series proposed by Kepler and the 15° aspects previously proposed by both Glahn and von Elmensberg:

Für die gewöhnlichen und nicht ausgezeichneten 15°-Aspekte, z.B. 15°, 75°, 105°, 165° würde entsprechend der Orbis unter einem Grad betragen, nämlich 45 Bogenminuten. Derselbe Orbis von 45' gilt auch für Dezil und Tridezil.[105]

Here it is unclear whether Dr. Koch is proposing 45 minutes of arc as the basic orb value for all these aspect types, to be multiplied subsequently by the planetary multiplier values he advocates, or whether he is proposing 45 minutes as a hard limit for the final orb assigned to such aspects between all planetary combinations, but the latter interpretation perhaps seems more likely in view of his decision to exclude these classes of aspect from his table of aspect orbs altogether, considered together with his evident view that these are much less important aspects. Otherwise, if the planetary multipliers were to take effect on the 45' orb, then for a tridecile or quarti-sextile involving the Sun, an orb of 2°15' would be allowed – which seems excessive.

The following section of Dr. Koch's book is dedicated to the Number Theory of Aspect Doctrine (*Die Zahlentheorie der Aspektlehre*). Here, he gives extensive treatments of all numbers from 1 to 10 in application to the related circle division factors used in deriving aspects. In the process, he therefore considers the Septile series of aspects as well as the Novile series, which in common with Simmonite and Brandler-Pracht he calls the Nonagon.[106]

After this, under the heading *Die Bedeutung der Aspekte*, Koch separately interprets the general meaning of most of the major and minor aspect types, devoting almost a page to the quintile, and a whole paragraph to what we have proposed to call the quartisextile series, commencing thus:

> *Betreffs der Aspekte von 15° und ihrem Vielfachen, soweit sie noch nicht besprochen sind, nämlich den Aspekten von 75°, 105°, 165°, dürfte bei keinem fortschrittlichen Astrologen ein Zweifel bestehen, daß sie tatsächlich wirken; man muß nur ihren Orbis sehr klein, höchstens 1½° nehmen. Ihre Wirkung ist erregend und doppelwertig. Sie schwankt zwischen Annäherung und Sackgasse, Beitrag und Schröpfung. Die Qualität der aspektbildenden Planeten gibt den Ausschlag....*[107]

Like von Elmensberg, and much more so than Glahn, Koch is arguing for the meaningful importance of these aspects in astrological interpretation. He follows von Elmensberg in using the names *Trilin* for the 105° aspect and *Tao* for that of 165°, but notes that she was silent regarding the 75° aspect, and himself nominates the name *Bilin* for this, but does not propose a name for the base aspect of 15° itself.[108]

vii. Wider adoption of quartisextiles – the testimony of Thomas Ring

In his *Astrologische Menschenkunde Band I: Kräfte und Kräftebeziehungen* (1956), Thomas Ring, a leading German astrological thinker and writer for 45 years – from the appearance of his first major publications in 1938 until his death in 1983 – devotes a substantial chapter, *Die Kräftebeziehungen (Die Aspekte)*, comprising pp. 245–87 of the volume, to the theory of the astrological aspects.

In Ring's main table of aspects on p. 250, only the Ptolemaic aspects and six of Kepler's eight new aspects are shown, excluding the decile and the tridecile and all his 'borderline' aspects. However, in the foregoing text, Ring makes further reference to a series of aspects that neither Kepler nor Wilde had acknowledged but that Glahn, von Elmensberg, and Koch had all since given attention in the 20th-century German literature (as seen above): those stemming from the division of the 360° circle into 24 parts, which Ring advocates as being useful to evaluating the fine structure of the horoscope:

> *Schließlich kann für Beurteilungen der Feinstruktur über die Zwölfteilung hinausgegangen werden zum Vierundzwanzigeck, mit den Winkeln von 15°, 75°, 105°, und 165°.*[109]

He adds (p. 278):

> *Wird die zwölfstufige Ordnung durch weitere Aufspaltung verdoppelt im Vierundzwanzigeck, so entsteht eine regelmäßige Figur mit 15°-Aspekten, worin neben sämtlichen Aspekten der Zwölferordnung die schon dargestellten [Halbquadrat] und [Anderthalbquadrat] mit umfaßt sind. Als neu sondern sich 15°, 75°, 105°, 165° aus.... Als besonders eigenartig sei nur der 165°-Aspekt herausgehoben, charakterisierbar als feiner, trennender Schnitt, bei analogen sonstigen Anzeichen deutbar als Beitrag zu schicksalhaften Trennungen, seelischen Amputationen usw. Aspekte dieser Ordnung gelten lediglich als Bestätigung von Tendenzen, die in normalen Aspekten schon angezeigt sind.*

It is incidentally to be regretted that the label *Quindecile* has been widely misapplied by English-speaking astrologers since the 1980s to refer to the 165° aspect, when the term already existed and had remained in frequent and widely cited use since Kepler's time to refer to the 24° one that it justly describes by virtue of its representation of the division of the ecliptic circle by fifteen to form it.

The aspect of 165° was transmitted from the writings of Ring to the work of the late Noel Tyl, one of the most prolific American astrological authors of the late 20th century and early 21st centuries, who used it widely and adopted the name *Quindecile* for it, incorporating this into his teachings and influencing a student of his, Ricki Reeves, into writing an entire book about it with this name.[110]

While the transmission of German-sourced developments in astrological theory to English-speaking astrologers by Tyl is only to be lauded, the 165° aspect that von Elmensberg and Koch called the *Tao* should never even have been considered for the name *Quindecile*, seeing as it derives from the division of the zodiacal circle by 24 and not fifteen. This was certainly not a mistake that Ring himself, Tyl's primary source for the doctrine, ever made, as he referred to the series consistently as *Vierundzwanzigeck* (twenty-four-sided figure).

All the base aspects resulting from the division of the circle by three or more have traditionally been named according to the number by which the zodiacal circle has been divided to form them. It is on this basis that we use the term quintile (360°/5) for an aspect of 72° and not for an imagined one of 175°, and that we use the term sextile (360°/6) for one of 60° and not for an imagined one of 174°. Consistency in the system of astrological aspect nomenclature should preferably be cultivated as far as possible.[111]

I have personally proposed the name *Undecaquartisextile* in preference to von Elmensberg's idiosyncratic usage of *Tao* for the aspect of 165°, for the reasons given under the discussion of A. Frank Glahn above; and articles adopting this accurately geometrically descriptive name have in recent years been published in the mainstream astrological press by well-established astrologers such as Michelle Young, who wrote for many years in the now-discontinued *Horoscope* magazine.

viii. Harmonic Theory Revisited: the Integrally Harmonic Astrological Philosophy of John Addey

In the introduction to his important book *Harmonics in Astrology* (1976), the late John Addey argues for an understanding of all astrological doctrine in terms of 'the harmonics', which he defines as 'the rhythms and sub-rhythms of cosmic periods'.[112]

Addey's work conceptualises astrological signs, houses and aspects in terms of wave forms with positive and negative polarities, stating for example that a twelve-fold division would correspond to the sixth harmonic, since each of the six waves has a positive and negative phase.[113] After the research of Michel and Françoise Gauquelin that was prominent in his time, he calls upon statistical evidence of the distribution of aspects among representatives of different professions, and uses this evidence to argue that the conventional twelve-fold division upon which the Ptolemaic aspects are based is inadequate to describe real-world astrological distributions, in some of which, he contends, a fourth harmonic will be apparent and an eight-fold division of the circle must therefore be invoked. This, he says, is a revealed feature of much of the Gauquelin research, especially in relation to the diurnal circle that delimits the twelve astrological houses.[114]

Like Carter before him, Addey links the interpretation of the different circle division factors to numerological inferences. For example:

> When we... move to the idea of two, we may view this number as representing the idea of polarity, or of opposition, or of complementariness, or of positive and negative, or of subject and object, or of that which acts and that which is acted upon, or in countless other ways, but all these different ways imply the idea of duality and are derived from it. But when we proceed again to the idea of threeness we must leave this set of ideas behind because we are now involved with a triangular relationship.... A third factor has been introduced....[115]

Whatever the number involved, Addey insists that at equal distances between the points marked out by the division of the circle by that number will be a negative pole with the opposite energy.[116]

Addey decries the 'traditional emphasis on the number twelve' in astrology as being too limiting to describe the full range of real astrological relationships, arguing that 'all numbers play their part' in these, including 5, 7, 9, and even the numbers beyond 12.[117]

In proposing the application of this principle specifically to aspects, Addey goes on to argue that, even allowing for the semi-square and sesquiquadrate widely accepted by modern astrologers,

> ... a wholly unreasonable choice has been made in favour of certain numbers for dividing the circle (twelve and eight).[118]

A tool for chart analysis that Addey utilises is the harmonic chart, whereby the positions in absolute degrees longitude from 0° to 360° of the planets and points within a standard astrological figure are multiplied by the number of the harmonic that is to be investigated, and consequently spread over a like number of revolutions of the same circle composing the figure, and the aspects presenting in the rearranged figure are then assessed.

So for example, in a fifth harmonic chart, a planet at 11° of Gemini (71° of absolute longitude from the vernal point) would in fact appear visually at (71° * 5) 355° on the resultant chart. It would then appear in this fifth harmonic chart to be in partile opposition to another planet that was found at 5° degrees of Taurus in the original figure, because the position of latter planet at 35° degrees of absolute longitude would be converted to (35 * 5) 175° degrees in the resultant fifth harmonic chart.

A fifth harmonic opposition is equivalent to either a decile aspect (36°) or its multiple the tridecile (108°) in the original figure. From the perspective of Addey's harmonic theory, the interpretation of these two aspects is identical because they are both derived from the circle division factor of ten (2 * 5), so showing them alike in the fifth harmonic chart is no hindrance to meaningful interpretation.

Nonetheless, it remains the case that harmonic charts are essentially visual tools to aid the astrologer and are not strictly needed to comprehend or interpret the harmonic aspects. Nor was Addey the first to propose them in any application, as both the fourth harmonic chart and the eighth harmonic chart had already been in use among the Hamburg School astrologers of

Germany since the early-to-mid-20th century,[119] and visual tools called the 90° and 45° discs or dials had been popularised to represent them.[120]

One of Kepler's 'borderline' series of aspects that Addey regards as being important is the quindecile (24°) series, which, though without expressly naming it, he refers to descriptively as:

> *the third subharmonic of the quintile, which gives us the aspect of 24° and its multiples. This is the 15th harmonic, the third of the fifth or the fifth of the third.*[121]

Unlike Kepler, Addey proposes a clear interpretative guideline to the quindecile series, as follows:

> *These aspects are indicative of the enjoyment of and facility in some form of activity as shown by the planets involved.*[122]

So in contrast to Wilde, who was the first I have found to have adopted Kepler's other series of 'borderline' aspects, i.e., the 22.5° series based on the division of the circle by sixteen, Addey has sought to take Kepler's quindecile series into the mainstream.

With regard to the vexed question of aspect orbs, Addey's proposed solution is somewhat radical and exceedingly simple, being based on the direct arithmetic division of the allowed orb for the conjunction (however much that may be declared to be) by the circle division factor used to form the base aspect of the aspect series involved.[123] Based on his granting a 12° orb to the conjunction, Addey therefore proposes that the orb of the opposition be 6°, that of the trine only 4°, that of the square only 3°, that of the sextile only 2°, that of the semi-square and trioctile (or sesquiquadrate) only 1.5° and that of the semi-sextile and quincunx only 1°.

This method results in a far steeper disparity between the orbs for the Ptolemaic aspects than any previously recorded astrologer has advocated, with the conjunction having *four times* the orb of the square and *six times* that of the sextile under Addey's system.

Perhaps most controversial among the effects of this calculation method is that the quintile gets an orb of 2°24' (greater than that of the sextile) and the septile one of 1°43' (greater than that of the semi-square),[124] in marked difference from the conventionally lesser allowances for what have hitherto been regarded by most astrologers as being among the most minor of the new aspects (the quintile and septile series).

Afterword: the Statistical Research of Karl-Ernst Krafft

The late James Herschel Holden remarks that a similar work to *Harmonics in Astrology* was earlier penned by the Swiss statistician Karl-Ernst Krafft, apparently without Addey's knowledge.[125]

Krafft's *Traité d'Astro-Biologie* (1939) is full of a multitude of statistically based astrological research, and examines the distribution of the statistical peaks and troughs in its results, typically noting the geometric intervals between the peak occurrences in the overall distribution – a similar class of observation to that made by Addey in his examination of the later Gauquelin research.

Krafft's main book[126] is furnished with an index of 'notable intervals'[127] that encompass ones corresponding to a host of both Ptolemaic and harmonic aspects, including those of the quintile, novile, decile, and vigintile series and those of 22.5° and 15°, as well as more obscure and still lesser distances such as 10°, 9°, 6°, and 5°. However, while I have perhaps yet to digest it sufficiently thoroughly, it seems to me that no cohesive attempt is made in the text of the book to synthesise these findings into a coherent doctrine applicable to the interpretation of natal astrological aspects, so it is arguably of limited direct relevance, which is why it has not been featured as a direct contribution to aspect theory in Part Four of this chapter.

Appendix: Addey's System Moderated: The Graves Method of Orb Calculation

In 1996, the present author, in a flight of enthusiasm for contributing to the development of aspect theory, wrote and submitted to the Astrological Association of Great Britain a paper seeking to moderate Addey's system of orb calculation to bring the aspect orbs closer in line with astrologers' experiences and grant proportionately more weight to the lower prime number circle division factors, while holding true to Addey's principle of using a coherent mathematical methodology for the rationally consistent derivation of orbs, albeit one divided into two steps, each comprising subtler arithmetical processes, instead of the simple one advocated by Addey 20 years earlier.

My rationale for this was detailed in the retained last draft before the sending of my letter to the Association, here selectively abbreviated as follows:

I note Sue Tompkins's comments regarding allowed orbs for aspects, on p. 67 of her excellent work Aspects in Astrology *(1989). She mentions (a) that the routinely allowed orbs for major aspects are too large; (b) that various minor aspects are mistakenly altogether overlooked; and (c) that Addey proposed that orbs should diminish in direct proportion to the number used to divide the circle.*

In my experience..., Tompkins is correct in all three cases. Yet Addey's proposition as quoted is not especially helpful: it would lead to aspects of 8/11,[128] for instance, being awarded a greater orb than the [quincunx] at 5/12, and ultimately to the circle becoming awash with zones counted as representing aspects resulting from the division of the circle by obscure prime numbers having no likely representation at the physiological / psychological level of the subject; it would lead to every point on the circle becoming covered, often by an overlapping multiple, with aspects of one sort or another, unless the orbs granted initially to the major aspects were so small as to negate the very real and strong effects of such aspects outside these orbs.

For some time now I have been using a methodological system for determining every aspect to be noted and the orb to be allowed for it....

The guiding principles of my aspecting system are:

(a) to be truly comprehensive in the mapping of minor aspects, so that the relationships between factors so linked are not overlooked for synthesis purposes, and a more complete picture of how integrated the chart is can be gained;

(b) to avoid borderline orb allowances altogether, so that speculative 'spheres of influence' are not a licence for the astrologer to make any interpretation wished;

(c) to recognise the particular significance of the natural 2*2*3 zodiac relative to other subdivisions, including further '2's and '3's;

(d) in the event of other subdivisions, to recognise the geometrically progressively lessening importance on a biological / physical / psychological level of prime numbers as they arithmetically increase;

(e) in the event of major aspects partially overlapping in their orbs of influence with minor ones, <u>both</u> aspects should be noted;

(f) to name minor aspects logically and systematically in accordance with the precedents set by existingly named aspects, and to glyph them accordingly.

Although the editor of the *Astrological Journal* of the time did not select the article in question for publication, I believe with hindsight that it remains a relevant and serious contribution to the modern debate over how aspect orbs should be derived, and I have therefore reproduced the calculation method from the retained final pre-submission draft below without further comment:

Stage A: The Natural Zodiac

The conjunction orb is nominated at 9°. For each further prime number factor by which the circle is to be divided, starting with the lowest, the orb is divided by the factor with the subsequent addition of one third of the result, to provide the orb applicable to the aspect(s) formed by the circle division in question. Hence, in descending order of orb, the natural zodiac aspects are as follows:

DIVISION:	ASPECT(S):	ORB CALCULATION METHOD:	ORB:
1	0°	NOMINATION	9°
2	180°	[9°/2] * 4/3	6°
3	120°	[9°/3] * 4/3	4°
2,2=4	90°	[6°/2] * 4/3	4°
2,3=6	60°	[6°/3] * 4/3	2.6R°
2,2,3=12	30°; 150°	[4°/3] * 4/3	1.7R°

Stage B: All other aspects

For every other integral circle division in turn, starting with 5 and working upwards with 7, 8, 9, 10, 11, and 13 to 72, which is the highest division to qualify as a producer of aspects under the procedure below, apply the following steps:

1) Identity the prime number factors which compose the integer.

2) Intersect as many of these as possible (at most, two 2s and one 3) with the factors constituting the natural zodiac divisions, as specified above; and adopt the orb corresponding to the natural zodiac division intersected, as a starting point.

3) For each remaining (non-intersected) integer-composing factor, in turn, starting with the lowest, divide the orb hitherto standing by the factor to the power of 1.5. Thus, for a factor of 2 divide by 2.8284; for a 3, divide by 5.1962; for 5, by 11.1803; for 7, by 18.5203; for 11, by 36.4829; for 13, by 46.8722; for 17, by 70.0928; and for 19, which is the highest prime number to qualify as a producer of aspects under this procedure, by 82.8191.

4) If the resulting orb is less than 0.1°, reject the circle division as it does not qualify to produce aspects. Move to the next integer.

5) Multiply the orb by ⅚ as a fixed penalty for the division integer not forming part of the constitution of the natural zodiac.

FROM KEPLER TO ADDEY:
A CHRONOLOGY OF DEVELOPMENTS IN ASTROLOGICAL ASPECT THEORY FROM 1602 TO 1976

A photographic scan of the author's original 1996 manuscript table of harmonic aspects

6) To determine the aspects produced by the division integer, divide 360° by it, note the base aspect formed, and continually add the base aspect on, as far as 180°, noting every further aspect, but excluding any duplicates of aspects formed by lower division integers.

As seen in the table reproduced above, the orbs for the quintile and septile work out (to the nearest two decimal points) to 0.67° and 0.41° respectively. So in contrast to the results from Addey's system of orb calculation, the orbs resulting from the system adopted here put all quintile-series and septile-series aspects in their place as ones of lesser strength compared with the semi-sextile and the semi-square, the latter of which works out to an orb of 1.18° based on ⅚ [4° / 2.8284].

This was an essentially mathematical theoretical exercise, and I do not propose today that practising astrologers (still less, traditional astrologers) should adopt such an intricate array of minor harmonic aspects as are featured in the table that resulted from the coherent orb calculation method I developed in the mid-1990s. In particular, please note that the expression of the orb allowances in the above table to four decimal places was purely for the purposes of presenting the mathematical results of the calculation operations to a high degree of accuracy. It would be manifestly absurd to attempt to calculate orbs to such a high degree of precision in practical astrological chart delineation!

However, the aim of my mathematical experiment in counteracting the seemingly undue importance granted by Addey's method to the *minor prime number* harmonic aspects as compared with those derived from the division of the circle by prime number factors comprising 2s and 3s was essentially accomplished.

Was Addey in fact justified in breaking so completely with tradition? That is arguably a question above all for the working astrologers of today to decide, although theoreticians may still be entitled their views.

The Harmonics after Addey – A summary Bibliography, 1977 to 2019

Addey's work on the harmonics remains the pioneering text that defined the modern 20th-century perspective on harmonic aspect theory that all others since have followed. To cover the contributions of his successors in detail would extend the scope of this chapter beyond its temporal brief.

However, the development of interpretations and theory around harmonics did not stop in 1976. For those wishing to get a more up-to-date perspective on the topic, there have been numerous other detailed treatments of the subject since 1976 that are worth consulting for further reading. These include, in chronological order:

Williamsen, James S.; Williamsen, Ruth E. *Astrologer's Guide to the Harmonics* Second Printing, with Revisions and Format Changes. Green Bay, WI: Cambridge Circle, Ltd., 1977.
Greig, John E. *Astrology and Planetary Harmonics*. London: Astrological Association and John E. Greig, 1979.
Tierney, Bil. *Perceptions in Astrology*.[129] Lynchburg, VA: Mercury Hour, 1980.
Addey, John, ed. *Harmonic Anthology*. Third Printing. Tempe, AZ: AFA, 1983.[130]
Hamblin, David; intr. Harvey, Charles; 'Harmonic Charts: Understanding and Using the Principle of Harmonics in Astrological Interpretation' London: Aquarian Press, 1983.
Jay, Delphine. *Practical Harmonics*. Stated First Edition. Tempe, AZ: AFA, 1983.
Tierney, Bil. *Dynamics of Aspect Analysis: New Perceptions in Astrology*. Second Edition. Sebastopol, CA: CRCS, 1983.
Ishikawa, H. M. "Gen", *Divisional Harmonics: the Easiest Way to Focus on the Details in a Horoscope*. Stated First Printing. Tempe, AZ: AFA, 1984.
Hannan, Charles and Hannan, Lois. *Predictive Techniques in Annual Harmonics: Predictive Techniques and the Annual Harmonic Chart; Harmonic Progressions and Life Cycles*. Stated First Printing. Tempe, AZ: AFA, 1986.
Harding, Michael and Harvey, Charles. *Working with Astrology: the Psychology of Harmonics, Midpoints and Astro*Carto*Graphy*. London: Arkana, Penguin, 1990.
Donath, Emma Belle. *Minor Aspects Between Natal Planets*. Fifth Printing. Tempe, AZ: AFA, 1990.[131]
Press, Nona Gwynn. *New Insights Into Astrology*. Second Printing. San Diego, CA: ACS, 1992.
Pesavento, Larry. *Harmonic Vibrations: a Metamorphosis from Traditional Cycle Theory to Astro-Harmonics*. Greenville, SC: Traders Press, 1996.
Pesavento, Larry. *Planetary Harmonics of Speculative Markets*. Greenville, SC: Traders Press, 1996.
Addey, John. *A New Study of Astrology, together with Astrology Reborn and The Discrimination of Birth Types*. London: The Urania Trust, 1996.
Bolton, David. *Harmonics: Schlüssel zur astrologischen Aspektdeutung: Einführung und praktische Anwendung*. Tübingen: Chiron Verlag, 2009.
Hamblin, David. *The Spirit of Numbers: A New Exploration of Harmonic Astrology*. Bournemouth: Wessex Astrologer, 2011.
Hamblin, David. *Harmonic Astrology in Practice*. Swanage: Wessex Astrologer, 2019.

Endnotes

1. For a concise introduction to the theory and terminology of aspects in astrology, see the author's three-part article *Introduction to Astrological Aspects* (2002–3), freely available online at https://www.astrolearn.com/astrology-articles/aspects1/
2. See the author's definition of these terms within his earlier extended discussion of this topic in 2003 at https://www.astrolearn.com/astrology-articles/aspects3/
3. See J. Lee Lehman, *Classical Astrology for Modern Living* (Whitford Press, 1996), p. 195.
4. See also Dr. Lehman's table of all antiscial and contra-antiscial sign pairings, including those in mutual square aspect, on p. 191 of her *op. cit.*
5. *Op. cit.*, p. 109
6. London: Tara Astrological Publications, 2002.
7. Al-Bîrûnî was writing in the early 11th century CE. It is beyond the purposes of the present chapter, which is concerned with the timeline of changes to astrological aspect theory only since 1602, to check every medieval source before Al-Bîrûnî in order to trace this practice back to its origins. Suffice it to say that numerous texts by the Arabic astrologers have become available in English translations for the first time since 2002 thanks to the assiduous efforts of Benjamin N. Dykes PhD.; and those interested in establishing the timelines for the variable use of planetary orbs more precisely are recommended to consult these translations
8. William Lilly, *Christian Astrology* (1647), p. 107.
9. These records have not been cross-checked with the original sources for the purposes of this chapter, but the sources concerned are all widely available.
10. Maurice McCann, *Astrological Essays*, p. 15.
11. Anonymously translated as *Concerning the More Certain Fundamentals of Astrology* for Clancy (New York, 1942); and later separately translated by Mary Ann Rossi as 'On the More Certain Fundamentals of Astrology', in *Proceedings of the American Philosophical Society*, Vol. 123, No. 2 (April 27, 1979): pp. 85–116.
12. *Sesquiquartile* – as translated in the Clancy edition; the later APS edition gives *sesquiquadrature*. In the APS edition of Kepler's later work *Harmonices Mundi*, it is instead called the *trioctile*. Many modern 20th-century astrological sources prefer *sesquiquadrate* or *sesquisquare*.
13. Clancy edition, p. 15.
14. Musical correspondences are recorded by the scholars J. Bruce Brackenbridge and Mary Ann Rossi in their extensive *Note 31* to the APS edition, pp. 113–15.
15. Translated into English as *The Harmonies of the World* by Charles Glenn Wallis for *Great Books of the Western World 16: Ptolemy. Copernicus. Kepler*, published by Willam Benton (1952), and again by E. J. Aiton, A. M. Duncan and J. V. Field as *The Harmony of the World* in *Memoirs of the American Philosophical Society held at Philadelphia for Promoting Useful Knowledge*, Volume 209 (1997).
16. See APS edition of *H.o.t.W.*, pp. 326–57.

17 It should be noted that he had already hinted at the importance of the semisextile in the intervening years in a small part of his general introductory astrological treatise *Tertius Interveniens* (1610), within the section headed Thesis 59. Most of this book, including the whole of Thesis 59, has recently been translated by Ken Negus as *Kepler's Astrology* (Amherst: Earth Heart, 2008) – see especially p. 129, wherein mention of the revealed importance of the semi-sextile is made.

18 This came to be known more commonly in the 20th century as a semi-square.

19 *H.o.t.W.*, Book IV, Chapter V, Proposition IX – see APS edition, p. 340.

20 *H.o.t.W.*, Book IV, Chapter V, Propositions X–XIV – see APS edition pp. 341–47.

21 *H.o.t.W.*, Book IV, Chapter VI – see APS edition, p. 356.

22 *H.o.t.W.*, Book IV, Chapter V – see APS edition, pp. 347–48.

23 *H.o.t.W.*, Book IV, Chapter VI – see APS edition, pp. 351–54.

24 His explanation for his change of view is lengthy and uses an analogy with a piece of string; those wishing to explore it further should consult one of the available translations of *Harmonices Mundi*.

25 *H.o.t.W.*, Book IV, Chapter VI – see APS edition, p. 354.

26 Dr. Walter A. Koch, *Aspektlehre Nach Johannes Kepler: Die Formsymbolik von Ton, Zahl und Aspekt* – Neudruck, Hamburg, 1952 (after the original of 1950), p. 31.

27 Lilly's own spelling varies within his text.

28 William Lilly, *Christian Astrology* (1647), five listed on p. 32 and seven (including four of the same ones) at pp. 511–12, so eight in total.

29 James Wilson, *Dictionary of Astrology* (1819), pp. 56–59.

30 His proposed name *Quadrasextile* is ill-fitting because the 150° aspect is not derived from four times the sextile or even of the semi-sextile. Four sextiles would be 240° (a trine).

31 *Ibid.*, p. 59 and pp. 99–101.

32 *Op. cit.*, p. 75.

33 *Op. cit.*, p. 101.

34 Originally entitled *The Herald of Astrology* before its name evolved to *Zadkiel's Almanac*.

35 Zadkiel, *The Grammar of Astrology* (1833), pp. 17–18.

36 This was a novel proposition in the early 1830s; but as we shall go on to see, some twentieth century writers would eventually adopt this aspect, and it has become known as the *novile* or *nonagon*.

37 Zadkiel, *The Grammar of Astrology*, p. 19.

38 [sic]. Here Chaney, or perhaps a typesetting working for him, has given the degrees of separation to the decile or semi-quintile but mislabelled it the semi-quartile. This error may conceivably have resulted from his original intention to include both these aspects, but because the names of the semi-quintile and semi-quartile look almost identical at a glance and because they occur in succession within the order of the

zodiac among all the aspects considered by Chaney, at 36° and 45° respectively, he has somehow managed to mix and merge their records, publishing the degrees of the first but the name of the second.

[39] W. H. Chaney, *A Primer of Astrology and American Urania* (1890), Part 1, p. 27.

[40] It is here assumed that the semi-quintile he has falsely labelled the semi-quartile was meant to be included as the semi-quintile since he has given the degrees (36°) of the semi-quintile, although an alternative reading might be that he had truly meant to include the semi-quartile at 45° over and above the semi-quintile, but simply mislabelled its number of degrees.

[41] Chaney is referring mockingly to a purely hypothetical proposal he has dreamed up in his own rhetorical mind for an aspect of 75° (half a quincunx of 150°) here in a bid to show that aspect inventions have already reached an absurd level. It is ironic to note that in the mid-20th century, as we shall go on to see, he was proved partly right as a 75° aspect was indeed proposed by some astrologers, but not with the name of semi-quincunx or in connection with the quincunx.

[42] W. H. Chaney, *op. cit.*, pp. 59–61.

[43] *Ibid.*, p. 61.

[44] Those published from 1928 onwards bore the extended name of *A-Z Horoscope Maker and Delineator*.

[45] Llewellyn George, *A-Z Horoscope Maker and Delineator* (Portland, OR: Llewellyn, 1913), p. 41.

[46] *Ibid.*, p. 353.

[47] *Ibid.*, p. 356.

[48] Zadkiel Tao Sze, *The Hand-Book of Astrology Vol. I* (London: G. Berger, 1861), p. 8.

[49] *Ibid.*, p. 95.

[50] *Ibid.*, p. 103.

[51] W. H. Chaney, *A Primer of Astrology and American Urania* (1890), Part 2, pp. 63–64.

[52] *Ibid.*, p. 67.

[53] *Ibid.*, Part Four, p. 109.

[54] *Ibid.*, Part 5, p. 137. Chaney is not the first 19th-century astrologer to criticise Kepler's aspect doctrine, but is perhaps unaware of Wilson's previous criticisms of it.

[55] *Ibid.*, Part 6, p. 177.

[56] London: Catty & Co., 1877.

[57] A common alternative spelling for what arguably should be Tridecile to denote three *times* ten, akin to Biquintile (and not Duoquintile) denoting two *times* five.

[58] Maurice McCann, *The Sun and the Aspects* (London: Tara Astrological Publications, 2002), p. 67.

[59] *The Astrologer's Magazine*, Vol. I, No. 6, (January, 1891): p. 140.

[60] McCann, *The Sun and the Aspects*, p. 81.

[61] Not to be confused with Alan Leo, whose real name was William Frederick Allan.

Green was a prominent member of Alan Leo's circle who would become the author of several specialised astrological books including *The Theoretical Value of the Degrees of the Zodiac* (1898); *Theoretical Astrology* (1903; revised as *The 'Reason Why' in Astrology* in 1910); *Directions and Directing* (1905); *Mundane or National Astrology* (1911); and *Weather Predicting by Astro-Meteorology* (1912).

62 *The Astrologer's Magazine*, Vol. 2, No. 8, (March, 1892): p. 464.

63 *Ibid.*, pp. 464–65.

64 *The Future: a Monthly Magazine of Predictive Science & Events of the Day*, Vol. I, No. VII (August 1, 1892): pp. 102ff.

65 G. Wilde and J. Dodson, *A Treatise of Natal Astrology* (Halifax: The Occult Book Co., 1894), p. 6.

66 *Ibid.*, p. 7.

67 Alan Leo, *Practical Astrology*, stated Second Edition, Revised (= the first full-length edition and the first under this title) (London: Modern Astrology Office, [1897]), p. 13.

68 Lehman, *Classical Astrology for Modern Living*, pp. 187–97.

69 Leo, *Practical Astrology*, stated Second Edition [1897], p. 15.

70 *Ibid.*, p. 203.

71 Old is better known by his usual pen-name of 'Sepharial', although in the first edition of this, his main general astrological text-book, he used his real name, adding 'Sepharial' only between parentheses. Later editions of the same book from 1903 onwards are credited only to his pen name.

72 W. Gorn Old, *The New Manual of Astrology in Four Books* (London: George Redway, 1898), p. 48.

73 *Ibid.*, p. 49.

74 *Ibid.*

75 Berlin: F. W. Peters-Verlag, 1955.

76 W. J. Simmonite, *The Scientific and Literary Messenger* (London: Simpkin and Marshall, 1842), p. 46; Simmonite, *The Celestial Philosopher: or, the Complete Arcana of Astral Philosophy, being Genethliology Simplified, or the Doctrine of Nativities*. Vol. I (London: Simpkin, Marshall, [c. 1849]), p. 2.

77 Karl Brandler-Pracht, *Astrologische Bibliothek Band I: Kleines Astrologisches Lehrbuch* (Leipzig: Theosophisches Verlagshaus Dr. Hugo Vollrath, 1910), p. 31.

78 *Ibid.*, p. 33.

79 *Ibid.*, pp. 35, 37.

80 Geo. Wilde, *A Primer of Natal Astrology for Beginners*, Third Edition (Halifax: Rexo, 1911) [NB: Earlier editions of this title are vanishingly scarce and could not be sourced at the time of my research for this study.].

81 *Ibid.*, pp. 9–10.

82 This is half a semi-quartile, or $1/16^{th}$ of the zodiacal circle, and could alternatively be called a quarti-quartile or a quarti-square.

[83] This is three times the vigintile, so we might reasonably call it a Trivigintile.

[84] This is three times Wilde's semi-demi-quartile, or 3/16ths of the circle, and we could reasonably call it something like a Triquarti-quartile or Triquarti-square.

[85] Wilde gives 112°, but this is clearly half a degree off as the aspect in question must be five times his semi-demi-quartile, or 5/16ths of the circle, which we could reasonably call something along the lines of a Quintaquarti-quartile or Quintaquarti-square.

[86] Wilde mistakenly gives 157° as the exact separation for the Triseptile, almost three degrees off. It seems he has confused the position of the nearby septile with that of the 157.5° aspect proposed by his student W. Kruse.

[87] This is seven times Wilde's semi-demi-quartile, and we may reasonably refer to it as a Septaquarti-quartile or Septaquarti-square accordingly.

[88] More normally known as the vigintile.

[89] This is seven times a vigintile, and we could reasonably call it a Septavigintile accordingly.

[90] This is nine times a vigintile, and we might therefore reasonably call it a Novavigintile.

[91] A. Frank Glahn, *Erklärung und systematische Deutung des Geburtshoroskopes*, 2. Durchgesehene Auflage (Bad Oldesloe: Uranus-Verlag Max Duphorn, 1925), p. 184.

[92] Multiplier prefixes loosely proposed on the basis of the Latin names for five (quinque), seven (septem) and eleven (undecim).

[93] Friedrich Sieggrün, 'Die Fliegerbombe: Astrologische Skizze' in *Die Hamburger Astrologenschule* (1925). The original printing is not to hand, but the article was reprinted half a century later in the compilation volume *Der Mensch: eine Empfangsstation kosmischer Suggestionen*, published by Ludwig Rudolph (Hamburg: Witte-Verlag, 1975), and in this edition the table of aspects appears under the heading *Aspekte* on p. 336.

[94] A. Frank Glahn, *Erklärung und systematische Deutung des Geburtshoroskopes* (Bad Oldesloe: Uranus-Verlag Max Duphorn, 1924), p. 52.

[95] K. W. Von Elmensberg, *Astrognostica Rediviva: Alte Tempelweisheit in Neuer Fassung*, 2. Lieferung (Berlin: Verlag Ora, 1930), pp. 134–37.

[96] *Ibid.*, p. 134.

[97] *Ibid.*, p. 136.

[98] *Ibid.*, p. 140.

[99] Charles E. O. Carter, *The Astrological Aspects* (London: L. N. Fowler, 1930), pp. 8–9.

[100] *Ibid.*, p. 9.

[101] Charles E. O. Carter, *The Astrological Aspects* (Tempe, AZ: AFA, 1992) (a photocopy-based reprint of the Revised and Enlarged Edition of 1951), p. 9.

[102] Dr. Walter Koch, *Aspekt-Lehre nach Johannes Kepler* (neudruck, Hamburg, 1952), pp. 64–68.

[103] *Ibid.*, pp. 70–73.

[104] A close examination of his later articles and writings may help to resolve this point.

[105] Walter Koch, *op. cit.*, p. 73.
[106] *Ibid.*, pp. 73–82.
[107] *Ibid.*, p. 89.
[108] *Ibid.*, pp. 89; 92.
[109] Thomas Ring, *Astrologische Menschenkunde I: Kräfte und Kräftebeziehungen* (Zürich: Rascher Verlag, 1956), p. 250.
[110] Ricki Reeves, *The Quindecile: the Astrology & Psychology of Obsession* (St. Paul, MN: Llewellyn, 2001).
[111] For further reading, see the present author's live text debate of the issues involved in this topic at Skyscript astrology forum with fellow-contributor 'Atlantean', postings dated January 3rd to 4th, 2010, conserved in the second and third pages of the thread at http://skyscript.co.uk/forums/viewtopic.php?t=4828 at the time of writing.
[112] John Addey, *Harmonics in Astrology: An Introductory Textbook to the New Understanding of an Old Science* (Cambridge Circle Ltd., 1976), p. 5.
[113] *Ibid.*, p. 34.
[114] *Ibid*, pp. 26–30; p. 34.
[115] *Ibid.*, p. 35.
[116] *Ibid.*, pp. 35–36.
[117] *Ibid.*, pp. 36–37.
[118] *Ibid.*, p. 67.
[119] Hamburg School astrology, often known as Uranian astrology, is a further rich seam of astrological theory developed in the twentieth century. However, because it makes extensive use of midpoints in place of conventional interplanetary aspects, it constitutes a mine of unconventional astrological theory that was felt to exceed the scope of this chapter, and has therefore been left out of the central discussion, which is not in any way to understate its importance.
[120] It is also worth noting here that prior even to the invention of the 90° dial, a 360° dial marked out in 15-degree gradations with aspect glyphs including glyphs for proposed aspects of 15°, 75°, 105°, and 165° matching the ones previously used by Sieggrün in 1925, was being sold separately by the publisher, Witte-Verlag, of the first edition of Alfred Witte's main interpretative guidebook to midpoints, including those involved with hypothetical Transneptunian planets, *Regelwerk für Planetenbilder: Die Astrologie von morgen* (1928), and described in its pages.
[121] John Addey, *op. cit.*, p. 126.
[122] *Ibid.*, p. 127.
[123] *Ibid.*, p. 130.
[124] *Ibid.*, p. 131.
[125] James Herschel Holden, *A History of Horoscopic Astrology from the Babylonian Period to the Modern Age* (Tempe, AZ: AFA, 1996), p. 201.
[126] He also wrote several shorter books and pamphlets, a number of conference papers,

and numerous magazine articles in both French and German that were widely published in the international astrological magazine press of the 1920s and 1930s.

[127] K.-E. Krafft, *Traité d'Astro-Biologie* (Paris: Amedée Legrand/ Lausanne: V. Porchet, 1939), p. 350.

[128] By which I meant eight elevenths of the circle, or the eight-times multiple of the undecile base aspect.

[129] The second edition of the work above. It would form the core of what would become Tierney's successful later book *Dynamics of Aspect Analysis*, see above.

[130] First published by Cambridge Circle Limited in 1976, and comprising an anthology of the author's published magazine articles of relevance to harmonics since 1958, of which those since 1961 are more directly relevant. Thus constituting a useful companion volume to the synthesis of his ideas presented in his main book *Harmonics in Astrology*.

[131] Originally published in 1981.

Part Two:
Astrologers' modern treatments of the Sun,
and integration of the outer planets and Lilith

Chapter Three
The Rise of the Sun:
The Natal Sun Emphasised, 1887–1959

Part 1: A Summary of Sun Sign Writings before 1887

In astrological text-books published until the mid-1880s, the Sun is usually considered on an approximately equal footing with the Moon and all planets through to Saturn, and accorded a similar amount of interpretative paragraph space to all of them. Although as Kim Farnell has previously documented, some traditional interpretations of the Sun signs for human appearance, character and destiny known as *Zodiologia* can be traced back as far as the ancient Babylonian period and flourished in classical times alongside horoscopic astrology,[1] the chief domain in the early modern period in which the Sun was accorded prominence as expressed through the signs of the zodiac was a long-established breed of casual popular writing aimed at non-astrologers and existing entirely outside the framework of formal astrological teaching and practice – indeed, belonging more to folklore than to astrology, although perhaps having its roots in the ancient *Zodiologia*.

One of the best-documented examples of this is *Le Miroir d'Astrologie Naturelle* by Sinibal de Spadacine, believed to have been penned by an astrologer based in Milan.[2] The first printed edition recorded in libraries is from 1606, but it was reprinted frequently in the 17th and 18th centuries. This curious short tract gives rather vague and general descriptions of people born in each of the calendar months, without expressly attributing the influences of the months to the signs.

Another early example of popular Sun sign writing identified by Farnell, first published thus in 1506, was Richard Pynson's English edition of the originally French short popular book *The Shepherd's Calendar*, to which Pynson is said to have added Sun sign delineations that included prognostications for character as well as appearance.[3]

The continuing vestiges of such folkloric traditions were apparent in the modern era in works such as Margaret Johnson's finely illustrated zodiacal poetry book *The Procession of the Zodiac* (Boston, US, 1886) – a feast of beauty for the eyes and the spirit, but not an attempt to teach astrology.

One notable Renaissance text occupies a grey area between folkloric and serious astrology, but ultimately belongs squarely to the domain of a simplified popular introduction to astrology at best. In 1522, a broad-based divinatory manual by German theologian Johannes von Hagen (1467–1537), writing as Johannes ab Indagine, and one that would prove enduringly popular throughout the 16th century and much of the 17th, was first published in Latin in both Frankfurt and Strasbourg.[4] As the extended title of Indagine's book shows, it covered palmistry (chiromancy) and physiognomy together with natural astrology, all in the space of about 70 leaves of text.[5] This popularly pitched work was widely translated into modern European languages, with the first German edition appearing in 1523;[6] a Dutch edition in 1536,[7] a partial French one in 1545,[8] the first full French translation in 1549,[9] and the English translation of Fabian Withers in 1558.[10] The Withers translation was itself reprinted in 1575, 1598, 1651, 1656, 1676 and 1683, testifying to its enduring success in the marketplate. Even the Latin edition was widely reprinted, with fresh printings thus appearing in 1531, 1534, 1541, 1543, 1547, 1551, 1556, c. 1560, 1582, 1603, 1622, and 1630.

A newly retyped edition of Withers's translation of Indagine, annotated by Kim Farnell, was published in 2015. The chapter headed '*Brief introduction upon the faces of the signs, what effect the Sun works in every house or mansion*'[11] succinctly delineates the Sun in each of the thirty-six decans in terms of both appearance and character. A later chapter, headed '*Hereafter follow the natural judgments of astrology, according to the revolution of the Sun through the twelve signs of the Zodiac*', fills an additional 14 pages of Farnell's edition,[12] and interprets the Sun signs as a whole, chiefly in terms of character. The combined length of both sections of the book given over to the natal Sun in the tropical zodiac, at 28 pages, exceeds that of the section dedicated to delineating the signs on the Ascendant and other angles.[13] The planets are allocated only one page between them in general terms,[14] and four pages as 'lords of the birth'.[15]

We may reasonably cite the preferential attention given by Indagine to the Sun in the part of his book that deals with astrology, and the manifest international commercial success of the work in Western Europe for over 150 years, as an important precedent for the modern Sun sign astrology movement. Indagine was neither widely cited nor imitated by serious astrologers writing from the 16th to the 19th centuries, but the astrologers of this period must surely have been conscious of the widespread presence of his work in continuing circulation, and its function as a simplified popular taster of astrology.[16]

Farnell also cites the Renaissance text *De Occulta Philosophia Libri Tres* by German polymath Heinrich Cornelius Agrippa (1486–1535) as an influence upon modern Sun sign astrology on account of Sun sign delineations. This seems to be based on Robert Cross Smith, writing as Raphael, apparently claiming to have extracted the Sun sign delineations appearing in his last book *The Familiar Astrologer* (1831) 'verbatim' from Agrippa.[17]

But did he? While researching for this essay, I have found no evidence for any of Smith's Sun sign citations coming from Agrippa's famous book or even from the *Fourth Book of Occult Philosophy* originally spuriously attributed to Agrippa. In fact, searching for extracts from Smith's Sun sign delineations online brings up only one source – Raphael's *Familiar Astrologer*!

To put this in context, let us briefly examine the publishing history of Agrippa's work. First published in the original Latin in partial form only in 1531, *De Occulta Philosophia* had been printed in its entirety by 1533,[18] with reprints following in 1538, 1541, 1550, 1551, 1567, and circa 1600, and other uncertainly dated printings also recorded. The first English translation, by a J. F.,[19] appeared in 1650 according to library records (though it was dated 1651). A new annotated edition of the first book only of this translation, by American heliocentric astrologer and occultist Willis Whitehead, would eventually appear in 1897–98, but in Raphael's day, and even in the day of Hiram E. Butler (whom we shall go on to discuss later), the original 1650 printing of J. F.'s translation was still the only English edition available.

Nor can I find any Sun sign delineations at all in the modern annotated Llewellyn edition of the sole 17th-century English translation of Agrippa's main book, which strongly suggests that there is no such content in the work and never has been. Since the text of J. F.'s translation is the same text that is used in the Llewellyn edition of 1993, which purports to be complete, we have sound reason to believe that there were no Sun sign delineations in the 1650 printing either. So unless a substantial section from the original Latin edition was omitted from the English translation of 1650 and from the new edition of the same published by Llewellyn in 1993, we can draw only one conclusion: Smith took his text from elsewhere! Furthermore, a brief leaf through the table of contents of the critical edition of the Latin text published by Brill in 1992 shows up nothing that looks as though it could be expected to contain Sun sign readings.

Smith's actual words are:

> *Amongst the various Astrological authors, Arabian, Persian, and Italian, who have written upon the effects of the '****Solar Horoscope****,' the most conspicuous*

are Taisner, Junctinus, Haly Abenragel, Indagine, and Agrippa, from whom the following is extracted verbatim; and first we begin with Sol in Aries....[20]

This form of words is open to a degree of interpretation. Smith does not specify whether the 'from whom' refers only to Agrippa, as the last author in his list, or to all the authors listed collectively. If he is referring to them collectively, then since most of these authors wrote in Latin and some of them had not been translated into English at all, we might perhaps conclude that he made, or commissioned, his own translation from a selection of Latin observations on the Sun signs distributed across several or all of the authors, or else that he quoted from the available English translation of another of the works he had listed. A thorough investigation of all the above sources to determine Smith's source or sources would be a valid line of future research, but for present purposes it is sufficient to say that we find no evidence in his most widely available works that Agrippa was a Sun sign astrologer or penned Sun sign delineations that influenced generations of astrologers to follow.

Instead, we see Smith's depictions of the Sun signs in the early 1830s in the context of a popularly pitched work of his own that was not a serious astrological teaching manual. As such, they belong more to the folkloric traditions of Sun-sign astrology, even if he did in fact cobble them together from serious astrological books of the past. This is a sign of the mixed market for astrological writing in England in Smith's day, which comprised a very serious, traditional framework and (largely separately from this) a popular underbelly. As an almanac writer and editor of various divinatory games in book form,[21] Smith had already straddled both markets in his work for several years by the time *The Familiar Astrologer* was published. In any case, it was not an astrological text-book and was unrepresentative of the serious astrological writing currents of his day.[22]

The 1880s and 1890s saw a boom in the volume and frequency of astrological publishing in England that surpassed any witnessed there since the late 17th century, simultaneously with a parallel and altogether unprecedented boom in like publishing in the US; and alongside a flurry of more traditional works, these developments collectively brought a new breed of natal astrological writing to the fore, one that gave far greater prominence to the Sun at birth.

While some examples of such work merely gave extended delineations of the natal Sun in the signs compared with their antecedents, but still in the context of more-or-less complete primers on natal astrology, others went much further and amounted to complete books covering nothing but delineations of the natal Sun, appealing in the process to a mass popular readership that did not need to have studied astrology at all or to have learnt how to use an ephemeris in order to comprehend the readings.

In the remaining parts of this essay, supported by a close examination of the relevant literature, we shall identify the chief historical strands in the shift towards a greater focus on Sun signs in natal astrology that began in those final decades of the 19th century and has remained a feature of popular astrological writing ever since. We shall categorise and shortlist examples of the breed spanning the early-to-mid 20th century, taking as our cut-off point the end of the 1950s, in order to exclude from the picture the New Age boom of the late 1960s. The latter explosion in astrological publishing was both epitomised and substantially driven by one of the most extensive and successful exponents of Sun-sign astrology on record, the late Linda Goodman. The astrological publishing boom that began in 1968 with the publication of her million-selling book Sun Signs has its own distinctive character and influences, and by ending our survey in the late 1950s, I seek to keep the account strictly to developments in Sun-sign astrology before New Age counter-culture took the world, and the astrological writing market with it, by storm.

A separate development to emerge some decades after the increased use of the Sun in natal astrology was its increased use in predictive astrology, and more particularly the practice of Sun sign–based forecasting. The next chapter in this volume is devoted to exploring how and when this came about, and the cultural context that allowed it to flourish.

Part 2: Butler's Revolution:
Solar Biology and the Soli-Lunar Polarities unleashed

I regard 1887 as the watershed year that both marked and sparked the movement towards giving greater prominence to the Sun in natal astrology, chiefly on account of a landmark natal astrology primer that was first published that year and enjoyed such sustained success that it was still in print over 80 years later in the late 1960s, having reached its 39th printing in 1967. The work in question is by Hiram Erastus Butler, and was first published by the Esoteric Publishing Company of Boston, Mass., in 1887. By the time of the 1967 printing, the publisher had become known as the Esoteric Fraternity and had relocated to Applegate, California, but it was a direct continuation of the same organisation.

Prior to 1887, the text-books of the 19th-century astrological revival, which were published chiefly in England, had departed relatively little from the overall balance of techniques taught by the 17th-century English and Latin texts.

We must acknowledge at this juncture that certain changes to astrological practice are manifest in the literature of 19th-century astrology. Chiefly, Uranus had been added to the roll call of planets considered, and astrologers had begun to use circular diagrams instead of the traditional square ones for astrological maps from 1830 onwards. Additionally, arch-modernist James Wilson had fiercely criticised the notions of the ancients in his *Dictionary of Astrology* (1819); Lilly's *Christian Astrology* had been abridged and revised by Zadkiel, and a popular astrology movement had been centred around various short-lived magazines and long-running, successful prophetic almanacs.

Nonetheless, the actual methods taught and practised around genethliacal astrology had not radically been altered; and the 19th-century astrologers for the most part were loyalists to the teachings of those of the 17th century, if sometimes outspokenly critical thinkers with it.

In 1887, however, New York-born Hiram E. Butler,[23] a member of the Theosophical Society,[24] radically departed from tradition with the launch of his book *Solar Biology*, whose extended title reads: '*a Scientific Method of Delineating Character, Diagnosing Disease; Determining Mental, Physical and Business Qualifications, Conjugal Adaptability, etc., etc., from Date of Birth*'. The book was edited by a John Latham from the starting point of Butler's manuscript; and Latham, unusually for an editor, openly lays claim to having put many of Butler's ideas into his own words, and also to having extended them with his own thoughts and added illustrations.[25] A possible inference from this was that Butler's writing in its manuscript form was not very polished, and Latham felt he had to do quite a bit of work to get the book into shape in a commercially viable form. But perhaps Latham was himself an earnest intellectual who was actively involved with Butler in the background in developing his system and felt it his duty to add his own thoughts and observations to those of the author so that the finished product was one of collegiate teamwork of which he could feel proud.

Because no traces allowing us to distinguish between Butler's words and thoughts from those of Latham have been left in the final book outside Latham's preface, we shall refer to the author consistently as Butler, while remaining conscious of the fact that the final text is that of Latham from the starting point of Butler's manuscript. Since we cannot be sure to what degree Latham has put his stamp on different parts of it, when we refer to 'Butler' we are in fact referring to a composite published voice or brand that comprises the combined work of the minds of Butler and Latham, operating together as a team from the starting point of Butler's ideas.

Referring to himself in the third person, Butler frames his work with an idealistic statement of purpose in his own preface,[26] to the effect that he has:

> but one general object in view; viz., to be of the greatest possible service to the world in which he lives,

adding that:

> the great confusion that now exists in the world arises wholly from the ignorance of persons as to their true nature and real sphere of use.

He goes on to state that inharmony is caused by people either pursuing professions to which they are not suited but into which their parents push them, or misunderstanding each other's motives; and the system he teaches is designed to help parents understand their children's individual needs. He further adds that he believes his teachings to be especially important to physicians (i.e., doctors) in diagnosing and treating their patients according to the needs of their individual constitutions.

In later printings, a *Special Notice to Astronomers and Astrologers* that was absent from the first edition, undersigned by The Author, is added after the *Author's Preface*, and seeks to address letters received since the first publication of the book regarding the planetary positions appearing in the integral ephemeris, which differ from those used in geocentric astrology and astronomy. In the process, Butler altogether dissociates his system of solar biology from the label of astrology, stating:

> *Those who study the science of Solar Biology thinking it will amalgamate with astrology, or aid in astrological prognostication, will find that it can not [sic] be so used, as it is a distinct science, using different data and arriving at entirely different conclusions. It reads character in human life completely, but in no case predicts coming events.*[27]

Thus, by his own account, Butler was not trying to simplify or modernise astrology, but rather to establish a new, separate, scientific discipline whose focus, unlike the traditional one of natal astrology (which was heavily geared to predicting events in life), was both centred upon and limited to character delineation.

The main text of his book begins with a lengthy philosophical preamble in which he refers back to evidence of the symbolic representation of the signs of the Zodiac by ancient writers in the books of the Bible, a common theme of earlier 19th-century writers. By appeal to written evidence from the distant past, he seeks to present his novel ideas as amounting to the revival of a much older tradition in spite of their pronounced differences from recorded astrological tradition.

Butler views what he calls *solar biology* as a natural science that is best understood in terms of the physical nature of the solar system, at the heart of which is of course the Sun. In Chapter II, *The Mechanism of Solar Biology*, he claims the zodiac in its influence on human life as an empirically established fact in these terms:

> *Our own observations conclusively prove that the solar fluid of the ecliptic, in which the earth and other planets move, contains the elements of the human organism, corresponding to the twelve departments of the human body.*[28]

He subsequently defines the solar fluid as follows:

> *The Solar Fluid is an ethereal atmosphere or sea of fluidic element pervasive of, and limited by, our solar system; the sun being a reciprocal centre for the interchange of forces, while this ethereal atmosphere, or sea, forms a natural and necessary medium for the transmission of their motions and potencies from planet to planet, and also holds in solution the primal and basic elements of all possible life and thought to be evolved within the confines of our solar system. These thought and life forces have a gravity or attraction towards the respective planets in a degree proportioned to the quality or function of the planet and the adaptability of the forces to find expression therein. Thus each planet is a progressive electro-vital or mental battery of a specific kind, receiving and emitting the elements of life and thought formation, varied in kind and degree by their ever-changing positions from department to department in the zodiac, so that whatever may be the position of a planet, its own nature, together with the polarity or added qualities derived from its position, are impressed upon all the worlds of our system through the pervasive, delicate, and perfect conductivity of the solar ether or fluid.*[29]

In keeping with this mechanistic causal cosmology, Butler advocates the consideration of the Earth in what he calls the 'Sun's zodiac' – in other words, its heliocentric position, saying that:

> *The position of the earth in the sun's zodiac at the time of a person's birth, forms the basic or innate principle of the physical nature and nerves of*

sensation; and the life forces start from this sign, and then tend toward the sign in which the moon was at the person's birth.[30]

When it comes to the Moon, whose position as viewed from the Sun is largely indistinguishable from that of the Earth, Butler instead advocates using the geocentric tropical zodiac, which he terms the 'earth's zodiac'. This zodiac, according to Butler,

Controls the reasoning faculties more than the intuitions, and acts upon the intelligence and life forces like a magnet upon a needle.[31]

Thus, Butler is advocating the use of a hybrid heliocentric-geocentric system of astrology, but with geocentric positions reserved for the Moon. The ephemerides integrated into his book are correspondingly limited to the heliocentric sign positions and ingress dates of the planets from Mercury through to Uranus. The separate table of lunar positions is geocentric. In neither case is degree information provided, so these ephemerides are blunt instruments limited in their usefulness to reference to the whole-sign natal delineations in the text of the book. In keeping with the dictates of this limitation, there is no treatment of astrological house placements or interplanetary aspects in the book – both essential elements of conventional natal astrology even if it is considered without any predictive focus.

Although Butler has thus far from a theoretical standpoint preached the consideration of the heliocentric Earth signs, when he comes to delineating the influence of the natal zodiac signs, perhaps for the sake of convenience of understanding by the general public, he lists the Sun signs under their conventional names in the geocentric tropical zodiac, rounded up to the nearest typical range of dates, thus Aries from the 21st March to the 19th April, etc..[32]

Butler adopts the label *polarity* to refer to the natal Moon sign in its own essence, setting in motion a modern tradition that would persist throughout the 20th century, typically in application to the consideration of the geocentric Moon signs in tandem with the Sun signs with which they happen to coexist in each individual birth chart.[33] He deems that:

The mind is directed toward subjects relating to the nature of the sign in which the moon was at birth, which we denominate as the POLARITY OF THE NATURE OF THE PERSON.[34]

This observation becomes the basis for Butler arguing for the division of the human population into 144 basic personality types, one for each of the combinations of heliocentric Earth sign and geocentric Moon sign.

Twelve later chapters of the book, collectively comprising 122 pages, are given over to the delineation of these combinations.[35] Although the text of these chapters does not expressly state whether the heliocentric Earth sign positions or the (exactly oppositely designated) geocentric Sun sign positions are being delineated in their combination with the geocentric Moon sign positions, potentially causing confusion, the text of the much later Chapter XXVII, *Direction for Reading Character by the System of Solar Biology*, contains an example of a native born March 21, 1820, for which the reader is directed to find the page for 'Aries with the Moon in Gemini'. The reading of 'Aries' for March 21st in this example shows that the 144 delineations are in fact intended to be read wholly geocentrically, although this is not expressly stated as a rule outside the context of this example; and we might reasonably protest the shortfall in editorial clarity on this point!

Thus, it can be said that, far from being just a Sun sign astrologer with a heliocentric theoretical worldview, Butler had in fact developed a natal astrological chart reading system emphasising in effect the geocentric soli-lunar combinations, and one that would influence generations of leading astrologers in his wake, including Alan Leo and Grant Lewi, to do the same.

Still, as we have seen earlier, Butler devotes a substantial separate chapter exclusively to the natal Sun signs; and even in this, we see a major departure from conventional natal astrological teaching. An average of 2–3 pages of text is given over to every Sun sign; and most of it is focused on observations of personality, with only cursory reference to the parts of the body ruled by the sign at the beginning.

It is only when it comes to the reading of the planetary signs that the heliocentric positions are used throughout Butler's book. Thus, the chapters given over to brief delineations of Mercury through to Uranus in the signs, which between them fill only 38 pages (a small fraction of the total page count allocated to the Sun and Moon), should be read as relating to their heliocentric sign placements.[36]

The hybrid system of part-geocentric and part-heliocentric natal astrology taught by the book *Solar Biology* would prove influential primarily to a generation of American astrologers operating in the 25 years or so following its first publication, with Frank Earl Ormsby,[37] Frederick White,[38] Willis F. Whitehead[39] and Holmes Whittier Merton[40] being among the foremost exponents of what was branded as 'heliocentric astrology' during this period.

Butler's whole astrological system had a revolutionary, ground-shaking impact upon modern natal astrology in spite of his protesting that it did not belong under the label of astrology at all; and the extended and personality-focused delineation of the natal Sun is arguably the part of his revolution that has gained the most sustained traction in modern astrological writing ever since.

Part 3: The Solar Revolution Reverberates: Increased Solar Prominence in General Astrological Writings, 1889 to 1952

To demonstrate the speed with which Butler's revolutionary system had an impact on modern astrology, we need look no further than the chronology of astrological text-books appearing in the United States in the decade following the first publication of *Solar Biology*.

Thomas Burgoyne and Frank Earl Ormsby were among the leading American astrologers of the period who had published general natal astrology books that took after Butler's example of giving added emphasis to the natal Sun, with Burgoyne's delineations averaging about 50 lines per Sun sign,[41] and Ormsby's[42] about 45, only slightly less than Butler's average of a little over 60 lines per sign in his chapter dedicated just to the Sun signs.

But while Burgoyne and Ormsby delineated the natal Sun in the context of serious, weighty esoteric philosophy and broader astrological theory, by the early-to-mid 20th century, examples of astrology books in which typically upwards of half the overall space was given over to the delineation of the Sun signs proliferated. These books stopped short of focusing only on Sun signs, but their Sun sign readings were their main feature, with the other chapters appearing to be something of an afterthought aimed at whetting the appetite of the novice for the possible further study of proper astrology. The market for most of these works was the general public.

A chronological source list of many of the most notable books in this category that are found in our library follows:

- [Anonymous], *The Practical Solar Biology*[43] (Undated [by 1896]).[44]
- Alan Leo, *[Astrological Manuals No. 1:] Everybody's Astrology* (London: L. N. Fowler/ Boston: The Occult Publishing Co. / Bombay, India, 1901).
- Margaret Mayo, *Our Fate & the Zodiac: an Astrological Autograph Book* (New York: Brentano's, 1901).

- I. M. Pagan, *From Pioneer to Poet or The Twelve Great Gates[:] An Expansion of the Signs of the Zodiac Analysed* (London: The Theosophical Publishing Society, 1911).
- Jean Tucker, *[Renard's Popular Topics Library:] Read the Answer in the Stars* (New York: Charles Renard, 1925).
- Mme. Eberwein, *Astrology Applied to Practical and Modern Life* (No place or publisher stated, 1927).
- Llewellyn George, *Astro-Analysis: Twelve Studies in Astrology. The Science of Life's Reactions to Planetary Vibrations* (Los Angeles: Llewellyn George, 1927).[45]
- Evangeline Adams, *Astrology: Your Place in the Sun* (London: George G. Harrap, 1928).[46]
- Llewellyn George, *You and I and the Stars - The Zodiac: Its Influences; Your Possibilities – Lessons on what is indicated for you and for others by the 12 Celestial Signs – A Personal and Vocational Guide [–] The Vibratory Dynamics Of Life's reactions to Solar Radiations as affecting character, health, psychic urges, mental tendencies, abilities, latent talent, personal magnetism, vocation, location, friends, unions, finances, etc. [....]* (Los Angeles: Llewellyn George, 1930).
- Evangeline Adams, *Astrology for Everyone: What It Is and How It Works* (New York: Dodd, Mead & Co., 1931).[47]
- Geraldine G. Davis, *Student's Round Table: Compiled and devoted to the search for the fundamental varieties existing in the educational system of Astrology*. Stated First Edition ([No place or publisher stated], Sept. 1936).
- Stella Coeli, *Your Fate: Predictions of the Stars, Planets and Other Heavenly Bodies: Modern – Authoritative – Scientific* (London & Letchworth: PM [Productions],1946).[48]
- Violet Brezany, *Starlore* ([no publisher stated], 1952).

Of the above works, Isabelle Pagan's book is the odd one out, in that the central content is an in-depth symbolic study of the zodiac signs couched in the language of theosophy. It is too meditative and complex to qualify as popular astrology writing. The book would probably have been of most interest to members of the Theosophical Society and other followers of theosophical thought, including serious astrologers practising esoteric astrology from a theosophical perspective, such as the primary target readership of *Modern Astrology* magazine.

Part 4: Solely the Sun:
The Unstoppable Rise of the Sun-Sign Primer, 1894 to 1959

The integration of lengthier and more personality-focused Sun-sign delineation content into general astrological textbooks was at the milder end of Hiram E. Butler's spectrum of influence. By the mid-1890s, a new breed of book focused on *nothing but* the natal Sun sign had come into currency. The pioneer of this genre was also one of the first woman astrologers to have an astrology book published in the United States: New York-based Eleanor Kirk.

Kirk's book *The Influence of the Zodiac on Human Life*[49] in its original edition runs to 179 pages. The average number of lines of text devoted within to each of the Sun signs is around 200, or more than thrice the length accorded to each of them by Butler (not counting his separate treatment of the Sun-Moon combinations). This was thus the first example of what we might call *extremely expansive* writing on the natal Sun signs, going far beyond the already revolutionary precedent set by Butler seven years previously. And it paved the way for many other astrologers to follow with their own long treatments of the Sun signs in similar dedicated books. Kirk's book therefore marked the birth of a new form of popular astrology in book format, far simpler even than what Butler had put forth: the Sun-sign primer.

Not only was Kirk the first successful exponent anywhere in the world of this new genre of astrology book devoted exclusively to the extensive delineation of personality from Sun signs, but also she was at the vanguard of the first wave of woman astrologers breaking through into the United States astrological writing market alongside their established (and new) male counterparts. By the end of the 19th century, she had been joined in the limelight by Ellen H. Bennett[50] and Catherine Thompson.[51] The turn of Evangeline Adams, probably the most widely-familiar name among all pioneering woman astrologers in the United States today, would come over a quarter of a century later: she did not have any books published before her autobiography *The Bowl of Heaven* appeared in 1926.

Kirk's book remained in print well into the early 20th century, although later printings prior to the formal copyright renewal date were not declared thus in print. Those after 1901 or thereabouts[52] were amended by the addition of separate character readings for the 'cusp dates' at the frontiers between the successive Sun signs, creating a controversial theoretical talking point in relation to which astrologers have continued to wage intellectual disputes ever since, with most professional astrologers typically denying that there is any such thing as a Sun-sign cusp region that blends the influences of two signs.

In 1895, the year after *The Influence of the Zodiac Upon Human Life* was first published, another, similar book appeared in print in the United States. This was *Our Places in the Universal Zodiac*[53] by W. J. Colville, a British esotericist who had emigrated to the United States in his adulthood after finding his writings more popular there than in his native homeland.

Colville's Sun-sign primer has a very similar page count (172 pp.) to that of Kirk, but more lines per page, and consequently averages in excess of 250 lines per Sun sign, making it even longer in its overall estimated word count per sign. Unlike Kirk's book, it does include brief mentions of the modifying influence of certain planets if found rising or otherwise prominent when the Sun is in each sign, as well as of the standalone influence of some planets in the signs, showing that Colville knew about the whole of the birth chart; but only very brief space is given to these readings.

It is notable that Colville was aware of the astrological works of Butler, Burgoyne, and Kirk before his went to print only the following year, and also that he seeks to distinguish it from all of them, setting out his purpose for the book within the philosophical framework of active human participation in destiny, thus:

> *Some years ago a large book... by Hiram Butler, entitled* Solar Biology, *excited considerable notice among thoughtful people, as it called attention to what was then quite a new field of speculative inquiry for the masses, viz.: the distinctive characteristics of twelve distinct manners of people dwelling all about us, and among whom we must of necessity, if the theory be true, classify ourselves.*
>
> *A little later... appeared* The Light of Egypt[....] *In this work the twelve varieties of the human family were somewhat elaborately considered, and in our judgement, often somewhat erroneously, by reason of the pessimistic strain which ran through a considerable portion of the volume.*
>
> *Very recently indeed, Mrs. Eleanor Kirk,... a singularly bright and progressive woman, has launched upon the sea of literature* The Influence of the Zodiac upon Human Life; *which... has already secured quite extensive reading. All these books are fascinating, and they are useful; still in our opinion, though the latter is in many respects greatly in advance of the two former, even that does not express in all things the particular view of the subject which we desire to place prominently before the ever increasing number of students of Mental Science and cognate themes, who ply us with questions concerning the true relation between Mental Science and astrology.*
>
> *We have recently given courses... on this subject..., and so great has been the demand for a general gist or outline of these teachings in cheap and portable form, that we have decided to write out a concise synopsis of each lesson, hoping that the hints and suggestions thrown out in this greatly condensed form may accomplish the double purpose of inviting deeper research in the same general direction, and clearing away the fog of pessimism or the mist of fatalism which beholds the intellects of many who have not yet risen to a consciousness of the*

power vested in human individuality; a force latent in every one of us, but awaiting acknowledgement on our part before it will flash forth from its age-long obscurity and demonstrate the mighty truth that man is creator and not creature, sovereign and not slave of circumstance.

The decided difference between our school of thought and that represented by the title of Mrs. Kirk's book will be at once evident to the reflective reader. Our reading of the subject is that we have a place in the Zodiac; that it includes us; and that we are working individual entities embraced within the sweep of its comprehensive activity. To take this stand is to differ radically from those who speak of the influence of the Zodiac **upon** *human life, as though it were entirely external to ourselves, and controlled us from without, leaving us no active influential part to play with reference to its movements.*

After the success of these books by Kirk and Colville, with both running to multiple printings, there was no turning back for popular astrology writing. The genie was out of the bottle: Sun-sign primers were a proven commercial success with the masses, and much as many serious astrologers might despise them for oversimplifying astrology into a series of potted character portraits based on one astrological factor alone, it was no use crying over spilt milk.

A chronological shortlist of some notable later Sun-sign primers published in the United States and Great Britain up to and including 1959 follows:

- H. F., a Fellow of the Universal Brotherhood, [*The People's Handbook Series No. 54: April, 1898:*] *Astrology Made Easy; or, the Influence of the Stars and Planets upon Human Life* (New York: F. M. Lupton, 1898).[54]
- Charlotte Abell Walker, *Under a Lucky Star: Explaining characteristics, tendencies and possibilities, choice of partners*[55] *and employees, suggestions on marriage and government of children* (New York: G. W. Dillingham, 1901).[56]
- Katherine G. Brown, *My Stars: Are they Lucky or Unlucky?* (New York: Charles E. Bentley, 1902).
- Dr. J. R. Phelps, *Our Astrological Birthday Book: Character Readings* (Chicago: Goldthwaite Publishing House, 1903).
- Lela Omar, *Your Future: the Zodiac's Guide to Success in Life* (Philadelphia: Penn Publishing, 1904).[57]
- Isabelle M. Pagan, *Astrological Key to Character: the Twelve Zodiacal Types Interpreted* (London: Theosophical Publishing Society, 1907).
- Prof. Alfred F. Seward, *Humanity and the Zodiac: a Study of Planetary Influences Upon the Physical, Mental and Moral Nature of Mankind*. Stated Second Edition (Columbus, OH: Prof. Alfred F. Seward, 1909).[58]
- Elizabeth Towne;[59] Catherine Struble Tring, *How to Read Character*[60] (Holyoke, MA: The Elizabeth Towne Co., 1909).

- Beatrice Baxter Ruyl, *The Zodiac Birthday Book* (New York: Baker & Taylor, 1910).
- Cheiro, *When Were You Born? A Book That Will Bring Success. Your Character Told[;] Your Tendencies Explained[;] Your Future Indicated[.] With engravings illustrating Life's Mysterious Triangles* (Chicago/New York: Rand, McNally, 1912).
- Madame M. Martell, *Guide to Gold, Glory, and Birth Reader* (St. Louis, MO: Madame M. Martell, 1912).
- Astor,[61] *Drawing Room Astrology or Solar Horoscopes*[62] (Hong Kong: Brewer, 1915).
- Prof. A. F. Seward, *The Zodiac and its Mysteries: Vocational Training or A Study of Planetary Influences Upon the Physical, Mental and Moral Nature of Mankind* (Chicago: A. F. Seward, 1915).
- Prof. Alfred F. Seward, *Astrological Bureau of Information for Business Men*[63] (Chicago: A. F. Seward, 1916).
- Rapoza, *Planets of the Months: Your Lucky Stars; Astral Colours; Lucky Days; etc.* (London: Weldons, undated).[64]
- Louise Brightman Brownell, *Your Destiny in the Zodiac and Its Mastery* (Los Angeles: The Aquarian Ministry, 1919).
- Belle Bart, *Thru the Stars to Success: Astrology Today* (East Aurora, NY: Roycrofters, 1923).
- Hazel L. M. Fauber, *The Astrology Birthday Book* (Chicago/New York: Laidlaw Brothers, 1923).
- R. G. Howells, *The Zodiac and You*[65] (Miami, FL: R. G. Howells, 1924).
- Polly Patterson, *The Zodiac: Destiny's Celestial Cycle – Reprinted from 'Fashionable Dress'* (New York: Fashionable Dress Publishing, 1926).
- Prof. A. F. Seward, *Seward's Planetary Hand-Book*[66] (Chicago: A. F. Seward, 1926).
- Ethel Bret Harte, *Zodiacal Influences from Seed to Flower* (London: The Theosophical Publishing House, 1927).
- Maryln Hamilton, *Romance of the Stars* (Los Angeles: Wetzel Publishing, 1931).
- Ada Muir, *[Astrology and Health No. 1:] Health and the Sun Sign – Dealing with the physical uses of certain mineral salts present in food and herbs, and their correspondence with the signs of the zodiac* (Vancouver, BC: [undated]).[67]
- Manly P. Hall, *Psychoanalyzing the Twelve Zodiacal Types* (Los Angeles: Philosophical Research Society, 1937).[68]
- C. Hilda Pagan, *Star Dust* (London: The Theosophical Publishing House, [1938]).
- Miss Gilher, *Golden Gems of Psychological Astrology*[69] (Beverly Hills, CA: No Publisher Stated, 1940).
- Dane Rudhyar, *The Pulse of Life: New Dynamics in Astrology*[70] (Philadelphia: David McKay Co., 1943).[71]
- Grant Lewi, *Your Greatest Strength* (Philadelphia: David McKay Co., 1946).[72]
- Edward Lyndoe, *Plan with the Planets* (London: Herbert Jenkins, 1949).
- Sydney Omarr, *Dial Your Lucky Number: Your Pocket Solar Horoscope with Astro-Hand Chart* (Ardmore, PA: Fresta Press, 1949).
- Sydney Omarr, *Secret Hints…For Men and Women* (Hollywood, CA: Ninth House Publishing, 1958).

A variation on the single-volume Sun-sign primer of which examples began to appear as early as the 1900s in the United States was the pamphlet focused on a natal reading for a single sign of the zodiac, issued as part of a set of twelve such pamphlets that were sold individually. Even more than the Sun-sign primer, this type of publication was geared at readers who lacked any kind of prior astrological initiation and possibly lacked even the appetite to read about other people's Sun signs, only wanting to digest their own (and perhaps those of a few people close to them), and buy one individual pamphlet (or at most a few different pamphlets) accordingly.

Twelve-volume sets of this kind also subsequently took off in France, where the format would prove extremely common in the mid-late 20th century and there developed an increasing tendency for authors to write substantial books on each of the Sun signs that exceeded the length of the pamphlet format previously witnessed in the United States. Examples within the time-frame of our survey on both sides of the Atlantic include, in chronological order:

- F. W. Wilson, *Were You Born Between [December 21st and January 20th – November 22nd and December 21st]?* - [Set of 12 pamphlets] (Poughkeepsie, NY: The Astrological Society, 1910).
- Alfred J. A. Straughan, *Your Birth Reading [No. 1 If from March 21 to April 19 – No. 12 If from Feb. 18 to March 20]* – [Set of 12 pamphlets] (Pittsburgh, 1920).
- Evangeline Adams, *Evangeline Adams' Own Book of Astrology: The World's Most Famous Astrologer Interprets What the Stars Reveal About You Your Mental Physical and Emotional Characteristics Your Business Abilities and Prospects about Love and Home [...] [If You Were Born Between March 22nd and April 20th – If You Were Born Between Feb. 20th and March 21st]* – [Set of 12 pamphlets] (New York: Tower Books, 1931).
- Maurice Privat, *Ceux qui Sont Nés [du 22 mars au 20 avril – du 20 février au 21 mars]* – [Set of 12 pamphlets] ([no place stated]: Éditions Stock, [undated; B.N.F. records 1937]).
- André Barbault, [Bélier – Poissons] [Set of 12 books] (Éditions du Seuil, 1957–1959).[73]

In some cases, the Sun-sign concept was further simplified by books or sets of pamphlets that nominally gave readings for the *calendar month* instead of the solar zodiac sign. Examples include:

- Margaret Mayo, *Fate Autographs: Birthday Book* (Philadelphia: Jas B. Rodgers, 1899).
- [Anonymous], *Were you Born In... [January to December]* – [Set of 12 pamphlets] (Pittsburgh, PA / New York: The Great Aim Society, 1909).
- [Anonymous], *Ce que vous devez savoir avant de vous Marier si vous êtes né en [Avril – Mars]* – [Set of 12 pamphlets] (Paris: l'Administration, undated).[74]

Sun-sign synastry, the analysis of relationship compatibility based on Sun signs alone, was a topic that would also become an increasingly common feature of popular astrology writing in the latter part of the 20th century but made its first notable appearances right at its beginning. Charlotte Walker's aforementioned *Under a Lucky Star* (1901) covers the theme briefly, but other authors took it much further; and by the outbreak of World War II, it had become the main theme of two complete books, both of them published in 1937:

- Pharos [pseud.], *Successful Marriage*[75] (London: Richard Arling, undated).
- Vivian E. Robson, *Your Affinity: the Astrological Guide to an Ideal Marriage and to Greater Happiness in Marriages Already Contracted* (London: W. Foulsham, [1937]).

The genre would reach its zenith in terms of the extent of writing on each Sun-sign combination outside the period of this survey, with the appearance of Linda Goodman's *Love Signs* in 1978.

The early 20th century also saw the appearance of works that explored the symbolism of the zodiac signs (or, in some cases, that of the zodiacal constellations) in depth, without specifically relating them to astrological effects from the passage of the Sun through them. Many of these works were theosophical in tone; and some of their authors took pains to dissociate their work from astrological applications altogether, although it is difficult to conceive that the books would not have been consulted by astrologers of a theosophical persuasion for use in astrology. Notable examples include:

- J. Henry Van Stone, *The Pathway of the Soul: a Study in Zodiacal Symbology* (London: Modern Astrology Office, 1912).
- Rev. Holden Edward Sampson, *The Twelve Houses of the Zodiac in their Relation to the Twelve Organic Structures of the Human Constitution* (Birmingham: The Ek-Klesia Press / London: William Rider & Son, undated [1926 or 1927]).
- Walter H. Sampson, *The Zodiac: a Life Epitome[,] being A Comparison of the Zodiacal Elements with Life-Principles: Cosmic, Anthropologic and Psychologic* (London and Leicester: Blackfriars Press, 1928).
- Katharine R. Logan, *The Call of the Stars* (Los Angeles: Wetzel Publishing, 1930).
- Manamea [Tamalelagi], *Star Symphony* (Sunland, CA: Cecil L. Anderson, 1949).
- Mabel Baudot; intr. Charles E. O. Carter, *The Charmed Circle: the Zodiac* (London: The Theosophical Publishing House, 1957).

Part 5: Law of the Lights: Works on the Sun and Moon Sign Combinations after Butler

The precedent set by Hiram E. Butler in offering 144 separate delineations for all the possible combinations of the Sun and Moon signs at birth is one that has been followed enthusiastically by other authors from time to time ever since.

The most historically noteworthy exponent of this practice after Butler was Alan Leo, who devotes a whole 52-page chapter of his book *Astrology for All* (1899) to what he calls 'The Solar-Lunar Combinations'.[76]

Thirty years after Leo, we find the book *Solar Psychology* by Alan M. Emley published in the United States.[77] Emley is clearly a disciple of Butler and his work, to which he refers in the text, although he also criticises it for being difficult to understand for those uninitiated into the thinking of the Esoteric Fraternity, hence the need for his own book to bridge that gap. Even the title of his book is closely derivative from *Solar Biology*; and he adopts the same use of the word 'polarity' as Butler to describe the Moon sign, and delineates the 144 soli-lunar combinations in his own words within the text of his primer.

Four years later, the first edition of S. R. Parchment's lengthy esoterically slanted astrological text-book *Astrology Mundane and Spiritual* was published in California.[78] This mammoth volume of 906 pages, which would be reprinted by the American Federation of Astrologers in the early 1970s, includes succinct delineations of the 144 natal soli-lunar combinations, though they form a relatively small part of the vast overall work.

Another two years on, the first edition of Grant Lewi's first book *Heaven Knows What*[79] appeared. Both the initial edition of 1935 and the second of 1937 were credited to his pen-name of the time, *Scorpio*.

The majority of the text of *Heaven Knows What* is given over to delineating the 144 Sun-and-Moon-sign combinations in considerable detail, leaving other astrological considerations, such as interplanetary aspects, to the final chapters in a way that makes them appear something of an afterthought. The book makes use of simplified tables to direct any reader to look up which paragraphs to read without needing to understand how to read an ephemeris. Commercially, this easy-to-use format proved a winning formula for Lewi, as, thanks in no small part to Lewi's gift for lifelike character portraiture through his mercurial writing style, the book became a best-seller and has been reprinted many times since his premature death in the early 1950s.

Lewi's work was certainly not the last word on the natal Sun-and-Moon-sign combinations, with several further notable examples appearing in the late

20th century, outside the time span of this essay, by Robert A. Hughes (1977), Jefferson Andersen (1978), Charles and Suzi Harvey (1994), and Derek and Julia Parker (1996). Butler's legacy in this respect has proven long, rich, and enduring.

Part 6: The signs of the zodiac divided: The Draw of the Degrees, 1879–1953

Bridging the territory between a subcategory of the Sun-sign primer and a subcategory of the study of general zodiacal symbolism is a genre of text that seeks to give separate readings for different degree areas, or subdivisions, of each sign of the zodiac. While some works on the symbolism of the individual degrees existed in medieval times, there was a marked revival of interest in this area at the end of the 19th century and the beginning of the 20th, one that owes partly to the heightened interest in the Sun signs at this time. Some of the new degree-area expositions indeed clearly take the form of readings for the degrees of the Sun, while others make no particular reference to the Sun and are designed for wide application across astrology. In the subcategory of Sun degree-area readers we may place the following works newly published in this period:

- Sepharial, *The Birthday Book of Destiny. – Compiled from Ancient Hermetic and Rosicrucian Sources, Arranged and Interpreted* (London: Nichols & Co., [1904]).
- Dr. J. R. Phelps, *Birthday Horoscopes: Character Readings by Dr. J. R. Phelps* (New York: Barse & Hopkins, 1908).
- Leo Bernart, *Ogilvie's Astrological Birthday Book: Is Your Birthday To-Day? A Character Reading for Every Day in the Year Compiled from Observations of the Effect upon Character-Making, of the Aspect of the Heavenly Bodies at the Moment of Birth* (New York: J. S. Ogilvie, 1915).
- C. C. Zain, *[Course X-A, Serial No. 103:] Natal Astrology: First Eighteen Decanates Analyzed* (Los Angeles: The Church of Light, 1922).
- C. C. Zain, *[Course X-B, Serial No. 104:] Natal Astrology: Last Eighteen Decanates Analyzed* (Los Angeles: The Church of Light, 1923).
- Leonid, *The Stars and Your Future: the Symbols of Esoteric Astrology Explained for Everybody. What to do: What to avoid: Careers to Adopt: Matrimonial Guidance and Natal Influences*[80] (London: Herbert Jenkins, 1933).
- Muriel Hasbrouck, *Pursuit of Destiny – With Thirty-six Tarot Cards and an Endpaper Chart of the Cycles* (New York: E. P. Dutton, 1941).

The works by Sepharial [Walter Gorn Old], Bernart, and Leonid from the shortlist above deserves special mention on account of their presentation of readings for every calendar date of the year, rather than specifically for the degrees of the Sun.

Sepharial is not fully transparent regarding the methodology he uses to arrive at his readings, but my tentative investigations to date tend to suggest that, at least for some of them, he took into consideration the positions in the tropical zodiac according to sources he had access to at his time of writing (which may in certain cases have been out of date and not duly updated for precession) of a number of prominent fixed stars.

The approach in much later 20th-century works individually interpreting calendar dates of birth has been branded *personology*,[81] and expressly integrates principles of astrology and numerology, but I have not found any manifest evidence that numerology was a part of the basis for Sepharial's readings, although a fuller investigation is called for on this point.

The book by Muriel Hasbrouck instead divides the Sun signs into decans, giving separate readings for each of the thirty-six solar decans. She further links these decans to tarot cards; but it is not necessary to be acquainted with the tarot to derive purely astrological meaning from her readings.

Elbert Benjamine, who used the pseudonym of C. C. Zain in many of his works, also analyses the solar decans, in two individually published pamphlets that formed small parts of a wide-ranging esoteric course[82] published in instalments over many years. These particular pamphlets were first published in 1922–23 but would seem to have been reprinted without the updated printing date being declared; and I have found clear evidence to indicating that the text was amended in places in later printings. In the printing to hand of the pamphlet *Last Eighteen Decanates Analyzed*, which is likely to post-date World War II, Benjamine declares the importance of interpreting the natal solar decan in these terms:

> *Next to locating the Dominant Planet, the most important single factor to be considered in determining the individual's natural bias is the decanate in which the Sun is found at birth. It is so important because it maps the section of the astral body where those most deep-seated of all experiences, those relating to the desire for significance, called the Power Urges, are organised into a dynamic stellar structure. Analytical psychology proves that these Power Urges, which included the mental factors that go to make up a person's pride, firmness, approbativeness, and self-esteem, are the most strongly fortified and persistent of all the energies within the soul.*[83]

It is interesting to see Benjamine justify his separate delineation of the solar decans on theoretical grounds related to modern concepts of psychology. Whereas popular writers typically merely describe the characteristics of the Sun signs for a general readership, Benjamine feels the need to intellectually justify this practice in his serious body of work, but he adopts it nonetheless. This exemplifies the diversity of Sun-sign writing in the early 20th century. While some was decidedly popular in slant, other examples were primarily theosophical, and still others linked into the theoretical worldview of modern psychology.

In the subcategory of general degree symbolism readers, the following works belong:

- Raphael, The Astrologer of the Nineteenth Century (ed.), *A Description of the Faces and Degrees of the Zodiac, as Given in the Ancient Authors, Being Applicable to Genethliacal and Horary Astrology* (London: The Author, 1879).[84]
- 'Charubel', *The Degrees of the Zodiac Symbolised*, to which is added H. S. Green, *The Theoretical Value of the Degrees of the Zodiac* (London: Nichols & Co. / Boston, MA: The Occult Publishing Co., 1898).
- 'Charubel' [and Sepharial], *[Astrological Manuals. No. VIII:] The Degrees of the Zodiac Symbolised* (Second Edition), *to which is added a translation by 'Sepharial' of a Similar Series Found in 'La Volasfera'* ([London]: Modern Astrology Office/ Boston, MA: F. Spenceley, 1907).[85]
- Isidore Kozminsky, *Zodiacal Symbology and its Planetary Power, in which the Planetary Influence for Each Degree of the Zodiac Accompanies the Symbol for the First Time* (London: William Rider & Son, 1917).
- Marc Edmund Jones, *Lecture-Lessons: Symbolical Astrology – Lesson 849, Issued 5/18/31 – Lesson 874, Issued 11/9/31* ([Sabian Assembly], 1931).
- Ada Muir, *The Degrees of the Zodiac Analyzed* (British Colombia: The Author, 1940).[86]
- Marc Edmund Jones, *The Sabian Symbols in Astrology* (New York: Sabian Publishing, 1953).

Jones's Sabian degree readings were first published in his set of *Symbolical Astrology* lessons in 1931 and then again in *The Sabian Symbols in Astrology* in 1953. They would further later be adopted by, among other authors, Dane Rudhyar in his work *An Astrological Mandala*, but that falls outside the temporal scope of this survey, having been published in 1973.

Muir indicates that her degrees are meant to be read for the Sun, Ascendant and Midheaven in particular, declaring:

The position and aspects to the degree of the Sun will tell of the soul struggle for freedom against the thraldom of the senses. The rising degree indicates the personal outlook and the degree on the Midheaven shows the scope of the individuality....

It is also possible through the study of the interpretation of the Ascendant and Midheaven degrees to check the birthtime and so get it more exact. In some instances where the exact day of birth was not known it has been possible to decide this by studying the interpretation of the degree of the Sun on the possible dates.

She further relates (pp. 5–6) the planetary degrees to past lives, exemplifying a subculture of karmic astrological thinking that had developed on the esoteric fringes of astrological practice by 1940, although it would not become mainstream within astrology before the 1970s.

Part 7: Lustre of the Luminaries through the Lens of Leo: Alan Leo's teachings around the natal Sun and Moon, 1896–1913

We give special attention here to the place of the Sun in the work of William Frederick Allan (1860–1917), best known by his pen-name of Alan Leo,[87] chiefly because of the misconceptions abounding among contemporary astrologers and historians to the effect that he was primarily responsible for the rise of modern Sun-sign astrology. Both the contextual chronology of his work in relation to that by other astrologers published before and alongside it, and the close textual inspection of his own corpus of work, serve clearly to demonstrate that this is not so.

Having examined the available histories of astrology covering the modern period that have been published from the mid-20th century onwards, I have concluded that these misconceptions about Leo's legacy were absent from the histories published up to and including the 1990s,[88] and seem instead to have been introduced more recently, and propagated only in the representations of the history of astrology that have newly been published since the beginning of the 21st century.

Benson Bobrick's *The Fated Sky: Astrology in History* (Simon & Schuster, 2005) is a prime example. In the six pages he devotes to discussing Alan Leo (pp. 266–71), Bobrick, citing Leo's decision to change his surname, declares:[89]

Thus, Sun-sign astrology, in his own person and in the kind of astrology he purveyed, became confused with astrology itself. Before long, he would become the most famous and influential astrologer in the world.

Bobrick is here implying both that Sun-sign astrology was the type of astrology Leo sold and (by extension) that he influenced others into doing so more than anyone else did. Quoting prominent British media astrologer Neil Spencer, Bobrick adds (p. 268) that Leo,

> *In order to make astrology accessible to the masses,... "made the Sun sign into the astrological catch-all it is today".*

As we shall go on to see, I find no evidence in support of this perception either as to Leo's use of the Sun or as to his motives for treating it as he did, and regard Bobrick's reporting as tapping into a misconceived, revisionist straw-man view of Leo in currency in the late 20th and early 21st centuries that portrays him as some kind of an unscrupulous bogeyman singly responsible for ruinously casting aside centuries of astrological tradition and setting up a dark age of simplified modern astrology.

David Ovason,[90] writing in *The History of the Horoscope* (also published in 2005), does not go so far as to blame Leo for Sun-sign astrology, but is nonetheless severely critical of him, even ascribing mercenary motives to his publishing activities (p. 188):

> *More destructive of future horoscopy, Leo was prepared to change the traditional basis of astrology in order to make the practice more acceptable to non-specialists. For pecuniary reasons, Leo published a large number of books under his own name, not all of which were written by him.*

Ovason's judgemental first assertion here, and the assumptions implicit in it both with regard to Leo's reasons for reforming astrological doctrine and with regard to his impact on future astrological practice, are not supported by any cited evidence and are historically unsound. With regard to his second claim, in fairness to Leo, it should be pointed out that the authorship of every volume in his series of small books collectively entitled *Alan Leo's Astrological Manuals* is clearly credited to its actual author within, so Ovason's remark is arguably an unjustly negative reading of Leo's conduct in producing this series of books aimed at beginners under coherent branding.

The contrast between Bobrick's and Ovason's negative early-21st-century views of Leo and the esteem in which he was held by Ellen McCaffery as recorded in her history of western astrology in 1942 could not be starker. McCaffery writes:

> His text-books on astrology reflect his theosophical interests, a matter which apparently irritates certain astrologers who do not believe in theosophy. As one reads his books one is reminded of the Neo-Platonic theories on 'Emanations.' However, Alan Leo was a very profound astrologer and mathematician, who travelled all over the world, to India and to China, to confer with astrologers of various systems.... Alan Leo was a very lovable personality who had the gift of drawing all kinds of people around him, and among these many of very high intellectual calibre, who were prepared to study astrology, which meant that they took up all phases of higher mathematics, spherical geometry and astronomy, in order that they might understand thoroughly what they were actually doing when they made horoscopes.[91]

As applies to the other 20th-century histories of astrology I have examined, no mention of Alan Leo in relation to Sun-sign astrology is made by McCaffery, who ostensibly recognised that it was not of the essence of his legacy – indeed, in her time, no one was even claiming it to be.

A more nuanced and better-balanced early-21st-century reading of Leo's view of the Sun in astrology than we glean from Bobrick is subsequently recorded by Nicholas Campion in his *History of Western Astrology Volume II*.[92] In particular, Campion usefully accounts for Leo's idealised view of the Sun with direct reference to the teachings of the founder of theosophy, Helena Blavatsky.[93] Campion, unlike Bobrick, also incidentally attributes Leo's change of surname to his identification with his ascendant sign and not his Sun sign. If Campion were correct, this would remove a central plank of Bobrick's argument from his thesis and leave it tumbling unsupported like a house of cards, although even if not, the argument would still be a tenuous one at best. In this writer's view, however, Campion's portrayal of Leo still places more invention and influence in the realm of Sun-sign astrology at Leo's door, as compared with that which stems from Butler and subsequent writers in the United States, than is merited by the evidence of the literary record, and potentially gives the misleading impression that Leo was singly responsible for the reform of Sun-sign descriptions along the lines of both content and length in 20th-century astrology when he writes:

> [Leo] embarked on a programme of deliberate invention without which modern astrology would be simply unrecognizable. Leo's description of Aries was typical. At almost four times the length of Zadkiel's version, Leo's

completely ignored physical characteristics and set the tone for all future descriptions of the sign.[94]

The 21st-century myth of Leo's central responsibility for modern Sun-sign astrology continues to be perpetuated in the present day, further supported by the appearance of Alexander Boxer's new history *A Scheme of Heaven*[95] in 2020. Boxer, quoting part of the same paragraph I have cited above from Campion along the way in support of his position, asserts (p. 234):

> *Moreover, according to Leo, the best way to forecast how someone's inner cosmos would respond to changes in the outer universe was to examine that person's "Sun Sign."... Traditionally,... the Sun sign was only one quantity among many that went into a birth horoscope, and by no means the most important. All that changed with Alan Leo....*
>
> *From Alan Leo's astrological improvisations, it was a quick progression to today's familiar format.*

By 'familiar format', Boxer is referring to the 12-column format of newspaper Sun-sign forecasts. Thus, he is implying that Leo was responsible for setting the scene for the introduction of Sun sign–based forecasting. Not only is the assertion that natal Sun-sign writing begets Sun-sign forecasting intellectually dubious in the first place, but pinning the blame for this development on Alan Leo demonstrates a serious lack of relevant factual research on this point by the author. Further, in his implication that Leo was responsible for eliminating the consideration of all other factors in the birth chart in favour of the Sun, Boxer evinces a disappointingly shallow acquaintance with the text of Leo's own books. More so even than Bobrick before him, Boxer is feeding the reader a straw-man caricature of Leo and his work, one that bears almost no recognisable relation to their reality.

So in what measure was Alan Leo truly an originator and influencer in the domain of Sun-sign astrology? Like many astrologers active from the 1890s onwards, he was undoubtedly heavily influenced by the work of Hiram E. Butler, whose book *Solar Biology* was a towering presence among recent astrological text-books at that time. This is apparent in Leo's extensive delineations of the natal Sun signs and of the soli-lunar combinations in certain books of his. We have seen in previous sections of this chapter how his books *Everybody's Astrology* and *Astrology for All* fit into categories of literature focused predominantly upon Sun signs, and partly on soli-lunar combinations, respectively.[96]

But Leo's corpus of work was diverse; and even those works in which he does cover the Sun and the soli-lunar combinations in detail represent only parts of the approach to astrology that he taught and practised.

When it is considered as a whole, and compared with the often singular volumes that we have referenced by other authors in Parts 2 to 4 above, we find on the contrary that Leo's corpus of work provides one of the more serious and complete general courses of instruction in natal astrology aimed at the beginning or intermediate student in his day, and leaves many of his contemporaries looking like populist dabblers or wanton commercial exploiters by comparison.

Let us first look at Leo's views on the astrological Sun by picking out some representative quotations from his own books, before analysing how much of his written work was given over to the understanding and delineation of the natal Sun in the signs of the tropical zodiac.

From his comments about the Sun scattered through his early works, it is possible to get a clearer view of Leo's views on Sun-sign astrology and of the degree to which he may have been influenced by publications before his.

A notable example is found in Lecture III of his *Four Lectures on Astrology* (1901), in which he states (pp. 43–50):

> *In America about four or five years ago, some of the principal newspapers took up the subject of the Sun in the sign[97] and the character of persons born during a particular month, and there were several books written on this subject. In the horoscopes of people the sun and the sign it is in will govern the individual characteristics. In fact, when I first gave my rendering of that in Modern Astrology, many people wrote me to say how marvellously true the descriptions were. Yet, if you were to ask a person in what month he was born and gave a reading of the character from the Sun in the sign, he might not [recognise] it altogether as accurate. To-night I wish to explain the reason of this....*
>
> *When I first studied astrology the science was in a most chaotic condition, and you had to discover for yourself what the planets in the signs meant. I set to work, therefore, to classify the whole and I found the Sun really indicated the individual character; that is, the character that is at the root of us, behind our personality; that which, on self analysis, would be found to express the individual part of us. But in the ordinary, every-day life, the Moon or lunar characteristics only are apparent.*

> *Practically, if we allowed the spiritual nature to act more frequently in our common life, it might be said we were living up to the expression of the Sun in the sign, and we should be acting without the limitations of our personality. We are all subjected to these limitations caused by the planets and the signs of the zodiac; we identify ourselves with the different influences, but the true life is hid, as it were, with the Sun.... If you could concentrate the whole of your mind and turn it in towards the diviner part of your nature, you would find that in itself was a veritable spiritual Sun, a ray from which penetrating your personal self, constituted its very life and being, and that it was with this ray that you identified yourself. No person in a thousand ever lives up to what the Sun in the sign indicates.*

From these extracts we can see both that Leo was aware of some of the complete books written on the Sun signs in the United States in the mid-1890s, and that he himself regarded the Sun as representing a higher part of the self that people should aspire to embody, but believed this goal to be one that is very difficult to attain because all the other features of the individual birth chart are powerfully influential. From this account, we are not left with any sense that Sun-sign delineations by themselves were considered by Leo to be adequate or sufficient as a portrait of human personality in spite of whole American books previously having been focused upon them.

In his very first book, *A Simple Method of Instruction in the Science of Astrology* (1896), which was originally serialised in the pages of *Modern Astrology* magazine before being separately published in a workman-like paperback binding, Leo refers to the natal Sun in these terms (p. 7):

> *The Sun is the most important planet, for he rules not only our vital energy, but is the medium through which our moral character is denoted, for we must be moral before we can be wise. Therefore the Sun is POWER.*[98]

Here, his characterisation of the Sun as the 'most important' planet should not be misconstrued as primary evidence that Leo was a Sun-sign astrologer. He is instead making an evaluative judgement of its greater importance based on his assessment that the *moral* nature is indicated by the Sun and his belief that morality is the most important of all human attributes to which to aspire, in the quest for wisdom.

In the definitive extended version of the same book, retitled as *Practical Astrology* the following year (1897), Leo further adds (pp. 121–22):

> ... *the place of the Sun at birth indicates the kernel, or root, out of which the real character springs, and the sign in which it is found will mark off the chief characteristics of the Individuality, or real internal person, and in accordance with the position of the Moon its signs, and aspects, with the ascending sign, so will the character be expressed. To make this idea as clear as possible think of the Sun, Moon, and ascendant as spirit, soul, and body respectively. The Sun, as the spirit, will require the Moon, as the soul, to express it in addition to that which is permanent in the body through the ascendant.... Now from the polarization of the Moon to the Sun we learn the true nature of the personality, and as there will be 144 different polarities we shall at once see that there are 144 totally different and distinct characters irrespective of the other planetary configurations. We will now consider the polarities, but it must be distinctly remembered that they are general and not always particular, for much will depend upon the part of the map in which the polarity falls, and the aspect, but in a general way they will indicate the trend of the character.*

Here, we see how he is using the same term as Butler, 'polarity', in application to the Sun-and-Moon-sign combinations, but with a slightly different emphasis: whereas Butler calls the Moon sign by itself the 'polarity', Leo is referring to the mutual interaction of the Sun and Moon signs thus – which is arguably a more logical reading of the word. Hair-splitting over the definition of *polarity* aside, we can clearly see Butler's influence coming through in Leo's work published just ten years after the first edition of *Solar Biology*.[99]

It is also apparent here that Leo regards the Sun, Moon, and Ascendant as being objectively similarly important parts forming the basic personal nature in spite of his personal moral preference for individuals seeking to accentuate and more fully embody the characteristics represented by their natal Suns. Elsewhere in his writing, he groups them together as 'the three centres'.

In his book *How to Judge a Nativity Part II* (1904), Leo adds these insights regarding the Sun (p. 173):

> From the standpoint of the feelings the Sun governs the heart, with its sensations and emotions, and gives life to these feelings, from the fiercest passion up to the purest love and friendship.

> From a mental standpoint the Sun is the heart of Wisdom, the life of the intelligence, the self-conscious centre on the plane of the mind.

> *The importance of the Sun's position and aspects can never be over-estimated in judging a nativity; for without its rays all would be dead and inert.*

In addition to adding considerable nuance to his earlier-taught solar associations, Leo here again testifies to the importance of the Sun in natal horoscopy, but not specifically the Sun sign, rather, its position in general (which we can take to include its house position as well as its sign position) and also its aspects. Far from showing Sun-sign-astrology leanings here, Leo is advocating the interpretation of the Sun in the complete context of its position and planetary aspects in the natal figure, which is a thoroughly traditional approach.

The last paragraph deserves special comment, however. Here, Leo, much like Butler before him, is using a naturalistic, physical cosmological argument to argue for the primary importance of the Sun in natal interpretation, as compared with all other celestial bodies.

In *The Key To Your Own Nativity* (1910), a more popularly-pitched textbook chiefly taking the format of a set of numbered delineations, with reference to which it was designed to be easy for anyone to obtain a cut-and-paste-based natal astrological reading, Leo differentiates his treatment of the zodiacal signs from the equivalent treatment in the popular newspaper press with these words:

> *In the popular articles on Astrology which appear from time to time in the weekly papers the term 'born under' such and such a sign usually refers to the sign occupied by the Sun, and not to the Rising Sign, a practice which is to be regretted as it often causes confusion.*[100]

His choice of words here is noteworthy on account of the note of negative judgement evinced in respect of the journalism of the popular press relating to Sun signs. In spite of his efforts to bring natal delineations within the reach of the mass public in terms of affordability, clearly Leo did not see himself as either a popular-press astrologer or a Sun-sign astrologer, and regarded the breed as relatively ignorant and as a source of public misconceptions regarding astrology. Nor did he regard the Sun sign as supplanting the ascendant sign in astrological practice. His expression of regrets within one of his major astrological textbooks over the term 'born under' being applied by astrological journalists to Sun signs, and not to ascendant signs, as he believed it should be, proves this.

Aside from his editorial features and articles in the monthly magazines he tirelessly edited, *The Astrologer's Magazine* (1890–1895) and *Modern Astrology*

(1895–1917), Leo's printed work comprises the following known books in the original English editions,[101] presented in chronological order of publication. In each case, I have shown the total page count of the main paginated section[102] of the first edition that is held[103] and can therefore accurately be counted; and, in parentheses, the number of those pages that are given over to Sun-sign-delineation content:[104]

- *A Simple Method of Instruction in the Science of Astrology, Containing the True Nature of the Planets – Part I* (1896): 73pp (1)
- *Practical Astrology – Being a Simple Method of Instruction in the Science of Astrology* (1897): 206pp (1)
- *Astrology for All: To Which Is Added a Complete System of Predictive Astrology for Advanced Students* (1899): 104pp (34)
- *Casting the Horoscope*[105] (1901): 83pp (0)
- *Everybody's Astrology* (1901): 78pp (56)
- *Four Lectures on Astrology, Exoteric and Esoteric* (1901): 72pp (8)
- *The Horoscope and How to Read It* (1902): 68pp (0)
- *How to Judge a Nativity*[106] (1903): 176pp (0)
- *Astrology Explained* (1903): 14pp (0)
- *How to Judge a Nativity Part II*[107] (1904): 190pp (1)
- [co-authored with H. S. Green] *The Horoscope in Detail* (1904): 94pp (0)
- *Complete Dictionary of Astrology* (1905):[108] 136pp (1½)
- *What Is a Horoscope and How is it Cast? A Book for Beginners* (1905): 94pp (0)
- [co-authored with Heinrich Däath] *The Progressed Horoscope by Alan Leo – A Sequel to How to Judge a Nativity Wherein the Progression of the Horoscope Is Exhaustively Considered, Both in Principle and in Practice[;] including also A Full Delineation of Each and Every Possible Progressed Aspect, With Its Influence on Character and Destiny, the Effect of Transits, etc.[;] To which is added 'The Art and Practice of Directing', a Complete Treatise on Primary Directions, by Heinrich Däath* (1906) : 316pp (1)
- *Horary Astrology* (1907): 138pp (0)
- *The Key to Your Own Nativity: Analytical Readings of Every Position in a Nativity, Based on Scientific Principles* (1910): 303pp (5)
- *The Astrologer and His Work[,] With some Remarkable Short Stories* (1911): 48pp (0)
- *Esoteric Astrology: A Study in Human Nature* (1913): 293pp (½)
- *Symbolism and Astrology: An Introduction to Esoteric Astrology* (1914): 78pp (0)
- *Mars: the War Lord* (1915): 99pp (0)
- *When the War Will End: a Scientific Prediction* ([1915]): 8pp (0)
- *A New Factor in Education: Astrology – The Zodiac as the Basis of Temperament* (1916): 28pp (2)
- *Saturn: the Reaper* (1916): 108pp (1)
- *Jupiter: the Preserver* (1917): 88pp (0)

Additionally, Leo penned a set of astrological correspondence lessons that adopted a systematic approach to the teaching of astrology, and was divided into nine nominal 'series' of seven lessons each. The complete set, when sold bound, filled six hardcover volumes, although because of the high price asked if retained, they were issued on a loan basis and then returned for redistribution to other students, so very few printings were ever made and still fewer are known to survive. Only three such original volumes are to hand, but without prejudice to the contents of the others, it can be said that this sample shows no particular favouritism for the natal Sun, although it does demonstrate Leo's pronounced preference for what he called *Esoteric Astrology*[109] – reflecting the theosophical doctrine to which he and more particularly his wife Bessie subscribed, as well as being in keeping with the previously established ideas of fellow-theosophist Butler.

Because the complete set of *Correspondence Lessons* was unavailable for the purposes of this exercise, no page count for any of the volumes is presented here. Further, in adding up the total number of pages of all Leo's qualifying works of which complete examples were available (thus excluding both his magazines and his correspondence course), mindful of the fact that *Practical Astrology* was revised from *A Simple Course of Instruction* and that *What is a Horoscope?* was revised from *The Horoscope and How to Read It*, I have counted only the later and lengthier of the two editions by page count in each case for those two works. This gives:

All books by Alan Leo: 2754 pages
(of which 111 pages on Sun signs = 4.03%).

I think this low percentage figure, standing as it does far beneath the equivalent percentage for many of his Sun sign–oriented American contemporaries and immediate antecedents, clearly demonstrates that Alan Leo does not deserve a reputation either as a Sun-sign astrologer in himself or even as a significant catalyst to the simplification of astrology along Sun sign–oriented lines, although, under the influence of the esoteric current of astrological writing popularised by Hiram Butler in his day and favoured by the Theosophical Society of which he was a follower, as well as quite probably the direct influence of the teachings of Helena Blavatsky herself, he still gave the Sun much more preferential treatment than did nearly all British 19th-century astrologers writing before him. That he did so was a product of the prevailing international English-speaking astrological and theosophical culture into which Leo grew up, one that had already adopted the practice. It certainly is not evidence of Leo desiring to simplify astrology as an end in itself in order to make it easier for ordinary people to follow, and nor is it evidence of his seeking to remove from consideration in astrological interpretation a full spectrum of pertinent astrological factors.

The caricatured portraiture of Alan Leo's astrological thinking and work that has become a mainstay of 21st-century historical accounts of astrology has been long overdue for rectification, and I hope this study will help to set the record straight as well as to shine a little more of the spotlight upon Hiram Erastus Butler, Eleanor Kirk, and W. J. Colville and their pivotal roles in developing the modern genre of Sun-sign literature in the late 19th century.

Endnotes

[1] Kim Farnell, *Flirting with the Zodiac: A True History of Sun Sign Astrology* (Wessex Astrologer, 2007), Chapter 1, pp. 1–9, *esp.* pp. 5–6.

[2] In a rare error, the late research director of the American Federation of Astrologers, James Herschel Holden, writing in his *Biographical Dictionary of Western Astrologers*, seems unaware of the 17th-century editions, of which the BNF records no fewer than four, and speculates that the author is an 18th-century Italian astrologer.

[3] Farnell, *op. cit.*, pp. 27–30.

[4] Johannes ab Indagine, *Introductiones apotelesmaticae elegantes in chyromantiam, physiognomiam, astrologiam naturalem, complexiones hominum, naturas planetarum. Cum periaxiomatibus de faciebus signorum, & canonibus de aegritudinibus, nusquam fere simili tractata compendio* (Argentorati Schott / Francofurtum Impressum apud Dav. Zephelium, 1522).

[5] In the original edition thus; later editions were typically reduced to a small octavo format and reset over hundreds of pages accordingly.

[6] As *Die Kunst der Chiromantzey*.

[7] As *Chyromantia*.

[8] As *Proposition astrologicque, et pronostication naturelle* – said to be a translation only of the astrological section entitled *Periaxiomata de faciebus* in the original work.

[9] As *Chiromance & Physiognomie Par Le Regard des Membres de l'Homme*.

[10] As *Briefe introductions, both naturall, pleasaunt, and also delectable unto the Art of Chiromancy, or Manuell divination, and Physiognomy: with circumstances upon the faces of the signes: also certain canons or rules upon diseases and sicknesse: whereunto is also annexed aswel the artificiall, as naturall astrologye, with the nature of the planets* (Apud

Johannis Day, Londoni, 1558).

[11] Johannes Ab Indagine, *op. cit.*, tr. Fabian Withers, pp. 103–16.

[12] *Ibid.*, pp. 167–80.

[13] *Ibid.*, pp. 147–66.

[14] *Ibid.*, pp. 141–42.

[15] *Ibid.*, pp. 186–89.

[16] See also Farnell's secondary commentary on Indagine in *Flirting* (*op. cit.*), pp. 32–35.

[17] See Raphael, *The Familiar Astrologer* (1831; reprinted several times in the mid-19th century), pp. 249–60.

[18] The early publication history is difficult clearly to ascertain from Worldcat records, since the edition of Christianus Wechelus in Paris, dated 1531, comprises only the first book, while that of Johannes Graphaeus of Antwerp, retaining the 1531 date, appears from its title to be the complete work, and that of the Beringos fratres in Lyon, which also appears complete, is variously dated 1531, ca. 1531, and 'after 1531' in library records. This is a question for a dedicated Agrippa scholar to resolve.

[19] The identity of this J. F. is disputed, with most library records on Worldcat identifying him as a John French, but in the Llewellyn edition of 1993 (reprinted many times since), he is instead named as James Freake. It is beyond the purposes of this essay to settle this dispute, but the reader is advised of it for the record.

[20] Raphael, *The Familiar Astrologer* (1835 printing), p. 249.

[21] E.g., *The Royal Book of Fate* (1828).

[22] See Farnell, *op. cit.*, p. 58.

[23] His date of birth is given in print as 29 July 1841, at 4 a.m., although the place is not stated; he is recorded to have died at Applegate, California, on 3 Nov. 1916.

[24] For a full account of Butler's activities and esoteric influences, see Farnell, *op. cit.*, pp. 73–80.

[25] *Solar Biology*, 'Editor's Preface', pp. iii–vii.

[26] *Solar Biology*, 'Author's Preface', pp. ix–xii.

[27] *Solar Biology*, 1969 printing, p. xiia.

[28] *Solar Biology*, p. 33.

[29] *Ibid.*, p. 39.

[30] *Ibid.*, p. 42.

[31] *Ibid.*

[32] *Ibid.*, 'Chapter III: The Twelve Signs or Functions of the Zodiac', pp. 49–79.

[33] See, e.g., Robert A. Hughes, *The Sun and Moon Polarity in Your Horoscope* (AFA, 1977), as well as examples within the time frame of this essay in Section iv below.

[34] *Solar Biology*, p. 43.

[35] *Ibid.*, Chapters VI–XVII, pp. 88–209.

[36] *Ibid.*, Chapters XIX–XXIV, pp. 217–54.

[37] Author of *The Law and the Prophets* (1894).

38 Author of *Heliocentric Astrology* (1896).
39 Lead columnist for the *Heliocentric Section* in the American esoteric periodical *Star of the Magi*, which ran from 1899 to 1903.
40 Merton wrote under the pseudonym of Yarmo Vedra and authored his own book *Heliocentric Astrology* (1899).
41 See Thomas Burgoyne, *The Light of Egypt* (1889), pp. 213–35.
42 See Frank Earl Ormsby, *The Law and the Prophets* (1894), pp. 16–27.
43 This scarce late 19th-century work is a 56-page digest of some of the principal notions in Butler's *Solar Biology* and in view of how closely it copies from the latter, it may reasonably be supposed to have been issued by the Esoteric Fraternity as a simplified introduction to the doctrine expounded in the main book, in spite of the absence of formal publication credits. The delineations within are limited to the Sun signs.
44 Our original printing of this tiny paperback bears a hand-signed notice of gift presentation dated April 21st, 1896. Publication therefore must predate this.
45 An expanded edition with an additional 52 pages subsequently appeared in 1930.
46 Published in the same year as the first US edition, by Dodd Mead.
47 Also commonly found reprinted in a book club edition by New Home Library from 1943.
48 After the original edition by Books Inc., 1940.
49 Idea Publishing Company, New York, 1894.
50 Author of *Astrology, Science of Knowledge and Reason* (New York, 1897).
51 Editor of *The Sphinx*, an ambitious astrological magazine published intermittently (with significant gaps) between September 1899 and at least December 1907 (the date of the last issue to hand).
52 No separate printing date is given, but the internal advertising on the copy to hand for a book first published in 1901 shows this as the earliest possible date for it; the amended version of Kirk's book, which she self-published under her own name, extends to 191 main pages and bears the added subtitle on its front board 'with Character Readings of Persons Born Upon the Cusp', differentiating it clearly from the original edition.
53 Freedom Publishing Company, Boston (1895; reprinted 1899); later republished as *The Significance of Birthdays* (New York: Macoy Publishing, 1911).
54 Also reprinted in unclearly dated contemporaneous editions by Holmes Book Co. (Los Angeles, CA), and I. & M. Ottenheimer, Publishers (Baltimore, MD).
55 This work includes a basic coverage of Sun-sign synastry. See further coverage below.
56 Later reprinted by M. A. Donohue & Company in an undated edition retitled *Your Fortune Told Under Your Lucky Star*.
57 Reprinted multiple times subsequently, and notable for taking after Eleanor Kirk's emphasis on separate delineations for 'sign cusp' positions of the Sun, thereby helping to perpetuate the then-recently-contrived notion that solar cusp areas have their own separate influence.

58 Also issued in a revised edition of 1915, itself reprinted with a new pictorial cover design in 1916.
59 Towne was one of the leaders of the New Thought movement in the United States in the early 20th century, and edited with William E. Towne the magazine *Nautilus* for many years, as well as authoring *The Life Power and How to Use It* (1906), *How to Use New Thought In Home Life* (1916), and *15 Lessons in New Thought* (1919).
60 This title appears on the front cover only. No overall internal title page is present, but there is an internal page serving as a title page by providing publication details, albeit without the proper title, only indicating the first of the Sun signs to be covered, namely Capricorn, in its place. The book is a Sun-sign guide but makes a feature of including quotations from representative famous individuals.
61 This name may be a pseudonym. We do not know the identity of the author of this brief popular tract.
62 A very brief and condensed guide to the Sun signs, with one page allotted to each, listing associated characteristics under seventeen different themes.
63 Despite the pretentious title, this tiny leather-bound pocketbook is not a work of financial astrology, but rather an elementary Sun-sign guide marketed at the businessmen of its day as though to make it more socially acceptable for them to show a passing interest in such a subject as astrology.
64 Presumed within a few years before or after 1916, the recorded date of another title by same author.
65 As the title would suggest, this is a simple Sun-sign primer aimed at the non-technical beginner. Approximately eight pages of text, two of noted celebrities and one of tabulated traditional associations are devoted to each sign in turn. The advertised asking price for the book at the time of publication was US $1. The advertising at the back of the volume focuses on similar mass-market-oriented esoteric and divinatory works, with prices ranging from $1 for Sepharial's *Astrology* to $2 for William Walker Atkinson's *Mind Power*.
66 Despite the name, this is just another Sun-sign guide by this author.
67 Presumed 1930s. This original edition is not in Worldcat. On our copy, the original printed publication credit has been pasted over with a later label reading: "The Torch Publishing Co., 657 E. Hastings St., Vancouver, BC". Like other works by Muir, it was later reprinted by Llewellyn, only in this case the title was amended to *Health and the Sun Signs*; the third printing is dated to 1968.
68 This slender pamphlet by one of the 20th century's most celebrated and prolific esoteric writers was compiled from articles by the author originally published in *Wynn's Astrology Magazine*. It had reached its fourth edition in 1946 after the second of 1941 and the third of 1944, testifying to the continuing popularity of the Sun-sign-primer formula with the American mass public throughout the mid-20th century.
69 A basic, Sun-sign-level publication.

70 This work is mostly focused on zodiacal symbolism in general but does implicitly relate its readings to the delineation of the Sun in places, lending itself more truly to the Sun-sign-primer category of work than the astrologically detached zodiacal symbolism category overall.
71 Reprinted several times since, most commonly under the altered title of *Astrological Signs: the Pulse of Life*.
72 Also reprinted as a paperback by Helicon Books of New York in 1950.
73 The late André Barbault's set of 12 Sun-sign publications was the first seen in France to exceed 100 pages per volume, and by virtue of its extraordinary combined length, singly set the trend for substantial books on individual Sun signs that would go on to proliferate there in the late 20th century. It was reprinted in a colourful miniature cloth-bound collectors' edition in 2004.
74 In the absence of internal dating or authoritative deposit library records, the two examples held are guessed from their appearance to date from approximately the 1920s.
75 An early Sun-sign synastry guide, divided along gender lines. For each Sun sign, separate sections are given over to the personalities of men and women born under the sign, followed by one on men born under the sign in relationship with women born under every sign in turn, with typically from half a page to two-thirds of a page given over to each combination. Thus, in all 144 combinations are described.
76 Alan Leo, *Astrology for All* (London, 1899), Chapter XVIII, The Solar-Lunar Combinations, pp. 60–101; in the second edition (1904), this spans pp. 71–126.
77 Alan M. Emley, *Solar Psychology* (Denver, CO: William H. Andre, 1929).
78 S. R. Parchment, *Astrology Mundane and Spiritual: A text-book giving a brief résumé of cosmogenesis and anthropogenesis; complete instructions for casting, progressing and reading the horoscope, with twenty-six example horoscopes illustrating the diagnosis of disease by means of star chemistry* (First Edition - Distributed by Rosicrucian Anthroposophic League, 1933).
79 A playful title inviting a double take, after a common expression normally used to indicate one's own ignorance; only the implication here is that the heavens (or stars) really do know.
80 A book of readings of the solar degrees, linked to birthdays. Both succinctly expressed symbols and multi-paragraph readings are included for each day of the year. The true identity of the author is not known.
81 Gary Goldschneider was the principal author of a series of best-selling books in this genre starting in the late 1990s.
82 The whole course, published by the Church of Light (Los Angeles, CA), runs to over 200 pamphlets and is also commonly found bound up in 22 nominal books in 24 volumes.
83 *Last Eighteen Decanates Analyzed*, unknown printing, pp. 42–43.

84 This work by Robert T. Cross (who served as *Raphael* for several decades and was a prolific writer under that name) is notable for its publication well before Butler's *Solar Biology*, which indicates that the trend towards degree analysis cannot be attributed solely or even chiefly to the influence of Butler's book. *The Faces and Degrees* was subsequently reprinted by W. Foulsham in a falsely backdated edition that must truly have been issued in the 1890s or thereabouts, and again in 1901, this time in a properly dated edition.

85 This edition, the first published by Modern Astrology Office, is separately listed here on account of Sepharial's degree series having supplanted and completely replaced that of H. S. Green as was found in the original Nichols edition, somewhat ironically in view of Green having been a closer associate of Modern Astrology Office than Sepharial ever was. The reformulated edition was the basis of all later reprints, of which there have been several, including undated ones by L. N. Fowler after 1908, and a US edition by the Aries Press in 1943.

86 Subsequent editions, published by Llewellyn, appeared in 1958, 1963, and 1967.

87 For a definitive, up-to-date biography of Alan Leo and his wife Bessie, see Kim Farnell, *Modern Astrologers: The lives of Alan & Bessie Leo* (2019).

88 To wit, Ellen McCaffery's *Astrology: Its History and Influence in the Western World* (1942); Ellic Howe's *Urania's Children* (1967), Eric Russell's *Astrology and Prediction* (1972), Zolar's *The History of Astrology* (1972), Manly P. Hall's *The Story of Astrology* (fourth edition, enlarged and revised, 1975, after the first of 1933); Derek and Julia Parker's *A History of Astrology* (1983); Patrick Curry's *A Confusion of Prophets* (1992); and James Herschel Holden's *A History of Horoscopic Astrology from the Babylonian Period to the Modern Age* (1995).

89 *Op. cit.*, p. 26.

90 Multiple eyewitness accounts hold that Ovason was an alternative pen-name of the author Fred Gettings (1937–2013), who had previously written under his own name an oft-reprinted *Dictionary of Astrology* (first published by Routledge, Kegan and Paul, 1985).

91 Ellen McCaffery, *Astrology: Its History and Influence in the Western World* (Charles Scribner's Sons, 1942), pp. 349–50.

92 Nicholas Campion, *A History of Western Astrology Volume II: the Medieval and Modern Worlds* (Continuum UK, 2009), pp. 232–34.

93 *Ibid.*, p. 232.

94 *Ibid.*, p. 233.

95 Alexander Boxer, *A Scheme of Heaven: Astrology and the Birth of Science* (Profile Books, 2020).

96 Additionally, 48 pages of Leo's later book *The Key to Your Own Nativity* (1910) are dedicated to delineating the 144 natal Sun-and-Moon combinations.

97 This sentence is clumsily constructed.

98 This text is also retained in the first edition of the renamed, expanded version of this book, *Practical Astrology* (1897), p. 7.
99 See also Leo's exploration of the term 'Polarity' in *The Key to Your Own Nativity* (1910), p. 203, and in his later book *Esoteric Astrology* (1913), Chapter XV, 'Esoteric Value of the Polarities', pp. 131–42.
100 Leo, *The Key To Your Own Nativity* (1910), p. 233.
101 Several were also translated into German, and some into Dutch and French, at the height of Leo's influence in the early 20th century.
102 That is to say, excluding prefatory pages represented by Roman numerals.
103 In all cases, this is believed also to be the true first edition under the title shown. Note however that *Practical Astrology* was nominally billed the second edition since it originated as a major expansion of *A Simple Method of Instruction in the Science of Astrology Part I*, which I have listed separately above it. Similarly, *What Is a Horoscope and How is it Cast?* was a reworking of *The Horoscope and How to Read It*.
104 This is based upon an approximate manual count while leafing through every page in every volume to assess its contents. For consistency's sake, the separate soli-lunar combinations have not been counted here, and nor have depictions of the zodiac signs in general or in their groupings such as elements and qualities, without reference to the Sun being posited in them. However, discussions of the influence of the Sun in the zodiac signs in general without reference to its particular sign placement are counted as being directly relevant and so included in the page count.
105 In the editions of 1904 and 1908, this work was temporarily renamed *Astrology for All Part II*, before reverting to its original name by the edition of 1912, which was billed the 'Third Revised Edition' of Astrology for All Part II although it was in fact the fourth overall edition of *Casting the Horoscope*.
106 In all issues from 1904 to 1908, this work was instead known as *How to Judge a Nativity Part I*, before it reverted by 1912 to its original title of *How to Judge a Nativity*.
107 In later editions from 1912, this work was renamed *The Art of Synthesis*.
108 The only edition to appear in Alan Leo's lifetime, and in spite of its title, incomplete thus, with the alphabetically arranged astrological terms that are defined ending on 'Horoscope' and excluding both 'Sun' and 'Signs of the Zodiac'. A posthumous revised edition spanning the entire alphabet was prepared by Vivian Robson and published in 1929, running to 205 pages, but there were no Sun-sign delineations added so the Sun-sign-related content is still limited to 1½ pages, the greater part of which relates to disposition to diseases.
109 Series 3, Lessons 1–7, *Esoteric Astrology*; Series 9, Lessons 1–7, *Special Instruction in Esoteric Astrology*.

Chapter Four
The Early History of Sun-sign Forecasting and Newspaper Astrology, 1890–1937

Introduction: What is Sun-sign Forecasting and Why is it so Controversial?

Almost everyone living today who was raised in North American and European cultures will have been familiar from an early age with a particularly superficial representation of astrology in the mass media, taking the form of potted forecasts for each of the twelve Sun signs in the upcoming period of time. This is what astrologers call *Sun-sign forecasting*. It is quite distinct from traditional personal astrological forecasting from the individual natal horoscope, which is based on the interpretation of a much more thorough and accurate set of astronomical measurements. As such, Sun-sign forecasting is often derided by astrologers as a very poor representation of astrology. Others, however, point to its success as a means of getting a taste of astrology before the masses through media channels that would be averse to running any more detailed and complex astrological content, and its consequent value as a source of widespread awareness of the existence of astrology, thereby stimulating the market for astrological consultations that support the livelihoods of professional astrologers, and potentially whetting the appetite of those curious enough to investigate astrology further and become student astrologers themselves.

Sun-sign forecasting as we know it in the press today typically takes the form of readings, compressed into a single paragraph, of the astrological influences expected to be experienced by those born under each of the twelve Sun signs in the day, week, month, or year ahead, depending on the nature of the publication in which they are printed.

For more than 80 years, Sun-sign forecast columns have been a popular feature of weekly and monthly newspapers and lifestyle magazines, including the weekend magazines issued with Sunday newspapers. For much of that time, if not nearly all of it, they have also appeared in portions of the daily newspaper press. In some western cultures, daily Sun-sign forecasts have even been a feature of breakfast-time television shows, a notable example in the UK being those given by Russell Grant on *BBC Breakfast Time* from 1983 to 1986 and then on *TV-AM* from 1986 to 1990; and weekly ones have been included on teletext services.

Such is the ubiquity of the Sun-sign forecast in mass media outlets that when the general newspaper and magazine press features astrology at all, a Sun-sign forecast is nearly always the essence of the feature. Only occasionally do we see other articles about astrology in the mainstream press, and then they are usually ones written from a sociological, sceptical, or historical perspective, and almost never instructive upon astrological techniques. As a result, astrology and Sun-sign forecasts have become almost synonymous in the minds of the astrologically uneducated general public. Likewise *horoscopes* and Sun-sign forecasts: although they are not the same thing at all, such is the degree of public confusion and misunderstanding of the word *horoscope* that sceptical members of the lay public are sometimes seen or heard to argue against horoscopes on the misapprehension that horoscopes *are* Sun sign forecasts, while having absolutely no understanding of the meaning of the word *horoscope* as understood by astrologers.

The basic technical methodology around Sun-sign forecasting is an open secret among astrologers. The natal Sun sign is treated as the effective ascendant sign, and the current transiting planets are placed by the astrologer in whole-sign solar houses starting from the natal Sun sign. They are then interpreted according to their positions in the twelve solar houses, taking into close consideration their mutual aspects as modifying influences upon their effects in the houses.

My esteemed colleague Kim Farnell, one of the most accomplished researchers of modern astrological history from primary sources, has previously given a thorough exposition of the earliest traces of solar house methodology, demonstrating in her book *Flirting with the Zodiac*[1] that the use of solar houses in astrology has centuries-old roots. But how far back do we need to go to find when Sun-sign forecasting began to take root in the popular press?

The simple answer in broad terms is to the 1930s, for, as has been well-established in the existing historical narratives on the development of modern astrology, this was the decade when the twelve-paragraph-format Sun-sign forecasts began regularly to appear in widespread elements of the general press as well as in the specialised popular astrology press.

However, this answer is somewhat vague and also simplistic, and we need to look further back in time to trace the origins of Sun-sign forecasting in the periodical press.

A myth that we may as well dispel at the outset, however, and one we shall go on to explore in detail later, is the one that attributes the invention both of Sun-sign forecasting and of newspaper astrology to the astrologer R. H. Naylor writing for the British newspaper *The Sunday Express* in 1930, which is incorrect on both counts. Naylor was not by a very long stretch the first newspaper astrologer, he was not the inventor of Sun-sign forecasting, and he was not the first astrologer to write Sun-sign forecasts for the press either. We shall come to Naylor and his true place in the historical narrative towards the end of this chapter.

Sun-sign forecasting was not Dane Rudhyar's idea either. One of the more fanciful notions to have entered some of the history books since 2000 was that he suggested the idea to Paul Clancy as a vehicle for popularising astrology, a notion for which no documentary evidence has been presented, and one that is incompatible with the timeline of the acquaintance of Clancy and Rudhyar as well as with Rudhyar's intellectual and philosophical approach to astrology. This account seems most likely to have been based on an inadvertent *bona fide* misreading or misrecollection of elements of an interview with Rudhyar late in his life, perhaps one he gave in *Astrology Now* magazine, No. 13, June 1976.[2]

Part 1: Precursors to Sun-sign Forecasting in the late 19th-Century Astrological Press

To understand the origins of Sun-sign forecasting in the general press, we need to look back at least as far as the late 19th century, and to the United States astrological magazine press. In 1884, Mr. O. D. Bragdon of Boston launched his monthly magazine *Signs of the Times*,[3] which had soon become known as the leading astrological magazine in the United States and was mentioned from time to time in such a light in newspaper reports.

In every issue of *Signs of the Times*, there are multi-page readings in plain English of what astrologers today often call the astrological weather (current astrological transits) for the headline month, divided by calendar days. These readings are not Sun-sign-specific, but they do set an important precedent for daily readings of the current astrological weather, which is a central element of the methodology used in Sun-sign forecasting. Bragdon's magazine continued until 1891 (with occasional interruptions) and kept this feature going throughout.

As we shall go on to see, daily readings of the current astrological weather for everyone irrespective of Sun sign, using much the same methodology, had spread to the general American newspaper press by 1910.

Meanwhile, in the UK, P. Powley, a British astrologer who was a pivotal figure in the UK astrological community from 1887 to 1890 thanks to his editorship of the major monthly national astrology magazine published in London during that period, *The Astrologer*,[4] had introduced as a regular feature in his magazine, starting in August 1887, a type of annual Sun-sign forecast. This style of forecast takes the form of predictions for the whole of the year ahead for anyone whose birthday is today. In effect, it is using the exact Solar degree corresponding to the calendar date in an average year as a basis for forecasting using the solar return chart set for this date, but it amounts to a whole-year Sun-sign forecast for those born on that date.

Neither Bragdon's format nor that of Powley is exactly what we are familiar with today, but both are arguably partial methodological prototypes for what, upon integration into a single methodology centred upon the whole Sun signs instead of either the degrees or the generality of the whole population, later became the twelve-paragraph Sun-sign forecast.

Anniversary readings for the year to come for everyone born on a particular calendar date were also featured in the short-lived weekly *Bland's Astrology*[5] (1889), alongside a third type of forecast in the form of succinct whole-life readings for newborn infants born on the current date in this year (which is of course a potted natal astrological forecast and not a Sun-sign forecast).

All three of the aforementioned types of popular content in the specialised astrological magazine press would make their way into the astrology columns of the non-specialist newspaper press in due course.

Part 2: Representation of astrology in United States Newspapers before 1910

Thanks to the open-access project *Chronicling America* run by the United States Library of Congress, researchers now have unprecedentedly easy access to archives of a wide range of out-of-copyright newspapers published in the United States before 95 years ago.

When we look at these digital archives, we find very little evidence of *regular* newspaper astrology columns in the US general press before 1910. We do however find plenty of evidence of public interest in both natal astrology and astrological forecasts by the 1890s, a time when astrology was booming in the United States, as reflected in a greatly increased proliferation of new astrological publications from the late 1880s onwards. The evidence for this in newspapers typically takes the form of isolated articles rather than regular columns, but it is still valuable historical documentation of the public status of astrology in America in its day, and we shall discuss some of the more interesting examples below.

In the edition of San Francisco newspaper *The Morning Call* for May 2nd, 1890, there is an extensive column quoting from both *Raphael's* and *Zadkiel's* almanacs for 1890 their mundane forecasts for the month of May. This shows that the major British astrological almanacs of the time not only were being distributed to the United States, but also were attracting sufficient public attention there for their forecasts to be considered as newsworthy by portions of the general newspaper press.

However, astrology gets a very mixed press in United States newspapers of the late 19th century where it is mentioned at all, with only some editors bestowing upon it an uncritical open exposition, and others feeling the need either to overtly decry it as a form of lingering irrational superstition, or else to satirise it with a nudge and a wink, as though appealing to their readers' sense that they are sufficiently well-educated to know better than to believe in this kind of supposed nonsense without needing to be directly told not to!

For instance, a more sceptical tone regarding mundane astrological forecasts is evoked in the article 'Star-Gazers' in the issue of *The Advocate*, published in Topeka, Kansas, for June 13th, 1894, [p. 7], which reports in a mocking tone on a mundane forecast for the month of June made in *The Prognostic Star-Gazer*,[6] which was a brief monthly astrological newspaper published at Boston, Mass..

There is, however, some purely factual reporting on astrology, usually in a spirit of looking upon it as a primarily historical curio. An example of very simple factual reporting is the article 'The Zodiac: A Brief Explanation as to its Twelve Signs' in *The Sedalia Weekly Bazoo* for March 4th, 1890.

More sophisticated than this is a potted natal delineation for the newborn second daughter[7] of President Grover Cleveland, published in *The Blackfoot News* for September 16th, 1893, under the heading 'Baby's Horoscope'. The reading is credited to 'Prof. Leonis',[8] said to be a 'New York Professor'.

In the *Sunday Herald* of Salt Lake City, Utah for June 24th, 1894, we find a serious and substantial three-column article headed 'Read from the Stars. – An Astrologer Draws Solemn Horoscopes of Public Men', which gives unsolicited personal forecasts for a selection of well-known public figures including Queen Victoria, President Cleveland, and other prominent US politicians of the day.

And occasional journalistic expositions of the public interest in astrology provide valuable historical documentation of the culture of the times.

On June 30th, 1891, a journalist writing in *The Waterbury Evening Democrat* an article headed 'Horoscopes to Order – Old Astrologer Makes Them In New

York', which is said to have first appeared in the *New York Sun*, reports on having met a bearded elderly male astrologer at his office in New York, and includes quotations from him.[9]

On July 19th, 1891, there appears in the *Salt Lake City Herald* a lengthy article reproduced from the *Sunday Herald*,[10] undersigned J. H. Connelly and headed 'The Stars Tell It – Your Fortune and Your Fate Can Be Read'. This piece gives significant insight into the public status of astrology in the United States at the time and also into the contemporaneous sense among its practitioners of a need to modernise the traditional subject along more rigorously scientific grounds. Among the more interesting observations made by Connelly are:

It may possibly be mildly surprising to [scientific materialists] that astrology has to-day not only more believers but more who understand a good deal of its strange and difficult computations, laws and jargon, than have existed at any one time within at least three hundred years. Such is nevertheless the fact. Several years ago, a New York Sunday newspaper established an astrological department, devoting a column each week to the deductions and forecasts drawn by a thoroughly competent astrologer from the horoscopes of individuals sending in simply the place and exact time of their birth and statement of their sex. The applicants for attention to that column were from one to five hundred a week.... That eagerness has continued up to the present time, and the letters received are in themselves sufficient demonstration that those who ask the casting of their horoscopes are by no means the ignorant and vulgar, but in a great majority of cases persons of intelligence, education and culture. [...]

There are better evidences of the hold astrology has as a fin du siècle fad. In New York and Boston there are numbers of shrewd, practical men, speculators in the stock, produce and cotton markets... who pay regularly $5 per month for forecasts of the days and even the times of days, when operations[11] are advisable and when it will be best for them to carefully refrain from doing business. And they govern themselves accordingly. [....]

Here is something more. There are three astrological journals (monthlies) published in this country, three in England, one in France and one in Germany.[12] They are strictly technical publications, appealing only to the interest of those who have gained some insight into the mysterious art, and are very rarely seen by anybody but the subscribers, who receive them by mail. You will not find in them any such promiscuous horoscoping of the multitude as in the newspapers before spoken of. When a horoscope appears in them it is cited for demonstration of some affirmed principle of resultant effects from certain given planetary causes; or to illustrate the reading of some unusual aspects. There are serious and able articles on the planets, their co-relations and influences upon mundane affairs. Sometimes instructions in new methods of 'directions' are given. The ephemeris for the month, and general indications of the prevalent conditions on each day, are indispensable....

The bibliography of astrology is increasing rapidly, and it is noteworthy that the works of to-day are really scientific, by eminent mathematicians and cogent reasoners, such as Pierce[13] and Goold,[14] who swept away relentlessly the sacred dust and superstition of the past ages.... Patient, painstaking scientists, all over the world, are diligently comparing observations, notes and inferences on the still undetermined influences of Neptune and Herschel in their various aspects with the outer planets. Probably Prof. Oliver Ames Goold's re-issue of James Wilson's Dictionary of Astrology[15] has done more than any other one book to command the respectful attention of reasoning and inquiring minds, and in it are smashed without mercy whole basketfuls of superstition laid by Ptolmy,[16] Placidus and their successors down to Sibley,[17] Coley, and Lilly. At the same time the dealers in old books find that they have no stock which commands surer and better prices than the ancient works of astrology. Students seize them eagerly, partly from curious interest in their vagaries, partly from the good grains that they believe may be sifted from the bushel of chaff they contain.

The latter part of Connelly's testimony as quoted here is especially important as contemporaneous witness evidence of the thriving second-hand market for centuries-old astrology books in the United States as early as 1891, and strikes a further nail into the coffin of the discredited historical narrative that astrological tradition had been altogether forgotten by the end of the 19th century.

On June 3rd, 1894, the *New York Sun* gives over almost a whole broadsheet page to an article headed 'Fortunes in the Stars. The Horoscopes of Nine Celebrated Men Accurately Cast'. This gives readings, with printed birth chart wheels, for a host of prominent American public figures of the time. But most interesting are the introductory remarks of the much more sceptical editor of the paper in introducing the anonymously authored article:

The belief in astrology did not die out, as many suppose, centuries ago; but that ancient science has a large number of votaries in Europe and America to-day. It would probably greatly surprise those who think that the casting of horoscopes is a lost art to know how many persons of good reputation and good position in life, people of education, too, in some cases, nourish a secret belief in the influence of the stars and planets, and covertly consult astrologers at the outset of important undertakings.

The editor then makes his own position with regard to astrology abundantly clear in his choice of words, when he writes:

In order to illustrate the methods and mysteries of this pretended science, which has imposed upon the ignorant and superstitious in all ages, and which a few hundred years ago numbered such men as the great astronomers Tycho and Kepler among its practitioners, and was universally believed in by the monarchs and ruling classes of Europe, The Sun has obtained the dates of birth of nine well-known citizens, and submitted them to astrological judgment.

So it is apparent that the inclusion of this article is not intended as an endorsement of the practice of astrology, which is regarded by the editor as a product of ignorance and a form of superstition. It would seem instead to be designed merely to satisfy people's historical curiosity with a measure of detachment. But perhaps on analysis there was also a begrudging commercial realisation in the background that such features helped to sell papers even if they were considered the stuff of superstitious nonsense.

On December 30th, 1894, the *Salt Lake Herald* and the *Omaha Daily Bee* both report on the increasing interest by this time in both London and New York in astrological readings, especially among women, in an article penned by a Dahlia Hughes[18] headed 'Casting of Horoscopes: Modish Women Deeply Engaged in Studying the Stars':

Astrology is the dominant occult attraction in London at the majority of West End 'At Homes'. No hostess is considered a success at such unless she provides an astrologer as one of the attractions.

In New York the art is practiced sub rosa,[19] and although hosts of society women devote much precious time to the study of their fate, as revealed by sun, moon, and stars, very little is said about it to the outside world. Intimate friends form a coterie which meets once a week, possibly more frequently, to listen to lectures on astrology and incidentally, so they say, have their fortunes revealed in the heavens....

With many ladies it is simply pastime; with others it might be called a matter of business, social life, philanthropies, and dress even being regulated for them by messages from the spheres.

> *To attend an astrological lecture, or séance, is at least to pass an entertaining hour. In one Fifth Avenue residence, my lady's boudoir, luxurious and sweet with burning incense, which lends an oriental touch to the occasion, is often the rendezvous of half a dozen friends for whom everything cabalistic has a charm.*
>
> *The high priestess is a woman who divides her time between Boston and New York,[20] and so much are her services in demand, for lectures, casting horoscopes, and nativities that it is extremely difficult to see her unless an appointment is made in advance. She has her regular 'clients' or patrons in New York, and although willing to foretell $2 worth of fate in the stars, so to speak, $5 and $10 is her usual charge, while for a very elaborate and carefully prepared horoscope which prognosticate everything that can possibly happen in a life time, $100 is not an unusual charge.*

We have already seen in Connelly's previously quoted article from 1891 his testimony to the effect that a New York Sunday newspaper had set up an astrological department several years earlier. I have unfortunately not been able to identify the Sunday newspaper to which he refers from searching the Library of Congress archives, but if we presume his account to be reliable, then the timeline of newspaper astrology in the United States needs to be pushed back at least to the late 1880s. But just how much further back does American newspaper reporting of astrology actually go?

In my searches to date, I have found the documentary evidence to be much thinner on the ground before the 1890s. However, there would seem to have been a little press interest in astrological forecasts affecting national American politics for decades already by this time, as evidenced for example in *The New York Herald* for November 13th, 1875, in which, under the heading 'The Star of Ulysses. – Horoscope of General Grant by Astrologer Lister', a personal forecast is made for then-President Ulysses S. Grant by an astrologer whose name is given only as Lister.[21] Nonetheless, this is not a typical article for its time, and in the 1870s, articles of genuine political astrology are vastly outnumbered by ones that use the term 'political horoscope' purely figuratively, either in journalistic reference to the political outlook in the time ahead, or seemingly to refer to a physical document consulted by politicians at that time—from the context in which it gets mentioned, it appears to have briefed them on strategy for upcoming electoral campaigns, presumably without any reference to astrology.

Part 3: The first regular newspaper astrology columns

Although I have not found any examples of *regular* astrological forecasting columns in the US press before 1910, there is, however, one notable exception: a long-running mock-astrological column in the *Scranton Tribune*, Pennsylvania, that was active at least from 15th March 1895.[22] This column promises a 'Daily Horoscope' but is quite evidently satirical in tone, even to the point where the columnist adopts the pseudonym of Ajacchus, identified by my esteemed colleague Christopher Renstrom[23] as a probable knowing corruption of the stock insult 'A Jackass'. The content reads as a tongue-in-cheek pastiche of the whole-life readings for newborn infants that we have previously seen featured in the likes of *Bland's Astrology* (but which may have become far more widespread in the intervening years), and of astrologers' advice in general.

Perhaps the next question we need to ask ourselves having come to that perception is what specifically the *Scranton Tribune* column was satirising? Were there any daily horoscopes in the general press of the 1890s under different names or that are not found in the Library of Congress's open-access digital archives? Or is the satire purely on the predictions for each day found in some popular almanacs or possibly magazine publications of the time? This remains for now an open question pending further research.

Still, it is evident that the editor of the *Scranton Tribune* saw a market for this kind of send-up among its readership, much as we have previously seen the editor of *The Advocate* (Kansas) saw one for his tone of mockery in addressing astrologers' mundane forecasts in 1894. The appearance of the satirical column in the *Scranton Tribune* is also a seeming sign that astrological columns in other publications (whichever they may have been) had begun to be more widely noticed and to attract the derision of sceptical elements of the American public by this stage. And the column in the *Scranton Tribune* must have been a local success, to judge from the fact that it continued to be run on a daily basis at least until May 1902.[24] A seven-year run for an astrological satire that might have come to feel old and stale after the first few days if it had been written in a way that its readers did not find perennially entertaining is no mean feat.[25]

What is also notable, however, is the early use of the specific term *Daily Horoscope* for the purposes of this column. This would appear to have set a trend (if it was not already symptomatic of a pre-existing one, for which hypothesis I have found no evidence to date) for similar headings for a great many other American newspaper astrology columns throughout the early decades of the 20th century. Indeed, such was the momentum built up around this heading that when Sun-sign forecasting proper was introduced, the term *Daily Horoscope* frequently continued to be used in relation to newspaper columns featuring it.

To this haphazard sequence of events we owe much of the confusion that persists to this day in the minds of the general public regarding the meaning of the word 'horoscope'. It was quite simply an established tradition of the American general newspaper press to refer to most or all regular astrology-related columns with elements, real or purported, of astrological forecasting in some connection with the current day, by the label *Daily Horoscope*.

Moreover, analysis of the archives from 1895 onwards shows that the use of the phrase *Daily Horoscope* as a heading for newspaper astrology columns increases in frequency over the period, to the point of becoming extremely widespread by the late 1920s, although the familiar twelve-paragraph Sun sign column format had not yet been widely introduced even then.

A point of particular irony to note here is that the term *Daily Horoscope* actually made sense according to the more proper modern use (if not absolutely the original one as understood in ancient astrology, which was the Ascendant) of the word 'horoscope' to mean 'natal astrological reading' when used in the satirical *Scranton Tribune* column, because even though its readings were all pastiches, they were essentially pastiches of natal horoscopes for those newborn on the date in question and not of current forecasts for the astrological weather affecting all those already living before that date. Could it be from the satirical application of the correct modern use of the word 'horoscope' that the incorrect one abounding today, by a process of corruptive editorial tradition, arose? This certainly seems a credible hypothesis in view of the available evidence.

By January 1910, we find that the use of the term *Daily Horoscope* has already changed in its effective meaning to a forecast for the general astrological weather for the day, as shown in a conserved example from *The Washington Times* for January 17th 1910, penned by a long-forgotten astrologer called Frances Carroll.[26] The very next month, *The Spokane Press* jumped on the trend, with its own similar *Daily Horoscope* feature starting up.[27]

Columns with this name had come to proliferate by 1913. In my research, I have found the following examples by the end of that year of columns that are either called *(The) Daily Horoscope* or at least referred to editorially as a 'Daily Horoscope', showing the earliest and in some cases also the latest-dated issues of each I have been able to access online, which are by no means necessarily at the limits of the true range of dates between which they were published, and should be regarded more as marking their minimum *proven* extents:

- *Daily Horoscope* by Cozette (sic), April 6 – May 14 1907, in the *Fort Worth Telegram*, Fort Worth, Texas; continues thereafter, without credit at head to Cozette, through to July 19th;
- *The Daily Horoscope*, July 20–30, 1907, in *St. Joseph News-Press / Gazette*, St. Joseph, Missouri (text looks identical in essence to format for Fort Worth News above, so perhaps this was syndicated)
- *The Daily Horoscope*, April 02, 1908 – still publishing at end of 1913, in *The Buffalo Times*, New York (appears terse and proverbial at first, but long-running; *McClure Newspaper* starts to be credited above the heading in print in late November 1912; occasionally the name given for the paper is instead *The Buffalo Enquirer*, but the content and format appear identical)
- *The Daily Horoscope* May 08–28, 1908, in *The Province*, Vancouver, British Columbia (content appears identical to that in *The Buffalo Times* on days for which scans of both have been conserved and made available online, e.g., May 28, 1908)
- Daily Horoscope feature, in *The Washington Times*, Washington, DC, January 17, 1910 (the title of the column itself is unclear, but it was first announced that day and referred to generically as a 'Daily Horoscope' feature)
- *Daily Horoscope* in *The Spokane Press*, Spokane, Washington, Feb. 11–21, 1910
- *The Daily Horoscope* in *The Daily Herald*, Port Huron, Michigan, March 08 – August 26, 1910 (content is identical to the *Buffalo Times* feature for the same date)
- *The daily horoscope* in *The Wichita Daily Eagle*, Wichita, Kansas: April 05, 1910 – (appears very brief and terse)
- Daily horoscope feature (title unclear) in *Altoona Times*, Altoona, Pennsylvania, announced as beginning in issue of January 17, 1912
- *The Daily Horoscope* in *The Washington Post*, Washington, DC, June 26 – Dec. 05, 1912
- *(The) Daily Horoscope* in *The Brooklyn Daily Eagle*, Brooklyn, New York, July 03 – October 03, 1912 (content appears identical to that of the *Washington Post* column shown above when scans of both are available for the same date)
- *Daily Horoscope* in *Harrisburg Telegraph*, Harrisburg, Penn. – from Dec. 21, 1912
- *Daily Horoscope* in *The Indianapolis Star* – from January 05, 1913
- *Daily Horoscope* in *The Star Press*, Muncie, Indiana – from January 07, 1913
- *Daily Horoscope* in *Quad-City Times*, Davenport, Iowa – from Feb. 13, 1913
- *Our Daily Horoscope* in *The Times Recorder*, Zanesville, Ohio – announced Feb. 28, 1913; running from at least March 04, 1913
- *The Star's Daily Horoscope* in *The Sacramento Star*, Sacramento, California, from March 10, 1913
- *The Daily Horoscope* in *Alton Evening Telegraph*, Alton, Illinois, from March 15, 1913
- *Daily Horoscope* in *Press and Sun-Bulletin*, Binghamton, New York, from Sept. 06, 1913
- *Daily Horoscope* in *The Capital Journal*, Salem, Oregon, from October 10, 1913

Some of these features show evidence of syndication among multiple regional press outlets, an increasingly common business practice for the sale and distribution of editorial content in the United States in the early 20th century.

By the mid-1910s, such columns were so widespread across the United States that opposing them was no longer merely the preserve of satirists' casual mockery. They had also become a subject of serious concern and discussion among the religious orthodoxy, with a Catholic journal being among the printed fora where articles decrying the genre are to be found.

It would seem plausible that the issuance of mass prognoses and advice from secular quarters was not considered by such religious objectors to be in keeping with either the spirit of the Bible or the Will of God; perhaps it may even have been considered a threat to the practice of sound spiritual counsel given by a priest in conversation with the individual parishioner. But whatever their reasons may be, to this day, over a century later, there remains a bedrock of theologically motivated opponents of newspaper astrology columns and of the wider practice of astrology, finding common cause with the scientific objectors, albeit from a different angle of intellectual attack.

Part 4: Early Solar Degree Area Forecast Columns

In the early 1920s, American newspaper astrological forecasting columns start to edge closer to the modern twelve-Sun-sign format without quite reaching it. By August 1922, the astrologer Marion Meyer Drew had begun to have published by the press monthly forecast columns that differentiated the forecast according to bands of time when the native was born. To begin with, the bands of time to which she refers are a combination of (firstly) calendar date regions in *any* year (which are clearly in effect solar degree areas, so she is forecasting from solar degree regions much as the British astrologers of the late 1880s were with their anniversary forecasts, albeit spread out over a wider band of dates) and (secondly) groups of different dates in multiple separately declared specific years (which would appear to be the result of her attempts to relate a current transit back to the approximate degree position of a natal planet other than the Sun).[28] The second of these practices, while diligent and precise, took up a lot of extra space with printed dates, and may conceivably have been abandoned for editorial reasons rather than for astrological ones.

By 1926, we see the Sun sign taking a more obviously prominent role in some of Drew's forecasts, although her columns are still presented as coherent essays and not divided into twelve paragraphs. This is exemplified in her column in the *Evening Star* (Washington, DC) for February 7th 1926, where she gives a prognostication for the whole of 1926 in general, but significantly if unevenly broken down by Sun sign, although in places still by non-sign-spanning solar degree area.[29] This would seem to mark a further transitional incremental phase towards the introduction of the full Sun-sign forecast column in the United States newspaper press.

However, there is new evidence in the British magazine press that at least one columnist had begun at the very start of 1926 to produce twelve-paragraph Sun-sign columns for a British magazine. Such a column was found by Kim Farnell in *Pam's Paper* magazine in the years since this essay was first completed in 2020. This finding is so important in modifying the proven sequence of developments culminating in the modern Sun-sign column that I felt it historically appropriate and indeed necessary to add in a mention here, while fully crediting her with the discovery.[30] To what degree, if at all, the Sun-sign forecaster writing for *Pam's Paper* in the UK may have either influenced or been influenced by Drew and her similar methods in evidence at about the same time in the US is as yet unascertained.

Another four years on, the American astrologer Sidney Bennett, better known in the press throughout his career by his pen-name of *Wynn*, had become active in his own right as author of a similar regular astrological column to that of Drew, one that was featured in the *New York Daily News*. Bennett was at one point married to Drew, and further historical research is called for to establish a clearer picture and timeline for their influence upon each other in terms of the solar forecasting elements of their respective columns.

In connection with Wynn's column, the *New York Daily News* also carried advertising for a set of 12 booklets penned by Wynn, one for each zodiac sign, promising to tell readers 'the Astrological Influences that are affecting you now, and will affect you in the near future'.[31] The commercial sale of twelve separate booklets with Sun-sign forecasts just for the individual Sun signs they were separately aimed at would appear to mark the final span in the bridge to the adoption of the full Sun-sign forecast column in the United States newspaper press; and Wynn was the astrologer who installed it.

Wynn is identified as the author of these pamphlets in the OCR transcript of a later advertisement in the *New York Daily News* for the same pamphlets, as found in the issue for Monday, February 2nd, 1931, which promises:

> *Twelve booklets, one for each sign of the zodiac, with informative chapters on psychology, health, occupation and matrimony as well as detailed explanation of the astrological influences that are affecting you now and will affect you in the next few years. Written by Wynn, eminent astrologer who*

conducts 'Your Stars Today' in The News; 32 pages, pocket-size; sold at cost, 10¢, as a service to News readers.

On this evidence, it appears quite plausible that detailed forecasts for single Sun signs were for sale in New York before the first twelve-paragraph columns in the US press compressed this commercial format into a regular free feature there.

By the end of 1930, Wynn had also penned his first book, a 96-page publication by the Dell Publishing Company[32] called *Your Future*,[33] which resembles a large newsstand magazine with its dual-columned text and pictorial paper covers. This was clearly meant as a primer of basic astrology for the masses. While the main Sun-sign content is natal, towards the back there is a simple primer of Sun-sign-forecasting methodology headed *Estimating the Future*, in which Wynn explains how transits from the slower-moving outer planets that were recognised and in common use among astrologers by that time, Jupiter, Saturn, Uranus, and Neptune, to the degree of the natal Sun, can indicate transient tendencies in life.[34] Interestingly, in the preface to the book, Wynn indicates that he began to write a magazine astrology column as early as 1919:

> *I was studying Astrology very hard throughout the five years up to 1919, at which time I began to run a regular department for one of our leading magazines, under the title "Your Stars Will Tell, by Wynn".*[35]

On this evidence, it seems credible that he and Drew may in fact have developed their astrological press column careers in parallel rather than his following after her, only his earlier efforts are not directly visible in the digital archives that I consulted while researching for this chapter. Separate Internet evidence records that Wynn wrote a column called *Your Stars Will Tell* for a pulp fiction magazine called *Love Story Magazine* at least between September 19th 1925 and January 24th 1931;[36] and although the magazine is recorded as having been introduced only in May 1921, it seems possible that the timeline of Wynn's account was very approximate and that he might have begun writing for it when it was first launched in 1921, barring the possibility that he first wrote a column with the same name for another magazine as early as 1919.

We cannot be sure of the start-date of Wynn's column in *Love Story Magazine* without having any early issues of it to hand. However, inspection of the scans now held on the Internet Archive for the issues for September 19th 1925 and June 12th 1926 reveals that at this stage, the predictive content was similar in tone to that of the forecasts written by Drew for the United States newspaper press during the 1920s, with brief daily universal forecasts only partially differentiated by ranges of birthdays as a proxy for solar degree areas.

Thus, we can definitively state based on the available evidence that Wynn had not yet adopted a 12-paragraph Sun-sign-forecast column by 1926, unlike his anonymous counterpart writing for *Pam's Paper* in the United Kingdom that year.

Further research is still needed to tie up the loose ends of this provisional summary account of the international origins and transmission of the methodology underpinning the modern Sun-sign forecast column.

Part 5: The first twelve-paragraph Sun sign forecast columns

All the foregoing is intended as background showing the timescale of developments and the momentum towards the regular appearance of the modern Sun-sign forecast format in the general press. Let us move now to the crux of the issue, which is when the first modern Sun-sign forecast columns put down roots.

Kim Farnell, in her pioneering research towards her book *Flirting with the Zodiac*, had previously identified the January 1932 issue of an American general occult magazine entitled *Your Destiny* as the setting for the first appearance of any regular monthly Sun-sign column in the specialist esoteric-interest press.

More recently, she came upon what appears to be a mere incidental aberration, a very early example of a newspaper horoscope column that includes differential potted forecasts for nine of the twelve Sun signs in relation to a particular period of time, though neither they, nor that period of time, are the sole focus of the column. The article in question is dated to July 1904, which is well before even the first non-satirical American newspaper columns commenting on the general astrological weather irrespective of Sun sign sprang up in the 1910s. This discovery would appear for now to be a case of a nearly-formed prototype of the wheel being invented with another purpose in mind well before the invention of the full wheel, and independently of it. Corroborating evidence would be needed for before it could be linked causally or in any other way to the much later general movement towards newspapers and magazines running twelve-paragraph-format Sun sign forecasts.[37]

The column in question is penned by an astrologer who is almost entirely unknown today, James Clyde Wallace. No astrological books in his name have come down to us, and he would seem to be a good example of the existence, beneath the body of known public astrologers who have put their names to books throughout recorded history, of an underbelly of astrologers hidden to history, some of whom may have contributed articles or simply letters to the press, while many others had private practices without being engaged in any kind of public discourse on the subject. In this case, it would appear from my archival searches to date that Wallace had cultivated for himself a public profile through the popular press as a celebrity psychic and clairvoyant in the very early 1900s, but had added astrology as a string to his bow, perhaps as something of an afterthought.

Wallace's column appears in the *Daily Oklahoman* for July 3rd, 1904. It is headed *An Astrological Horoscope and Predictions From the Ephemeris of 1904 and 1905*. After a preamble referring to Wallace's past predictions in the British and American press and defending the status of astrology as an 'exact science', the column continues with a general forecast of the conditions for late 1904 and the whole of 1905.

It is within this discussion, under the subheading *Better in September*, that Wallace moves to differentiate between what nine of the twelve Sun signs will experience from September to December 1904. The signs covered are Taurus to Capricorn inclusive, to the notable exclusion of Aries, Aquarius, and Pisces. It is not clear whether the other signs were excluded because of an editorial decision to chop them owing to a shortage of space (as seems possible in view of the included signs being consecutive ones), or whether Wallace simply did not feel he had anything relevant or important to say about them in this particular astrological predictive context.

Just one or two short sentences are given over to each Sun sign, and the description is very general. For instance:

> *All Leo persons will find the coming three months disastrous. October brings favourable influences for success.*

Although this is not yet a full Sun sign column, it does show that as early as 1904, occasional astrologers were already practising a form of Sun-sign forecasting that was general to the whole sign, and not specific to the individual solar degrees, as were the anniversary horoscope features previously seen in the British astrological press during the late 1880s.

Nonetheless, as yet no evidence has been uncovered to suggest that Wallace's differential predictions in this column of 1904 set or followed a wider trend in his day. Indeed, we have to wait until the early 1920s before we next see concrete evidence of differential predictions by Sun sign from the pen of Marion Meyer

Drew; but even these are not regular twelve-paragraph Sun sign forecast columns.

Nay, to date, Farnell's recent discovery of a twelve-paragraph column that ran in *Pam's Paper* magazine throughout 1926 remains the earliest example uncovered in any territory or context; and the one she previously discovered in *Your Destiny* in 1931 remains the earliest one found in the United States, though there is an open question pending future evidence as to whether there may have been others there beforehand that have not yet been identified.

Subsequent to the launch of the column in *Your Destiny*, the astrologer Paul Clancy was a significant mover in perpetuating the format within the specialist esoteric periodical press – most famously in the pages of the very long-running pulp newsstand astrological magazine *American Astrology*, which he edited from its launch in May 1933 until his death just over 20 years later, but which would remain in print ultimately until March 2003.

Having previously come across Clancy's extensive monthly Sun-sign forecast column within the pages of the issue of his second short-lived astrological magazine *Popular Astrology* for June 1932,[38] in 2016 I decided to follow up my curiosity regarding how far back in time this went by contacting Kris Riske at the headquarters of the American Federation of Astrologers in Tempe, Arizona, home to one of the best-stocked astrological libraries in the United States and even the world. Knowing that before *Popular Astrology*, Clancy had edited another magazine called *Astrological Bulletin*, I asked Riske that summer if she wouldn't mind checking the AFA library to see if it was present and whether and when Sun sign forecast columns had begun in it. She very kindly took the time to do so, and identified the first appearance of a Sun sign forecasting column in one of Clancy's magazines as being the issue of *Astrological Bulletin* for February 1932 – which is to say, the very month after the issue of *Your Destiny* already uncovered by Farnell.

In light of the relatively long lead times towards the publication of monthly magazines, it struck me as being most unlikely that Clancy would have had time to directly copy the format from a magazine whose nominal publication date was only a month earlier, raising the open question of a common source for both.

Whatever and whoever may have inspired him (and perhaps it was none other than the obvious candidate of Wynn, whose dedicated booklet-form year-ahead forecasts for each of the Sun signs, as we have already seen, were on sale to great fanfare at the end of 1930), with Clancy's successive dedicated astrological magazine publications gradually reaching a wider and wider audience on the ing, but whatever you commence at this time is likely to terminate in a battle royal. A violent conflict or other form of violence in your home might tend to wreck your domestic environment. Guard against accidents at your place of residence, also you may find yourself forced into close contact with some person (a man) who is very stubborn, contentious and most difficult to deal with or avoid. Mars in your fourth house in an intruder and an unwelcome guest. There is a tendency on the part of these opposed to you to carry the war right into your camp. Thus during the earlier part of June, we expect to find you on the defensive, meeting an aggressive attack — successfully, Later, in the month (after June 21st) you may expect to take command of the situation and force your affairs through to a successful conclusion. During the period that Saturn is transiting the natal position of your Sun (Saturn will be effective in your sign 1932, 1933, 1934). Some special tragedy or sorrow or unhappiness may touch your life through a personal loss of some kind, also this is a danger to your health and threatens your personal safety. The month of May and first three weeks of June 1932 is one of the periods when this influence is likely to be especially powerful. Under this influence in your personal attitude toward life, you are inclined to be implacable, unyielding and icily indifferent, cold as an Arctic winter and just as dark, mysterious and silent. A stubborn unyielding attitude constitutes a danger to you personally. It is not advisable to tempt Fate when directly under the ray of Saturn and especially is this true of a time when Saturn is in turn afflicted by Mars, as it is during May and the early part of this present month of June. The secret of success under this Saturn influence is "intelligent non-resistance". Guard your health at this time by taking special measures to see that the eliminative system is functioning properly. Later in June (after the 21st), these afflictions disappear for a time. Your health conditions and general circumstances undergo marked improvement. Any opposition to your personal plans which you may have previously experienced may be expected to fade away, and when you previously found powerful opposition, you may expect to find equally powerful, energetic and aggressive support. Therefore, it would be advisable to postpone important affairs until after June 21st., when victory in the battles of life may be confidently expected.

PISCES
February 20 to March 20

From June 3rd, to 16th, a garrulous gossipy Mercury in your domestic environment seems to threaten danger in a legal entanglement of some kind. This could be over a personal matter or through some business matter involving real estate. This is an unfavorable month to start legal proceedings of any kind, for dealings with lawyers, Courts of Law, for signing papers or for making domestic changes.

Mercury in the fourth department of your Solar Chart indicates that for the time, your field of activity will be of a Mercurial tone, highly intellectual or commercial bringing you into close personal contact with things and people of the above nature, or some such person may enter your place of residence for some special reason. This, also, indicates worry about domestic matters. Possibly some special problem involving the parents or parental home, and there may be a journey on this account. Family affairs will be the subject of free discussion by yourself and by others, but there is a warning in this square to Neptune. It would be advisable to avoid arguments and do not discuss your domestic affairs with strangers, some of this information is likely to be used against you in a manner that you little dream of, at the time, for Neptune, symbol of your outer social environment influences contacts and partnerships and legal advises during the next few years—is very subtle, oft times quite deceitful and treacherous. Use care in your social affairs and particularly such as involve your domestic life just at this time. A visitor to your home is a very interesting character but he has an axe to grind with some other person, and if you get mixed up in it, much discredit is likely to be your reward.

From June 16th to the end of the month, Mercury will be friendly to you and will conjoin Venus in your department governing pleasure and affairs of the heart and may bring you home special happiness through correspondence of a pleasant nature or with someone linked to you by the ties of affection. For those eligible for such, a proposal of marriage would be in order during this period, if such should be received, it may be favorably considered. Venus in your department during the entire summer (up to September 1st), promises quite a happy, emotional period, generally speaking, and especially during these last two weeks of June. This is, also, quite a favorable time for a pleasure trip.

This is not a time however, for favorable influences for speculative investments or for any matter that tends to combine pleasure with business, tho a fortunate change of residence may be made.

Briefly, June is during the first half, distinctly adverse for positive action of any kind, for those born in Pisces, but the last half of the month appears to be unusually fortunate.

Paul Clancy's detailed Sun sign column in Popular Astrology, June 1932, final page.

newsstands, could it be that his was the pivotal influence that eventually drew the general American newspaper press to copy the format?

Whether they may have been prompted by the example set by Clancy or that set by Wynn, or even that of whichever astrologer may have written for *Your Destiny*, the available evidence from digital archive searches strongly suggests that twelve-paragraph-format Sun sign forecasting columns did not take root in United States newspapers before January 1935.

Part 6: The first Sun-sign forecasting in the UK press

Geoffrey Dean and Arthur Mather have identified that another early British media astrologer after Naylor, Edward Lyndoe, began his first column in a weekly British newspaper called *The People* in October 1933 – which is a year and eight months after the first known appearance of Clancy's first modern Sun-sign forecast column, but almost eight years after the first one in *Pam's Paper*. They report that the content of Lyndoe's column, named *Plan with the Planets*, comprised a mixture of political forecasts, year-ahead forecasts for those with birthdays coming up in the next week, and personal forecasts for the upcoming week for those born within the date ranges of each of the twelve Sun signs, but without the Sun signs being named. In the absence of direct access to the source text, but presuming Dean and Mather's account to be accurate, Lyndoe is the first known astrologer to have adopted Sun sign forecasting as a part (though not the whole) of his column in the British newspaper press, predating R. H. Naylor by years on that score. Dean and Mather add that the names of the Sun signs were briefly added to the personal forecasting part of Lyndoe's column in May 1935 but discontinued not long afterwards, reading this as an indication that the British mass-market readership was not ready for the names of the Sun signs though it enjoyed reading the forecasts by date.[39]

But where did Lyndoe, as the first known British astrologer to adopt Sun sign forecasting as part of a newspaper column, get his idea for it, given that neither Naylor nor any other astrologer writing for the British newspaper press that we have thus far been able to identify had been practising the same methods within that context? One possibility would be that Lyndoe had come across either the column in *Pam's Paper*, or a similar one in another British magazine, and had taken after its methods. It also seems conceivable or even highly plausible that Lyndoe would have had access to early issues of Clancy's third and most successful monthly magazine, *American Astrology*, by the time he began his column, thanks to the well-established trail of international distribution for specialised astrological magazines on the occult and esoteric bookselling network, with word of mouth in the community and advertising also being factors that helped to spread news of new magazines in the field far beyond national borders, so the fact that Clancy's publications were produced on the other side of the Atlantic seems unlikely to have posed a major obstacle to examples coming before Lyndoe's gaze by the time he produced his first column of this nature. It is also remotely possible that Lyndoe would have come across some of Wynn's earlier forecasts, although any hypothesised distribution trail for these outside the USA seems more tenuous because Wynn's own monthly astrological magazine, which he launched in August 1931, did not attain nearly such a large-scale distribution, especially in its early years, as American Astrology did from the outset.

Part 7: The true role of R. H. Naylor in the history of newspaper astrology

As mentioned above, Richard Harold Naylor (1889–1952) does not feature among the pioneers of newspaper Sun-sign forecasting by any reckoning. He was predated in the practice not only by multiple American newspaper and magazine astrologers, but also by a fellow writer for the British press in the form of Edward Lyndoe and at least one British magazine columnist.

If you have previously come across received ideas on the origins of the Sun-sign column, you may very reasonably be wondering at this stage how those inaccurate received ideas may have arisen. Certainly there is no available evidence to suggest that Naylor was one of the pioneers of Sun-sign forecasting and ample evidence that he was not, so the very idea long crystallised in astrologers' minds that he was *the* pioneer of the genre may now be declared a wholly discredited myth.

Farnell has herself found no evidence of Sun-sign forecasts by Naylor before 1936, when according to her research he was writing for the British popular occult monthly magazine *Prediction* that had then just recently been launched. This is over five years after the first of those forecasts by Wynn for which I have found firm evidence, four years after the first by Clancy, and even three years after the first partial ones by Lyndoe.

Naylor's history is, however, a little more complicated than this. As so often with inaccurate historical narratives, behind the myth lies a kernel of truth that has been distorted over time.

In August 1930, Lyndoe was invited by the editor of the *Sunday Express*,

John Gordon, to write an article for the same newspaper about the birth of Princess Margaret, and did so. This took the form of a proper individual natal horoscope reading for the newborn princess. So it was far removed from Sun-sign forecasting or indeed from the daily-astrological-weather-type newspaper columns that had abounded in the United States for more than 20 years already by that stage.

A feature on the birth of a child to a prominent public figure in the national press was also nothing new generically, as we have previously seen in the example of the natal delineation for President Cleveland's second daughter in the US press in 1893. And yet, Naylor's article about Princess Margaret proved so popular with the British public, which typically attached great sentimental importance to its Royals, that Naylor had soon been invited by Gordon to contribute a regular astrological column to his newspaper.

Spurred on by demand arising from the popularity of his newspaper column, in 1932 Naylor also began to pen an almanac featuring a combination of mundane and personal forecasts. This appears from British Library records to have run for all years from 1933 to 1950, and again for 1954. The very first issue is to hand, and seems the most relevant to consider in evidence for his early forecasting work.

In the inaugural edition of Naylor's annual *Naylor's Year Book*, for 1933, Naylor loudly proclaims the magnitude of his own status as an influence in the first chapter, which is dated to September 1932, declaring that:

> My weekly article 'What the Stars Foretell' is now in its third consecutive year in one of the leading London Sunday newspapers. It is not too much to say that so far as the general public are concerned, those articles have entirely revolutionized the popular conception of Astrology. Week by week have appeared therein predictions which in eight cases out of ten have actually materialized. On my files are tens of thousands of letters from readers who have been impressed by the accurate way in which the Birthday Predictions have applied to their particular cases. Lastly (as imitation is the sincerest form of flattery) many periodicals are running astrological features.[40]

From his own testimony, as well as from established secondary accounts, it would appear that Naylor's *Sunday Express* column combined political or similar mundane forecasts for the world with solar degree-based whole-year forecasts for individuals born on particular dates in the period ahead. The latter type of content is a form of solar forecasting but it is not a Sun-sign column, and it had been done before in the UK, as we have already seen, much earlier, indeed as early as the late 1880s, by both P. Powley and R. Bland, in their dedicated British astrological magazines.

What Naylor offered was not in any way novel. But thanks to the forum in which it was published, it got noticed far more widely than previous examples, both by the public living at the time and by historians reviewing the modern history of astrology since, to the extent of generating the illusory abiding popular myth that he was a pioneer in ways that are simply not true.

Further, in spite of the high public profile afforded by his newspaper articles, Naylor does not rank as one of the more notable published astrological writers of the 20th century. His corpus of astrological text-books is limited to a couple of simple, superficial books aimed at members of the general public having no particular intellectual aptitude for learning even basic astrology, rather than at the serious novice student of astrology; and they appear seriously lacking in depth, substance, and structure compared with the beginner-oriented astrological text-books of the major contemporaneous British astrologers. One of Naylor's mass-market books that is still common today, *Home Astrology*, was published in 1933, and later reproduced with other material in a volume entitled *The R. H. Naylor Omnibus*. Naylor was a charismatic journalist and a successful self-publicist, and may even have been a competent astrological forecaster, but the primary evidence in the form of the contents of his own books strongly suggests that he was not an outstanding astrological writer or teacher.

In Chapter V of his *Year Book for 1933*,[41] we find that Naylor offers more extensive individual forecasts for the whole year ahead than he would have had space for in his newspaper column. These are divided not by solar degree, nor by whole Sun sign, but into thirty-six groups of calendar dates spanning ten days each, thus in effect by solar decan, though with the date spans starting mid-decan, e.g., Dec. 26th to Jan. 5th, equivalent to approximately 5°–15° Capricorn; and Jan. 16th to 25th, equivalent to approximately 25° Capricorn to 5° Aquarius.

This sign-boundary-traversing degree-related methodology does not differ significantly in spirit from the arbitrary working differentiations employed by Marion Drew for her forecasts in her newspaper column back in the 1920s; and while it certainly doesn't qualify as true Sun-sign forecasting, it *is* solar forecasting of a sort, and extensive at that; and it is clear that Naylor must have written the content in late 1932, almost a year before Lyndoe began his first column with Sun-sign forecasting content in it. So in this one respect, Naylor might lay claim to have had Sun-based astrological forecasts published in Great Britain before Lyndoe first did. But neither is it whole Sun-sign forecasting, nor did it appear in the press; and on both of those scores, Lyndoe predated Naylor.

Naylor's first known solar forecasting material is in any case still significantly later than the Sun-sign forecasts proper produced by Wynn in 1930 as well as those in *Pam's Paper* in 1926 and in both *Your Destiny* magazine and *Astrological Bulletin* early in 1932.

Prediction aside, its short-lived weekly sister publication in the Link House publishing stable, *The Weekly Horoscope*,[42] unleashed a lengthy Sun-sign forecast column from its very first issue, that of September 18, 1937.[43] This was initially penned by Colin Bennett.[44] The equivalent of a dense whole column of text within this large-format publication is given over to detailed forecasts for each and every Sun sign in the coming week. This shows that by this point, the art of the Sun-sign-forecast column was well-established, and indeed had gone into overdrive. By later standards, the amount of writing on each Sun sign in *The Weekly Horoscope* to cover the period of just a week appears extraordinary and excessive. But it is strong testimony to the popular art of Sun-sign forecasting having attained a wide audience in the mass marketplace in the UK by 1937. And it is conceivable that the influence exerted by Naylor through the mainstream newspaper press upon the British public at large in the domain of its interest in astrological forecasts may indeed have helped to create a public demand and appetite for writing of this character, even though it was not exactly what he did in his column, at least not in his first five years as a newspaper columnist writing on astrology.

Conclusion

The true history of the origins of the modern Sun-sign forecast column is a remarkably complex, tangled, and messy web of strands to unpick. The invention of the format owes to a wide range of influences with roots in both the popular forecasting content found within the specialist British astrological magazines of the late 19th century and the dramatic rise in popularity of astrology in the United States in the same period.

It was arguably only when the US press began running its regular daily horoscope columns in the early 1910s that the pathway to the invention of the Sun-sign forecast column was fully cleared; and it took several incremental developments from there to its final staggered international realisation between the mid-1920s and the mid-1930s.

Marion Meyer Drew, Sidney K. Bennett (Wynn), and Paul Clancy rank foremost among the known astrologers who saw to the creation and perpetuation of the format, all of them Americans, with the unidentified writers of the 1926 column in *Pam's Paper* and the January 1932 column in *Your Destiny* magazine also playing important supporting roles, and Edward Lyndoe serving as a bridge to its mainstream adoption in the United Kingdom.

Richard Naylor does not even figure among the true pioneers of Sun-sign forecasting, though he did help newspaper astrology columns to become popular in the UK starting in the early 1930s and introduced a solar forecasting element to popular almanacs from 1933 onwards.

Dane Rudhyar played no role as a pioneer of either Sun-sign forecasting or newspaper astrology, though his articles for Clancy's successive astrological magazines did support their long-term success by adding a level of philosophical and psychological depth that they might otherwise have lacked.

Endnotes

[1] Kim Farnell, *Flirting with the Zodiac: A True History of Sun Sign Astrology* (Bournemouth: Wessex Astrologer, 2007).

[2] I have previously explored this point in detail in my article 'Five Myths on Modern Astrology Reviewed' (2016; expanded version in *Infinity Astrological Magazine*, May / June 2019, with further revision forthcoming in the second volume in my 'Studies in the History of Astrology' series with Revelore Press), q. v. – see *Myth 5: Dane Rudhyar originated Sun sign forecast columns in the 1930s by giving the idea for them to Paul Clancy*.

[3] See fuller account in Philip Graves, *A Brief History of Astrological Journals Part 3: 1860– 1886* (forthcoming in Volume 3 of my 'Studies in the History of Astrology' series with Revelore Press).

[4] *The Astrologer. Composed of 12 Monthly Parts Treating on the Science of Astrology, Medical Botany, etc. – Contains Lessons on the Science, Comments and Remarks by Various Authors, Household and Medical Recipes, Birthday Information, Letters from Correspondents, together with a Fund of Useful and Valuable Information, much of which cannot be found in any other Work* (London: W. Foulsham, July 1887 to June 1890).

[5] *Bland's 'Astrology', with Supplement* (London: Foulsham / Hull: R. Bland, February 9th to April 20th, 1889).

[6] No holdings of this publication are found in Worldcat, and survivals are very scarce, but a ragged original printing of the edition for July 1905 surfaced on an online auction website in 2024. This was just four pages long and was indicated as Number 245, suggesting that it had been in publication for about 20 years of mostly monthly issues by that time. It was perhaps distributed mainly locally within the Boston area. The editor of *The Prognostic Stargazer* is named in a separate article in *The Argus* (Albany, NY, July 15th, 1888) as a Thomas A. Bearse.

7   Esther Cleveland, September 9, 1893 – June 25, 1980 – though she is not named, being merely referred to as 'Baby Ruth's sister', Ruth having been President Cleveland's first daughter.
8   This unknown Prof. Leonis has not left any books or periodicals in his name and is presumed to be one of the many less historically visible practising astrologers who did not produce such a body of written work for posterity. No mention of him is found in the late James Herschel Holden's authoritative *Biographical Dictionary of Western Astrologers* either. In 1887, scandal had attended the high-profile case of an astrologer named John de Leon, known to L. D. Broughton. De Leon had been convicted of conspiring to induce very young women or teenage girls to move to Panama to get work only for their true employment there to turn out to take the form of what was euphemistically referred to in the press as 'immoral purposes'. De Leon was sentenced to 15 years in jail, however, so Prof. Leonis must have been an altogether different astrologer in spite of the common element to his chosen name.
9   The astrologer is not named and could therefore be anyone, though it is appealing to think based on the description that it might possibly be L. D. Broughton.
10 Also of Salt Lake City – not to be confused with the national British newspaper of the same name.
11 From the context, this should be read as referring to trading operations and not surgical operations.
12 It is a pity for the historical record that Connelly has not named the publications to which he refers. There are not known to have been any dedicated astrological periodicals in either France or Germany as early as 1891, though there were multiple mixed occult-interest periodicals in France, and it may be to publications of this kind that he is referring here. Similarly, in the United States, only *Signs of the Times* and *The Prognostic Star-Gazer* are known to have been active at this time, and it would be interesting to know which other publication he may have had in mind here.
13 A misspelling of the surname of British astrologer [A. J.] Pearce.
14 The identity of this Goold is not entirely clear, but given the subsequent contextual discussion it is probably a mis-spelling for Gould, the publisher of a new edition of James Wilson's *Dictionary of Astrology* at Boston in 1885.
15 Wilson's *Dictionary of Astrology*, originally published in England in 1819, was first published in the United States by A.H. Roffe & Co. at Boston, Mass., in 1885, in an edition prepared by Oliver Ames Goold. Wilson is notable for his acerbic and critical writing upon some of the concepts of the astrologers of the past, including Ptolemy. No tradition was sacred to him if it flew in the face of his sense of reason.
16 [sic] – i.e., Ptolemy.
17 [sic] – i.e., Ebenezer Sibly.
18 Although she is credited by name in only one of these two publications, the content is identical so it is clearly her work in both. It seems to have been much more common

practice in the press at this time than it has since become for the authors of individual articles not to be credited by name.

[19] *Sub Rosa*: in secret. Literally, under the rose – a reference to the rose's traditional association with secrecy in ancient Roman times. Roses are said to have been placed on the ceilings of Roman dining-rooms to remind those present to keep secret anything discussed around the dinner table. See p. 112 of Eugene Ehrlich, *Nil Desperandum: A Dictionary of Latin Tags and Phrases* (Guild Publishing, 1986; after the original Robert Hale edition of 1985).

[20] This 'high priestess' is not named. A probable candidate in view of her known connections to both cities and prominence in astrology as a stock market forecaster by the late 1890s would be Catharine Thompson, the eventual editor of *The Sphinx* magazine published at Boston starting in September 1899. Evangeline Adams also had connections to both cities later in her life but was only 24 years of age at this time, did not move to New York until later in the 1890s, and was not sufficiently well-established in 1894 to command such high fees – see Karen Christino, *Forseeing the Future* (2002), p. 55 – so she is not at all a plausible candidate for the identity of the said *high priestess*. Eleanor Kirk was a well-established astrologer in New York and might be considered an outside possibility, and Ellen Bennett was close to attaining prominence, but Catharine Thompson seems overall to be the most likely candidate among woman astrologers with connections to New York who are known to history today.

[21] In reality this seems sure to be Thomas Lister, an émigré from England to the US in the 1840s or earlier. He was known by L. D. Broughton and has been recorded as settling in New York. Lister had become a national celebrity in the 1860s in connection with his having cast a horoscope for President Abraham Lincoln in advance of Lincoln's assassination on April 15th, 1865. According to the testimony of Lister's ex-wife after his death, as reported in *The Argus* (Albany, NY, July 15th, 1888), which gives his name instead as Lester, Lister's horoscope for Lincoln had included an instruction to 'beware of the 14th of April, and to avoid firearms'. She also testifies that he sent the horoscope to Lincoln in advance of his death. See also entry on Lister in James Herschel Holden, *A Biographical Dictionary of Western Astrologers* (2013), p. 450.

[22] See example at https://chroniclingamerica.loc.gov/lccn/sn84026355/1895-03-15/ed-1/seq-4/

[23] A prominent contemporary American astrologer who is also a dedicated historian of the early history of astrology in the United States.

[24] See further example published on May 10th, 1902, shown in the middle of the third column of p. 4 as scanned at https://chroniclingamerica.loc.gov/lccn/sn84026355/1902-05-10/ed-1/seq-4/

[25] A century later, the Scranton Tribune column would find a parallel in a spoof horoscope feature credited to Psychic Psmith in the *Sunday Telegraph*, which sent up Sun-sign forecast columns using the comic device of absurd levels of pretended

specific precision in concrete forecasting for each of the Sun signs. This also ran for several years and is presumed to have appealed to the more reactionary elements of the politically Conservative and culturally conservative newspaper's audience, for whom having a good old laugh at the expense of the irrational beliefs of the ill-educated, stupid commoners (according to their perceptions) was meat and drink.

[26] See article headed 'Daily Horoscope is Started for Delvers into the Occult' at https://chroniclingamerica.loc.gov/lccn/sn84026749/1910-01-17/ed-1/seq-10/

[27] See article headed 'Will Tomorrow Be Lucky For You?' at https://chroniclingamerica.loc.gov/lccn/sn88085947/1910-02-11/ed-2/seq-1/

[28] See for example Drew's forecast in the Evening Star (Washington, DC) for August 13th, 1922, column headed 'Saturn's Power in August to bring Earthly Sorrow, Astrologer Says' at https://chroniclingamerica.loc.gov/lccn/sn83045462/1922-08-13/ed-1/seq-53

[29] See scan of article headed 'Lucky and Unlucky Birthdays for 1926, According to Astrology of Ancients', as conserved at https://chroniclingamerica.loc.gov/lccn/sn83045362/1926-02-07/ed-1/seq-74/

[30] The earliest instalment of this Sun-sign-forecast column that Farnell has documented is 'Will January Bring You Luck?' in *Pam's Paper* (January 1926): pp. 18–19.

[31] A low-resolution thumbnail of the advertisement for these brochures in the *New York Daily News* for December 19th, 1930, with integral photographic image of the booklet for Capricorn and list of the twelve Sun signs (visible in outline) in a column on the right side of the advertisement, is free to view at https://img.newspapers.com/img/thumbnail/413588106/200/290/0_0_3611_4681.jpg

[32] The Dell Publishing Company did not launch its long-running magazine *Horoscope* for another five years until October 1935, so *Your Future* was truly a one-off publication within its genre at the time for this publisher.

[33] Wynn, *Your Future: a Guide to Modern Astrology* (New York: Dell Publishing, internally undated, but integral five-year ephemeris for 'the coming five years' spans 1931 to 1935, and this combined with internal advertising for another magazine first published in 1930 show probable publication date as late 1930 or very early 1931).

[34] Ibid., pp. 92–94. Pluto had only just been discovered earlier that year, and Wynn was apparently in no hurry to force it into his working methods.

[35] Ibid., p. 4.

[36] See entry for Wynn on this page: http://www.philsp.com/homeville/fmi/s/s8910.htm#A230717

[37] Kim Farnell informs the author that her research into this is still ongoing in 2024, so we may yet expect the announcement of further important discoveries from her in the future.

[38] *Popular Astrology and Astrological Bulletin* Vol. 2, No. 1 (June, 1932).

[39] See their account at http://www.astrology-and-science.com/s-hist2.htm, which has been expanded from an article first published in *The Astrological Journal* (May-June

1996): pp. 143–55. There are some historical inaccuracies elsewhere in the article, which should not be taken as entirely reliable. In particular, it should be pointed out that the claim made in this article by Dean and Mather to the effect that that the first astrology column of *any* character in the US press appeared in 1931 in *The Boston Record* is, as can clearly be seen by all the references to earlier ones elsewhere in my study of the topic, unambivalently false, and would appear to be a discredited historical meme that formerly helped prop up the now long-disproven Naylor-first narrative before today's 21st-century online research facilities allowed researchers outside the United States to access scans of early-20th-century American newspapers.

40 *Naylor's Year Book: A delineation of What the Stars Foretell for 1933* (Hutchinson & Co., 1933), p. 23.

41 *Ibid.*, pp. 130–205.

42 *The Weekly Horoscope*, edited by a pseudonymous Orion (whose true identity is unknown and seems unlikely to be in any way connected to the last of the former editors of the by then long-defunct *Orion's Almanac*), lasted for only 39 weekly issues from September 11, 1937 to June 4, 1938 before being subsumed within *Prediction*.

43 *The Weekly Horoscope*, No. 1 (September 18, 1937): pp. 36–39.

44 Nowadays little-remembered British astrologer who left us a short beginner-oriented book entitled *What Is Astrology?* (Rider, [1935]).

Chapter Five
The Earliest Astrological Conceptualisations of the planet Uranus, 1781–1839

When was Uranus first discovered?

The planet Uranus is widely acknowledged as having first been discovered by the astronomer William Herschel[1] in 1781,[2] although he was not the first to recognise its status as a planet. He initially observed it through a telescope at his residence in the city of Bath, England, on the night of March 13th, 1781, and presumed it to be a comet.

Herschel's tentative discovery then came under the scrutiny of senior astronomers, among whom the Astronomer Royal based at Greenwich, Nevil Maskelyne (1732–1811), was the first to suggest based upon its apparent motion that it was more likely to be a planet than a comet.[3] A succession of others, notably including French astronomer Jean-Baptiste Gaspard Bouchart de Saron (1730–1794) and mathematics professor Anders Lexell (1740–1784), concurred with Maskelyne after undertaking their own studies.[4] Writing in or soon after July 1781 in the *Berliner Jahrbuch*, Johann Elert Bode (1747–1826), who was based at the Berlin Observatory, formally declared Herschel's discovery to be that of a planet.[5] Only in November, on the occasion of being awarded a medal by the Royal Society for his discovery, did Herschel himself admit that he had probably been mistaken in judging the object to be a comet.[6]

The historian René Bourtembourg has recently presented evidence indicating that the planet was first observed in ancient times by the astronomer Hipparchus but mistaken for a star, and that this observation was subsequently incorporated into Ptolemy's star catalogue, the *Almagest*, which also identified the planet as a star in the constellation Virgo.[7]

In 1985, D.C. Wright recorded that there were 22 further sightings of Uranus between 1690 and 1771 by the astronomers John Flamsteed[8] (in 1690), Pierre Charles Le Monnier[9] (from 1750 to 1769), James Bradley[10] (in 1748 and 1750) and Tobias Mayer[11] (in 1756).[12] The main source for Wright's report is a book by A. F. O'Donel Alexander, *The Planet Uranus: A History of Observation, Theory and Discovery* (1965). It is also worth noting that the existence of an outer planet plotting an extra-Saturnian orbit around the Sun was anticipated by some astronomers before the discovery of Uranus. James Wilson records both [Edmond] Halley[13] and Bradley as being among them.[14]

How and when did Uranus come by its name?

Uranus was not commonly called *Uranus* in the 70 years after its discovery. Herschel himself named it *Georgium sidus* (Latin for 'star of George') in honour of King George III; but this proposal did not meet with widespread approval outside Britain; and until the mid-19th century, it was more widely referred to as *Herschel* after its discoverer, on the suggestion of Jérôme Lalande,[15] who is also credited with proposing its abiding astrological glyph as early as 1784.

The name Uranus was first suggested by the astronomer Johann Bode[16] in an essay he read before a local scientific research society on March 12th, 1782. In his book *Von dem neu entdeckten Planeten* (Berlin, 1784), Bode recalls this and goes on to argue at length for the name, primarily on the grounds that he believes it is necessary to follow the mythology after which the ancient names of the other planets were taken, and that it would be conspicuous and anomalous in the context of this tradition to name a planet after a recent person or event (the implication of which is that the names Georgium Sidus and Herschel are equally inappropriate).

In ancient mythology, argues Bode at length, Uranus was the father of Kronos or Cronus (Saturn) and the grandfather of Zeus (Jupiter); its name is therefore appropriate for the next outer planet after Jupiter and Saturn in terms of the succession of their average orbital distance from the Sun:

> *Bereits in der am 12ten März 1782 bei der hiesigen naturforschenden Gesellschaft vorgelesenen Abhandlung, habe ich den Namen des Vaters vom Saturn, nemlich* Uranos, *oder wie er mit der lateinischen Endung gewöhnlicher ist,* Uranus *vorgeschlagen, und habe seit dem das Vergnügen gehabt, daß verschiedene Astronomen und Mathematiker in ihren Schriften oder in Briefen an mich, diese Benennung aufgenommen oder gebilligt. Meines Erachtens muß man bei dieser Wahl die Mythologie befolgen, aus welcher die uralten Namen der übrigen Planeten entlehnet worden; denn in der Reihe der bisher bekannten, würde der von einer merkwürdigen Person oder Begebenheit der neuern Zeit hergenommene Name eines Planeten sehr auffallen. Diodor von Cicilien erzählt die Geschichte der Atlanten, eines uralten Volks, welches eine der fruchtbarsten Gegenden in Africa bewohnte, und die Meeresküsten seines Landes als das Vaterland der Götter ansah. Uranus war ihr erster*

König, Stifter ihres gesittetern Lebens und Erfinder vieler nützlichen Künste. Zugleich wird er auch als ein fleißiger und geschickter Himmelsforscher des Alterthums beschrieben; er entdeckte zuerst die nähern Umstände der Fortrückungen der Himmelskörper, bestimmte die Länge des Jahres nach dem Umlauf der Sonne und theilte die Monate nach dem Mondlauf ab. Seiner astronomische Vorhersagungen und seine Verdienste um die bürgerliche Gesellschaft erwarben ihn die größte Hochachtung seines Volks; es glaubte in ihm mehr als einen Menschen zu sehen, er wurde nach seinem Tode vergörtert, und der höchste Theil des Universums, der Himmel, nach seinem Namen genennet.... Noch mehr: Uranus war der Vater des Saturns und des Atlas, so wie der erstere der Vater des Jupiters. Hiernach entlehnten die drei entferntesten und hinter einander folgenden obern Planeten, Jupiter, Saturnus und Uranus ihre Namen gerade von drei zunächst vor einander hergehenden Personen der ältesten Mythologie, und der Planet Uranus, entzöge sich in den Räumen des Himmels unsern Augen fast auf eine ähnliche Art, wie die Geschichte desjenigen, von dem er den Namen führt, sich in jene dunkele Zeiten der fabelhaften Vorwelt verliert, da nach die Götter oder vielmehr die Atlantier den Erdboden beherrschten.[17]

Bode is additionally arguing here that the name Uranus is appropriate because the first King of the Atlases bore the name Uranus and was reputed as a skilled astronomer as well as giving his name to the sky, and that there is a meaningful parallel between the previous failure of astronomers through the ages to identify the planet Uranus and a myth connected with the ancient King Uranus being lost in dark times. Although he was an 18th-century astronomer, Bode's arguments by mythological analogy have a ring that is remarkably familiar from those of astrologers of the 20th century seeking to determine the influence of newly discovered celestial bodies such as Pluto.

However, the name *Uranus* was not officially accepted in Britain until 1850, when it replaced *Georgium Sidus* as the name used by Her Majesty's Nautical Almanac Office, 30 years after the death of King George III and 20 years after that of his successor George IV.

Before then, as we shall go on to see, a transliteration of the ancient Greek equivalent of the name *Uranus*, as *Ouranos*, was occasionally used by British astrologers.

How did astrologers react to the discovery of Uranus?

In the decades immediately following the discovery of Uranus, there was a revival in the publishing of astrological textbooks in England after half a century in which almost nothing more substantial or permanent than almanacs appeared.

For the purposes of researching for this chapter, I have searched the OCR layers of scans I previously took of original printings of numerous books and several magazines published over the 55-year period spanning 1784 to 1839 for references to *Georgium Sidus, Herschel, Uranus* and *new planet*, in order to track the development of thinking related to Herschel's discovery. Some books of this period are mere modern translations of works by Ptolemy and Placido de Titis, and it is therefore to be expected that they include no references to the new planet, so the the most part I have passed by these. The rest are new works, and these have been searched thoroughly, but have proven to be a mixed bag, with some enthusiastically integrating Uranus into the scheme of astrological judgement, and others making only cursory passing reference to its discovery or completely ignoring it.

It is possible that some references will have been missed as a result of inaccuracies in the optical character recognition process within Adobe Acrobat, especially when the text to be deciphered is in old fonts and the paper is aged, or where the planet was referred to only by its glyph and not by any name in words (though some such instances have been located by manual searching), so this account should be considered indicative and not exhaustive.

I was unable to find any references at all in the early edition to hand of Ebenezer Sibly's voluminous *Complete Illustration of the Celestial Science of Astrology* (1784–90) or in his *Key to Physic and the Occult Sciences* (c. 1794). This may possibly reflect the first work having been in preparation in manuscript form before the discovery of the new planet was widely considered a significant event by astrologers. Perhaps more probable an inference is that the absence of reliable ephemerides for Uranus in the early years after its discovery precluded its extensive astrological study by all but the most mathematically ingenious astrologers at such an early date, with the result that it had not yet been incorporated into the astrological practice of old hands like Sibly, who had learnt astrology comfortably before it was discovered, even if they might otherwise have been so minded.

There were also no references found in the pseudonymous C. Heydon Jun.'s *The New Astrology* (2nd edition, 1786) or his subsequent work *The Wisdom of*

Solomon in Miniature (1792), and likewise none in Manoah Sibly's two-volume edition of one of the major Latin works of Placido de Titus in English translation as *Astronomy and Elementary Philosophy* (1789) and *A Collection of Thirty Remarkable Nativities* (1789). Even a decade later, none is to be found in John Worsdale's *Genethliacal Astrology* (2nd edition, 1798).[18]

In fact, we have to fast-forward to the early 19th century before we see Uranus mentioned in any astrological book other than a magazine; and even then, some authors continue to produce complete new works without any mention of the new planet at all. A notable case in point is that of John Worsdale Jr., whose work *Celestial Philosophy* (1828), believed to have been edited and amended from a manuscript of the same name that was first prepared by his late father John Worsdale Sr.,[19] appears to contain no references to Uranus, Herschel, or Georgium Sidus at all, and conspicuously omits the glyph from the natal figures that are studied in the volume. This may again reflect the fact that Worsdale Senior was of an older generation of astrologers who, like the Sibly brothers, had learnt astrology before Uranus had even been discovered, and, content with the methods to which he was accustomed, saw no compelling case for changing them to include the new planet whose influence remained, by general astrological consensus, at a fairly speculative stage of early study. In turn, Worsdale Junior may have seen no just cause to radically depart from his late father's accustomed methods of chart delineation to fit in with the customs of his contemporaries after his father's death.

Interspersed below with the references to Uranus found in astrological books are several drawn from the typically short-lived astrological magazines that occasionally appeared during the period under study.

The Conjuror's Magazine (1791–93)

The *Conjuror's Magazine*,[20] which began as a relatively broad-based publication, devoted increasing attention to astrology in response to the interest of its subscribers over the course of its two-year run. References to Uranus within its pages are few, but those that are found show at least that some astrologers were beginning to consider the planet as a potentially important astrological factor by this time. In the issue for June, 1792, in a letter dated June 8th, an astrologer signing himself *Mercurius of Bath* remarks in the context of a discussion of the nativity of Mr. Pitt[21] that:

> ... *the position of the Georgian planet, (which I believe to be of the nature of Saturn) is a circumstance by no means in his favour.*[22]

This is the earliest example I have found to date of an astrologer either making a statement of the general astrological influence of Uranus or citing it as a factor in the judgement of a nativity.

In the issue for May, 1793, a letter by a John Overton of Gravesend, dated May 20th, is published. In this, he remarks:

> ... I present... the two annexed schemes for the time of the Sun's entering Aries for the years 1805 and 1806.... My chief motive for so doing, is on account of Saturn and the Georgian[23] being in conjunction at those two particular periods, in what is termed an angular situation, and the Georgian being now considered of the nature of Saturn, and consequently agreeing with those particular parts of the zodiac that he agrees with, renders the conjunction (particularly if a vernal scheme is of any use) very remarkable!
>
> I acknowledge the smallness of the apparent diameter of the Georgian cannot render him of much consequence with the rest of the planets, but as the earth is acted upon by his gravity and attraction, and as she receives his light as she does the rest of the planets', of course his influences will be proportionable to his apparent magnitude and distance with the rest of the planets that compose our system....[24]

Overton's astronomically grounded arguments for the fact and degree of astrological influence from Uranus are notable as a sign of a background of uncertainty among astrologers of the day as to whether the new planet should be considered astrologically important or not, and if so, to what degree. His citing of apparent magnitude as an arbiter of the degree of influence of a celestial body exemplifies the desire of many astrologers of the time to take a scientifically informed and measured approach to the study of new astronomical discoveries.

No references to Uranus under any of its names could be found in the scan to hand of a bound set of the first six months of *The Astrologer's Magazine and Philosophical Miscellany* (August 1793 to February 1794), which was the immediate successor to the *Conjuror's Magazine*, the change of name reflecting the progressive shift in emphasis to its contents, with astrology by then taking centre stage. It continued to appear for several more years. Unfortunately, all later issues are extremely rare, and none was available to inspect for the purpose of this chapter.

Thomas White (1811)

On page 24 of Thomas White's *Beauties of the Occult Sciences Investigated* (1811), the customary glyph for Uranus appears in the list of planets alongside the name *Georgium Sidus*; and two paragraphs are devoted to the planet on pp. 58–59, of which the first alludes purely to its astronomical characteristics, while the second discusses its place in astrology thus:

> *He has no Houses alloted him, but participates of the nature of the malevolent Planet Saturn, in the highest degree; and is therefore equally unfortunate, according to the place in which he falls, in the Radical figure.*[25]

P. J. Swift (1812)

The following year (1812), P. J. Swift's tract *Destiny of Europe* appeared as a study of the nativity of Napoleon Bonaparte. In his preface, Swift makes passing reference to *the Georgium Sidus*, citing its discovery by Herschel as an example of the 'advantages now possessed for the cultivation of astrological knowledge'.[26]

In the following introduction, Swift criticises the previously published nativity of Napoleon by Thomas Orger on the grounds that both 'the Georgium Sidus' and the Part of Fortune were incorrectly placed by Orger.[27] Swift lays claim to a more accurate calculation of the former using 'Vince's Tables',[28] a resource to which Orger may not have had access, since his own study was published in 1805. Swift proceeds to refer to the aspects to Uranus found in Napoleon's nativity. Under the heading 'Of the Quality of Death', he writes:

> *No one can infer from this any thing like violence, but, [the Sun] is in mundane quartile of the Georgium sidus. I know experimentally, that this Planet is a great malefic, but I doubt very much, whether opposed as he is by Jupiter, he is sufficiently malevolent to occasion a violent death; what he contributes however will be very remote, and exceeding [sic] obscure; and as he is as well as the Luminary of the time in fixed and violent signs, I conclude that his Influence may tend to accelerate the end of the native by unfair means.*[29]

Under the heading 'Honour and Grandeur', Swift modifies his interpretation of Napoleon's natal Sun in Leo as follows:

> *The mundane square of Jupiter and the Georgium sidus to the Sun, farther illustrates the native's opening the way to Grandeur, by treachery and violence.*[30]

Swift also interprets the influence of several primary directions involving Uranus upon Napoleon's life – for example:

The Sun came to the Sesquiquadrate of Georgium sidus, a little past [the age of] 38, under the baneful Influence of this aspect, he carried War and Ruin into the Peninsula, and of course has been unsuccessful and will not succeed in it.[31]

The Monthly Correspondent on Physical and Prognostic Astronomy (1814)

In 1814, there appeared a short-lived monthly magazine called *The Monthly Correspondent on Physical and Prognostic Astronomy*.[32] The first eight issues (probably all that were published), comprising 374[33] consecutively paginated pages, have been conserved in a few major UK-based libraries; and a photographic scan of one such set has been made available online by the Bodleian Libraries, Oxford.[34] Although this scan did not have searchable text at the time when I downloaded it in 2016, I have manually inspected it to locate significant references to Uranus by any of its known names.

The very first issue begins with a poem headed 'Introductory Lines', which mentions the planets in turn, and includes the following couplet, referring to the 84-year orbit of Uranus in relation to human lifespan:

Beyond moves Herschel; man decrepid grows Ere his vast round the distant traveller goes.[35]

An extensive footnote beneath discusses the new planet and its six already-known satellites in purely astronomical terms, giving credence to the title's physical astronomy theme.

Each issue ends with monthly ephemerides for a selected year, including the longitude, latitude, and declination of 'The Georgian, or New Planet' every ten days, which suggests that the editors felt that Uranus was a valuable subject at least for astronomical observation and perhaps also for astrological study. The first year chosen is 1812; and subsequent issues of the magazine take the previous years in reverse chronological order, so the eighth and last presents ephemerides for 1805.

A separately cumulatively paginated supplement called *Mentor Stellarum, or a Complete System of Starry Science*, was supplied with each issue of *The Monthly Correspondent*; and its purpose seems to be an educational exposition of the traditional principles and methods of astrology. A particularly lengthy treatment is given to the luminaries and planets. However, there are just a couple of paragraphs headed 'Of the Georgium Sidus or Herschel'; and the first of these is purely astronomically descriptive, while the second has only this to say:

> *With respect to his specific nature he is found most like the planet Saturn, and therefore similar influences are to be expected from him in the Genesis.*[36]

Within the main magazine are fairly frequently found studies of natal astrological figures. A glyph for Herschel, sometimes apparently in simplified form,[37] is typically included in them,[38] whether or not the planet is specifically mentioned in the accompanying interpretative text, though it is sometimes cited therein as a source of affliction to other planets;[39] and the ages of life at which primary directions to it will take effect are occasionally listed among others.[40]

A recurring theme of the astrological content of the magazine, one that would undoubtedly appear macabre and socially inappropriate to early-21st-century western sensibilities, but that to the British astrologers of the day was a valid subject for astrological research, is the analysis of the nativities of children who died in infancy, some of whom are even named. The first of these does not include any mention of Herschel or even its glyph.[41] The second, that of an R. Etherington, said to have been born on November 16th 1812 at 9:37 a.m., and to have died on June 12th, 1813, appears as a case study[42] with the following remarks:

> *This nativity, elucidating the causes of a short life, was transmitted to us by that ingenious and profound mathematician, Mr. James Wright,*[43] *who having obtained the moment of birth correctly, predicted the termination of the child's existence within the year; for which he assigns the following reasons:-*
>
> *[Sun] and Herschel in [conjunction], and nearly in mundane [square] to the ascendant.*
>
> *The same planets in mundane sesquiquadrate to the Moon, and in semi[square] to Mars.*

In the May issue, a correspondent undersigned J.W.[44] writes in with an analysis of the nativity of 'the infant Marr', another child who died in infancy,[45] observing:

> *... we find both the infortunes Saturn and Mars in the house of death, and Saturn is within half a degree of the middle of the eighth house, and of course in sesquiquadrate of the ascendant and fourth house, and in semiquartile*

> to the midheaven, thereby denoting death of a most violent nature, both to himself and parents...; and the Georgium Sidus is nearly in opposition to the ascendant, and in mundane semiquartile to Venus, and in zodiacal sesquiquadrate to Jupiter, so that both the benefics were vitiated, and unable to save life; and besides the moon was nearly in mundane semiquartile to Mars, and near the mundane quartile of Mercury, who is afflicted by being in semiquartile to the Georgium Sidus, so that upon the whole it affords the most positive and unequivocal testimony of a violent death...

In the June issue, a correspondent identically undersigned as J. W., whom we can reasonably suppose to be the same individual who submitted the infant death study for the May issue, proffers his opinion on the nativity of a child born on April 26th, 1814 and still very much alive at the time of his writing.[46] And yet, J. W. predicts a short life for this infant:

> ... both the luminaries are afflicted by the infortunes... and the Moon who is hileg [sic] or giver of life, is without the least support from either of the benefics; neither is the ascendant befriended by them, and though the Sun is within 6 degrees of the trine of Jupiter yet they are separating, and Jupiter is weak and afflicted by the quartile of Herschel, and Mars lord of the ascendant is on the cusp of the eighth house, therefore... I am convinced the child cannot live long, and I shall be much surprised if it survives the first year....[47]

It is not only infants for whom affliction by Uranus is cited as a sign of an early death, however. In the April issue, J. W. writes in with comments on the nativity of a Mr. Timothy Marr, said to have been born on July 7th, 1787 at an estimated time of 6 a.m., and to have been murdered, together with his family, during the night between the 7th and 8th of December, 1811:[48]

> The testimonies of a violent death are numerous and striking: the Moon, who is giver of life, is in semi-quartile to Mars from violent signs, and is greatly afflicted by the mundane quartile of the Georgium Sidus from the twelfth house....[49]

In the June issue, J. W. also submits his analysis of the nativity of an astrologer named William Elder, said to have been born on October 2nd, 1739 at 3:30 p.m.[50] He argues that Uranus was 'partly the cause of [Elder's] death':

> ...at the time he died the ascendant arrived to the sesquiquadrate of the Georgium Sidus....[51]

In the August issue, the conclusion of a lengthy article by J. W., headed 'Remarks upon the Nativity of Mr. John Lambert', discusses the possible place of the new planet in the scheme of the essential dignities (p. 350), proposing in effect that it be given the joint domicile rulership of both Capricorn and Aquarius alongside Saturn, but more particularly the rulership of Capricorn, at variance with later opinion; and also that it be introduced into the traditional scheme of triplicity rulers:

> ... here it may not be amiss to notice, that notwithstanding the little apparent derangement produced in the system of astrology, by the introduction of the Georgium sidus, it happily fills up a chasm of greater consequence [than its addition to the system of the terms], if we allow it to preside with Mars, over the watery triplicity, as one planet was certainly wanted before the discovery of Herschel, to complete the system in this respect. As the dignity of triplicity is of infinitely more power and consequence than the terms, therefore the ancients were less liable to err in the triplicity than in the terms; and without destroying the ancient system of astrology transmitted to us by the ancients, according to the best means of information they possessed; it would make it more agreeable to nature and reason, to allow Saturn and Herschel to possess the two signs opposite to the houses of the luminaries; so that Saturn, though perfectly agreeing with the nature of Capricorn, being cold and dry, may possibly be strong there, yet the Georgian planet may perhaps possess the supreme rule of Capricorn, which would make the system with the introduction of the Georgian planet perfectly harmonious.[52]

Yet J. W. concedes that the received system of dignities should not be disrupted lightly:

> ... the ancient system of astrology resulted from long experience, and laborious observation, and should not be subverted, or suffer the least detraction upon slight grounds. But if we allow the Georgian planet to have influence, it must be admitted the system of the ancients was a little defective.[53]

Also in the final issue, there appears an anonymous article in florid prose headed 'Observations on the influence of the Georgian, communicated to the Editor through a private channel', hailing the discovery of Uranus as opening to the view of astrologers 'a vast field of scientific enquiry'. The writer continues by reflecting upon how differently astrologers would have conducted their art if they had known of its existence previously, and further alludes to scoffing attitudes to astrologers from non-astrologers being prevalent at the then-present time, on the grounds of astrologers' past ignorance of the existence of the planet and consequent failure to take it into consideration:

> How deeply genius regrets, how sincerely science deplores the absence of this immense orb[54] from the calculations of planetary influence....
> But vain are the regrets – vain are the wishes of the student of astrology; our forefathers in the most towering rise, of the eagle-flight of their intellect never observed the sphere of the Georgian, though the spirit of their boundless mind sought the confines of creation. ...
> Led by such a light, and under the guidance of such wisdom, those who have sought a knowledge of things below by a contemplation of things above,[55] would have long since given a mortal blow to the base endeavours of their enemies; then would astrology have raised the lofty turrets of its fabric to the elevation of perfection, gilded by the rays of celestial truth.
> Neither would they have had to lament the disappointment of their own best hopes, and the failure of many ingenious calculations, as the knowledge of the existence of the Georgian, comprising an acquaintance with the sphere of his influence, seems now to have been all that was wanting in the elucidation of sidereal power. ...
> Yes, it is too true, that in the place of a noble candour, declaring its want of information to enable it rightly to decide on the merits or demerits of astrology, the most foul and opprobious abuse is levelled without mercy on students, and science; and the very reason that should induce all to make allowances for the partial imperfection of its details, (the absence of the Georgian from all the calculations up to this period) is converted by many into a means of ridicule, and as final proof of astrological absurdity.[56]

James Wilson (1819)

James Wilson, writing in the first edition of his *Complete Dictionary of Astrology* (1819), refers to the new planet as *Ouranos*[57] in his introduction and at places in the main text,[58] but occasionally also as Herschel in the main body of text.[59] Under the heading 'Houses', Wilson distinguishes the two accustomed uses of the word 'house' in astrology, referring to what the ancients sometimes called *places* but modern astrologers call simply *houses* as 'mundane houses', and to planetary domiciles as 'planetary houses'. It is in his discussion of the planetary houses that Wilson uses the discovery of Uranus as ammunition in a characteristically irreverent, caustically witty attack on the traditional system of domal dignities, which assumed seven planets:

... Had there been 14 signs, the luminaries would have had two as well as the rest, but there being but 12, they have but one each. The planet Herschel was then unknown, else he would have dislodged some of them by a writ of ejectment. Few seem to have been more aware of this absurdity than Placidus, but, not wishing to contradict Ptolemy, he preserves an almost profound silence respecting exaltations and dignities.... It is with regret I am obliged to confess that the chief part of Ptolemy's system is founded on this ridiculous, cabalistic nonsense of the domal dignities of the planets, a mere human invention and arrangement, and one of the worst that ever was known, being neither agreeable to nature, nor reason, nor consistent even with itself. The existence of an eighth planet unveils the absurdity at once; but allowing there were but seven, and even admitting for argument sake, that the planets really possessed such domal dignity and strength in certain signs, they could have no effect in such places when not posited there....[60]

With regard to the question of the astrological influence of Uranus, Wilson deems that it:

no doubt has some kind of influence hitherto undiscovered, and if there be any truth in the doctrine of colours, its influence must be evil and somewhat resembling that of Saturn.[61]

Under the heading 'Planets' he adds:

Whatever its influence may be, we are unacquainted with it at present, but, if any judgment may be formed from the colour of a planet, it does not appear very malignant. Some think it can have no power because its distance is so great, but if distance were an object in these cases, Saturn's effect would be much inferior to that of Mars or Jupiter, whereas they are all considered as possessing an equal degree of influence.[62]

Wilson's references to the doctrine of colours as a possible indicator of the astrological influence of the new planet seems a curious aberration from his position as a reformist critic of traditional astrological doctrine, or at least one that does not conform to modern standards of scientific method any more closely than much of what he rejected.

What is perhaps more remarkable is Wilson's total failure to acknowledge in his dictionary any of the previously recorded ideas pertaining to the astrological influence of Uranus. He was perhaps unacquainted with such recent sources as *The Monthly Correspondent* at the time when he compiled it, and was instead leaning more on the major books of the past, albeit in a critical spirit.

The Straggling Astrologer

Ten years on from *The Monthly Correspondent*, there appeared in London another short-lived astrology magazine that is nonetheless rich in astrological history and references to Uranus, entitled *The Straggling Astrologer*. This was published in 22 weekly issues spanning just four calendar months, from June to October, 1824.

In the issue for June 26th, there appears a letter from an R. C. S. (almost certain to be Robert Cross Smith)[63] headed 'The Nativity of the Late Unfortunate Aeronaut Harris'.[64] This is a natal study of the English balloonist Thomas Harris, said to have been born on May 24th, 1792 at 5 a.m.,[65] who had then recently been killed in a high-profile ballooning accident on May 25th, 1824. Smith remarks:

> *And lastly, the most fatal position of all is, as I judge, Herschell [sic] in Leo, in the fourth house, or end of all things!*[66]

The nativity of another balloonist, George Graham,[67] said to have been born in London on November 13th, 1784 at 10:10 p.m., is analysed by an astrologer signed *Raphael*[68] in the issue for September 11th.[69] The author of the article remarks:

> *Mars with Mercury, and the Moon with Venus, denote a surprising degree of mechanical genius and inventive ideas, while the trine of Herschell [sic] to each of these significators sways the mental faculties to pursuits of no common or ordinary kind, but mostly out of the reach of custom, and those remarkable for strangeness or eccentricity.*[70]

This description is notable for being one of the earliest accounts of the psychological influence of Uranus, and one that is recognisable to this day from the received ideas of the 20th century. Raphael goes on to cite the 'opposition of Herschell and Saturn' as a possible contributory factor to Graham's pursuit of 'aerial experiments'.[71]

In the issue for July 10th, afflictions of Uranus by Mars from cardinal signs are suggested as a sign of ill-fortune for the established church if other factors agree.[72] In evidence, two then-notorious events of July 19th, 1822[73] and June 8th, 1824[74] are cited. The unsigned author of the article notes that on the former date,

> *Mars had just entered Libra, and was applying to a quartile of the Georgium Sidus, the latter being retrograde, and beholding one another from cardinal signs.*[75]

On the latter date:

> *Mars, also, has just ingressed, as before, into Libra, and, as in the former instance, is applying to a quartile with Georgium Sidus, the latter now retrograde as before; and the aspect still being from the same cardinal signs... to which may be added, the quartile of the Sun and Georgium Sidus, on both days within orbs, and from the same cardinal signs.*[76]

In a later part of the same article, the author discusses 'celestial omens coinciding with the time of trial' in the trial of a Captain O'Callaghan on June 14th, 1824.[77] During this discussion, the author writes:

> *... from a number of observations on the effects of Georgium Sidus, on public bodies, I am convinced that murmuring and discontent are among the effects of his influence. He is excessively morose and sullen; and his conjunction with the Moon, on the present occasion, will account for the extended and almost general impulse which has been given to popular irritation.*[78]

Uranus invoked as a contributory cause of major fires

In the issue of *The Straggling Astrologer* for July 17th, an extended discussion headed 'A Comparison of the Signs and Aspects under which Some of the Chief Destructions by Fire have taken Place' commences.[79] Uranus is considered by the unsigned writer (perhaps the editor) as a factor in several of the fires referred to, including the destruction of Astley's Amphitheatre on September 17th, 1794 (when 'Mars,... entering the disastrous degrees of Sagittarius, is applying to an opposition of Georgium Sidus, which sufficiently marks the calamitous nature of the event');[80] and of St. Paul's Church, Covent Garden, on September 19th, 1795 (when 'Georgium Sidus and Saturn are in a platique [sic] conjunction in the ominous degrees of Gemini... and Mercury is seen applying to a trine with Georgium Sidus and Saturn');[81] a second devastating fire at Astley's Amphitheatre on September 21st, 1803 (when Jupiter and Mars, conjunct in Libra, were both 'quartile to Georgium Sidus from cardinal signs');[82] and the destruction by fire of a theatre called The Circus in St. George's Fields on August 12th, 1805 (when 'the conjunction of Saturn and Mars in Libra' made 'quartile configurations with Georgium Sidus from cardinal signs').[83]

In the issue for July 24th, the discussion of factors involved in major fires resumes under the heading 'A Continuation of the Retrospect of Great Fires with the Coinciding Aspects Beneath Which they have Severally Happened'.[84]

Within this study, reference is made to the burning down of the Theatre-Royal, Covent-Garden, on September 20th, 1808. It is mentioned, among other indications, that:

> *The Georgium Sidus was also in the ominously flagrant degrees of Libra.*[85]

Further reference is made to 'the apartments appropriated to the Duke of Cambridge in St. James's Palace' having been 'destroyed by fire' on January 17th, 1809. The seriousness of the fire is again attributed to Uranus:

> *The accident at St. James's was somewhat more serious than [another recent fire], and this may, without much hesitation, be ascribed to the degree of Libra, occupied by the Herschell [sic] planet at the time.*[86]

Uranus is again held partly to blame in the analysis of the burning down of the Old Custom-house in London[87] on February 12th, 1814:

> *In attending to the celestial signs corresponding to this great catastrophe, it will be observed, that the Georgian planet was within very little more than one degree of the sign Sagittarius, in which Saturn was at the time Drury-lane theatre was consumed:*[88] *thus was the ascendant of London, on each occasion, opposed by a planet similar in nature, and general influence. While in this ominous sign, we see Georgium Sidus meeting a retrograde quartile of Jupiter from a sign no less malignant in these violent combustions, namely, Virgo....*[89]

Additional fires are discussed in a further continuation of the article in the issue for July 31st, with oppositions to Uranus (from Mars and Jupiter, respectively) being invoked as a factor in two of them: the theatre of the Odeon, Paris, on March 20th, 1818;[90] and a fire said to have consumed 'a great number of houses' at Edinburgh on June 24th, 1824.[91]

In the issue for August 7th, a correspondent undersigned *Sidrophel* writes in with remarks upon three further notable fires,[92] including firstly the Great Fire of London, which, he notes, occurred when Uranus was at 2° Sagittarius:

> *The Georgium Sidus, we may also add, occupied a place in the ominous sign Sagittarius.*[93]

He then remarks that two other fires occurred on successive days in June 1789: the Opera-House in the Haymarket[94] on June 17th, and the Manchester Theatre on June 18th.[95] Among his observations on the prevailing planetary configuration at the time of both fires is:

The planet Herschell is, also, within orbs of opposition of Saturn: and the latter of these planets is within one degree of the place of Jupiter at the fire of 1666; a strong testimony that the degrees you mention are very apt to cause fires.[96]

Uranus as a cause of death by transit

In the issue of *The Straggling Astrologer* for July 31st, oppositions to Uranus by transit are hinted at as being possible indicators of death when coinciding with transits by the opposing planet to the South Node of the Moon, in an article headed 'Remarks upon the Signs which Prevailed over the Deaths of the King and Queen of the Sandwich Isles and the Chinese Lady, Calculated to Evince the Anaretic Influence of the Dragon's Tail'.[97]

The unsigned author notes that the 'Queen of the Sandwich Islands'[98] died on July 8th, 1824, the day after Venus transited the Dragon's Tail in Cancer while 'applying to opposition with Georgium Sidus';[99] and then the King[100] died on July 14th as Mercury transited the Dragon's Tail while applying to the same opposition of Uranus.[101]

On the question of the essential dignities of Uranus

In the issue of *The Straggling Astrologer* for September 4th, another pseudonymous astrological contributor, *Astrologus*, answers a question published in the previous issue regarding whether or not 'the planet Herschel' has 'any essential dignities' and if so, which,[102] with a rambling reply that explicitly advocates giving Uranus its domicile in Aquarius and, at the same time, implicitly favours making other arrangements for Saturn:

> *It being a fashionable theme among the astrologers of the present day to cry down essential dignities, probably but few students have paid any attention to the subject of this query. But from what I have been able to gather from experience, I consider that Herschel has great power in the signs Gemini, Libra, and Aquarius, but most power in the latter sign; from which circumstance it may be considered as his house, and the other signs as his triplicity. Neither is this robbing the planet Saturn of his dignities, for I believe that Saturn has very strong and powerful dignity in the sign Taurus. Although I despise equally the trammels of ancient customs, and the frippery of modern innovations, yet I do not think it right to pay that attention to the dignities of the planets (except in horary and mundane questions) which some pretend to belong to these celestial orbs, although I am aware that, in some instances, in nativities, they must be used.*[103]

In this context, the word 'may' implies certain entitlement based on reason, and not indecision or uncertainty. *Astrologus* is stating that it follows rationally from the observation of Herschel's greatest power in Aquarius that the sign could be considered its house, and therefore that it ought so to be considered. This citation from September 1824 can therefore be declared the earliest unequivocal claim attributing the domicile rulership of Aquarius to Uranus that has thus far been identified in print.

In the issue for October 2nd, Astrologus's belief is echoed by a correspondent signed I. V.,[104] who, writing a letter headed 'Letter from a Celebrated Amateur, on the Errors of Astrologers', refers in no uncertain terms to 'the planet Herschel and his domal dignities in Aquarius':

> ... *I will begin with the planetary dignities, which I am sorry to see are now attempted to be cried down. I say attempted, for every one who has had any rational experience in the science, must know, that the theory on which they are formed, is too well grounded to fall a prey to petty innovations, either of the past or present day.... Another cause, which might have given rise to the above erroneous notions,*[105] *has probably arisen from astrologers neglecting the planet Herschel and his domal dignities in Aquarius, whereby they have been often out in their judgments. For instance, suppose an artist should have neither Mercury nor the Moon exactly well placed, and yet is sensible he possesses clever abilities, – here he finds the science at fault. But suppose him to have in his nativity Herschel in Aries, and the Sun in Aquarius, here they are in mutual reception, and this at once accounts for his ingenuity and cleverness, without straining any point in the science.*[106]

The Spirit of Partridge (1824)

In the same summer that *The Straggling Astrologer* was active, a rival weekly astrological magazine called *The Spirit of Partridge* was launched. Although it outlasted its immediate forerunner, it too folded the following January, but not before recording a wealth of additional insights into the British astrological community of its day, including some detailed formulations of the astrological influence of the planet Uranus.

In the very first issue, under the heading 'Observations on the Nature of the Planets', the editor devotes a dense extended paragraph to the discussion of the astrological nature of Uranus:

> We shall now proceed to treat of the effects of the most remote planet in our system, called HERSCHEL, Georgium Sidus or Ouranos.... His nature is similar to the combined influence of Saturn and Mercury, and he infuses into the constitutions of those persons in whose nativities he is most powerful, a remarkable degree of eccentricity. He is decidedly malefic, and whatever he does of evil is always in the most strange and unexpected manner; if well configurated to Jupiter in a nativity, on a good direction, he will not unfrequently [sic] give a legacy, but it will always be from a quarter the least expected.... This star appears particularly inimical to the fair sex, and frequently leads them to those connexions which ensure disgrace and ruin. His evil aspects to the Hyleg, though not sufficient to terminate life of themselves, very materially contribute to hasten the effects of other malignant directions. He frequently causes the sudden death of some relation according to his position in the radix. If placed in the ascendant, the native will be very remarkable for odd and excentric [sic] actions. We have known a person in this case, to suddenly walk out of a room when surrounded by his most intimate friends, without taking leave of any one, or even knowing himself the reason of his conduct. Persons under his influence are generally of a romantic, roving, unsettled disposition, much addicted to travelling, meeting with many strange adventures, seldom experiencing much matrimonial felicity, subject to sudden reverses of fortune, and often terminating[107] their lives far from their native land.... When we consider how much this planet must have baffled the judgment of ancient Astrologers, and when we also reflect that there may be others yet undiscovered, we cannot help remarking the folly and ignorance of those persons who require from the Astrologer, what they expect from no one else, infallibility.[108]

Also in the first issue, there is a discussion of a 'dreadful tempest' said to have commenced about 8 p.m. on October 5th, 1784, leading to the loss of 'a number of vessels, together with their crews'. The writer remarks:

> ... we observe an opposition of Saturn and Venus, and both of them in square to Herschel. It has been observed, that whenever Saturn and Herschel have been in evil aspect with the concurrence of other discordant configurations, that some tremendous commotion has ensued.[109]

In Issue XII, under the heading 'Observations on the Nature of the Signs of the Zodiac', the following wit-infused remarks are made about Uranus in the context of the system of essential dignities recorded by Ptolemy:

> ... Herschel, at the time Ptolemy wrote, was undiscovered, although experience shows his power is scarcely inferior to any of the old planets, he has had no dignities alloted to him; therefore what becomes of the orderly arrangement which has excited so much imagination in the breast of some late Astrologers. Some learned correspondent in a late publication... proposed to rectify this by giving him some of the sign Aquarius, and recommended business to be carried on in future under the firm of Saturn, Herschel & Co..[110]

In Issue XIII, we find a discussion of the 'Position of the Planets At the Time of Mr. Harris ascending in his Balloon',[111] in which it is remarked that:

> Herschel... is in opposition to Jupiter from the third and ninth houses,... which shows a dangerous voyage.[112]

There are other case studies cited in which Herschel is implicated in death – for example, the revolutional figure for the 82nd year of the late King George III,[113] set for June 4th, 1819 at 9:29 p.m.,[114] is analysed with the following remarks, implicating the hard aspects of Uranus to Saturn as factors among others:

> In this Figure, we find the Moon in opposition to Mars, who is on the Radical Place of Jupiter: Herschel is in Square to Saturn in the Revolution, he is also in opposition to Saturn in the Radix, and the latter transits the Square of his own place, and the places of Mercury and Venus.... These combined with the powerful operating direction... we think quite sufficient to produce death.[115]

Robert Cross Smith (Raphael I) (1828)

The original editor of *Raphael's Prophetic Messenger*, Robert Cross Smith, routinely refers to Uranus as *Herschel*, although he also acknowledges that it is alternatively known as *the Georgium Sidus*[116] or as *Uranus*.[117]

In the Prefatory Remarks to his *Manual of Astrology* (1828), written under his accustomed pen-name of Raphael, Smith claims to have presented only information of 'real utility in a scientific way'[118] in the volume, and proclaims that his writings on the signs, houses and planetary orbs have been 'entirely divested of the superstitions and absurdities of the dark ages'.[119] He goes on to excuse the ancients for the 'absurdities which have hitherto been the reproach of Astrology' on the grounds that:

> ... *the vacuum in the system, which the discovery of Herschel supplies, might well be supposed to lead to the adoption of many erroneous rules, by those persons who found the science itself to stand the united test of reason and demonstration.*[120]

So like Wilson, Smith regards the discovery of Uranus as proof that some traditional astrological doctrine related to the planets was false, but unlike Wilson, he is forgiving of it on the grounds that astrologers of bygone times could not reasonably have been expected to know better.

We find similar views expressed in the main text, where, without attribution, Smith quotes directly from the previously cited reading given in *The Spirit of Partridge*:

> *When we consider how much this planet must have baffled the judgment of the ancient Astrologers; and when we reflect also, that there may be other planets equally powerful, beyond his orbit, as yet undiscovered, we cannot help remarking the extreme ignorance and folly of those persons, who require from the Astrologer what they expect from no one else, infallibility.*[121]

And on the specific question of the system of essential dignities (or, as Smith calls them, essential fortitudes), he elaborates on why earlier astrologers should be forgiven:

> *But as the recent discovery of Herschel, the stupendous planet has thrown new lights upon the science of the stars, it could never have been expected that the ancients should have been perfect in every part of their system; and therefore a blind obedience to every rule they laid down, would be little short of bigotry and credulity. Still, it must be acknowledged that the ancients are entitled to our warmest gratitude, for the wonderful discoveries they made in the theory of celestial influence; and it would ill become the author of this work, or his candid readers, to reject aught*[122] *that they advanced, without repeated proofs of its fallacy.*[123]

Smith proceeds to give a summary of his impressions of the astrological influence of the new planet that has more in common with modern interpretations than any recorded before him; but even this is prefixed with words of caution on the grounds that Uranus has been incompletely studied to date:

> Herschel... having been so recently discovered, that no one living has seen more than one half his celestial revolution through the fields of space, it cannot be expected that a complete system of his Astrological effects could possibly be given; but from the author's own experience, aided by what other observations he could gather from men of skill and science in celestial philosophy, this planet is peculiarly unfortunate in his nature[;] and of course his influence, when brought into action by aspecting the various significators in a nativity, is replete with evil, also. He may be compared to the combined effects of Saturn and Mercury. He is in nature extremely frigid, cold, dry, and void of any cheering influence....
>
> His effects are truly malefic; but what he does of evil, is always in a peculiarly strange, unaccountable, and totally unexpected manner: he causes the native born under his influence, to be of a very eccentric and original disposition. Those persons are generally unusually romantic, unsettled, addicted to change, and searchers after novelty. If the Moon or Mercury, and Herschel be well aspected, they are searchers after nature's secrets, excellent chymists, and usually profound in the more secret sciences. He gives the most extraordinary magnanimity and loftiness of mind, mixed with an uncontrollable and intense desire, for pursuits or discoveries out of the 'track of custom'.
>
> In Marriage, if in the seventh house, or afflicting the Moon, he causes every thing but happiness, want of order and [of] sociability in domestic concerns,[124] listlessness and coldness between man and wife, discord from the most entire, strange and unusual causes, death of relatives, &c. He is equally evil in love, and peculiarly inimical to the fair sex: his evil aspects to the Hyleg have also a tendency to materially lessen the space of life.
>
> As yet there are no peculiar houses assigned him, but we have reason to think (from several thousand observations) that the sign Aquarius, is one wherein he much delights; that he is fortunate in the airy trigon, Gemini, Libra, and Aquaries [sic]; and unfortunate in fiery, earthy, or watery signs...[125]

Towards the end of the volume, Smith judges a lunar eclipse that took place on November 3rd, 1827, at 5:07 p.m., noting that:

> the Georgian planet Herschel, is gloomily beheld by a malicious aspect of Saturn, the lord of the ninth, tenth, and eleventh houses....

He adds:

> From the position of Herschel, I fear many failures will take place in public buildings, edifices, and national works of importance.[126]

This is one of the earliest documented examples in an astrological textbook of a mundane astrological judgement using Herschel as a malefic.

Finally, under the heading 'Astrological Portents from the Appearance of Meteors, and Unusual Celestial Phenomena', Smith argues that the 'figure of the heavens' at the time when any new celestial body is first seen or discovered can serve as an indicator of the influence of the new planet in general. Thus, in the case of Uranus:

> This planet was first discovered on March 13th 1781, 10h. P. M.; and by casting the horoscope for that period, the student will perceive that the celestial stranger was in the ninth house of heaven, and Saturn in the twentieth degree of Sagittarius, in the second house or house of wealth. – The horoscope of his appearance of course most plainly indicated, that the influence to be expected from this newly discovered star would be eminently evil – and such, Astrologers have ever found it to prove. – Therefore it readily follows, that the same rules must be observed in every case, when a new celestial appearance or unusual phenomena [sic] is observed in the heavens.[127]

Thomas Oxley (1830)

In the main text of his work *The Celestial Planispheres, or Astronomical Charts* (1830), Thomas Oxley has very little at all to say about Uranus. However, in a glossary towards the end of the book, he categorises Herschel as a 'primary planet' alongside Saturn, Jupiter, Mars, Venus, and Mercury.[128]

A few pages later, he calls on the editors of *White's Ephemeris* to include the geocentric longitude and latitude of Herschel in future editions[129] – indicating that Oxley regarded Herschel as worthy of astrological study but felt that ephemerides for it were too frequently excluded from the annually published ephemerides and almanacs, and perhaps that it was necessary for him to reserve judgement on its influence before making bold pronouncements in a work that would carry his name for posterity.

Rupertus Stella (1832)

Rupertus Stella is the pseudonym used by an unidentified astrologer who wrote a book on horary astrology published in 1832. Herein, he devotes a substantial paragraph to characterising the influence of Uranus, which closely echoes many of the views expressed four years previously by Smith, but rephrases some of Smith's pronouncements so as to be specific to horary questions:

> *Herschel, or Uranus, being only discovered in 1781, no one can positively say what are its exact effects, but from the observations already made, we have every reason to consider him replete with evil; possessing the combined effects of Saturn and Mercury: but this evil is always peculiarly strange and unaccountable. A person born under Herschell influence is of a very eccentric disposition, romantic, unsettled, and incessantly searching after novelty. If he be joined in good aspect with [the Moon] or [Mercury] the natives, or those born under him [sic], generally prove excellent chemists, and often great admirers of the occult sciences, endowed with extraordinary magnanimity and loftiness of mind. If [the Moon] be afflicted by him, or he be in the seventh house of the figure in a question of marriage, he causes every thing but happiness, at the same time producing these effects from the most strange and unnatural causes. In love he has the same tendency, and appears to be 'sworn foe' to the fair sex.*[130]

When considering horary questions specific to each of the twelve houses, the pseudonymous Stella sometimes treats Uranus as a malefic equivalent to either Saturn or Mars. For example, in questions proper to the twelfth house, the lord of the first house afflicted by Uranus, Saturn, or Mars 'shows long imprisonment';[131] and in questions proper to the tenth house, Uranus, Saturn, or Mars in the MC, and afflicting the lord of the ascendant, 'denotes very little hope to the inquirer of obtaining the office or preferment desired'.[132]

Stella's readiness to incorporate Uranus into horary as early as 1832 exemplifies how the typical late-20th- and early-21st-century sensibilities of horary astrologers, according to which horary should be practised strictly along traditional lines as taught up to and including the 17th century, which is to say without the use of the outer planets, were uncharacteristic of the mindsets of horary astrologers practising in the early-to-mid-19th century.

Richard Morrison (1833)

Commander Richard Morrison, the original editor of *Zadkiel's Almanac*, was already using his accustomed pseudonym of *Zadkiel* at the time of the first publication of his pocket-sized *Grammar of Astrology* in 1833. In Chapter III of his *Grammar*, entitled 'The Natures of the Planets', Morrison describes the astrological influence of Uranus in these terms, which again seem to owe a debt to the earlier writings of Smith:

The nature of Herschel is extremely evil. If ascending at the time of birth, he causes the native to be of very eccentric disposition, pursuing extraordinary and uncommon objects; one who despises the track of custom, and is very abrupt in his manners. Whatever good he may produce, when well aspected or situated, will be of a sudden description, and quite out of the common course of things. Persons whose minds are influenced by this planet are unsettled in life, partial to travelling, witnessing many strange scenes, and very romantic and extraordinary in their ideas, and partial to the study of antiquity, but yet likely to strike out[133] many novelties.[134]

Morrison adds, however, that Saturn is even more evil than Herschel. Thus, he holds to the traditional view that Saturn is the greater malefic. Regarding marriage, he asserts:

Herschel in the 7th is evil; and if he afflict the Moon in a man's nativity, or the Sun in a woman's, he destroys domestic happiness.[135]

Under the heading 'The Kind of Death', Morrison indicates:

Herschel cannot kill by himself, but his ill aspects assist to destroy life; and where they concur, will produce something sudden, singular, or extraordinary in the nature of the death.[136]

The Horoscope (1834)

The very next year, Morrison launched and edited his own short-lived weekly astrological magazine called *The Horoscope*,[137] wherein we come to learn considerably more about his views on the planet Uranus. In the first issue, he analyses the death of the ancient Greek playwright Aeschylus, observing:

It had been foretold to Aeschylus that he should die by the fall of a house or other building, about a certain period; and he,... to avoid this danger, went away from all buildings, to pass his time in the open fields, until the evil influence should be passed over. But the Astrologer, though he could foresee the general nature of the accident by which Aeschylus perished, could not tell the precise thing itself which should cause the poet's death. It was probably caused by evil aspects of the planet Saturn, the planet being situated in Gemini, an airy sign. But the Astrologer could only judge that it would be something which would fall on and crush the head of Aeschylus that should cause his death. He was killed as he sat in the fields, by the fall of a tortoise, which an eagle dashed against his bald pate, mistaking it for a stone.... The extraordinary nature of the death leads us to judge that the planet Herschell was a joint cause of it; as he always acts in a very uncommon manner. If so, the Astrologer who foretold the death of Aeschylus, could not know its exact character, as Herschel had not then been discovered.[138]

Uranus in the prediction of weather

In the third issue of *The Horoscope*, we find one of several early examples of Morrison using aspects to Uranus to predict the weather, as he declares regarding May 18th:

The Sun and Moon are in trine aspect, and Mercury approaching the body of Jupiter, while Sol is leaving the latter and in square to Herschel. These are testimonies of rough weather, with high winds and cool, wintry air.[139]

In the sixth issue, under the heading Atmospherical Astrology,[140] Morrison outlines as a principle for astrological weather prediction:

...that the Sun should be observed in the first place, whenever we desire to foresee the nature of the weather. Whatever planet the Sun is in conjunction, or Zodiacal parallel, with, it will cause the weather to be of its nature at that time. The next powerful aspect to a conjunction is the opposition aspect, if it be one of the evil planets; and then the square, then the sesquiquadrate, and last the trine and sextile.

In the case of aspects from the Sun to Uranus, he adds:

Herschel causes cold and sudden showers, and changeable weather, in Spring and Autumn; cloudy, and cool air, with sudden changes, in Summer; frost and snow, and much cold weather, in winter.

In the seventh issue, Morrison cites as a general observation for weather prediction the following rule:

It has been observed, that whenever Saturn and Herschel are in ill aspect, (with other evil configurations,) excessive commotion ensues in the atmosphere.[141]

Uranus in the prediction of Earthquakes

The fourth issue of *The Horoscope* begins with an astrological analysis of an earthquake said to have occurred at Cadiz around 8:30 p.m. on April 13th, 1834.[142]

The chart printed gives Uranus at 25°40' Aquarius, conjunct the cusp of the fourth house at 26°30'. Morrison remarks:

> *And it is a remarkable fact, that five out of the six shocks of earthquakes recorded in England, within these few months, (and of which a list was given in last week's HOROSCOPE) occurred while the sign Scorpio was ascending; and while the planet Herschel was close to the meridian. In this figure Herschal [sic] was exactly on the meridian at the time of the shock, and Jupiter (in Taurus) had just passed the western horizon, and formed a mundane square aspect with him....*[143]

In the fifth issue, under the heading 'A Terrific Earthquake', an earthquake said to have buried 70,000 people at Philipoli,[144] Romania, and to have been felt as far away as Bencoolen [in Sumatra, present-day Indonesia], with 'the sea receding, leaving vessels dry, throwing down walls, &c.', on March 17th, 1818,[145] is analysed astrologically. Among the testimonies cited are:

> *Herschel is in opposition to Mars, and in square aspect, also, to the Sun and Venus.... In addition... we find Herschel and Jupiter in precisely the same declination....*[146]

In the seventh issue, under the heading 'The Great Earthquake in Syria', an earthquake said to have killed 20,000 on 13th August, 1822[147] is analysed, in relation to both its own figure and that of the previous lunar eclipse of August 3rd, 1822 at 0:17, Morrison considering both to be important. Of the chart for the earthquake itself, he notes, among other observations:

> *At the earthquake, Herschel was in exact opposition to the moon, and sextile of Mercury, and close trine of Saturn.... The Sun, also, at the time of the shock, had exactly reached 45 degrees, (a semiquartile aspect,) from the place of Venus at the eclipse, in which place we find him in close sesquiquadrate aspect (135 degrees) to Herschel at the same period....*[148]

On the following page, Morrison lists a set of 'Rules for Predicting Earthquakes', including:

> *Third. – Earthquakes happen more frequently when there are planets, (especially the larger planets, Herschel, Saturn, Jupiter, and Mars,) in the signs Taurus and Scorpio.*[149]

Uranus in Mundane Astrology

In the sixth issue of *The Horoscope*, in a column headed 'Predictions for June, 1834', Morrison invokes a square to Uranus to make a mundane prediction:

About the 12th, the square of Jupiter and Herschel will bring an important event connected with the Irish church.[150]

In the seventh issue, under the heading 'Prediction', Morrison also makes a forecast for the United States from the position of Uranus at the time of the solar eclipse of June 7th, 1834:

The Sun and Moon had just risen at New York, at the new moon; and Mercury, in sextile to Mars, and trine to Herschel, was rising. Herschel was on the meridian. We judge that a sudden change will occur among the ruling powers. The President will probably resign his office, or a general election in the United States will occur this month....[151]

This prediction would appear from public records to have fallen flat, although riots took place in New York City from July 7th to 10th, and there would be an assassination attempt against the President the following January.

Debates over the influence and essential dignities of Uranus

In the fifth issue of *The Horoscope*, under the heading 'Objections to Astrology, with Answers thereto', Morrison responds to the question 'How could the old astrologers be correct, when they knew nothing of the planet Herschel?' as follows:

The existence of Herschel, unknown to the old astrologers, did, of course, cause them to err more or less in all those cases wherein his influence was felt; but as his power is far inferior to any other planet, and as no one planet comes into operation at all times, either in nativities or atmospherical Astrology, the errors would neither be very frequent, nor very extensive.... But we contend that he has influence.[152]

He then responds to another question related to Uranus: 'If the Herschel planet have so much influence while it is at such an immense distance, why is not some – why is not much attention paid to the adjacent asteriods [sic], Ceres, Pallas, Juno, and Vesta?' as follows:

> *Answer. – The asteriods [sic] are very small (the smallest is only 80 miles in diameter, and the largest only 1425 miles), whereas Herschel's diameter is 35,000 miles. Yet, this alone would be no sufficient reason why they should have no influence; and we are of opinion that they may have some, but very trifling, power.... The distance of Juno from the Earth is 157 millions of miles, which is far beyond the relative distance of Herschel, as regards their mutual size. Herschel's diameter is 35,000 miles, his distance from the Earth, 1705 millions of miles, but Juno's diameter is only 1425 miles, therefore, to be at a proportionate distance from the Earth, it should be only 69 millions of miles away; whereas, it is 157 millions of miles distant, or 88 millions of miles beyond its due distance. If the asteriods be observed when all four are in conjunction, probably some influence may then be detected.*[153]

Morrison's response to this question is notable on account of both his being open to the idea that the asteroids may have some astrological influence and of his consideration of the relative apparent magnitudes of celestial bodies as viewed from Earth as an indication of how much influence they ought to have – a scientifically cautious, astronomically measured position at odds with the views and practices of most astrologers using the asteroids and centaurs since the 1970s, but in line with the views expressed by John Overton of Gravesend in his letter to *The Conjuror's Magazine* published in its issue for May 1793.[154]

In the eighth issue of *The Horoscope*, an anonymous correspondent undersigned simply 'A STUDENT' reacts in turn to Morrison's responses to the previously cited theoretical objections to astrology, and additionally asks:

> *Why has not Herschel a house assigned to him in the Zodiac?*

before adding:

> *Kepler, to whose fertile intellect Astronomy is so much indebted, made many of his discoveries by following up a pre-conceived notion of harmony; and an intelligent friend of mine, who is imbued with the same spirit, insists that as there are twelve signs, so we might expect twelve planets. Singularly enough, in favour of his hypothesis, we have, including the newly discovered planets,*[155] *already eleven.*[156] *As far, therefore, as this reasoning extends, we may presume that another heavenly body, belonging to our system, is yet to be found; in which case, in harmony with the principles of equitable adjustment, each planet might have its own house, instead of the present seemingly confused*

arrangement, according to which two signs are, without any obvious pretext, given to single planets.[157]

In a cursory footnote of his own, Morrison proposes to 'defend' the traditional arrangement of the domiciles in a future article.[158]

It is historically noteworthy from the foregoing discussion that as late as 1834 the assignation to Uranus of its domicile in Aquarius, which had been firmly proposed as early as 1824 in *The Straggling Astrologer* (*see above*) and again by John Varley in 1828,[159] had not yet been accepted by other astrologers, with neither Morrison nor one of his most eager correspondents evincing the opinion that Herschel had been assigned a house at all by then, although the student in question clearly felt that perhaps it should be assigned one!

Morrison's promised response to *A Student* arrives in the tenth issue, and seeks to account for the tradition of *houses* being assigned to the planets with reference to posited ancient Egyptian origins.[160] The details of his lengthy historical narrative are beyond the scope of this essay, but he concludes:

If, then, such was the origin of the houses of the planets, there is good reason why the astrologers have not given a house to Herschel.[161]

In a footnote to this, he adds the following concession:

We have no opinion of the power of the houses, or other essential dignities of the planets, in nativities; nor have we even mentioned them in the Grammar of Astrology.[162]

Uranus in nativities and as a cause of critical illness and death

In the sixth issue of *The Horoscope*, within an article entitled 'Nativity of King Leopold's Son', a birth chart set for 24th July, 1833 at 4:30 a.m. is analysed.[163] At the end, Zadkiel remarks critically upon an analysis of the same nativity in an annual publication he does not name:

We have been partly induced to give this Nativity, from its having been published in a very incorrect manner, in a yearly publication, wherein the position of Mercury is very erroneous; and, moreover, the author evidently does not understand the true principles of the doctrine of Nativities, as he thinks that Herschel afflicting the Hyleg may be fatal, whereas this planet may assist to destroy, but can never kill of itself. He has omitted the ill aspect of Mercury to the Sun, the chief cause of death! It is this manner of handling Nativities which brings the science into disrepute. In this instance, the Native was[164] *to live till about 25 years of age, and then die without any direction to the Sun but one of Herschel – a manifest error.*[165]

This remark is notable both for the open peer criticism and possible hints of rivalry apparent in Morrison's sharp words, and for his relatively conservative intellectual position that an aspect from Herschel by itself can only be a contributing factor to death and not the main cause of it – this from the pen of an astrologer often derided by traditional astrologers of the late 20th and early 21st centuries for having widely broken with tradition and corrupted the text of William Lilly's *Christian Astrology* when abridging it for republication the following year (1835). There were different degrees of modernism in 19th-century astrological thinking; and Morrison did not position himself as the most radical reformer among his contemporaneous peers.

In the fifth issue, a writer using the pen-name *Stellarius* reports that his son was '[seized] with convulsions' on November 26th, 1833, and cites the Moon being in the 12th house 'in square of Herschel' as one of several 'strong testimonies of evil' in the figure he drew for the time of illness.[166]

In the tenth issue, Morrison analyses the 'Nativity of a Child who lived only Half-an-hour', this being a girl born in Liverpool on May 28th, 1834 at 8:30 p.m.. Uranus is extensively invoked as being complicit in the poor baby's almost immediate demise:

Here is an instance of the power of the evil planets to destroy life at once, if there be no assistance from the benefic planets.

The Sun had just set, and Saturn had just passed the meridian, while Mars was exactly thereon; hence the Sun was in close square aspect to both Saturn and Mars. The evil Herschel was in the middle of the second house, and was, therefore, four houses and a half (a mundane sesquiquadrate aspect) from the Sun. Mercury, being 46 degrees from Mars, had just passed the semiquartile of him, and partook of his nature, and being conjoined with the Sun afflicted him still further. The Moon was in sesquiquadrate to Saturn, both in the Zodiac and the world,[167] *being only 1 degree past the 135 degrees from Saturn: she was in mundane semiquartile (a house and a half) from Mars, and was in sesquiquadrate to both the Sun and Mercury, and in conjunction with Herschel. The ascendant (the hyleg on which the life chiefly depends) was opposed by the Sun, in semiquartile to Herschel and the Moon, and had the exact square of Mars, who was just on the meridian, being extremely powerful and desperately evil, from being in ill aspect to both Saturn and Herschel.*

On the other hand, not a single benefic ray intervened. The Sun had no aspect of either Jupiter or Venus, nor had the ascendant. The Moon lay, it is true, in the declination of Jupiter; but Jupiter was alone and afflicted by a square of Herschel, and was aspected by both Saturn and Mars, of whose nature he largely partook.... This figure shows all the three hylegiacal points – Sun, Moon, and ascendant – dreadfully afflicted, without any assistance by good planets. Immediate death was the result, and such will ever be the case.[168]

This example shows that the natal analysis of babies who died in infancy, which would surely be considered heartless and inappropriate by today's standards, was not a pastime peculiar to the astrologers who wrote for *The Monthly Correspondent* in the early 19th century, but was in fairly widespread currency in early-19th-century astrological practice, as also was the reputation of the planet Uranus as a frequent contributor to sudden death.

David Parkes (1839)

In 1839, the astrologer David Parkes, writing under the pseudonym of *Ebn Shemaya*, had a book published called *The Star; being a Complete System of Theoretical and Practical Astrology*.

In his introduction to *The Star*, Parkes cites the fact of Halley having anticipated the discovery of Uranus from perturbations to the orbit of Saturn, to argue for the scientific plausibility of astrological influence in general:

The philosophers observed an irregularity in the motion of Saturn, which they found impossible to explain by the known laws of nature. At length they endeavoured to do this by supposing, that another planet existed beyond the orbit of Saturn, acting continually upon him by an attractive force, so as to impede or accelerate his orbicular motion, according to their relative situations; and, from the midnight labours of Dr. Herschell [sic], the planet now bearing his name was discovered, proving, beyond dispute, the truth of the former conclusions, and at the same time powerfully illustrating the mighty laws of attraction. Now, as it is proved that such a small planet as Herschell comparatively is, has such very powerful influence on Saturn, as to impede or accelerate his motion, notwithstanding the vast difference in the extent of their orbits; why cannot Saturn and Jupiter, which contain many times the quantity of matter that the earth contains, whose diameters are many times greater than that of the earth, and which are much nearer the earth than Herschell is to Saturn, I say, why cannot these immense orbs affect the earth, and consequently every being existing upon it in a very considerable degree? Thus every objection to planetary influence, in all its modifications, is completely obviated.[169]

The main focus of the book is the mathematical calculations involved in calculating directions when casting a nativity, and the interpretation of those directions. However, it becomes apparent that Parkes regards Uranus as a malefic alongside Mars and Saturn, with the power to inflict episodes of severe ill-health by direction:

I had a sudden and very severe illness at the age of eighteen years and three months, followed at intervals by several others; by these I proceeded to rectify the nativity. I observed the positions of Mars, Saturn, and Herschell, and I judged that when these formed their evil aspects to the ascendant, illness would inevitably take place.[170]

Under the heading 'Rules for Determining the Particular Qualities of the Mind', Parkes discusses the influence of the planets on the mind when found 'in partile aspect' with the Moon or Mercury, including:

Herschell causes strangeness, waywardness, romantic ideas, eccentricity, a perpetual wish for the discovery of secrets in science and art, a love of things out of the track of custom, as antiquities and mystic learning, or enthusiastic reveries.... In these cases, also, the Moon or Mercury in aspect to Herschell never fails to produce astrologers and antiquaries....[171]

In the section of his book headed 'On the Effects of Directions', Parkes leaves Uranus out of the delineations, but saves a paragraph for it at the end:

The planet Herschell was unknown to the ancients, not having been discovered until 1781. Its nature and influence are thought to be similar to a combination of Saturn and Mercury, that is, in some degree malific [sic]. His evil effects are always of a strange and extraordinary kind, and, as before stated, persons born under his influence are romantic, unsettled, eccentric, and extraordinary characters, though magnanimous and noble-minded. Being only a small orb, and at an immense distance from the earth, his evil effects are neither so powerful as those of Mars, nor of such long duration as those of Saturn.[172]

In a footnote to the following table of the Essential Dignities and Debilities of the Planets, in which Saturn is accorded its domicile in both Capricorn and Aquarius as per the tradition, Parkes remarks tersely:

[Herschel] has the same fortitudes and debilities as [Saturn].[173]

Here again we see clear evidence that the opinions advanced by some astrologers as early as 1824, whereby Uranus should be considered to have its domicile in Aquarius alone, had not met with universal peer acceptance 15 years later.

Conclusion

The uptake of the study of the planet Uranus by astrologers in the decades following its discovery in 1781 was neither immediate nor universal; but within 35 years (by 1816) it was being widely and generally enthusiastically studied, and over the following two decades (to 1834), readings of its astrological influence that are more or less familiar from modern practice became widespread in the mainstream British astrological literature.

Nevertheless, there was considerable diversity in the opinions of the astrologers of those times with regard to its place in the system of planetary domicile in particular, and also with regard to the extent of its influence, and in the finer details of its interpretation.

Endnotes

[1] Frederick William Herschel (1738–1822), a German astronomer who settled in Britain in early adulthood, the first President of the Royal Astronomical Society.

[2] See, for example, Simon Schaffer, 'Uranus and the Establishment of Herschel's Astronomy', *Journal for the History of Astronomy*, Volume 12, Part 1 (February 1981): pp. 11–26.

[3] Maskelyne is cited in William Sheehan, *et al.*, *Neptune: from Grand Discovery to a World Revealed* (Springer, 2021), p. 46, as having made this suggestion in writing on April 4th, 1781.

[4] Sheehan, et al., *Neptune*, p. 46.

[5] *Ibid.*, p. 47.

[6] *Ibid.*

[7] René Bourtembourg, 'Was Uranus Observed by Hipparchus?', *Journal for the History of Astronomy*, Volume 44, Issue 4 (November 2013): pp. 377–87.

[8] English astronomer John Flamsteed (1646–1719), the first Astronomer Royal, and a

Fellow of the Royal Society, best known for his star catalogue *Catalogus Britannicus* and star atlas *Atlas Coelestis*.

9 French astronomer Pierre Charles Le Monnier (1715–1799), author of several books on astronomy in the 18th century.

10 The Reverend James Bradley (1693–1762), English astronomer and Fellow of the Royal Society, who succeeded Edmond Halley as Astronomer Royal in 1742.

11 German astronomer Tobias Mayer (1723–1762).

12 D. C. Wright, 'Uranus in Antiquity', *Quarterly Journal of the Royal Astronomical Society*, XXVIII (1987): p. 79.

13 Edmond Halley (1656–1742), successor to Flamsteed as Astronomer Royal, who observed and calculated the orbit of the comet that has since come to bear his name.

14 James Wilson, *A Complete Dictionary of Astrology* (1819), 'Introduction', p. xiv.

15 French astronomer Joseph Jérome Lefrançois de Lalande (1732–1807).

16 German astronomer Johann Elert Bode (1747–1826), a Fellow of the Royal Society from 1789, is best known today for having popularised what has become known as 'Bode's Law' (though this was first discovered by another astronomer, Johann Titius, in 1766), and for his star atlas called *Uranographia* (1801); Bode is also credited with having been the first to calculate the orbit of Uranus, with reference to earlier sightings such as that of Flamsteed.

17 Bode, *Von dem neu entdeckten Planeten*, pp. 88–90. I have transcribed and checked the relevant text from the Google Books scan, found at the time of writing starting at https://play.google.com/books/reader?id=ZqA5AAAAcAAJ. Some of Bode's spellings and forms of word endings are archaic and obsolete by modern German standards, but have been retained as printed for authenticity.

18 Expanded from the first of 1796.

19 See, for example, the extensive article *The Two John Worsdales* by Marc Demarest (2019), online at http://ehbritten.blogspot.com/2019/02/rogues-vagabonds-part-seven-two-john.html at the time of writing.

20 Printed for W. Locke, No. 12 Red Lion St., Holborn, London, August 1791–July 1793.

21 The Right Honourable William Pitt, born May 28th, 1759, who was the long-serving British Prime Minister at the time, having been appointed on December 19th, 1783. He is usually referred to by historians as William Pitt the Younger to distinguish him from his father, who had also served as Prime Minister. His nativity is given in the issue of *The Conjuror's Magazine* for February, 1792 on p. 205 and analysed on the following pages to p. 209 by an astrologer undersigned B.. To this article, Mercurius of Bath responds critically in the June issue.

22 *The Conjuror's Magazine*, [Vol. I No. 11], (June, 1792): p. 435.

23 I.e., Uranus.

24 *The Conjuror's Magazine*, [Vol. II No. 10], (May, 1793): p. 406.

25 Thomas White, *The Beauties of Occult Science Investigated* (1811), p. 59.

[26] P. J. Swift, *Destiny of Europe* (1812), 'Preface', p. ii.
[27] *Ibid.*, 'Introduction', p. ii.
[28] A presumed reference to tables produced by Samuel Vince (1749–1821), an astronomer and mathematician connected with the University of Cambridge, who wrote a three-volume work, *A Complete System of Astronomy* (1797–1808).
[29] Swift, *Destiny of Europe*, p. 12.
[30] *Ibid.*, p. 20.
[31] *Ibid.*, pp. 26–27.
[32] In the 19th century, astrology was sometimes referred to descriptively as 'prognostic astronomy'. A notable later example is to be found in W. J. Simmonite's book on horary astrology, first published in 1851 under the name *The Prognostic Astronomer*. The term 'prognostic astronomy' could be viewed psychologically as bearing the air of a wish by 19th-century astrologers for astrology to be recognised as being established scientifically from astronomical observations, which is to say, that it was a mark of their desire for their art to be respected as much as astronomy was by society at large. In this light, the present publication is especially notable for its combination of physical astronomy and prognostic astronomy under one title.
[33] Pages 335–42 are mispaginated as 235–42.
[34] At http://dbooks.bodleian.ox.ac.uk/books/PDFs/590692599.pdf
[35] *The Monthly Correspondent*, Vol. I, No. I (January 1, 1814): p. 12.
[36] *Mentor Stellarum*, [1814], p. 73. This cursory reading matches that of the first astrologer to proffer one in *The Conjuror's Magazine* in 1792, see above.
[37] It is perhaps worthy of note that in the first two issues that the glyph used resembles little more than a capital H, without a fully discernible cross and circle, at least in the monochrome scan to hand; however, by the time we get to the March issue, the familiar full-fledged glyph is in use, for example in the natal figure on p. 110; and thereafter it appears regularly.
[38] *The Monthly Correspondent* [1814]; see, for example, pp. 64; 70 and 73.
[39] See, for example, pp. 71 and 163.
[40] See, for example, pp. 71–72.
[41] *The Monthly Correspondent*, Vol. I, No. I (January 1, 1814): p. 28.
[42] *The Monthly Correspondent*, Vol. I, No. II (February 1, 1814): pp. 73–74.
[43] See also the reference to Wright in the footnote below.
[44] In subsequent issues, the address of this J. W., a frequently published correspondent with the magazine, is given as 18, Mead's Row, Westminster Road. In the July issue, we find a letter published by a James Wright of a differently formulated address, 18, Meadrow, Lambet.. However, Mead Row is a street in present-day Lambeth, very close to what is now called Westminster Bridge Road, so we can reasonably suppose that these two addresses are one and the same, and that J. W., wherever he appears in this magazine, is none other than James Wright. Since J. W. was a common set of initials

among British astrologers of the early 19th century, shared also by such enduringly well-known writers of the period such as John Worsdale and James Wilson, we can be grateful for historical posterity that the J. W. writing in *The Monthly Correspondent* at length saw fit to identify himself in full.

45 *The Monthly Correspondent*, Vol. I, No. V (May 1, 1814): pp. 194–95.
46 *The Monthly Correspondent*, Vol. I, No. VI (June 1, 1814): pp. 240–1.
47 *Ibid.*, p. 240.
48 *The Monthly Correspondent*, Vol. I, No. IV (April 1, 1814): pp. 167–69.
49 *Ibid.*, p. 168.
50 *The Monthly Correspondent*, Vol. I, No. VI (June 1, 1814): pp. 264–66.
51 *Ibid.*, p. 265.
52 *The Monthly Correspondent*, Vol. I, No. VIII (August 1, 1814): pp. 350–1.
53 *Ibid.*, p. 351.
54 A common old-fashioned term for planet.
55 I.e., astrologers – the expression is alluding to the reading of terrestrial events from celestial configurations.
56 *Ibid.*, pp. 359–61.
57 See earlier discussion of the names by which Uranus was first known.
58 Wilson, *A Complete Dictionary of Astrology*, pp. xiv, xxii, 74, 313.
59 *Ibid.*, p. 274.
60 *Ibid.*, pp. 274–75.
61 *Ibid.*, p. 74.
62 *Ibid.*, p. 313.
63 From the later inclusion of articles signed *Raphael* in the same magazine, this can reasonably be presumed to be Smith, who later became the first in a succession of astrologers to edit the long-lived almanac *Raphael's Prophetic Messenger*, in connection with the pen-name he had by then adopted (*see below*).
64 *The Straggling Astrologer*, [No. 4], [June 26th, 1824]: pp. 61–62.
65 Smith claims that Harris's time of birth was supplied to him personally by the aviator only a few weeks previously.
66 *The Straggling Astrologer*, [No. 4], [June 26th, 1824]: p. 62.
67 Graham (1784–1867?) and his wife, Margaret Graham, became celebrity balloonists in 19th-century England.
68 One of the first appearances in print of the pen-name of Robert Cross Smith, the future editor of *Raphael's Prophetic Messenger* – see note above and further mentions below.
69 *The Straggling Astrologer*, [No. 15], [September 11th, 1824]: pp. 226–28.
70 *Ibid.*, p. 226.
71 *Ibid.*, p. 227.
72 *The Straggling Astrologer*, [No. 6], [July 10th, 1824]: pp. 87–89.

73 A date on which the Anglican Bishop of Clogher in the Church of Ireland, Percy Jocelyn (1764–1843), is recorded to have been found in a compromising state of undress with a soldier in a back room of a public house in London, causing a national public scandal by the mores of the times, when homosexuality remained criminalised.

74 On this date, 'the trials of Carlile's shopmen commenced'. This is a reference to the trials of William Campion, Thomas Jefferies, Richard Hassell, John Clark, William Haley, William Cochrane, and others for the sale of 'anti-Christian publications' in the shop of Richard Carlile of 84, Fleet Street, London.

75 *The Straggling Astrologer*, [No. 6], [July 10th, 1824]: p. 88.

76 *Ibid.*, p. 89.

77 In a case heard in Surrey, Captain Luke Carlos O'Callaghan was convicted of assaulting the Reverend James Saurin, and sentenced to a month in prison as well as a fine.

78 *The Straggling Astrologer*, [No. 6], [July 10th, 1824]: p. 93.

79 *The Straggling Astrologer*, [No. 7], [July 17th, 1824]: pp. 109–12.

80 *Ibid.*, p. 110.

81 *Ibid.*

82 *Ibid.*, p. 111.

83 *Ibid.*, p. 112.

84 *The Straggling Astrologer*, [No. 8], [July 24th, 1824]: pp. 118–21.

85 *Ibid.*, p. 118.

86 *Ibid.*, p. 119.

87 This building was situated at a site called Wool Quay in the parish of All Hallows, Barking. Its replacement was already under construction nearby at the time of the fire.

88 A reference to a fire that destroyed the third Drury Lane theatre building in London on February 24th, 1809.

89 *Ibid.*, p. 120.

90 This theatre (whose replacement, opened in 1819, still stands at 2, rue Corneille, in the 6th arrondissement) was officially called the *Théâtre de l'Impératrice*, and had been standing only since 1808, having replaced the original building, itself destroyed by an earlier fire on March 18th, 1799.

91 *The Straggling Astrologer*, [No. 9], [July 31st, 1924]: pp. 133–34.

92 *The Straggling Astrologer*, [No. 10], [August 7th, 1824]: pp. 156–57.

93 *Ibid.*, p. 156.

94 This theatre was originally known as the Queen's Theatre when opened in 1705. Its replacement is nowadays known as Her Majesty's Theatre, and stands on a street still called Haymarket in the City of Westminster.

95 The Queen's Theatre, Spring Gardens, Manchester, which opened on June 5th, 1775, and is said by some modern sources to have burned down soon after midnight on June 19th, 1789, though whether or not the fire had already broken out on the 18th is not

immediately clear.
96 Ibid., p. 157.
97 *The Straggling Astrologer*, [No. 9], [July 31st, 1824]: pp. 130–32.
98 I.e., the Queen consort of the Kingdom of Hawaii, c. 1802–1824, who died of measles while on a state visit to London.
99 Ibid., p. 130.
100 Kamehameha II, c. 1797–1824, the second king of the Kingdom of Hawaii, who is believed to have perished from the same cause as his wife.
101 Ibid., p. 131.
102 *The Straggling Astrologer*, [No. 13], [August 28th, 1824]: p. 208.
103 *The Straggling Astrologer*, [No. 14], [September 4th, 1824]: p. 222.
104 Although the identity of I.V. is not expresly given, John Varley would appear a plausible candidate since he is known from his later work *A Treatise of Zodiacall Physiognomy* (1828) to have firmly attributed the rulership of Aquarius to Uranus, in keeping with the advocacy of this I.V. in 1824. In Latin, the initial I. could stand for Ioannes, the equivalent of John.
105 I.e., notions that the system of the essential dignities of the planets is false.
106 *The Straggling Astrologer*, [No. 18], [October 2nd, 1824]: p. 286.
107 I.e., finishing, not by suicide, but by happenstance.
108 *The Straggling Astrologer*, [No. 1], [Thursday, Aug. 5th, 1824]: pp. 13–14.
109 Ibid., p. 20.
110 *The Straggling Astrologer*, No. XII, p. 245.
111 *The Straggling Astrologer*, No. XIII, pp. 258–59.
112 Ibid., p. 258.
113 The year in which King George III would die.
114 *The Straggling Astrologer*, No. XII, p. [237].
115 *The Straggling Astrologer*, No. XIII, p. 261.
116 Raphael, *A Manual of Astrology* (1828), p. 43.
117 Ibid., p. 70.
118 Ibid, p. v.
119 Ibid., p. vi.
120 Ibid.
121 Ibid., p. 72. It is not certain that his failure to attribute the source indicates that Smith himself was an early contributor to *The Spirit of Partridge* and the unacknowledged author of the source text from which he has now quoted. But the possibility, however remote it might appear, is an intriguing one. The editor of *The Spirit of Partridge* is recorded in British library records as having been a Mr. Dixon, but Smith had not yet manifestly joined the staff of *The Straggling Astrologer* when *The Spirit of Partridge* commenced publishing and the source article appeared in it.
122 Meaning 'anything at all', or in this context, 'absolutely everything'.

123 Raphael, *A Manual of Astrology* (1828), pp. 132–34.
124 This sentence is confusingly structured, but can be read as meaning that in domestic concerns, Uranus causes unhappiness, and also disorder and a lack of sociability.
125 *Ibid.*, pp. 70–71.
126 *Ibid.*, p. 238.
127 *Ibid.*, p. 246.
128 Thomas Oxley, *The Celestial Planispheres* (1830), p. 291.
129 *Ibid.*, p. 299.
130 Rupertus Stella, *The Astrologian's Guide in Horary Astrology* (1832), p. 30.
131 *Ibid.*, p. 202.
132 *Ibid.*, p. 199.
133 I.e., to engage in, as in the familiar expression 'to strike out in new directions'.
134 Zadkiel, *The Grammar of Astrology* (1833), p. 8.
135 *Ibid.*, p. 57.
136 *Ibid.*, p. 62.
137 *The Horoscope; A Weekly Miscellany of Astrology, Containing Complete Answers to Every Objection to the Science*, published by Willmer and Smith, Liverpool, from May 3rd to September 6th, 1834. The title was revived by Morrison as a monthly in 1841.
138 *The Horoscope*, No. 1 (May 3, 1834): p. 6.
139 *The Horoscope*, No. 3 (May 17, 1834): p. 21.
140 *The Horoscope*, No. 6 (June 7, 1834): p. 47.
141 *The Horoscope*, No. 7 (June 14, 1834): p. 54.
142 No records of such an event can readily be found online, so this may be presumed to have been a relatively minor tremor by historical standards, if indeed the report is accurate, although major earthquakes have been recorded at other dates in southern Spain.
143 *The Horoscope*, No. 4 (May 24, 1834): pp. 25–26.
144 The city nowadays known as Plovdiv, in present-day Bulgaria.
145 It is curious in view of the magnitude of the reported event that there are no online records matching this date in reference to any earthquake reported to have affected Bulgaria or neighbouring Romania, but there is reliable documentation of an earthquake centred on what is now called Bengkulu, Sumatra, the following day, March 18th, 1818, accompanied by a tsunami, and preceded by hourly shocks on March 17th. It could therefore be that Morrison was leaning on confused records or second-hand oral reports, and ended up blending two different events into a single one in his mind. A 7.9-magnitude earthquake struck the Vrancea Mountains of Romania on October 14th, 1802, reportedly causing near-total destruction to the cities of Ruse, Varna and Vidin; and a smaller magnitude-6.0 earthquake was reported at Sofia on April 25th, 1818; but it is difficult to ascertain any reliable basis in fact for his report about Plovdiv.

146 *The Horoscope*, No. 5 (May 31, 1834): p. 37.
147 This earthquake is well documented, and is generally known as the Aleppo Earthquake, although some more recent estimates place the death toll in Aleppo city itself at closer to 10,000.
148 *The Horoscope*, No. 7 (June 14, 1834): p. 50.
149 *Ibid.*, p. 51.
150 *The Horoscope*, No. 6 (June 7, 1834): p. 44.
151 *The Horoscope*, No. 7 (June 14, 1834: p. 56.
152 *The Horoscope*, No. 5 (May 31, 1834): p. 38.
153 *Ibid.*, p. 39.
154 See citation from it above.
155 This is presumed to refer to Ceres, Pallas, Vesta, and Juno, all of which were discovered in the 1800s.
156 How exactly *A Student* arrives at this figure is not clear: Mercury, Venus, Mars, Jupiter, Saturn, Uranus, Ceres, Pallas, Vesta, and Juno together make ten, but with the luminaries, twelve, and it does not seem plausible in this context that the Earth is being counted, so perhaps Juno is being discounted on grounds of its relatively small size, and the luminaries are being included, or perhaps A Student has simply miscounted.
157 *The Horoscope*, No. 8 (June 21, 1834): p. 62. Despite the mathematical vagueness displayed, *A Student*'s reasoning here foreshadows the opinions often encountered in 20th-century works, to the effect that there should be one domicile for each luminary and planet, but with hypothetical planets such as Vulcan often invoked to make up the numbers, even after Neptune and Pluto were discovered, and the asteroids then being either treated as fragments of a single lost entity or excluded altogether from the system.
158 *The Horoscope*, No. 8 (June 21, 1834): p. 62.
159 Varley, writing in his *Treatise of Zodiacal Physiognomy* (1828), the original text of which is regrettably not to hand, has been quoted by Kim Farnell thus: '*Capricorn is the house of Saturn; and Aquarius is governed by the Herschel planet*'. See the citation in context in her article 'When & why did Uranus become associated with Aquarius?' at https://skyscript.co.uk/ur_aq.html. Although my more recent discovery of references predating Varley's book by four years that assign Uranus to Aquarius in the system of domiciles has arguably superseded Farnell's statement that 'John Varley decided that Uranus ruled Aquarius in 1828' as an answer to the question posed by the title of her paper, it remains valuable for its pioneering research into the question and contains many useful references.
160 *The Horoscope*, No. 10 (July 5, 1834): pp. 77–79.
161 *Ibid.*, p. 79.
162 *Ibid.*

[163] *The Horoscope*, No. 6 (June 7, 1834): pp. 45–46.
[164] I.e., was supposed or expected, according to the writer in the unnamed annual publication to which Morrison refers.
[165] *The Horoscope*, No. 6 (June 7, 1834): p. 46.
[166] *The Horoscope*, No. 5 (May 31, 1834): p. 36.
[167] I.e., *in mundo*.
[168] *The Horoscope*, No. 10 (July 5, 1834): pp. 73–74.
[169] Ebn Shemaya, *The Star* (1839), p. 10.
[170] *Ibid.*, p. 133.
[171] *Ibid.*, pp. 168–69.
[172] *Ibid.*, p. 179.
[173] *Ibid.*

Chapter Six
When Did Astrologers First Associate Neptune with Pisces?

Introduction: When and how was Neptune discovered?

The planet Neptune was first formally discovered by the German astronomers Johann Gottfried Galle (1812–1910) and Heinrich Louis d'Arrest (1822–1875) in September 1846,[1] marking the culmination of a succession of investigations by different astronomers and mathematicians dating back to 1820. In 1820, the French astronomer Alexis Bouvard (1767–1843) began to undertake the challenge of calculating a complete set of tables of planetary motion for the planet Herschel (since known as Uranus), which were published in 1821. Herschel was observed by Bouvard to have been deviating unexpectedly in recent years from its predicted orbit, giving rise to his suspicion at first that previous observations of its position had been very inaccurately recorded.[2]

However, by 1832, Bouvard's own tables were already proving inaccurately representative of up-to-date observations of the position of the planet, which had drifted off-course by half a minute, as noted by the British mathematician and astronomer Sir George Biddell Airy (1801–1892), who served as director of the Cambridge Observatory and subsequently became Astronomer Royal in 1835.[3] These observations led to widespread speculation among astronomers as the the cause of the deviation, with the more fanciful hypotheses including that Uranus had entered an area of space containing a mysterious medium that introduced resistance to its motion, and that it had been thrown off-course by a collision with a passing comet.[4]

The Reverend Dr. Thomas Hussey (1792–1866), a rector at Hayes, Kent who also kept his own private astronomical observatory, was among the first to suspect that Uranus was in fact receiving a gravitational tug from an undiscovered celestial object, a suspicion he conveyed to Bouvard, who acknowledged that he had also entertained the possibility. Hussey subsequently relayed the idea to Airy, who responded that it was premature to seek to identify the source of any external pull on Uranus and that the position of Uranus would have to be observed for several successive revolutions first (which given its 84-year orbit would have taken several centuries). Following a serious accident in 1838, Hussey had to retire from his active pursuit of astronomy, so nothing further came of his line of enquiry.[5]

By 1841, the deviation of Uranus from its path predicted by the tables of Bouvard had increased to two minutes of arc, and publications speculating on an undiscovered planet to account for its perturbations were widely available. John Couch Adams (1819–1892), a young student at the University of Cambridge, challenged himself to discover the hypothesised seventh extra-terrestrial planet (after Mercury, Venus, Mars, Jupiter, Saturn, and Uranus), and set to work on this following his graduation in 1843. His first attempt led to him correctly identifying 1822 as the date of a conjunction between the unknown planet and Uranus, but his estimate of the current position of the unknown planet in 1843 was about 16 degrees out.[6] This was successively refined based on further calculations, with his third attempt dated April 28th, 1845, his fourth September 18th, his fifth October, and his sixth August 1846.[7] The fourth of these was sent to James Challis, who had succeeded Airy as director of the Cambridge Observatory, in September 1845, but Challis responded that he did not have time to investigate the matter, and referred Adams on to Airy instead.[8] The following month, Adams dropped his fifth solution through Airy's letterbox. This one gave positions for Neptune that were accurate to within two degrees. Airy responded by requesting clarification of a technical point having to do with the radius vector of the planet Uranus, but no further reply from Adams was forthcoming, as a result of which Airy did not make any attempt to follow up Adams's solution with observations.[9]

By November 1845, in France, Urban Le Verrier (1811–1877), the director of the Paris Observatory, had begun to work on his own prediction for the position of the planet perturbing the motion of Uranus.[10] His solution was announced to the French Academy on August 31st, 1846, and subsequently mailed on September 18th to Galle at the Berlin Observatory. The very same evening that he received the letter, Galle, together with his colleague d'Arrest, observed the planet Neptune within a degree of the position predicted by Le Verrier.[11]

Part One:
Why did it take so long for astrologers to incorporate Uranus and Neptune into their practice?

The discovery of Neptune in 1846, following on from that of Uranus in 1781 and that of the dwarf planet Ceres in January 1801, with other asteroids having followed soon after, prompted astrologers of the later nineteenth century into a fresh reappraisal of their working methods. Aside from the consideration and study of the possible astrological influence of these newly discovered celestial bodies on purely empirical terms, as was the rationally-based inclination of the leading astrologers of the day, the question remained as to whether or not these newfound planets should or even could satisfactorily be incorporated into the existing systems of planetary dignities such as domicile and exaltation. In the decades immediately following the discovery of Neptune – that is to say, the 1850s, 1860s, and early-mid 1870s – the publishing of new astrological works went through a relatively barren period before starting to pick up again in the late 1870s. It is therefore not entirely surprising that there is relatively little literary evidence with regard to opinions on the use of Neptune in astrology to be found on record in these decades.

In the case of Uranus, however, there were quite a few new major astrological treatises first published in the decades following its discovery. And yet, debate on its influence and speculation as to its rulership did not gain much print space at all before the transient English astrological magazines of the mid-1820s afforded a convenient opportunity – which was over 40 years later. Following this, references to what was then still most often known as Herschel began to be made in early issues of Raphael's *Prophetic Messenger* in the late 1820s.

So why were astrologers so slow to get off the ground in interpreting Uranus in astrology? Was it just because they were set in the ways of the old texts and reluctant to accommodate it? Or did they feel that much more time was needed to study it first? The latter interpretation tends to be the most usually cited by astrological historians today. But we must also consider astrologers' limited access to astronomical ephemerides for newly discovered planets as a factor counting against their study and application to astrological delineation. If the record for Neptune is anything to go by, it can reasonably be supposed that it was difficult for astrologers to access accurate ephemerides for Uranus for decades after its discovery. Planetary positions for Uranus (better known in the decades after its discovery as either Georgium Sidus or Herschel) began to be incorporated into Raphael's *Prophetic Messenger* from the very first year that it was expanded from a prophetic tract into a full almanac with an integral monthly ephemeris, which was that for 1834 – more than half a century after the planet's discovery.

In the simpler but much earlier-established *Moore's Almanac*, which lacked a full planetary ephemeris, Uranus, Ceres, Pallas, Juno, and Vesta were all being listed with their glyphs by the issue for 1821, with the dates on which exact aspects to Uranus would fall further being noted in the calendar pages with which each issue commences. The inclusion of Uranus thus was new since the issue for 1818, although unfortunately I have not yet been able to pinpoint the exact year when the changeover occurred since I lack access to those for 1819 and 1820. We can in any case see that it had taken nearly 40 years from its discovery in 1781 for Uranus to begin to be regularly included in any astrological almanac, and slightly more than this for it to be cited as an influence in worked astrological figures. When we come to Neptune, we find a similar though slightly shorter delay from the moment of discovery to that of there being documented records of any significant study of the planet by astrologers; and the available evidence strongly lends itself to a conclusion that the main reason for this delay is a lack of access to ephemerides for Neptune for almost thirty years following its discovery.

I have found no reference to Neptune in the ephemerides integrated into *Raphael's Almanac* in any year up to and including that for 1865. Unfortunately, I have not been in a position to consult any issues from 1866 to 1875 inclusive for the purposes of writing this chapter. However, it is notable that by the 1876 issue, the ephemerides accompanying the publication have begun to give Neptune's longitude, latitude, and declination on the 1st day and 15th day of every month; and from the 1877 issue, its longitude is given daily and its latitude and declination once every three days, putting it on a level playing field with the other planets for the first time in terms of the availability of full ephemerides to astrologers.

The picture is similar in the case of *Zadkiel's Almanac*, with which *Zadkiel's Astronomical Ephemeris* was optionally available, though the almanac is often found bound without it. In the 1875 issue of Zadkiel's ephemerides, no data for Neptune are included at all. By the 1878 issue, Neptune's longitude and latitude are given once every six days only. And by the 1882 issue, its longitude is given daily and its latitude and declination once every four days. Again, I'm prevented from ascertaining the exact dates of the changes from the absence of access to the in-between years.

In the United States, astrologer W. H. Chaney published *Chaney's Ephemeris from 1800 to date* at Salem, Oregon in 1877. This very early example of an astrologers' ephemeris book spanning almost a whole century of daily positions includes summary data on the longitudes and latitudes of Uranus throughout, but no data at all on Neptune. It is evident that the move towards including full data for Neptune in ephemerides designed for astrologers did not occur before

1876; and one of the two leading astrological almanac publications still gave none at all as late as 1875, with the other providing only very limited data for that year. Thus, we cannot blame the astrologers of the day for their failure to study the astrological influence of Neptune or speculate on its essential dignities before the late 1870s. They simply lacked access to accurate data on its position through time, a prerequisite for any empirical astrological study.

Part Two:
The first published sources on the question of Neptune's sign rulership

1. Alfred Pearce (1880)

In 1880, just a few years after astrologers gained access to ephemerides for Neptune, Alfred Pearce's first astrological magazine *Urania* ran for nine months. In each issue, full daily longitude positions for Neptune are included, as is its latitude every three days. Frequent references are made to Neptune in articles featured within this magazine, indicating that the planet is now being seriously studied with a view to ascertaining its possible astrological influence. We find for instance in the article 'Epidemics and Planetary Influence' attempts to link mundane Neptune aspects in conjunction or opposition to Saturn with the outbreak of large-scale disease epidemics.[12]

In the editorial article on horary astrology commencing on p. 137, the writer (presumed to be Pearce) declares:

> *Neptune is as yet a "houseless wanderer," but as he is considered to resemble Venus in his influence, we shall, probably, shortly find some horary astrologer forcing Neptune's company upon Venus, and giving him a "dignity" in either Taurus, Libra, or Pisces. Had Aquarius not have been already assigned to Uranus in so hasty a manner, it is possible that the name of Neptune (although it was not given to the planet for any astrological reasons) might have suggested that this sign should be given to him.*

Thus, at this point in time, no determinate dignity is being assigned to Neptune, but the author of the article testifies to an opinion among astrologers that Neptune resembles Venus, and speculates, without directly advocating this, that a dignity in one of the signs of the domicile (Taurus and Libra) or exaltation (Pisces) of Venus may be proposed for Neptune by other astrologers.

In the following issue, guest author R. H. Penny, appearing under his accustomed pseudonym of 'Neptune', provides a nine-page study of the influence of the planet Neptune in mundane astrology,[13] but makes no attempt to assign to the planet essential dignities.

2. Friend of J. T. Campbell (1888)

J. T. Campbell, the little-known author of a letter to the editor (P. Powley) of the English astrological journal *The Astrologer*, is the first source I have found in print to have testified to any proposal that Neptune should have its domicile in Pisces in particular – albeit with reference to the opinion of an unnamed friend, rather than as a committed advocate for this proposal. He simply writes:[14]

> A friend informs me that Neptune's house and habitation are in Pisces, and his detriment and fall in Scorpio. Can any student add anything pro or con to this?

3. John Ackroyd (1890)

The late, great Research Director of the American Federation of Astrologers James Herschel Holden, writing in his *A History of Horoscopic Astrology*, cites John Ackroyd as the source of the primary account of astrological Neptune in the literary record, although it in fact comes ten years after the treatments of Neptune in medical and mundane astrology by Pearce and Penny respectively.

The account attributed to Ackroyd by Holden is a letter penned by a Prof. J. A. to late-19th-century Sheffield-based astrological bookseller John Story,[15] and published in Story's 1890 reprint of W. J. Simmonite's main natal astrological treatise *The Celestial Philosopher*,[16] which was retitled by Story under the name *The Complete Arcana of Astral Philosophy*.

J. A., in his letter to Story, is ambivalent, stating simply:[17]

> According to Ptolemy's theory, Aquarius should be Neptune's house, but Scorpio or Taurus might answer well, as they are both of an obscure and mystical nature, but it will require more experience, observation, and practice to settle the matter.

Thus, J. A.'s account of Neptune's dignities is ultimately non-committal, but testifies to the tension between tradition and empiricism as the guiding basis for astrological tenets in the late 19th century, with the author expressing a distinct preference for the empirical approach.

4. Nemo (pseud.) (1892)

Nemo (meaning 'no-one' in Latin) is the pseudonym of a regular columnist for the astrological journal *The Future*, which Pearce launched in 1892, over a decade after the short-lived Urania folded. From the second issue of *The Future* (March 1, 1892), Nemo authors a regular column called *Astrological Notes* within the magazine, and in the very first instalment of this he writes:[18]

> One suggestion has been made that, as these planets [Uranus and Neptune] are more remote from Sun than Saturn, they should have the same dignities as Saturn; while another would depose Saturn from Aquarius and Jupiter from Pisces, and declare that Uranus and Neptune respectively reign in their stead. Both these suggestions involve serious difficulties, nor do they settle the question once and for all with regard to any planets of our solar system yet to be discovered. It seems incredible that planets of such diverse natures as Saturn, Uranus, and Neptune (to say nothing of any still more distant), should all bear equal rule in the same two signs. Furthermore, to depose Saturn and Jupiter from their thrones, pre-supposes a grave error on the part of the ancients, whose teaching on this point has been handed down with complete unanimity from the dim past; it, moreover, necessitates a further process of dethronement and a further ignoring of the teachings of antiquity, whenever further planetary discoveries shall be made. Consequently I am compelled to reject both of these hypotheses.

But he goes on to compromise:

> The difficulty in which modern astrologers have found themselves involved, seems to have originated in their error in rejecting the ancient division of the houses of the planets into the diurnal and nocturnal. By observing this distinction, Uranus and Neptune easily find their houses, with room to spare for their yet undiscovered brethren. Thus Aquarius, which is the diurnal house of Saturn, is the nocturnal house of Uranus. Virgo, which is the nocturnal house of Mercury, is the diurnal house of Uranus. Pisces, which is the nocturnal house of Jupiter, is the diurnal house of Neptune. Gemini, which is the diurnal house of Mercury, is the nocturnal house of Neptune.

Thus, in summary, Nemo gives Neptune diurnal rulership only over Pisces, and nocturnal rulership over Gemini. This is a half-way measure compared with that advocated by the friend of J. T. Campbell or indeed the anonymously attributed second suggestion referred to by Nemo at the start of the first paragraph I quoted above.

5. Thomas H. Burgoyne (1892)

Thomas H. Burgoyne (1855–1894) was a Scottish late 19th-century astrologer who moved to the United States in his 20s, and eventually founded an esoteric order called the Hermetic Brotherhood of Luxor. His books *The Light of Egypt* (in two volumes, 1889 and 1900), *The Language of the Stars* (1892) and *Celestial Dynamics* (1896) were internationally successful enough to be translated into posthumous French editions, although Burgoyne himself had died before two of his books had even been published in the original English.

In *The Language of the Stars*, Burgoyne writes:[19]

> *The planet Neptune, so far as I have been able to find out, gives very beneficial rays when in Pisces, but the reverse in Aries, and therefore Pisces is a natural sign for Neptune, so it seems to me.*

But he stops short of specifically declaring it to be the domicile ruler of Pisces!

6. "Sagittarius" (1894)

The Astrologer's Magazine, edited by Frederick Lacey and Alan Leo, was the leading monthly British astrological periodical from 1890 to 1895, running continuously during these five years before it was replaced by *Modern Astrology*, which was edited solely by Leo after he parted company with Lacey.

Within the pages of *The Astrologer's Magazine*, considerable space was given over to contributions by guest authors. One such was a correspondent adopting the pen-name of "Sagittarius", who contributed an article called *The Houses and Exaltations of the Planets* that was serialised over multiple issues of Volume 4. In the March, 1894 issue, this "Sagittarius" argues for Pisces being 'the chief house of Neptune' and deduces that it must be stripped from Jupiter, leaving Sagittarius as the sole domicile of the latter planet:[20]

> *It is admitted by all astrologers that Uranus has great influence in the airy triplicity (Gemini Libra Aquarius) and that his chief domal dignity is Aquarius, also that Uranus is of the nature of Mercury and Saturn combined, and it has been repeatedly proved that Uranus evolves negative electricity (like Saturn), and always lowers the temperature when in aspect*

to Sun, Venus, Mercury, or the Moon, therefore since the discovery of Uranus and Neptune, modern astrologers have acted wisely in dethroning Saturn from Aquarius (Ptolemy's system), and giving that sign as the chief house of the eccentric Uranus. Pisces for the same reason is the chief house of Neptune, and poor old Jove must be satisfied with Sagittarius in future. The following are no doubt the reasons why Uranus should rule in Aquarius and Neptune in Pisces.

The Sun fountain of light and life to our system rules in Leo as his own house; the first planet revolving round him (rejecting the inter-mercurial planet Vulcan of R. A. Proctor) is Mercury who consequently gets Virgo the next sign to Leo, as Mercury's sphere is next to the Sun; then comes Venus next in order, who, of course, gets Libra for her house; passing the Earth, the next in order is Mars who gets Scorpio; the next sign in rotation then, omitting the asteroids (Ceres, Vesta, etc.) in toto, Jupiter gets Sagittarius the next in order; then comes Saturn who follows on with Capricornus the next sign. Here Ptolemy turns around and goes backward Saturn, Jupiter, Mars, etc., from the circumference to the centre, but we moderns who have Uranus and Neptune to complete our system and deal with, must advance and not recede as Ptolemy did for he knew nothing of these two planets Uranus and Neptune; therefore the next planet in the order of nature to Saturn who has Capricorn only is Uranus, who must of necessity have Aquarius; the next sign, and the last of the spheres is Neptune, so he for the same reason must have the last sign (Pisces) for his 'domal' dignity. Aries, the vernal equinox and the first sign of the circle, is given to Mars who is akin to the earth in nature, the principle of wrath and selfishness predominating over the principle of love, hence Mars gets Aries next to Pisces in the zodiac. Returning to the Sun Leo the sphere of Venus comes next, so she gets Taurus the next sign for her other house, then below Venus is Mercury, so consequently he gets Gemini for the same reason. Then comes the Moon, swiftest of all the heavenly wanderers, so the fair Luna gets the next sign Cancer for her house, then the Moon joins the Sun Leo, and from the conjoint principles of heat and moisture in union another gestation commences and so on ad-infinitum.

'Steady, my friend', says an objector, 'why should the inferior planets Mercury and Venus and the small planet Mars (with his two recently discovered moons) have two houses allotted to each of them?' Why, my friend? because they move so swiftly. Mercury is only about a fortnight in a *sign when not stationary in it, and for this reason has two signs for houses, and Venus likewise, and Mars, although really a superior, as he moves beyond the earth's orbit, must, as far as his swift motion and small magnitude is concerned, be considered an inferior, unless he be stationary, being only about six weeks in a sign, hence Mercury, Venus, and Mars being swiftly moving planets, compared to Jupiter, Saturn, Uranus and Neptune, have for the aforesaid reason two houses each allotted to them, but the giant planets Jupiter, Saturn, Uranus, and Neptune, on account of their slow and ponderous motion, have only one house each. The Sun and Moon being passive planets, and, according to Ptolemy, the most essential significators translating the influences of all the planets to our earth, have for this reason one house each only, even though the lesser luminary is the swiftest in motion of any of them.*

In the second part of the same article, starting on p. 241, "Sagittarius" argues for the exaltation of Uranus in Gemini and that of Neptune in Scorpio, concluding:

To summarise, Uranus is in his own house in Aquarius, in his 'exaltation' in Gemini, and in triplicity in Libra. Neptune is in his own house in Pisces, in his exaltation in Scorpio, and in his triplicity in Cancer.

So, unlike Burgoyne and Nemo, "Sagittarius" is unambivalent about making Neptune the sole ruler of Pisces. Thus, his position is identical with that of the anonymous friend of J. T. Campbell as cited by Campbell in source 2 above. But at variance with that of Campbell's friend, the position of "Sagittarius" is stated directly by the person who believes it, in first-party form, and at length in a proper article, so it is arguably the first fully formed exposition of this position in print.

Conclusion

From the available evidence, it would appear that the pioneers of the modern movement to accord Neptune its domicile in Pisces are both anonymous astrologers whose true identities are lost to history: the first being the friend of J. T. Campbell in November, 1888; and the second "Sagittarius" in March, 1894, although Alfred Pearce had hinted at Pisces as a possibility among three others back in 1880. Nemo's contribution in the pages of *The Future* in 1892 (*see 4. above*) was also considerable, but different in its analysis and conclusions from modern practice. Ackroyd's views as expounded in 3. above have nothing in common with the consensus of the contemporaneous writings cited in 2, 5, or 6. They should therefore be regarded as constituting an atypical anomaly in the early literary record on astrological Neptune, at least insofar as the author's advocacy of Neptune's dignities is concerned.

What is notable by marked contrast to early assignments of sign rulership to Pluto is that in the case of Neptune, astrologers waited until after it was discovered and after ephemerides became available before studying it empirically with a view to deducing both its general influence and its sign rulership. Reference to mythology as a basis for deduction, which, as we shall see in the next chapter, which explores the early sign rulership assignments for Pluto,[21] was a popular approach by 1930, is almost nowhere to be found in the early record of astrologers' reactions to the discovery of Neptune.

Endnotes

[1] See William Sheehan, *et al.*, *Neptune: From Grand Discovery to a World Revealed* (Springer, 2021), p. xi.
[2] *Ibid.*, p. xvi; pp. 63–68.
[3] *Ibid.*, pp. 68–73.
[4] *Ibid.*, p. 74.
[5] *Ibid.*, pp. 74–75.
[6] *Ibid.*, pp. 119–25.
[7] *Ibid.*, p. 130.
[8] *Ibid.*, pp. 135–36.
[9] *Ibid.*, pp. 139–46.
[10] *Ibid.*, p. 151; pp. 165–69.
[11] *Ibid.*, p. 169.
[12] *Urania: a Monthly Journal of Astrology, Meteorology, and Physical Sciences*, London, (May, 1880): pp. 129–33.
[13] "Neptune", The Influence of Neptune, in *Urania: a Monthly Journal of Astrology, Meteorology, and Physical Science* (June, 1880): pp. 173–82.
[14] *The Astrologer* Vol. II, No. 5 (November, 1888): pp. 119–20.
[15] Story re-edited and, in collaboration with London publisher W. Foulsham, saw to the posthumous republication in the 1890s of four of Simmonite's works, changing most of their names in the process; and some of the new editions went through further reprints over the decades to follow.
[16] Originally published in 1847.
[17] W. J. Simmonite, *The Complete Arcana of Astral Philosophy*, (London, 1890), Appendix, p. 8.

[18] *The Future* Vol. I, No. II (March 1, 1892): p. 29.
[19] Thomas H. Burgoyne, *The Language of the Stars: a primary course of lessons in Celestial Dynamics*, Third Edition, (Denver, CO, undated while retaining original copyright date of first edition of 1892).
[20] *The Astrologer's Magazine*, Volume 4 (March 1894): p. 170.
[21] Philip Graves, 'About the Sign Rulership of Pluto', *Infinity Astrological Magazine* 24 (March/April 2019): pp. 30–43. Re-edited for the following chapter here.

Chapter Seven
The First Published Assessments on the Sign Rulership of Pluto, 1897–1931

This chapter will attempt to pinpoint and present in strict chronological order as many as possible of the first published astrological assessments of the sign rulership of Pluto in both English- and French-language sources. Comparably early German sources, while avowedly important, will be investigated at a later date when a more complete spectrum of publications in which they may have appeared is to hand. Some relevant English and French sources may remain to be discovered.

Select, sometimes quite extensive citations from the original sources have been made, in order clearly to show the thinking of the astrologers concerned in their own words. In some cases, their preliminary assessments of the influence of Pluto have been included separately from their assessments of its sign rulership, where this is of clear historical interest.

References to so-called *Pluto-Wemyss*, the hypothetical planet proposed by Duncan Macnaughton[1] in advance of the discovery of the real Pluto by Percival Lowell, but then denied by him as being that Pluto after its discovery, have been omitted from the main body of this article in order to avoid confusion of unlike themes.

It is a curious fact of the history of modern astrology that, even with Macnaughton's hypothetical *Pluto-Wemyss* disqualified and excluded from this survey, the first few published assessments of the sign of the zodiac to be accorded rulership by Pluto appeared before the real physical Pluto was itself discovered, in connection with astrologers' prophecies of the discovery of a planet of that name.

1. Fomalhaut: Aries (1897)

The first known such example is found in the main textbook of Fomalhaut, the pen-name of Abbé Nicollaud. On p. 317 of the first edition of his *Manuel d'Astrologie Sphérique et Judiciaire* (1897), Fomalhaut grants Uranus to Capricorn, Saturn to Aquarius, Neptune to Pisces, Jupiter to Sagittarius, the asteroids to Libra, Venus to Taurus, Mercury to Virgo and the hypothetical planet Vulcan (said to orbit between Mercury and the Sun) to Gemini, before affirming that the planet beyond Neptune exists and is called Pluto:

> La planète au-delà de Neptune existe, elle se nomme Pluton....

He continues to argue (out of step with later astrologers) that Pluto is a benefic analogue to Mars:

> Mars et Pluton, cette dernière apporte les bons effets de Mars....

Finally, he argues that Uranus, Neptune, and Pluto were all known by the ancient Chaldeans, but that as a result of human eyesight having weakened, they had since become invisible. And from this he reasons that the ancient Chaldeans ascribed only one sign to rulership by any one planet – with Pluto as ruler of Aries:

> Rien n'est plus simple que d'admettre que chez les Chaldéens, Uranus dominait au Capricorne et Saturne au Verseau; Neptune aux Poissons et Jupiter au Sagittaire; Mars au Scorpion et Pluton au Bélier....

This is one of the earliest examples of an attempt to reduce all planets to one domicile each, in this case using the hypothetical Vulcan, the asteroids, and the then-yet-to-be-discovered-for-33-years Pluto to make up the numbers.

2. Isabelle Pagan: Scorpio (1907; 1908; 1911)

Ten years later, in 1907, a short treatise on the signs of the zodiac by the notable Scottish astrologer Isabelle Pagan, entitled *Astrological Key to Character*, was published by the Theosophical Publishing House. In this small-format book of barely forty printed pages, Pagan expresses her belief, in common with that Fomalhaut, in the existence of both Vulcan and Pluto as undiscovered planets. But in contrast to his view as expounded a decade previously, hers as given here (pp. 9–10) is that Pluto rules Scorpio and Vulcan rules Virgo.

In a footnote to her nomination of Pluto as ruler of Scorpio (p. 10), she succinctly writes by way of explanation:

> Planetary influence surmised as existent. Name chosen as classically appropriate to the sign of discipline and regeneration. Traditional ruler, Mars.

The following year (1908), she begins to contribute a more detailed series of articles on the same topic entitled 'The Signs of the Zodiac Analysed' to the pages of *Modern Astrology* magazine, starting in the April issue. This is eventually completed in 1909; but the part on Scorpio appears in the November, 1908 issue (from p. 497).

Here, she expands her view of the sign, arguing at variance with Fomalhaut that Pluto corresponds with the "negative side" of Mars and therefore with Scorpio:

> *Astrological tradition describes the influence which rules this sign as 'The negative side of Mars', which suggests that it cannot be positively associated with the god of war in his most familiar guise, though when he is looked upon in his sterner aspect, as destroyer and regenerator, we come near to the true spirit of Scorpio. It is possible that some planet as yet unknown represents this aspect of deity in our solar system.... Careful analysis of the type associated with this Power carries our thoughts back a generation in the story of the Gods, and brings before our minds a statelier and sterner deity than Mars, viz., Pluto, the god of the underworld, the brother of Neptune and of Jupiter. He is represented in ancient mythology as the just and incorruptible judge, dealing out the discipline which strengthens and purifies, and giving to each soul the sorrow and suffering that is due.*

In 1911, these articles were further expanded into the fullest edition of Pagan's work on the twelve signs of the zodiac in the form of her book *From Pioneer to Poet, or the Twelve Great Gates*, again published by the Theosophical Publishing House, but now extending to 318 large-format main pages. As a book, this work was unprecedentedly expansive in its coverage of the single theme of the signs of the zodiac in its day. In the text, she repeatedly names Pluto as the ruler of Scorpio, on pp. 101, 208, 210, and 245; and the above citation from her 1908 article in *Modern Astrology* is retained intact.

Pagan's view as more fully expounded in 1908 and 1911 is later closely echoed by Kevah Deo Griffis (born Lillian Griffis) in her article 'Popular Astrology: The Sign Scorpio' in *Modern Astrology*, November 1926. She writes:

> *Certainly the mystery and secretiveness of Scorpio would seem to reflect more of Pluto, the god of the underworld regions, the incorruptible judge, brother of Neptune and Jupiter. So perhaps some planet as yet undiscovered is the real ruler of this most magnetic and powerful of all the signs of the zodiac.*

Because Griffis's view ostensibly lacks any originality, I do not regard it as a distinct prophecy of the discovery of Pluto, and have filed it here with that of Isabelle Pagan.

3. A. E. Thierens: Aries (1911 / 1931)

Also in 1911, the Dutch astrologer and occultist A. E. Thierens argues in the first edition of his Dutch-language book *Cosmologie: Elementen der Practische Astrologie* for the existence of an undiscovered planet called Pluto, which he names therein as ruler of Aries (p. 47):

> *Wij willen echter vermelden, dat o. i. de beheersching dezer vier sferen als volgt is:*
>
> *Ariës door Pluto (heeft overeenkomst met Mars). [....]*

In the considerably later English-language revision of the same book, now entitled *Elements of Esoteric Astrology* (1931), Thierens accepts the appropriateness of the name Pluto for the planet discovered by Lowell the previous year, and connects it to the mythical Osiris, again proposing it as the ruler of Aries, on the basis of a theosophical argument:

> 'Before Osiris became the "One" and the Highest God of Egypt', says H.P. Blavatsky, 'he was worshipped at Abydos as the Head or Leader of the Heavenly Host of the Builders belonging to the Higher of the three Orders' (S. D., I, 471). This is absolutely appropriate with regard to the three positive centres in the lunar body, viz. Uranus, Pluto-Osiris, and Mercury-Hermes, of which Pluto, lord of Aries, may well be called the Head. Considering the tabula of categorical formation of the physical plane (p. 36), we find Aries at the head of it, which clearly demonstrated why its god or planetary ruler might well be considered to be 'the Head or Leader of the Heavenly Host' with regard to this plane, closely related with the nature and function of the positive electricity in this world. This consideration finds confirmation in the Secret Doctrine, where Pluto-Osiris is called 'Lord of the Lower Kingdom' (I, 501).

4. A. M. Wrey: Scorpio (1913)

In 1913, a pocket-sized, distinctly esoteric primer of questions and answers on astrology by the little-known A. M. Wrey (a woman astrologer, but her first name is not given) was published in London under the title *The Reading of the Stars for Those Who Love Them: A Primer of Astrology*.

Without contextual explanation, Wrey assigns Pluto as ruler of Scorpio (p. 18), the Earth as ruler of Taurus, and Vulcan as ruler of Virgo. This scheme is in fact the same as the one used by Isabelle Pagan in 1907 for all three of these signs. It is reiterated on p. 24 of Wrey's book; but on pp. 50–51, she presents a chart indicating that since the year 1910, which she defines as the start of the Cycle of Aquarius, Scorpio has come under the temporary influence of Mars instead of Pluto, while Pisces has come under that of Jupiter instead of Neptune, and Virgo under that of Mercury instead of Vulcan.

Wrey's book comes in for uncharacteristically scathing criticism from Alan Leo in his review in *Modern Astrology*, July 1913 (p. 303), on account of its 'unqualified statements'.

5. Sepharial: Aries or Scorpio (1918)

Five years after Wrey, and seven after Thierens, Sepharial (the pen-name of Walter Gorn Old), writing in the first edition of his book *The Science of Foreknowledge* (1918), became the fifth astrologer and fourth one of major repute to anticipate the coming discovery of a planet called Pluto in an original book. But unlike the four writing before him, he declines to determine which sign it will rule, only conceding that it must be one or the other of the signs currently assigned to Mars (p. 38):

> *Later, it will be found that Mars will have to yield one of its signs to Pluto, as Saturn has already yielded one to Uranus, and Jupiter one to Neptune. But until Pluto is located beyond the orbit of Neptune we cannot do better than devote our closest attention to the nature and attributes of the ocean deity and his representative among the spheres.*

6. E. Caslant: indeterminate, probably Aries (undated, before 1926)

Featured in *Le Voile D'Isis* No. 73, Janvier 1926, is an article by P. Genty entitled 'Les Planètes Hypothétiques' that indirectly draws attention to an additional prophecy of a planet named Pluto by the well-known mid-20th century French astrologer Eugène Caslant.

The source for Genty's reference is not given, but the attribution is in no doubt. He links it to the contemporary beliefs by two prominent astronomers, Gaillot of France and Lau of Denmark, that there are two planets beyond Neptune, and goes on to remark that some French astrologers share their conclusion. Caslant is named as one of them, and said to have given the two hypothetical planets the names Pluton and Proserpine (p. 72):

> *C'est d'ailleurs la conclusion de quelques astrologues français, Caslant entre autres, qui ont nommé ces Planètes Pluton et Proserpine. Pluton est de la*

nature de Saturne, Mars, et Mercure; Proserpine, de la nature de Saturne, la Terre, et la Lune.

There is unfortunately no reference made to what sign rulership, if any, Caslant accorded to his hypothetical Pluto.

The only published article by Caslant referencing Pluto before 1926 that has surfaced so far,[2] which is found in *La Science Astrale*, 2ᵉ Année N° 1, Janvier 1905, pp. 1–12, makes no mention of its rulership, merely repeating (without attribution) Fomalhaut's affirmation that the planet exists and had been known to the ancients, which strongly suggests that Caslant was directly influenced by Fomalhaut's then-recent 1897 book into making these assertions, though he did not make space for coverage of Pluto's domicile. There is, however, no mention of Proserpine in this 1905 article by Caslant, which casts doubt upon it being specifically the source for Genty's references.

In *La Revue Belge d'Astrologie Moderne*, 21 avril, 1930, writing shortly after the discovery of Pluto but before its naming, Gustave-Lambert Brahy recalls Genty's article four years earlier. Two months later, in the issue of 21 juin, by which time news of the name given to the new discovery has reached him, he congratulates astrologers collectively (but by implication, Caslant in particular) on having anticipated the name of Pluto before astronomers:

> *La nouvelle planète transneptunienne – au fait cette neuvième venue est-elle définitivement cataloguée? – vient d'être baptisée du nom de Pluton. Les astrologues seront tentés de conclure: naturellement!*
>
> *On sait en effet – voir l'article paru dans le numéro 2 du 21 avril – que certains d'entre eux utilisaient déja cette planète sous le même nom. Voilà une occasion, pour les astrologues susceptibles, de mettre la science officielle à la remorque en proclamant qu'une fois encore l'astrologie a devancé l'astronomie.*

In a later article on Pluto featured in the annual publication *Almanach Astrologique*, 1932 edition, Genty again refers to Caslant's views on Pluto, affirming that Caslant assigns Pluto to the second half of Aries; but how long ago the views he refers to at this point in time were conveyed to him or written down by Caslant is not immediately clear:

> *Uranus est en bon état céleste dans les signes d'Air, Neptune dans les signes d'Eau, Pluton dans les signes de Feu, et Proserpine dans les signes de Terre.*

Quant aux domiciles, Caslant leur donne respectivement la second moitié des: Verseau, Poissons, Bélier, et Taureau....

7. Francis Rolt-Wheeler: indeterminate (1930)

In the same week as Brahy's first editorial comment on Pluto mentioned above, which is to say, after its discovery but before its naming, the bilingual Carthage-based astrologer Francis Rolt-Wheeler, writing in the 21 avril, 1930 issue of his magazine *L'Astrosophie*, enthusiastically announces the discovery and expresses his conviction that the name Pluto will be chosen for it in due course (p. 49; p. 88). Like Brahy, he draws attention to astrologers having predicted that name before its discovery:

> *La deuxième question s'attache à la première. Que doit être le nom de la nouvelle planète? Son nom existait déjà. Les astrologues modernes, qui avaient prédit sa découverte depuis plusieurs années déjà, la nommaient Pluton (Pluto). La vraie raison est ésotérique. La voici: Il y a quatre triplicités: Terre, ou Plan Physique; Eau, ou Plan Emotif; Feu ou Plan Mental; Air, ou Plan Intuitif. Uranus régit le Plan Intuitif; Neptune le Plan Emotif; Pluton, devrait donc régir la triplicité de Feu ou le Plan Mental [....]*
>
> *La découverte d'une nouvelle planète, extra-Neptunienne, et qui, probablement, sera nommée 'Pluton' (Pluto), qui a été signalée peu de jours après la parution du dernier numéro de l'Astrosophie, peut bien être considérée comme l'événement astronomique le plus important de notre génération.*

Although at this very early stage, and within the timeframe of this study, Rolt-Wheeler does not propose a sign rulership in connection with Pluto, he would go on to side with Aries in 1934, at variance with the established view among his contemporaries by that time (see his article 'Uranus, Neptune et Pluton: Étude Occulte' in the Décembre, 1934 issue of *L'Astrosophie*).

8. Elizabeth Aldrich: indeterminate (1930)

One of the very earliest published editorials by an English-speaking astrologer speculating on the influence of Pluto after its discovery is given by Elizabeth Aldrich in Vol. 2 No. 2 (May, June, July 1930) of her magazine *The New York Astrologer*. Aldrich first strongly advocates that astrologers should study the planet astrologically before interpreting it, adding:

Of course speculation will be rife as to whether this planet rules a sign or not. Some students have suggested that it would rule Scorpio, Virgo, or Taurus. It seems to the Editor that it is too soon to discover its real rulership.

Nevertheless, she tentatively speculates on some of its areas of influence:

However, we can all surmise, and I believe, that it may be the planet of Justice. This might be what we have called, the Super Jupiter. Thus, it would be the representative of Real Justice, symbolizing the advent of Real Love. Together, they may bring out, through Real Love, and Real Justice, the greatest ideal of our future, Brotherhood.

It seems to us that it rules through its vast distance the extension of the finite to the infinite, the Fourth Dimension, the great skyscrapers, which presume to fling themselves upward, even to the Star. Also it rules the extension into the infinite spaces of the underworld, the twining, honeycombing, catacombs of the subway, which extends with infinite imagination, it might sometimes seem, to the bowels of the earth, the abode of unhappy spirits. Also it may mean the far-flung infinity of bridges and tunnels, which presume to span any spaces....

9. L. H. Weston: indeterminate (1930)

Another early reaction to the newly-discovered planet Pluto comes from the pen of the veteran American astrologer L. H. Weston. In the April-September 1930 double issue of the *Journal of the National Astrological Association*, Weston declines to propose a sign rulership assignation to the newly discovered celestial body, but opines that the name given to it by astronomers is fitting to its astrological functions, although his reasons for this view are not fully detailed.

He does, however, notably reason from mythology to argue along rather obscure lines that the ancient myths related to Pluto were based on occult knowledge possessed by the ancient astrologers of the existence of a real planet of this name although, unlike Fomalhaut before him, he does not contend that the ancients had the power of vision to see it.

In Greek mythology Pluto is the god of the nether world, anciently called Hades. He is feigned to rule over wealth, or, more correctly, over corn or food grain, for in ancient times corn or wheat was wealth. It grows up from the ground, in fact, comes out of the ground, that is, arises from the nether world. Pluto was the son of Saturn, because Saturn holds dominion in things earthly and rules the southern tropic, Capricorn, which was the nether world itself, being always in the south below the equator and the horizon.

We know that Greek mythology is based wholly on an ancient system of astrology, probably used in the time of the lost Atlantis and that the mythological stories are in reality dramatic adaptations of astrological doctrinals to Greek poetry.

For example, Pluto was said to have been particularly distinguished as the possessor of a wonderful helmet, or head-piece. This helmet rendered the wearer invisible, which means, of course, that Pluto is invisible. He really is, or was, to the Atlantean astrologers, yet they knew of him and described his actions, especially the incident in which he killed the gorgon Medusa.

Pluto struck off the head of the only mortal gorgon, Medusa, with a backward or retrograde movement of his sword while taking aim by the aid of a mirror. He was compelled to execute this maneuver on account of the fact that a direct view of any gorgon caused the one who was looking to congeal, or turn to stone.

Of course this is mythology, but it is based on certain astrological considerations: a retrograde movement, a view in a mirror or reflecting telescope, a gorgon, being a female personification having a head covered with snakes instead of hair, nearly an exact description of a comet. The orbit of Pluto being near the outward boundary of the solar system might be expected to contain an influence destructive to a cometary body as it rushed through the system. It might cut off its head!

I am in favour of using the word Pluto for the name of the new planet and adopting the conventional Greek helmet as his symbol.

In the next issue (October-December 1930), Weston reaffirms this view.

10. Llewellyn George: Scorpio (1930)

In the first edition thus (i.e., the first full-length edition and the first under its definitive title) of his book *How Planets Affect You*, as published in 1930, Llewellyn George apparently independently voices effective concord with Fomalhaut in proposing that Uranus, Neptune, and Pluto were conceivably known to the ancients (p. 92):

It is not taken for granted the planet is a newcomer in our solar system any more than Uranus and Neptune were newcomers at the moment of their discovery. Mythology provides plenty of references to justify a belief that the ancients were long aware of their presence. Likewise there are references to ultra-Neptunian bodies....

Whether or not he had previously consulted with the above-cited views of his long-time friend and associate L. H. Weston before arriving at this belief is unclear, though this seems quite possible.

But it is in any case in his magazine *The Astrological Bulletina* that George first spins out at length his thoughts on Pluto. In No. 187, July-August-September 1930 (pp. 83–88), he is already publishing views on themes or keywords to be associated with the newly discovered celestial body:

> *Marvelous as may seem the strides during the Uranian age, they will by comparison be dwarfed into insignificance by the greatly preponderant advance under the influence of Planet X. Through comparison and analysis correlating planetary influences and what has gone before in relation to the development of man and his environment, we are drawn logically to the conclusion that the influence of a new planet would ultimately be indicated by regeneration as the key word of what it can imply to the present limitations of mind. Through its rays man will be able to renew and perpetuate his mind and body until he is ready for new experiences and life on other planets. Gradually he will learn to demonstrate the spiritual values of levitation, transformation, materialization, metamorphosis, transfiguration, – regeneration.*
>
> *Truly, this planet (if no other) reveals that man possesses great potential powers. His possibilities are limitless. Not without reason did Edison proclaim that as yet man is using less than one millionth of his powers. The message of Astrology is one of hope, the hope that cheers one on to greater endeavor, for even now 'X' is working on the subconscious faculty of every living soul, endowing each with the power which helps make possible achievements little dreamed of. This interpretation of some of its influence will bring to mind Paul's great metaphysical commandment: 'Be ye transformed by the renewing (power) of the mind'....*

In the following issue, No. 188, Oct–Dec 1930, George reasons at length from the starting point of mythology for Pluto's rulership of Scorpio (pp. 81–86):

> *In the study of mythology it seemingly becomes apparent that the corruptions of time distorted the original meanings and indications of the myths. Where originally they bore significance to the heavenly bodies and their movements, their later treatments and interpretations became distorted to suit theological*

notions. Some careless writers confused Plutus (sometimes pictured as a boy with a cornucopia) the Greek god of riches, with Pluto, the god of the dead whose oldest name was Hades – 'the unseen'. In their pure rendition the myths were of astrological significance.

The sons of Cronus and Rhea, that is, Zeus (Jupiter), Poseidon (Neptune), and Pluto, having deposed Cronus, cast lots for the kingdoms of the heaven, the sea and the outer regions. Jupiter won the heaven, Neptune the sea, and Pluto the outer or infernal regions, which, from the original name of their ruler, were afterwards known as Hades. To some the 'house of Hades' was a dark and dreadful abode of spirits deep down in the earth. But according to another view the 'house of Hades' was a land in the far WEST, which to the Greeks was always the region of darkness and death; the east of light and life.

In the oldest Greek mythology the House of Hades was a place neither of reward nor punishment; it was simply the home of the dead, good and bad alike, who led a dim or shadowy reflexion of life on earth; akin to the present-day astral plane.

Pluto was simply the ruler of the house of death; in no sense was he depicted as a tempter or seducer of mankind, like the devil of Christian theology. Pluto was certainly depicted as stern and pitiless, but he was only so in discharge of his duty as custodian of the dead. But even Pluto once melted at the music of Orpheus when he came to fetch from the dead his wife Eurydice.

As it is so evident that mythology has drawn upon Astrology for its references to the planets, including the Sun and Moon, it will not be amiss for Astrology to draw upon mythology concerning 'the unseen' planet. Uranus, under favorable conditions, could be seen with the naked eye; Poseidon could be seen with a small glass or other means available to wise men of old; but Pluto, inhabitant of the 'outer regions' was Hades or 'the unseen'. In fact, so inconspicuous is it that modern astronomical photographs recorded it many times before astronomers recognized it and realized that it was a planet of the 'outer region', that is, a wanderer in an orbit farthest from the Sun.

One of the questions arising since this modern 'discovery' is, 'What house does Pluto rule?['] Mythology plainly says in no uncertain terms, 'The house of Hades (Pluto) is the home of the dead'. In Astrology this can refer to but one house – the eighth. The eighth 'house' in the natural or universal zodiac corresponds to Scorpio.

The theological notion placed the home of Hades deep down in the earth and called it Hell. Mythology designated it 'in the far west'. Astrologically the *eighth house is in the west (west by south). Astronomically, the constellation Scorpio is the abode of the many headed monster. (See mythological and bibliological references to Scorpio in the* A to Z Horoscope Maker and Delineator, *page 607, where the 'dog of hell' (Cerberus) is associated with the scorpion).*

The three headed dog is usually pictured with Pluto; said dog is actually pictured in the constellation Scorpio. Pluto is 'ruler of the dead'. In Astrology Scorpio and the eighth house rule the dead and matters relating to the dead.

Note: Pluto is usually pictured with a woman; Scorpio is termed a feminine sign. Cerberus is depicted variously as having three to one hundred heads, and body covered with snakes. Scorpio rules stagnant water and such places as are inhabited with scorpions, vipers, etc.

Until better evidence is found or better reasons advanced we believe Pluto rules Scorpio. This displaces Mars as ruler of one of the signs to which he has commonly been assigned. Mars is considered hot, dry, active; Scorpio, cold, moist, sluggish. While it requires some stretch of imagination to reconcile the two, there are characteristics in common between them sufficient to use Mars as ruler of Scorpio, and we may still continue to do so until more is definitely known of Pluto and until its ephemeris is calculated.

To this, George adds an intellectual justification for his use of reasoning by analogy from ancient mythology in the following terms, a justification that notably predates the first publication of C. G. Jung's essay 'On Synchronicity' in the original German by more than 20 years:

Man has only just now become keen and capable enough to 'discover' the planet and it will be some time yet before he becomes physically and mentally attuned sufficiently to manifest any reactions to the influence of its vibrations and in the course of time these will develop the ability to respond to its influence. In the interim researchers will be learning something about Pluto by means of analogy, that is, study of resemblance of properties or relations; similarity without identity; reasoning in which from certain observed and known relations or resemblances others are inferred; reasoning that proceeds from the individual or particular to a co-ordinate particular, thus involving both induction and deduction. In other words, analogy is specifically a resemblance of relations, a resemblance that may be reasoned from, so that from the likeness in certain respects we may infer that other and perhaps deeper relations exist. In fact, that is just what we have been doing in this article – comparing the known factors of Pluto with its mythological features and deducing its rulership of the sign Scorpio. It may be called masculine, stern, somewhat inscrutable, not itself malignant but dealing with high potencies; invoked by or responsive to music....

In the next issue (No. 189, January-March 1931), Mr. George adds this afterthought:

Just as mythology furnished the original clue to a starting point for surmising that Neptune was identified with Pisces, we find history repeating itself in that Mythology again furnishes the clue to the sign 'rulership' of Pluto, pointing directly to Scorpio.

11. Frederick Thoresby: Scorpio (1930)

In the December 1930 issue of *Modern Astrology* magazine, thus some months after Llewellyn George's nomination, the little-known Frederick Thoresby presents a scheme of sign rulerships in his article 'Zodiacal House Meanings' (p. 404). In this scheme, he assigns Pluto to Scorpio on the grounds that it is 'the universal energy of insight'. Virgo is granted to Vulcan and Libra to the Earth in Thoresby's scheme.

12. J. P. Gross: Leo (1930–31)

In a lengthy letter published in *Astrology, the Astrologers' Quarterly*, Volume Four, Number Four (December 1930 – February 1931), pp. 222–23, the similarly little-known J. P. Gross argues on a combination of mythological and mundane astrological grounds that Pluto should be considered the ruler of Leo:

Since this planet is trans-Neptunian, all who recognise Neptune for what he is, part ruler of Cancer with the Moon, will see the reasonableness of assigning Pluto to Leo. He would then represent the black inner core of the Sun, Sol, or Phoebus – Apollo the bright and shining envelope – 'Phoebus', of course, means 'shining'.

In mythology Pluto is always represented as wearing a crown, even in the underworld of the Shades, a characteristic that would certainly connect him with the royal sign. The only other 'Kings' are Apollo himself and Jupiter; but the latter was represented as such only during the 'Ptolemaic' period, when his original sign, Aries, replaced Leo as the first sign of the zodiac.

Since the discovery of this planet we have had the widespread emergence of dictators and autocrats ruling side by side with the kings in many countries; the dictator wielding the reality of power, the monarch presenting the outward show and splendour. Leo, being the fifth sign from Aries, the activity of this organiser par excellence has made itself felt in the creation of the world-wide Boy Scout Movement. The bringing up of coal to the surface of the earth is probably to be attributed to the return of Pluto.... Also since the Sun retired from the sole rulership of Leo in order to share the same with Pluto, we have seen the withdrawal of gold from general circulation.

Etymologically, Pluto is connected with Ploutos = Wealth, and this, too, would connect him with the gold sign, Leo.

Thus, astronomy, mythology, etymology, and world-events all concur in connecting Pluto with Leo.

Has any other sign equal claims?

I further believe that Pluto, ruling from his own original sign, will prove a benefic, if a stern one.

13. Bessie Leo; and 'E. S.': Scorpio (1931)

In the April, 1931 issue of *Modern Astrology* magazine, Bessie Leo and an unidentified 'E. S.', jointly reviewing the 1931 English edition of the aforementioned book by A. E. Thierens, openly disagree with the latter's assignation of Pluto as ruler of Aries (p. 132):

> *We cannot see eye to eye with him in giving Pluto to Aries, and it is unlikely all the older astrologers are in error, and to quote p. 94, 'Pluto rules second birth', this suggests the regeneration or transmuting element of Scorpio and contradicts the first statement.*

14. Karleen S. Lyon (*presumed*): Scorpio (*tentative*) (1931)

Also in April, 1931, but in the pages of a short-lived American magazine entitled *The New Frontier: Astrology Applied to Modern Conditions*, an unsigned writer, most likely to be the editor of the magazine, Karleen S. Lyon, quotes from Sepharial's earlier prediction in *The Science of Foreknowledge*, after marvelling at the foresight of astrologers of his generation in these terms:

> *The Quarter of a century search for a trans-Neptunian planet that finally focussed the public mind on a tiny Pluto was paralleled by advanced astrological students, who had already deduced its presence by analytical*

reasoning. They came close enough to the truth to guess its name and character, using in part the delicate aerial channels by which minds contact the unseen – still a mystery used without understanding, as we do the radio.

She goes on cautiously to argue in favour of Scorpio being Pluto's domicile in the following terms, while reserving final judgement for later:

Taking the presumed cycle of Pluto... it is interesting to see if world thought seems to have been influenced by this destroyer of the outworn when he was occupying, say, the house to which he is accredited, Scorpio, sign of death and regeneration.

We are impressed with the clean sweep of preparations for new religious thought that took place at these times, fitting when we consider that Sagittarius, where the soul reaches the pinnacle of spiritual enlightenment, is the next house in the symbolic journey around the Wheel of Life [....]

It is still too early to make definite decisions regarding the house and influence of Pluto, but not too early to be marshalling our evidence pro and con.

15. E. H. C. Pagan: Scorpio (1931)

After the discovery of Pluto, Elizabeth H. C. Pagan, a sister of Isabelle Pagan, implicitly endorses Isabelle's earlier detailed prophetic view that the planet rules Scorpio. In *Modern Astrology*, May 1931, starting on pp. 155–56, E. H. C. Pagan writes:

Now Lowell's planet is already being called Pluto. Can we discover why? Can we prove the appropriateness of this name as we have done with those of his elder brethren? Does he show power over things physical, the 'underworld' that was Pluto's domain in classical mythology; does he embody power, especially the wish to dominate, Will-power, in fact, with its concomitants of physical endurance and mental concentration?

The answer to these questions is found by filling it in to horoscopes that are well known to us, and finding how it solves the same problem in each. It will show us why some people have overcome serious disabilities and why others have failed inexplicably. It gives the clue, indeed, to the person's will, or power over circumstances; thus proving it to be the ruler of Scorpio. [....]

By placing Pluto in a horoscope we can now tell whether this faculty is weak or strong in the native, and whether it has a clear path or is thwarted by difficulties. Thanks to the careful calculations of astronomers, we now know where the ruler of all our Scorpionian friends will be found. We have never been satisfied that Mars should be regarded as the ruler of Scorpio; unless we very much emphasise that we refer only to the negative side of Mars. For there is a distinct difference between the ideal English soldier, ruled by Aries, and the Prussian militarist, ruled by Scorpio. The one is Wordsworth's 'Happy Warrior', the other is the ruthless superman.

And what is the negative side of martial qualities, the passive aspect of courage and enterprise? Is it not that endurance, the power to hold on, even against reason, when hope wanes and strength fails? Those are Scorpionian characteristics, such as we shall now expect to find associated with his new-found ruler, Pluto he can now observe in which individuals this endurance is found to be chiefly physical, or chiefly emotional, or chiefly mental, or which others cleave most to ideals; according to whether Pluto is in Earth, Watery, Airy or Fiery signs. The sign and house he is in will further indicate the nature of the things he sets his heart on; and the aspects from other planets will show how far he is likely to succeed.

16. C. E. O. Carter: indeterminate (connections with Cancer, Scorpio) (1931)

Having previously advised strong caution with regard to assigning characteristics of any kind to Pluto prior to its astrological study, the editor of *Astrology, the Astrologer's Quarterly*, Charles Carter, links it to both Cancer and Scorpio in his article 'Observations on Pluto, I', as published in the June – August 1931 issue of the same magazine. Earlier in this article, he also notably reports on the main findings of his initial careful study of the planet:

1. That Pluto is concerned with beginnings and endings. He is the planet of climax and crisis, and thus, in a sense, of upheaval. He brings matters to a head, ending one chapter of life and ushering in another.

2. In particular, he brings hidden things to light; he is a discoverer and revealer.

3. Since disease is usually of the nature of a climax, being the culminating effort of the body to cast off effete deposits, Pluto may be closely related to acute disease and even to death, which is the end of the chapter of physical embodiment.

4. Except inasmuch as climax is usually of a perturbing nature, Pluto is by no means necessarily a malefic, even in a mundane sense. Often his action is followed by much relief, as when a swelling is lanced.

Carter goes on to add to these points:

The action of Pluto does not seem to be quite so instantaneous as that usually associated with Uranus; he is an earthquake, but, like earthquakes, he sometimes gives a warning, if but a brief one. Even an earthquake is not so instantaneous as a flash of lightning.
   Politically, he causes revolutionary upheavals.
   In human psychology I am inclined to attribute to him a proclivity to abnormal and, so to speak, insatiate desires, and a thirst for that which is vast and beyond proper proportions. It gives not so much ambition as cravings, with restlessness, discontent, and dissatisfaction. [....]
   It is self-assertive, I suggest, and will not take a back seat or even such seat as is proper to its rank and endowments.

Later in the article, he addresses the issue of rulership, ultimately standing by the traditional rulership system, while lending some credence to the idea of Pluto ruling Scorpio:

Is Pluto a materialistic or a psychic or intuitional planet?
   I am inclined to think (and this is purely speculative) that he is an earth-water body and, as such, he would have a definitely common-sense or even hard-headed side, and also an astral or psychic aspect. Perhaps the latter will predominate. I tend to relate him to Cancer rather than Scorpio. In mythology, Jupiter, Neptune, and Pluto were brothers; this is in accordance with the undoubted connection between Jupiter and Neptune through Pisces, and I suggest that Pluto may be related to Jupiter through its exaltation, Cancer. On the other hand, Jupiter may rule Pisces, Neptune Cancer, and Pluto Scorpio.
   Cancer certainly shows a contradictory and dual nature, shrewd and prudent in some ways and sensational and unreasonable in others. But as we have not yet agreed on the rulerships of Uranus and Neptune, we ought, I think, to be in no great haste to 'fix' Pluto. In any case I am one who stands by the ancient and traditional rulerships and I regard the new planets as being at best not true rulers, but merely, as it were, 'interested parties'.

17. Mabel Baudot: Scorpio (1931)

In one of the lengthiest early mythologically-reasoned arguments concerning the sign rulership of Pluto, ranking alongside that given by Llewellyn George the previous year, a some-time contributor to the pages of *Astrology: the Astrologers' Quarterly* named Mabel Baudot also argues, in Vol. V No. 3 (September – November, 1931) of that magazine (pp. 123–36), that Pluto rules Scorpio. The article is much too long to quote in its entirety here, so only the central thrust is shown below; but taken as a whole, it serves as a fine example of how pervasive the use of elaborate astrological reasoning from mythology had become in English-speaking astrological culture by this point in time.

> *We firmly believe that Pluto is the overlord of Scorpio, as Uranus and Neptune are, respectively, the super-rulers of Aquarius and Pisces. It has frequently been borne in strongly to many well-known astrologers and earnest students that Mars alone could not bestow the deep, occult tendencies of this marvellous sign, with its sweeping range of thought, plummet-like probings into hidden things, intense preoccupation with the mysteries of Life and Death, intuitive realisation of the beckonings of the Beyond, its poignant verse and passionate prose, and, above all, its wonderful gamut of emotion.*
>
> *There seems to be, at times, all things contained in Scorpio at its best – colour, art, poetry, music; sounds ranging from the tremulous Æolian harp to 'thunder's deep and dreadful organ-note' which Shakespeare swept into his works.*
>
> *Scorpio's mechanical genius comes from Mars, but his metaphysical genius is the gift of his transcendantal ruler, who represents the power behind the throne. When the red hue of Mars fades into its complementary colour, and waves of ethereal sea-green tinge the sign of the Scorpion and the Eagle, then will the War God abdicate his throne, and his place will be taken by the great shadowy Ruler whose form is even now becoming slightly more distinct. Pluto was a king in Grecian lore, and the fixed signs have strong connotations with kinship, especially Leo and Scorpio. In the body of the Scorpion is the binary star, Antares, fiery red and emerald green. The name is from Anti Ares, similar to, or the rival of, Mars. It was one of the four royal stars of Persia in 3000 BC, when, as the Watcher of the West, it marked the autumnal equinox. Note that the colours of Antares correspond with the hues of Mars and Pluto mentioned above.*
>
> *Scorpio is the 8th octave – the sign of the Great Return. Here the soul, on its long pilgrimage, seeks desperately for wisdom – and shall not seek in*

vain. It is the sphere of martyrdom in many instances, of intense psychological crucifixion, and it has been said that all martyrdoms looked mean when they were suffered; but the soul rises from them like that in Masefield's verse: 'All smithied o'er with kingly gold'.

Pluto was the king of the underworld. His was the realm of shadows, of all the mysteries which took place below the surface of the earth (the soul is earthy in its first primitive gropings). He ruled from a throne over which black snakes crawled and writhed (the dark temptations and evil desires which beset the mind). This is undoubtedly a symbol of the Serpent Power inherent in Scorpio. Black bulls were grouped further back, and on each corner of his imperial seat stood deep-plumaged eagles with keen, penetrating amber eyes, typifying the upward flight of this bird into the empyrean. We should remember that the eagle is the only bird which is supposed to gaze unflinchingly into the Sun on its aerial journey – the power of Scorpio to seek the light and truth after his imprisonment in the realm of shades.

Conclusion

This study has been arbitrarily limited to opinions expressed by astrologers in connection with Pluto in print up to and including the end of the year 1931 purely in the interest of containing its length and demonstrating the fact that numerous such views were on the record at a very early stage, and certainly long before Fritz Brunhübner's famous early book on Pluto appeared in print in the original German (which was in 1935). If there is sufficient public demand, it could yet be productively extended with a second instalment covering the follow-up years from 1932 onwards, since there were many further interesting views registered in 1932, 1933, 1934 and beyond – indeed, throughout the 1930s, and into the 1940s and 1950s.

But I believe this chapter has served its primary purpose in showing that unity regarding the sign rulership of Pluto existed neither before nor in the immediate aftermath of its discovery, although whereas before its discovery there was a fairly even balance of views favouring either Aries or Scorpio, after its discovery, the opinion that it was ruler of Scorpio rapidly came to predominate, leaving the Aries hypothesis very much in the shade as a minority opinion alongside others that related Pluto to other signs altogether.

A secondary purpose of the study was to illustrate by way of copious examples the extent to which reasoning from mythology had pervaded astrological culture by the early 1930s, before C. G. Jung had had any influence on astrologers' theoretical thinking at all. Indeed, such reasoning was already abundantly evident in Isabelle Pagan's work as serialised in *Modern Astrology* in 1908-9, and seems to owe considerably to the influence of theosophical thinking in astrological circles at that time.

Endnotes

1. Macnaughton, writing under the pseudonym of Maurice Wemyss in Volume I (1927) of his multi-volume work *The Wheel of Life, or Scientific Astrology*, proposed no fewer than four hypothetical planets as part of a twelve-fold rulership scheme: Pluto as ruler of Cancer; Hercules as ruler of Leo; Dido as ruler of Virgo; and Jason as ruler of Sagittarius. His rulership scheme was also peculiar in that he omitted the Sun and the Moon altogether, then gave Uranus to Scorpio, Neptune to Libra, Jupiter to Aquarius, and the asteroids to Pisces. In fact, only Aries, Taurus, Gemini, and Capricorn are represented by their conventional rulers in his scheme.

    For several years prior to this date, initially writing under his real name, he had repeatedly referred to his hypothetical Pluto in articles in *Modern Astrology* magazine. In the February 1922 issue, he explains, in the context of the analysis of a horoscope (p. 48):

    > *Perhaps some will think that the affliction of Uranus, even though a weak sign was ascending, was scarcely strong enough to give such persistent ill-health as Mrs Prentiss suffered. I accordingly have inserted the position of a hypothetical planet Pluto whose position I have worked on for some time now. I shall refer to it in future articles. I consider it to be ruler of Cancer. [....]*

    But even this is not Macnaughton's earliest reference to his hypothetical Pluto in the pages of the magazine. A letter of his dated 30th July, 1919 (when he was just 27 years old) is printed in the November, 1919 issue (p. 347), casually referring to afflictions by Pluto without any further explanation.

    Because the real physical Pluto discovered by Lowell over a decade later had quite different characteristics from the Pluto that Macnaughton had envisaged and assigned to rulership of the sign Cancer, he disowned it, referring to it thereafter as Pluto-Lowell and to his own hypothetical one as Pluto-Wemyss in the pages of *Modern Astrology* magazine (of which he became the editor in 1931, retaining that position as late as 1940). Therefore, it seems only appropriate to exclude his hypothetical Pluto-Wemyss from consideration in the main body of this chapter alongside the real one, when the issue of the rulership of the real Pluto is the main focus.

2. My thanks to Serge Bret-Morel for drawing this to my attention in 2024.

Chapter Eight
Lilith in Astrology:
Second Moon, Asteroid, or Lunar Apogee?

In the astrology of the 20th century, confusingly, three astronomically entirely distinct concepts have all been named Lilith. This chapter will seek to clarify the sequence of events that culminated in the coexistence of the three different Liliths in use by astrologers at the end of the 20th century and continuing into the 21st. A particular focus will be the controversies within the world of astrologers that greeted the claims of the existence of a second natural satellite or Moon orbiting the Earth, nowadays known as Dark Moon Lilith.

Part One: Lilith as a Second Moon of the Earth: Speculations, 1898–1918

Divorced from its historical context, the notion of the Earth having two major satellites, the second of which should be called Lilith, may perhaps seem laughably fanciful from a typical early-21st-century perspective, given how far telescopes and astronomical knowledge have advanced today. However, the historical record tends to indicate that the origin of the concept of Lilith as a hypothetical second Moon to the Earth is closely bound up in the sincere scientific endeavours of late-19th- and early-20th-century astronomers to discover new planets beyond the orbit of Neptune. As a result of the discoveries of Uranus, Ceres, Pallas, Vesta, Juno, and Neptune between 1781 and 1846, there was heightened speculation in the late 19th century that more previously undetected celestial bodies would be discovered in due course.

While at the end of the 19th century and beginning of the 20th, the most attention was being focused upon the search for an additional outer planet or planets (which would eventually lead to the discovery of Pluto in 1930), there was also considerable scientific interest in other potential astronomical discoveries, including the possibility of a planet orbiting the Sun closer than Mercury (often referred to as Vulcan by astrologers from the late 19th century onwards), though the latter prospect has ultimately proved elusive.

Yet another area of speculation surrounded the possibility of unidentified, non-reflective, smaller terrestrial satellites. Since the early 17th century, a succession of reported sightings by astronomers of unknown bodies transiting in front of the Sun had engendered widespread speculation that there could be a smaller but still sizeable second satellite in orbit around the Earth. Most such reported sightings were of dark masses, fomenting speculation that there might exist a body so little reflective that it could not normally be seen against the backdrop of space, and could only be detected by telescopes when it formed a shadow in front of the Sun while making a direct transit over its face as viewed from Earth.

This climate of excitable anticipation came to a head in February 1898 when a German astronomer named Georges Waltemath attempted to deduce the orbital elements of such an undiscovered satellite from the dates of all the sightings he was aware of since 1618, and claimed its discovery. Waltemath's elements of the Earth's second Moon are said to have been published in the periodical *English Mechanic*, 11th February 1898.[1] For a few weeks following, the worldwide press reported on his claim, which caused an international sensation and sent public excitement into overdrive.

Sepharial's role in the naming of Dark Moon Lilith

Sepharial[2] is commonly credited by astrologers as being the original source for the astrological application of Dark Moon Lilith, but what exactly was his role? After all, he was not the astronomer who claimed to have discovered it. In his book *The Science of Foreknowledge*[3] (1918), we find three chapters that discuss Lilith. In one of them, he cites fourteen recorded sightings of objects passing in front of the Sun as being consistent with Dr. Waltemath's orbital elements; while a few of the others, which he did not find to be compatible, Sepharial construes as instead constituting evidence of a *third* terrestrial satellite. So far, Sepharial's demonstrable role is limited to that of a reporter on and propagator of an astronomer's claimed discovery.

It was however Sepharial himself who was the first to coin the name 'Lilith' for the hypothetical second Moon. This name did not arise immediately upon the publication of Waltemath's elements, but was adopted by the English astrologer soon afterwards, and indeed two decades before the publication of *The Science of Foreknowledge* in 1918, in which he justifiably claims the original responsibility for it.[4]

Waltemath, as an astronomer, was perhaps mainly interested in making astronomical discoveries, and it seems he did not trouble himself with imposing a name for his hypothetical celestial body.

To find out exactly when Sepharial first started referring to Dr. Waltemath's hypothetical second Moon as Lilith, we need to examine the astrological press from 1898 onwards in detail.

The claims by Waltemath had already reached the attention of Alan Leo in time for his going to press with the March, 1898 number of *Modern Astrology*, in which he reports indirectly under the heading 'A SECOND MOON':[5]

> According to the Rappel, an astronomer of Hamburg has made the discovery of a second moon, which will be visible on July 30th, 1898. The new satellite is said to be twice the distance from the earth of the moon with which we are acquainted.

Leo's report did not meet with universal approval among readers of the magazine. In the May issue, we find in the letters section this curt riposte:[6]

> Dear Sir, I hope you will not waste space on the pretended new satellite to the earth. At present there is no ground for supposing the alleged discovery to be more than a canard.[7] Yours sincerely, J. Wilson.[8]

It is in the August issue that the name 'Lilith' first appears, and not from the pen of Sepharial but from that of H. S. Green, one of Alan Leo's most prominent stablemates and fellow writers at *Modern Astrology* Office:[9]

> It is worth noting by the way that 'Lilith', the alleged second Moon of our earth, was at 29° Virgo in the horoscope of the Microcephalic Idiot, in conjunction with Mars and Mercury; which is an important fact for Sepharial.

This would appear to bear witness to Sepharial already having adopted the name 'Lilith' within six months of the first appearance of Waltemath's paper, and to having then interested Green in his discussion of the hypothetical body, although Green himself comes across from his language as remaining relatively guarded about the real corporeal existence or otherwise of the supposed satellite.

The first reference to Lilith by Sepharial that I have been able to find in print is indeed earlier, and occurs in the magazine he edited at that time, *Coming Events*. In the April, 1898 issue, the lead article is entitled 'The New Satellite – Lilith';[10] and within it Sepharial writes:[11]

> Dr. Waltemath, as everyone now knows, has definitely located the orbit of the second (? first) satellite of the earth, whom we will here call, for convenience, Lilith. In his article to the 'Globe', 7th February, 1898, he mentions various

observations of this unrecognised member of the Solar family, a number of which, taken for the dates of transit over the Sun's disc, enabled him to fix its synodical revolution at 177 days. We refer our readers to the 'Globe' for further particulars concerning the satellite, and here reproduce the dates of observation referred to therein:-

    1. *Lilith conjunct Sun* –   6th *June, 1761.*
    2.   "   19th *Nov., 1762.*
    3.   "   3rd *May, 1764.*
    4.   "   11th *June, 1855*
    5. *Lilith 148° elong.* -   25th *Oct., 1881.*

Sepharial goes on to add various astronomical observations and some methodological guidelines for the astrological study of Lilith, at the same time as proposing a symbol resembling a thick circle with a thick horizontal line across its diameter as a glyph for the pretended satellite. Also included is a purported 'Table of conjunctions of Lilith and the Sun' spanning the years 1854 to 1906 inclusive.

This entire article is reproduced and slightly extended in *The Science of Foreknowledge*[12] twenty years later. Thus we can see that within two months of all the sensational publicity greeting Dr. Waltemath's claims, and two decades before the publication of his book that is commonly taken as an original point of reference for astrological notions on the topic, Sepharial had both adopted the provisional name Lilith and accepted the proposition of the hypothetical satellite's factual astronomical existence.

From Two Moons to Three?

The following month, Sepharial leads *Coming Events* with an article headed 'A Third Earth-Moon', in which he reports on communications from Dr. Waltemath regarding a possible explanation for some recorded observations that do not match the orbital elements supposed of Lilith.[13] Sepharial adds:[14]

> *We are not yet in possession of sufficient facts regarding the Third Moon to give our readers any adequate notion of its movements in the zodiac, but if it be the body observed by Dr. Waltemath in 1897, it will have a synodical revolution of about 354 days, double that of Lilith, whose elements are already so well known that Dr. Waltemath was able to predict the date and position of its solar transit.*

In the same article, Sepharial also for the first time lists fourteen reported observations of purported Earth satellites between 1618 and 1898.

The whole article 'A Third Earth-Moon' is also reproduced, in only slightly modified form, in Sepharial's book *The Science of Foreknowledge*, under the same heading.[15]

The Influence of Dark Moon Lilith: first judgements

Later in the same issue of *Coming Events*, under the heading 'The Influence of Lilith', there appears the study of the nativity of a lady by another astrologer, who uses the pen-name *Asmothiel*.[16] Here, perhaps for the first time in a printed natal chart, the position of Lilith is invoked as an influence.

The next significant contribution by Sepharial himself, headed *Notes on Lilith*, appears in the issue for June.[17] Here we learn considerably more about his early speculations upon the astrological influence of the hypothetical second Moon:[18]

> *The influence of Lilith is undoubtedly obstructive and fatal, productive of various forms of catastrophes and accidents, sudden upsets, changes, and states of confusion. Falling in the 5th House of a horoscope, it has been found to indicate the insanity and death of a lover, loss of children, and death by childbirth. In the 3rd House, it has signified accidents and death to brothers and sisters, and a series of troubles arising out of correspondence. In four cases under observation, the presence of Lilith in the 6th House has produced dangerous occupation, ending in fatality.*
>
> *The name Lilith comes from the Hebrew word Lilah, which means the Night. In Kabalistic mythology, Lilith is the wife of Cain, as the Moon (Evah) is the wife of Adam. Lilith or Lilis is supposed to inhabit the upper regions of the air as a spectral being. Some authorities regard Lilith as the second wife of Adam after his fall from the angelic state. In this connection Lilith would certainly seem to bear a bad reputation and to be in such a way associated with a degraded and dark destiny.*

Most of the above extracts, and much of the rest of the original article, are also reproduced in *The Science of Foreknowledge* twenty years later, as the first part of the chapter 'The Astrology of Lilith',[19] which also includes some additional case studies and commentary.

In the issue of *Coming Events* for September 1898, Sepharial adds:[20]

> *Lilith's influence in a horoscope will not negative [sic] that of the other bodies, but it will modify their action when acting in combination with them. In short, it will disturb the caeteris paribus of our argument in regard to them.*
>
> *Research and tabulation of effects due to Lilith are what are now required, and every student is capable of conducting this enquiry....*

October's issue begins with an aspectarian for Lilith for the month. Sepharial then reiterates his call to students to study its effects, before remarking:

> *A writer in the English Mechanic endeavours to throw doubt upon the existence of the second Moon of the Earth, but the observations and figures cited in COMING EVENTS (April and May, 1898) remain untouched by either jealousy or scepticism. To Dr. Waltemath every honour is due for the luminous discovery he has made....*

This is the first hint of opposition to the acceptance of Dr. Waltemath's hypothetical satellite by the astronomical community to have been carried across into the astrological press, but at this early stage, Sepharial's tone in the light of such doubts remains triumphant and defiant.

I have checked all subsequent issues of *Coming Events* through to the end of Volume 4.[21] No significant further content on Lilith is found therein.[22]

Returning to *Modern Astrology* magazine, we next find Sepharial referring incidentally to Lilith in the course of discussing a nativity in his column 'Olla Podrida' in the issue for January, 1902:[23]

> *The premature birth of a child to Queen Wilhelmina of Holland, on the 12th November last, amply confirms her horoscope of the 31st August, 1880, at 6.30 p.m. .... In 1901 the Sun by direction was separating from Mars and applying to conjunction with Lilith, which holds the seventh house in Libra.*

This indicates that by the end of 1901, Sepharial was routinely using a postulated ephemeris for Lilith in his analysis of nativities, and was sufficiently persuaded of its utility to mention it in matter-of-fact terms even in outlets of the astrological press in which he did not serve as editor.

The following month, in his article 'A Vindication of the Pre-Natal Epoch', Sepharial refers to Lilith as:[24]

> *One of my astral protégées, Lilith....*

This adds evidence of his desire to develop and even promote its use by astrologers. He goes on to quote a reference to Lilith in an encylopaedia:[25]

> In the Encyclopaedia published by Cassell I find this pertinent little note on Lilith: 'A Rabbinical myth, Adam's first wife, changed for refractory conduct into a night spectre, especially hostile to new-born infants'.

This citation of an ancient myth connected with Lilith would appear to show that Sepharial's choice of the name in the first place was rooted in his consideration of its meaning in traditional Jewish mythology.

The Dark Moon Wars: Sepharial clashes with Wilson

These mentions do not go unnoticed by the previous detractor in the pages of the magazine against the claims of a second Earth Moon, J. Wilson, who, now choosing to refer to himself only by his initials, writes in to *Modern Astrology* again in a letter dated February 1st, 1902, to protest, this time supported by reasoned astronomical arguments:[26]

> *I see that Sepharial still believes in the bogus discovery of Lilith. The earth cannot have another satellite of appreciable size for the following reasons. If such a body existed it would seriously disturb the lunar motion, which is accurately known to a second. Further, such a body, even if non-luminous, would be easily traced by its passing between us and the stars and blotting them out....*
> *Yours truly, J. W.*

To this, Sepharial responds with courteous defiance:[27]

> *As to the existence of Lilith and my authority for the existence of other non-luminous bodies in space, I must refer J. W. to a special article on that subject, which will appear in this or a subsequent issue, at your convenience.*

The promised article does not materialise immediately, but in the meantime, Sepharial continues to refer freely to Lilith in his delineations featured within the pages of the magazine.[28]

When the heralded article does at length appear, in the issue for September 1902,[29] it is a lengthy one, suggesting that he had been biding his time to ensure that the task was accomplished to a satisfactory standard. I have selectively quoted Sepharial's key arguments and claims below:

> *It appears that in certain quarters the earth's second satellite, which I have christened Lilith from the ancient rabbinical tradition concerning the second wife of Adam, is held to be altogether mythical and to have no existence in fact.*

Apart from the consideration that there can be no myth (veil) without a basis in fact, something veiled in short, we have frequent record of observations of such a body by different persons of accredited veracity. I shall prove, not only that such a body as the earth's second satellite exists, but that it has been thoroughly located, and its orbit defined by Dr. Waltemath, of Hamburg; that its approximate longitude can always be found, and its influence upon sublunary things very accurately defined.

It has been urged that did such a body exist its action upon the Moon would be appreciable. To this I reply that its action will only be appreciable when all the elements are known. That there are a variety of unknown factors at work to produce disturbances in the Moon's motion in its orbit is proved by the various equations applied to the mean motion of that body in order to obtain its true place in its orbit. Burchardt's[30] equations are thirty-two in number for longitude and twelve for latitude of the Moon, of which only seventeen are theoretically requisite, while twelve are experimentally true, having been certified by over 4,000 observations. The remaining three are credited to the action of Venus and Jupiter upon the earth. In modern astronomy the unknown factor looms large and conspicuous....

As to the plausibility of the existence of such non-luminous bodies in the earth's orbit, I may refer the reader to Mr. Richard A. Proctor's Other Worlds than Ours.

But better than all theory in such matters is observed fact, and in regard to the existence of Lilith observations are sufficiently numerous, as the following list will show:-

At this point in his article, Sepharial cites 13 of the reported observations recorded between 1618 and 1898 that he considers to be evidence for the existence of the Earth's second satellite, before continuing:

The only bodies hitherto known as capable of obscuring the whole or a part of the Sun's disc are the Moon, Venus, and Mercury. Reference to the Ephemerides of these several dates of transit will show that none of the above bodies were concerned in the phenomena observed.

Now let us go a step further. By taking the number of days between any two of the observed transits, it will be found that it is a multiple of 177. Thus:- From 6th June 1761, to 19th November, 1762, are 531 days = 177 x 3. From 19th November, 1762, to 3rd May, 1764, are 531 days. It therefore appears that there is a body whose synodical period is 177 days. This may be accounted a *coincidence, and we are therefore justified in making a further test: from 3rd May, 1764, to 11th June, 1855, are 33,276 days = 177 x 188. This shows that after 188 revolutions, the position of the body is not affected by a single day, and hence we may conclude the body to have a mean synodical period of 177 days, or a mean orbital period of 119 days. Consequently the body will return to the same longitude about the same day of the year after a period of 126 years....*

It must not be thought that every conjunction is a transit of Lilith over the Sun's disc, any more than every new Moon is an eclipse of the Sun. This is a matter which is controlled by the inclination of the orbit of Lilith, and the Sun's distance from the Node at the time of conjunction; or, in other words, by Lilith's latitude at conjunction....

However, Dr. Waltemath has so far succeeded in defining the orbit of Lilith as to have predicted the date and position of its last transit....

The orbit of Lilith is greater than that of the Moon, its mean distance from the earth being between 960,000 and 1,230,000 miles, or about 1,080,000 miles. The time taken by the satellite to make a central transit of the Sun's disc fom W. to E. is about 2¾ hours.

Now as to its influence in sublunary affairs. I have already published several horoscopes in which Lilith in the sixth house produced a violent death when the subjects were engaged in their usual avocations. One was that of a porter killed in coupling a train; another that of a plate-layer on the railway knocked down by a shunting train; a third, that of a miner killed in the pit. I have also shown that its presence with the Moon or on the horizon at the pre-natal epoch produces either abortive birth or infantile inanition....[31]

I trust that, with the information before them, students will not continue to deny the existence of Lilith, but will instead make diligent research as to its influence on human life. That there is ample room for an unknown factor in astrological considerations is obvious.

However, Wilson will not be silenced by this display of authority, and holds to his guns, contributing a further letter dated September 1st, 1902, in which he remarks in somewhat scathing didactic terms:[32]

I come now to Sepharial's article on the bogus satellite. The table of transits appeared in the Daily Mail *in 1898, if I remember rightly. If reliable they are interesting as some evidence of the existence of the supposed Vulcan. In this case the periodic time would produce an eclipse and not a transit when crossing the Sun's disk. It is impossible that these can be appearances of another satellite for the two reasons I gave before. Sepharial fancies that astronomers calculate the Moon's motion by a set of guesswork equations in which an unknown factor figures largely, and yet they can calculate to a second. Surely he must see the absurdity of such a statement!! Let me assure him that there is no unknown quantity in the Moon's equations and such a body as Lilith would make a great difference in the result. If he still doubts my statement, I make the following challenge. Let him tell how he fancies that astronomers calculate the Moon's place, and then I will reply by telling him the real method.*

Again I remind your readers that if Lilith really existed it could be found by large telescopes as easily as if it were luminous. Seen through them the whole sky is a background of luminous points and an opaque body intervening would show its position plainly. So Sepharial need not trouble to debate the question but may search the sky with a large telescope in the region where he says his pet is to be found.

Yours sincerely, J. W.

Sepharial, perhaps a little shaken by this open attack on his level of astronomical knowledge, and not desirous of a protracted further argument with Wilson, seems to retreat from his previously bold, forthright position at this juncture, opting instead merely to defer authority to Waltemath:[33]

As to Lilith, I have no other authority than the claims of Waltemath of Hamburg, and I see that records of observations by various people at different times fall into line with his theory of the existence of such a body whose synodical period is exactly as stated. As to its dimensions, density, etc., I have no information, neither have I any knowledge of Waltemath's claims upon our notice. I have merely pointed the facts.

The debate then falls silent; and there is no further mention of Lilith in the pages of *Modern Astrology* for the next 4¾ years.

Three More Dark Moons? The mysteries deepen!

After such a long silence in the debate over Dr. Waltemath's fancied satellite, the astronomical controversy is suddenly reignited in the summer of 1907 by an article in the *Daily Mail* said to have been entitled 'Evil Influence of a Dark Moon'. The article in question reports on a Canadian meteorologist who had expressed a belief that a second terrestrial Moon had an influence on weather patterns. It is quoted verbatim in the pages of *Modern Astrology* as part of a brief aside headed 'Have We a Second Moon?':[34]

> *EVIL INFLUENCE OF A DARK MOON. – Professor E. Stone Wiggins, of Ottawa, who has carefully studied the weather of Canada for twenty years, believes that the cold and wet summer which is afflicting all parts of the world is due to the existence of an unrecognised satellite of the earth, in other words, a second Moon.*
>
> *Professor Wiggins claims to have discovered this second Moon in 1882. In the New York Tribune on June 6th, 1884, he claimed the discovery, and declared that the Sun was eclipsed on May 16th, the sky being perfectly cloudless and the visible Moon being in another quarter of the heavens. Astronomers laughed at him, but Major A. B. Rogers, who was surveying the projected line of the Canadian Pacific Railway, in a letter to Sir Sandford Fleming, said: 'Noticing the obscurity of the Sun on May 16th, I called the attention of the whole party to the striking phenomenon, stating it could not be a regular eclipse, as it lacked several days of the new Moon.'*
>
> *Professor Wiggins describes his dark Moon as having an immense carbon atmosphere, in which the Sun develops little or no light. Several times in New Zealand and North America the existence for about twenty minutes of 'a green crescent Moon of the most brilliant yet delicate shade' has been reported.*
>
> *Professor Wiggins ascribes the bad weather to the extra pull exerted on the earth when the dark Moon and the visible Moon are in line and nearest the earth.*

It is worthy of historical note that the *Daily Mail* headline uses the term 'Dark Moon', and the hypothetical terrestrial satellite Lilith has since come to be known by astrologers as 'Dark Moon Lilith' although it does not correspond by its supposed orbital characteristics to the 'Dark Moon' claimed by Professor Wiggins!

The unsigned editorial comment in *Modern Astrology* on this article from the *Daily Mail*, probably written by Alan Leo, notes that the date of May 16th 1884 does not match that attributed to the conjunction of Lilith with the Sun that year, which was July 8th. A balance of scepticism with open-minded consideration regarding purported new astronomical discoveries is advocated:[35]

> *It is well always to maintain a healthy spirit of scepticism in regard to sensational or alleged discoveries, but that should not preclude one from*

giving due attention to new theories or recognising the significance of well-attested observations.

In the same issue, seemingly by coincidence, is published a letter by the Welsh seer Charubel[36] in which he claims to have received by visionary experience knowledge of the existence of a second terrestrial Moon at a distance of 60,000 miles, and one to which he attributes 'evil influence'. He adds:[37]

Relative to my discovery of another Moon, which revolves about this earth at a distance of some 60,000 miles, as the name Moon may be objected to I may describe it as of a globe-like shape, a conglomeration of what I call dead or defunct matter, all being engulfed in a darkness exceeding the limits of the most elastic fancy....

In the very next issue of Alan Leo's magazine, there is a reference to a mythological second terrestrial Moon in the context of a book review. The book in question, credited to the pseudonymous 'Respiro', is entitled *The Brotherhood of the New Life – An Epitome of the Work and Teaching of Thomas Lake Harris, XIII: The Secret of Satan, or the Origin of Evil and the Fall of Adam-Eve*.[38] According to the review, the book claims that:[39]

the aforetime Moon of Oriana was swept into our orbit and became a second, and evil, moon to our earth.

The habitual association by astrologers of any hypothetical second Moon with evil influence is further reinforced by this reference, obscure though it may be. However, in the very next issue, the pseudonymous author of the book refutes the direct connection made to the supposed Moon of Oriana by this review, correcting the record with the following decidedly esoteric account:[40]

In one point you are in error; the former moon of Oriana is not the 'black satellite', but our own 'common or garden moon'. The black satellite is the world-soul of Oriana, distorted by the evil of its (former) inhabitants. Now that they are destroyed, I conclude the world-soul of this lost orb has shrivelled up, and has attracted some matter in the course of ages.

Also in the October issue, the discussion of Lilith proper returns to the fore in a new article entitled 'The Earth's Second Moon',[41] which quotes from an old article in the *Evening News* the orbital elements attributed by Dr. Waltemath himself to his hypothetical satellite, including, among other attributes:

- mean synodic revolution, 177.00593 days
- mean sideric revolution, 119.227434 days
- draconitic revolution, 118.003952 days
- anomalistic revolution, 120.5915 days
- mean daily motion, 3.0194393012 degrees
- inclination, 2.5 degrees
- eccentricity, 0.1587
- mean distance from the Earth, 1,026,000 kilometres (2.67 times the distance of the Moon)
- mean apparent magnitude, 140 arc seconds
- diameter, 700 kilometres.

The editorial comment in *Modern Astrology* advises caution with regard to the acceptance of Waltemath's claims:

It seems remarkable that such precision should have been arrived at with such scanty data, and a certain reserve should, we think, be shown in accepting them, since the 'moon' has not received the endorsement of official astronomy, so far as we are aware. But neither has Astrology for the matter of that!

A further letter by Charubel about his envisioned Dark Moon appears in the same issue.[42]

In 1908, a correspondent named E. W. Berridge, MD writes in to observe the similarity in the characteristics of the three 'Dark Moons' distinct from Lilith that have recently been under discussion:[43]

I am comparing Charubel's discoveries concerning the 'dark moon' and the 'ruined planet' with the statements in Respiro's recent book, The Secret of Satan. They mutually confirm each other. Charubel's 'dark moon' seems identical with Harris's 'black satellite', and also seems the same as Wiggins' 'dark moon'.

It is interesting to observe Dr. Berridge's attempt to rationalise three of the four different 'dark Moons' to have been proposed down to one; but his letter also reinforces the observation that at this time the term 'dark Moon' was not mainly associated with Dr. Waltemath's hypothetical satellite named Lilith by Sepharial, but rather with other, still more obscure notions in discursive currency at the margins of astrology and other esoteric fields of thought.

Fading Interest: Alan Leo Marginalises Lilith

After this, I have been able to find no further mention of astronomical or astrological Lilith in the pages of *Modern Astrology* for the next six years, until the publication of a question by a correspondent:[44]

Has 'Lilith', the earth's satellite, any influence in a horoscope?

The editorial response to this is brief and simple, and evocative of a hardening of opinion by Alan Leo against the idea that Lilith is a body of astrological value, which perhaps explains its absence from discussion in the previous years:[45]

We have not been able to trace its influence.

A further, similar question arises and is printed three years later, thus:[46]

> ANOTHER MOON.- *As certain people are of the opinion that the earth possesses a second satellite of very small mass, I would like to ask whether there is any astrological evidence of the existence of such a body, and if so, what effect it has on a nativity.*

The editorial response elaborates slightly on the previous one but mainly refers back to the lengthy article in the September 1902 issue by Sepharial (who by this time has been writing for about ten years for a newer rival astrological magazine originally called *Old Moore's Monthly Messenger*).[47] The editor, whom we may presume to be Alan Leo, comes across as detached from Sepharial's point of view as expressed at that time, and as merely recording the whole episode as a matter of marginal historical interest:[48]

> *Such a body is said to have been discovered, and its orbit defined, by Dr. Waltemuth, of Hamburg. Nothing has been heard about it lately, so whether it has been abandoned by science we cannot say. As to its astrological influence, an article on the subject appeared in MODERN ASTROLOGY for September, 1902, p. 140, with a table of conjunctions by which its position could be determined for any date. In this article the opinion was expressed that its influence was violent, or at least malefic. We do not think anything further has been published, save one or two earlier articles in Coming Events....*

This is the last reference to Lilith or other Dark Moons found in *Modern Astrology* to the end of 1918, the year in which Sepharial's book *The Science of Foreknowledge* was published.

Alfred Pearce on Lilith: Total Disinterest

Aside from *Modern Astrology* and *Coming Events*, one other British astrological magazine whose publication was active in the period of Dr. Waltemath's claims was *Star Lore and Future Events*, edited by Alfred Pearce.[49]

It is notable that Pearce gives Waltemath's claims no attention at all at the time they are made, though he later refers quite separately to the mythology of Lilith in an article headed 'Kronos and Capricornus':[50]

> As for the Moon, when at the full the ancients accounted her fortunate; but when she was horned, they considered her so malignant that if a child were born under certain configurations at such a time it soon died, or if it lived, that it would be guilty of crimes as great as its temper was black.
>
> This caused the Hebrew wise-women to write upon the walls of their bedchambers these words: 'Let not Lilith enter here' – the demon Lilith (derived from Lilah, the night), being certain evil influences of the Moon....

These remarks would appear to exemplify the popularity among cultured astrologers of studying ancient and mediaeval mythology at this time, but without giving any credence to its application to an unproven hypothetical celestial body.

Pearce is nonetheless aware of some of the claims, as he answers a question received from a correspondent thus:[51]

> The 'dark satellite' of the earth, to which reference was made in our last number, is not likely to possess any influence over the health, character or destiny of mankind. There are many dark bodies revolving in the Solar System.

His revealed total indifference to all such claims is striking in contrast to the interest shown by Sepharial. And yet, Pearce's matter-of-fact statement that many unseen bodies are revolving in the solar system has proved remarkably prescient given the huge number of Transneptunian celestial bodies invisible to the naked eye that have been discovered since his lifetime, of which Pluto would be the first.

Early French sources on Dark Moon Lilith (selection)

In the emerging astrological scene of early-20th-century France, Dark Moon Lilith received some attention too, at least up to and including the 1930s, since which Black Moon Lilith *(see separate treatment below)* has progressively taken over in popularity there.

An important article on hypothetical planets in general, *Les Planètes Hypothétiques* by P. Genty, appears in the long-running French esoteric monthly *Le Voile d'Isis* (1926).[52] Herein, Genty gives a fairly comprehensive-seeming account of 24 recorded sightings of unknown objects passing in front of the Sun between 1618 and 1898 – ten more than Sepharial had previously cited.

In this article, Dark Moon Lilith is discussed alongside the equally unproven intramercurial hypothetical planet Vulcan, and the then still-undiscovered transneptunian planets, which Genty estimates as being two in number, giving them the names Pluton[53] and Proserpine.

Four years later, a lesser-known astrologer, Marcel Gama, has an article on only Dark Moon Lilith published in the monthly French-language astrological magazine *L'Astrosophie* (1930).[54] Despite using the term 'lune noire', which has later tended to be exclusively reserved in the French astrological literature as a label for Black Moon Lilith, the article clearly refers to Dark Moon Lilith.

Gama states that before considering the influence of Dark Moon Lilith, it is necessary to prove that it really exists. He cites the 24 reported citings of objects passing in front of the Sun previously published by P. Genty,[55] and refers back to Waltemath's original claims regarding its orbital elements and size.

At this time, reports Gama, research is still ongoing at Utrecht in the Netherlands into the astronomical and astrological study of Dark Moon Lilith. He also notes that an ephemeris both of Lilith and of Waltemath's tentatively claimed third Moon, known by then as Lulu, has been published by Foulsham in London.

Another French astrologer who wrote on Dark Moon Lilith was popular astrological and occult writer Robert Ambelain (1907–1997), whose 32-page pamphlet subtitled *Lilith, le second satellite de la terre* (1938),[56] which he co-authored jointly with J. Desmoulins, includes ephemerides for its monthly position from 1870 to 1937 inclusive, as well as delineations for its influence in the twelve signs and houses and in major aspect to each of the luminaries and planets as far as Neptune, and brief guidelines on its interpretation in transits and directions.[57] This publication thus exceeds the extent of Sepharial's instructions for the reading of the pretended second terrestrial satellite.

Later American Sources on Dark Moon Lilith (summary)

Sepharial's 1918 book *The Science of Foreknowledge* has played a significant role in sustaining later interest in Dark Moon Lilith among English-speaking astrologers, even though the hypothesis of the astronomical existence of

Waltemath's body is now largely discredited and was already, as previously seen, highly controversial in the immediate aftermath of the claims made.

In the original edition of her book *The 144 'Doors' of the Zodiac*,[58] Thyrza Escobar describes how having first read *The Science of Foreknowledge* in 1932 aroused her curiosity and excitement to see how Lilith fitted into the astrological charts she studied. She was also intrigued by Sepharial's claims of a third terrestrial Moon, subsequently known as Lulu, and asked her research partner J. Allen Jones Jr. to compute ephemerides for them both. These ephemerides are found printed in his supplementary pages at the back of her book.

In the later 20th century, there also emerged in the United States several substantial interpretative astrological books focused exclusively on Dark Moon Lilith, notably *The Dark Moon Lilith in Astrology* by Ivy Goldstein-Jacobson (1961); *Lilith Insight* by Mae R. Wilson-Ludlam (1979); *Interpreting Lilith* by Delphine Jay (1981); and *The Book of Lilith* by Barbara Koltuv, PhD (1986).

Part Two: Black Moon Lilith: first conceptualisations, 1935–1943

In and since the mid-20th century, far more attention has been given by French- and German-speaking astrologers to an entirely different concept for Lilith, one that is most frequently referred to in the French literature simply as *Lune Noire*, while in the English-language literature it is known more fully as *Black Moon Lilith*.

Though hair-splitting distinctions abound in published definitions, to all practical astrological intents and purposes, *Lune Noire* or *Black Moon Lilith* refers to the apogee of the lunar orbit about the Earth – which is to say, the position at which it reaches its greatest distance from the Earth in its cyclical orbit, projected onto the ecliptic.

Jeffrey Kotyk, an active historian of Asian religions whose PhD thesis was on Buddhist astrology, has recently drawn attention to some uses of the lunar apogee in an old Chinese astrological tradition. Thus far, however, I am unaware of any equivalent uses in the western astrological literature before its adoption in the mid-1930s by French astrologer Maurice Rougié,[59] who habitually wrote as Dom Néroman.

Probably the first published discussion by Rougié of the point now known as *Black Moon Lilith* appears in his book *Les Présages à la lumière des lois de l'évolution*,[60] whose full table of contents is announced in advance of the book's release in the number of his magazine *Sous le Ciel* for February 1937,[61] and includes a section 99 entitled *Lilith, le trouble sexuel*.

In this section of the book, Rougié indicates that despite not having mentioned it in his work before, he has been studying the lunar apogee he now calls Lilith for some time, declaring that according to his study, the reality of the factor that people call 'Lilith' is simply the empty focus of the lunar orbit, which in an astrological chart is identical to the lunar apogee:[62]

> *Je n'ai jamais publié des travaux auxquels je me suis livré sur ce facteur, la nécessité de cette publication ne s'étant jamais imposé, mais voici que, dans cette étude d'une évolution générale, garder le silence sur Lilith serait introduire une lacune; je dirai donc ce que j'ai établi ou cru établir sur cet élément de la thème astrologique, me réservant de publier assez prochainement, sous le titre «Les luminaires noirs», l'étude qui m'a donné ces résultats.*
>
> *Le facteur qu'on appelle Lilith, c'est tout simplement, d'après cette étude, le foyer vide de l'orbite lunaire; donc sur le thème il se confond avec l'apogée de la Lune.*

He goes on to criticise the existing ephemerides for Lilith, which are based on a motion of about 3 degrees per day that does not correspond to any astronomically recognised body. Declaring that he does not know the origin of these tables, which he regards as 'traditional' documents, he hypothesises that they have been distorted:

> *On notera au passage qu'il existe des tables de Lilith (dont j'ignore l'origine) déplaçant ce facteur à la vitesse de 3° par jour. Comme ce facteur n'est pas défini astronomiquement, étant présenté comme un élément irréel et mythique, il est permis de penser que les documents traditionnels indiquant une marche de trois degrés par jour ont été, comme à l'ordinaire, défigurés, et que le «jour» dont il s'agit est lunaire.*

He is clearly referring to published tables for what we now call Dark Moon Lilith, and it would seem from his own testimony that he has accessed them without knowing the history of how they have been calculated or on what basis. He therefore would appear to have only a vague notion of what they are referring to, and no inkling of the extremely recent origin of the 'tradition' they are based on. Instead, he seems to be labouring under the illusion that they may be a distortion of a much earlier astrological tradition surrounding the daily motion of Lilith, a distortion he believes he has corrected in his study.

On this basis, we can affirm that Rougié's belief is that there is only one true Lilith, which is in effect the lunar apogee, and also that he believes this to be an older astrological tradition that he has only now rediscovered after it was distorted, leading to incorrect tables. His continuing text supports this reading:[63]

> *Rappelons ici que le mot 'jour'signifie constamment 'tour zodiacal' dans les textes anciennes; si c'est le méridien qui fait le tour, on a le jour usuel de 24 heures; si c'est la Lune, on a la révolution tropique de cet astre, qui dure 27 j. ½; si c'est le Soleil, on a l'année tropique de cet astre....*
>
> *Ici nous avons souligné la vitesse du foyer vide est 3° par «jour lunaire», pour montrer que la donnée traditionnelle sur Lilith s'accorde avec la réalité astronomique, à condition d'interpréter correctement le mot 'jour'.*

In zodiacal terms, Rougié states the true motion of what we now call Black Moon Lilith as being 0.1113° per day, equivalent to just over 3° per tropical lunar revolution of 27½ days, or 40.65° per year.

In the following section 100, headed 'Le couple lunaire occulte', Rougié considers the empty focus of the lunar orbit and the Moon's Node together as part of a system. He notes that both are virtual points, but cautions his readers against translating 'virtual' as 'unreal', giving in support of this principle the example of the centre of gravity of a system, which is often found outside any actual matter and yet is extremely important because it obeys the material law of gravitation.

Likewise, the Node and Lilith are two virtual factors in the lunar mechanism of influence. Rougié continues by describing them jointly as a liaison officer, a transmitter of influx between an emission system and a reception system, or a telegraph wire:[64]

> *Et ne l'oublions pas, ce couple n'est pas un émetteur d'influx, mais un tramsmetteur, exactement un agent de liaison, le seul agent de liaison entre le système émetteur, composé du Soleil et de ses planètes, et le système récepteur figuré par le sensitif; tout ce qui agit passant nécessairement par l'agent de liaison, on voit l'extrême importance de ce couple occulte: c'est celle de l'unique fil télégraphique entre un poste perdu dans la brousse et le monde civilisé.*

He goes on to explore how Black Moon Lilith and the Moon's Nodes move relative to each other, noting that the direct motion of Lilith (40.65° per year) works in tandem with the retrograde motion of the Moon's Nodes (which he gives as 19.35° per year) to cause the two points to return to their original positions relative to each other once every six years.

The next major feature on Black Moon Lilith I've been able to trace in connection with Rougié's work is an article in the November, 1937 issue of *Sous le Ciel* by a student at the Collège Astrologique de France identified as 'H. Guichard, élève 174'.[65] Guichard's article is entitled 'Le Rôle de Lilith – la Féminité' ('The Role of Lilith – Femininity'). It is a study of the nativity and life history of a woman born at Saône-et-Loire on 29th June, 1908 at 1:30 a.m.. Noting the presence of Lilith in Leo on the cusp of the 5th House, Guichard interprets it as bringing the subject a certain pride in her loves, a pride perhaps stronger than her actual passion or feelings. He later adds that Lilith seems to indicate a tendency to a certain sensual selfishness, with amorous abuses.

Rougié provides further extensive discussion of Lilith in his later *Traité d'Astrologie Rationnelle*[66] (1943), his most comprehensive general astrological textbook, which is also divided into numerous numbered sections. While references to Lilith are scattered throughout this volume, Section 68 comprises his main exposition of it. On pp. 66–67, he reiterates his earlier teaching on the vital importance of the combined system comprised by Lilith and the Lunar Nodes. His remark that the 'ancients' called the empty foyer of the lunar orbit 'Lilith' suggests that he still believes at this time that he has recovered a pre-existing astrological tradition:[67]

> *Le système essentiel Soleil-Terre-Lune n'est pas limité à ces trois corps célestes; il comporte deux éléments orbitaux dont le rôle est capital: le premier est le foyer vide de l'orbite lunaire, que les Anciens nommaient la 'Lune Noire', or 'Lilith'; le second est l'axe des noeuds lunaires, qu'ils appelaient le 'Dragon'.*

His statement that the ancients called the lunar nodal axis the 'Dragon' is less controversial, as this is well documented in translated older texts. Rougié adds that by this time his College has published ephemerides of Lilith[68] spanning 1860 to 1980, as well as a table allowing the user to find its latitude, among other useful tables.

After expanding on his earlier theme of the role of Lilith and the lunar nodes as mediators, he writes more specifically on Lilith's influence:

> *Au point de vue influentiel, Lilith représente l'antenne passive X, et le Dragon représente l'antenne active I, de tout ce qui est soumis à l'influence lunaire sur notre Globe, c'est-à-dire de tout l'ensemble vivant, de ce que l'on a appelé la biosphère terrestre. Lilith, antenne passive, donne donc une tonalité bestiale à l'antenne qu'elle couvre; elle rend le gourmet glouton, elle alourdit le charme en «sex appeal», les plaisirs en orgies....*

While his explanation in terms of antennas of lunar influence is not entirely easy to follow, Néroman appears to be characterising Lilith as conferring a bestial or animal tone to everything it contacts, so that it would turn a gourmet into a glutton, and intensify charm into sex appeal, and pleasures into orgies!

Later treatments of Black Moon Lilith: selected references

Since Rougié's time, a considerable number of astrological volumes in the French language alone have been wholly or in substantial part dedicated to the interpretation of Black Moon Lilith. Limited space precludes the detailed discussion of these. Here, however, is a select chronologically ordered list of relevant titles available in the astrological library I manage, which is not an exhaustive collection of everything published on the subject, but I think by itself is enough to demonstrate what a major concern of French-speaking astrologers the astronomical point whose importance Rougié championed during and before the second world war has become:

- Hadès, *Soleil et Lune Noire, ou les États Angéliques et les Lieux Infernaux*, 3ᵉ Édition (Paris: Éditions Niclaus, 1984).[69]
- Joëlle de Gravelaine, *Le Retour de Lilith: La Lune Noire* (Paris: L'Espace Blue, 1985).
- Jacques Coutela, *La Lune Noire: Interprétation Complète de Lilith* (Guy Trédaniel, 1986).
- Marie-Thérèse des Longchamps, *Les Noeuds Lunaires et la Lune Noire en Astrologie* (Paris: Éditions Fernand Lanore, 1989).
- Jacqueline Aimé, *La Lune Noire: Un Monde Interdit* (Éditions du Rocher, 1995).
- Philippe Granger, *La Lune noire et les destins de Vénus: Astrologie Psychanalytique Séminaires 2 et 3* (Monaco: Éditions du Rocher, 1998).
- Louis Millat, R. Dautremont, Max Duval, *Lune Noire* (Paris: Éditions Traditionnelles, 1998).
- Laurence Larzul, *Comprendre la Lune Noire: Vous et Votre Inconscient* (Éditions Grancher, 2002).
- Renée Lebeuf, *La Lune Noire, interprète du noeud originel* (Paris: Éditions Dervy, 2005).

English-language sources on Black Moon Lilith were few and brief before the 21ˢᵗ century, but now include the following recent major work by M. Kelley Hunter:

- M. Kelley Hunter, *Black Moon Lilith* (Tempe, AZ: AFA, 2010).

Part Three:
Lilith as Asteroid – early research, 1980–2000 (summary)

In February 1927, astronomer Benjamin Jekhowsky, working at an observatory in Algiers, discovered a small asteroid. Provisionally designated 1927 CQ, it was subsequently given the name Lilith by its discoverer in honour of a then recently-deceased young French composer he admired, Marie-Juliette Olga Lili Boulanger.[70]

The diameter of asteroid 1181 Lilith is about 23 kilometres. To put this into perspective, the fourteen largest asteroids all have diameters of at least ten times this (230 km or more), so Jehowsky's discovery was relatively small within the field of known asteroids even at the time it was made. Were it not for the interesting mythological associations of its eventually given name, it would arguably have been unlikely to have attracted the attention of astrologers as compared with the numerous much larger ones.

In fact, there was a general lack of application by almost all astrologers in studying any of the asteroids before the 1970s; and then it was the first four discovered (Ceres, Pallas, Juno, and Vesta) that received by far the most attention,[71] ostensibly as a result of ephemerides having become available for them before any others, even though Juno is actually only the eleventh-largest known asteroid. It was chiefly not before the early 1980s that a more extensive range of asteroids began to be actively studied and integrated by astrologers at the cutting edge of research in this area.

Asteroid Lilith became available to astrologers for more widespread study with the publication of *Ephemeris of Lilith* by J. Lee Lehman and the late Al. H. Morrison in 1980[72] as part of a project he had suggested to her the previous year.[73]

Even as late as 1986, however, the recent research and traditions of the 1970s remained sufficiently influential for Ceres, Pallas, Vesta, and Juno to be granted exclusive attention among all the known asteroids in the first edition of Maritha Pottenger's book *Complete Horoscope Interpretation*.[74]

In the same year, when Demetra George's ground-breaking and highly successful book *Asteroid Goddesses* was published,[75] there were two chapters on each of Ceres, Pallas, Vesta, and Juno, and one for all other asteroids combined, these being collectively classified as 'The Minor Asteroids'.[76] Within the chapter on 'The Minor Asteroids', George gives one of the first substantial astrological treatments of asteroid Lilith.[77] It is also included in the ephemerides of the zodiacal longitudes of 16 asteroids from 1931–1990 at the back of the book.[78] Her astrological ideas on asteroid Lilith are further developed in her later book

Finding Our Way Through the Dark (1995),[79] in which she considers it together with Dark Moon Lilith and Black Moon Lilith (*see above*) as part of the triple manifestation of the 'Dark Goddess' Lilith.

Dr. Lehman groups Lilith with three other asteroids, Artemis, Diana, and Walkure, under the heading 'Moon and Sky Goddesses', in her *Ultimate Asteroid Book* (1988),[80] devoting three pages to the astrological discussion of Lilith in particular.[81]

Also in 1988, the first edition of Martha Lang-Wescott's book *Mechanics of the Future: Asteroids* was published. In the revised second edition of 1991, to hand, a page is devoted to general concepts around the asteroid Lilith, followed by six pages of delineations of its aspects to other chart factors, making it the most exhaustive and extensive astrological treatment of the asteroid published at the time.[82]

In 1993, the late Nona Gwynn Press's book *New Insights into Astrology*[83] first appeared. While wide-ranging in its focus on innovative astrological methods and ideas, this popular book includes a major chapter on asteroids, within which a dense page of text is devoted to asteroid 1181 Lilith.[84] Here, she proposes astrological associations for it that are distinct from those for Dark Moon Lilith.

In his 1995 book *Asteroid Name Encyclopedia*,[85] which is introduced by Demetra George, Jacob Schwartz gives potted histories of the discoveries of a very large number of asteroids, together with suggested associations of their names. The book's attempt to cover so many different asteroids limits the available space for each, and his entry on Lilith runs to just 15 lines.[86]

In her pamphlet *Black Moon Lilith* (2000),[87] M. Kelley Hunter, who has since written more extensively on the different Liliths, also briefly discusses asteroid Lilith, together with Dark Moon Lilith and the star Algol, which she declares also to have been called Lilith by Hebrew astronomers,[88] raising the total number of Lilith concepts under astrological consideration from three to four – not counting the three long-forgotten disparate Dark Moons we previously encountered in the pages of *Modern Astrology*.

Endnotes

[1] As recorded by P. Genty in his article 'Les Planètes Hypothétiques' within *Le Voile d'Isis* No. 73 (1926): p. 73. This article is discussed more fully below.

[2] The prominent English astrologer and occultist, whose real name was Walter Gorn-Old.

[3] First edition (Foulsham, 1918), chapter headed 'A Third Earth-Moon', pp. 48–49.

4 *Ibid.*
5 *Modern Astrology*, Vol. 4, No. 2 (March, 1898): p. 60.
6 *Modern Astrology*, Vol. 4, No. 4 (May, 1898): p. 151.
7 A false or unfounded report or story.
8 An unknown regular reader, not to be confused with James Wilson (author of a notable *Dictionary of Astrology* in 1819), who was long gone from the world.
9 *Modern Astrology*, Vol. 5, No. 1 (August, 1898): pp. 26–27.
10 *Coming Events* (April, 1898): pp. 241–46.
11 *Ibid.*, p. 242.
12 *The Science of Foreknowledge* (1918): pp. 39–45.
13 *Coming Events* (May, 1898): pp. 280–81.
14 *Ibid.*, p. 282.
15 *Op. cit.*, pp. 46–49.
16 *Coming Events* (May, 1898): pp. 294–95.
17 *Coming Events* (June, 1898): pp. 354–56.
18 *Ibid.*, p. 355.
19 *Op. cit.*, pp. 50–57.
20 *Coming Events* (September, 1898): p. 458.
21 The final issue of Volume 4 is dated September 1900.
22 The magazine continued through a fifth year, and advertising in other astrological magazines suggest that it remained in publication for some months beyond that, but the later issues are not to hand.
23 *Modern Astrology*, Vol. XI, No. 1 (January, 1902): p. 27.
24 *Modern Astrology*, Vol. XI, No. 2 (February, 1902): p. 84.
25 *Ibid.*, p. 87.
26 *Modern Astrology*, Vol. XI, No. 3 (March, 1902): p. 174.
27 *Modern Astrology*, Vol. XI, No. 4 (April, 1902): p. 224.
28 See for example *Modern Astrology*, Vol. XII, No. 1 (July, 1902): p. 48.
29 *Modern Astrology*, Vol. XII, No. 3 (September, 1902): pp. 140–45.
30 This may be a misspelled reference to the German astronomer Johann Karl Burckhardt (1773–1825), said to have developed lunar theory and produced a new set of tables for lunar motion.
31 Exhaustion or lack of vitality or vigour, more commonly attributed to malnutrition.
32 *Modern Astrology*, Vol. II, No. 4 (October, 1902): p. 199.
33 *Modern Astrology*, Vol. XII, No. 5 (November, 1902): pp. 255–56.
34 *Modern Astrology*, New Series Vol. IV, No. 8 (August, 1907): p. 354.
35 *Ibid.*
36 Best known by astrologers for his authorship of a set of degree symbols said to have been obtained by channelling, in *The Degrees of the Zodiac Symbolised*, 1898.
37 *Modern Astrology*, New Series Vol. IV, No. 8 (August, 1907): p. 383.

38 Third Edition (Glasgow: C. W. Pearce and Co., 1907).
39 *Modern Astrology*, New Series Vol. IV, No. 9 (September, 1907): p. 426
40 *Modern Astrology*, New Series Vol. IV, No. 10 (October, 1907): p. 492.
41 *Modern Astrology*, New Series Vol. IV, No. 10 (October, 1907): pp. 475–76.
42 *Ibid.*, pp. 478–79.
43 *Modern Astrology*, New Series Vol. V, No. 2 (March, 1908): pp. 94–95.
44 *Modern Astrology*, New Series Vol. XI, No. 6 (June, 1914): p. 270.
45 *Ibid.*, p. 271.
46 *Modern Astrology*, New Series Vol. XIV, No. 6 (June, 1917): p. 184.
47 October 1907 to September 1914; subsequently renamed *The British Journal of Astrology*.
48 *Ibid.*
49 1897–1903.
50 *Star Lore and Future Events*, Vol. II, No. 19 (July, 1898): p. 109.
51 *Star Lore and Future Events*, Vol. II, No. 16 (April, 1898): p. 64.
52 *Le Voile D'Isis*, 31ᵉ Année, No. 73, *Second Numéro Spécial consacré à l'Astrologie* (1926): pp. 72–73.
53 French for 'Pluto'. Genty was one of several astrologers to predict the name Pluto years before its discovery and actual naming.
54 Marcel Gama, '"Lilith" – La Lune Noire', in *l'Astrosophie* Vol. III, No. 3 (21 mai 1930): pp. 105–13.
55 In *Le Voile d'Isis*, 31ᵉ Année, No. 73, *Second Numéro Spécial consacré à l'Astrologie* (1926): pp. 72–73.
56 J. Desmoulins; Robert Ambelain, *Éléments d'Astrologie Scientifique: Lilith, le second satellite de la terre* (Paris: Coutrai / Niclaus, 1938).
57 The co-authors also quote extensively from an unsigned editorial piece on Lilith in the French astrological magazine *Le Grand Nostradamus*, Septembre 1934, which is found at pp. 37–42 of that issue and is presumed to have been penned by its editor, Maurice Privat.
58 *The 144 'Doors of the Zodiac': the Dwad Technique* (Golden Seal Research Headquarters, 1974), pp. 49–52.
59 The real name of the prolific French astrological and esoteric writer best known for his pen-name Dom Néroman, although this was adapted from his earlier choice of Dom Nécroman. By profession, Rougié was a civil engineer with particular expertise in mining before his astrological work came to predominate.
60 Dom Néroman, *Les Présages à la lumière des lois de l'évolution* (Paris: Éditions Sous-le-Ciel, 1937), pp. 199–203.
61 *Sous le Ciel*, No. 10 (Février 1937): pp. 37–38.
62 *Les Présages à la lumière des lois de l'évolution*, p. 199.
63 *Ibid.*, pp. 199–200.

64 *Ibid.*, p. 201.
65 *Sous le Ciel* No. 18 (Novembre 1937): pp. 189–91.
66 D. Néroman, *Traité d'Astrologie Rationnelle* (Paris: Éditions Sous le Ciel, 1943).
67 *Ibid.*, p. 66.
68 Meaning Black Moon Lilith.
69 The original edition dates back to 1978 and the second edition to 1981.
70 Boulanger lived from 1893 to 1918, tragically succumbing at the age of just 24 to tuberculosis.
71 See for example Esther V. Leinbach, *Planets and Asteroids*, 1974; 2nd edition, 1976; and Emma Belle Donath, *Asteroids in the Birthchart*, 1976; 2nd edition, 1979.
72 A scarce book, said to have been published by CAO Times, 1980.
73 As disclosed in J. Lee Lehman, *The Ultimate Asteroid Book* (Whitford Press, 1988), p. [7].
74 Maritha Pottenger, *Complete Horoscope Interpretation* (ACS Publications, 1986).
75 Demetra George and Douglas Bloch, *Asteroid Goddesses* (ACS Publications, 1986).
76 *Ibid.*, pp. 185-202.
77 *Ibid.*, pp. 189–90.
78 *Ibid.*, pp. 301–20.
79 Demetra George, *Finding Our Way Through the Dark: the Astrology of the Dark Goddess Mysteries* (ACS Publications, 1995), pp. 135–36; 140.
80 *Op. cit.*, pp. 73–80.
81 *Ibid.*, pp. 76–78.
82 *Op. cit.*, pp. 178–85.
83 Nona Gwynn Press, *New Insights into Astrology* (ACS Publications, 1993).
84 *Ibid.*, pp. 193–94.
85 Jacob Schwartz, *Asteroid Name Encyclopedia* (Llewellyn Publications, 1995).
86 *Ibid.*, p. 135.
87 M. Kelley Hunter, *Black Moon Lilith* (ACS Publications, 2000).
88 *Op. cit.*, p. 6.

Index...

Abū Ma'Shar 28, 29, 30, 37
Ackroyd, John 228, 232
Adams, Evangeline 124, 125, 129
Adams, John Couch 224
Addey, John 63, 84, 91, 95–99, 102
Aeschylus 205, 206
Agrippa, Heinrich Cornelius 115–16
Ajacchus (pseudonym) 161
al-Bîrūnî 34, 35, 36, 42, 47, 65, 66
Aldrich, Elizabeth 241
Al-Khayyat, Abu 'Ali 26
Allan, William Frederick. *See* Leo, Alan
al-Qabîsî 30, 31
Al-Rijāl 31–35, 47, 116
Ambelain, Robert 270
Antiochus 8, 17
Aphorel. *See* Lacey, Frederick
Aspects
  Bilin 93
  biquincunx 70
  biquintile 66, 67, 68, 69, 70, 79, 81, 86, 91
  biseptile 86
  conjunction 63, 66, 67, 70, 73, 74, 77, 79, 81, 83, 85, 90, 91, 92, 97, 100, 186, 189, 195, 206, 209, 211, 224, 227, 257, 260, 263, 265
  decile 67, 68, 69, 71, 72, 85, 86, 92, 93, 96, 98
  inconjunct 64, 82

nonagon 85, 92
novile 85, 87, 90, 92, 98
octile 67, 78, 80, 83
opposition 39, 47, 63, 65, 66, 67, 70, 74, 77, 79, 81, 82, 83, 90, 91, 95, 96, 97, 190, 194, 195, 197, 199, 200, 206, 207, 227, 260
quadrasextile 69. *See also* quincunx
quartile 63, 65, 66, 67, 70, 73, 74, 77, 79, 82, 91, 187, 190, 194, 195, 196. *See also* square
quartisextile 88, 89, 92, 93
quarti-square 85
quincunx 64, 67, 68, 69, 70, 71, 72, 78, 82, 90, 91, 97, 99
quindecile 67, 68, 69, 71, 72, 78, 86, 94, 97
quintile 66, 67, 68, 69, 70, 71, 72, 73, 78, 79, 80, 81, 84, 86, 87, 90, 91, 93, 94, 97, 98, 102
semi-quadrate 68, 69
semi-quartile 69, 70. *See* semi-square
semi-quincunx 70
semiquintile 68. *See also* decile
semi-sextile 64, 67, 68, 69, 70, 71, 72, 77, 78, 79, 80, 81, 82, 83, 86, 90, 91, 97, 102
semi-square 66, 67, 70, 71, 77, 72, 78, 79, 81,
82, 83, 84, 90, 91, 96, 97, 102
septile 85–87, 92, 97, 102
sesquiquadrate 66, 68, 69, 71, 72, 77, 78, 79, 81, 82, 83, 84, 90, 91, 96, 97, 188, 189, 190, 206, 207, 211
sesquiquartile 66, 70
sesquiquintile 68, 69. *See also* tridecile
sextile 63, 65, 66, 67, 70, 74, 75, 77, 78, 79, 81, 82, 83, 90, 91, 94, 97, 206, 207, 208
sexti-sextile 91
square 66, 77, 78, 81, 83, 86, 90, 97, 118, 187, 189, 199, 206, 207, 208, 211, 212
Taoaspekt (Tao) 89, 93, 94
tridecile (trecile) 67, 68, 69, 70, 71, 72, 85, 86, 92, 93, 96
trigintasextile 91
Trilin 89, 93
trine 63, 65, 66, 67, 70, 73, 74, 75, 77, 79, 81, 82, 83, 90, 91, 97, 190, 194, 195, 206, 207, 208
trioctile 67, 97
tri-septile 86
undecaquartisextile. *See Taoaspekt*
vigintile 67, 68, 69, 71, 72, 78, 86, 98
vigintiquartile 88
Baudot, Mabel 252

Benjamine, Elbert 132–34
Bennett, Sidney. *See* Wynn
Blavatsky, H. P. 137, 144, 238
Bobrick, Benson 135–37
Bode, Johann 182, 183
Bonatti, Guido 28, 38, 39, 40, 66
Boxer, Alexander 138
Bragdon, O. D. 154, 155
Brandler-Pracht, Karl 85, 90, 92
Brunhübner, Fritz 253
Burgoyne, Thomas H. 123, 126, 230, 232
Butler, Hiram Erastus 117, 118, 119, 120, 121, 122, 123, 124, 125, 126, 131, 132, 138, 141, 144, 145
Campbell, J. T. 228, 229, 232
Campion, Nicholas xiii, xiv, 137, 138
Carroll, Frances 162
Carter, Charles E. O. 89, 90, 95, 250, 251
Caslant, E. 239, 240, 241
Chaney, W. H. 66, 70, 71, 73, 74, 75, 78, 79, 226
Charubel 134, 266, 267
Clancy, Paul 154, 169, 170, 171, 172, 175, 176
Colville, W. J. 125, 126, 127, 145
Cross, Robert T. 75, 78–83, 134, 156
Dariot, Claude 28, 42, 43, 46, 50, 66
Desmoulins, J. 270
Dodson, J. 82, 86
Dorotheus 9, 12, 13, 14
Drew, Marion Meyer 164, 165, 169, 174, 175

Dykes, Benjamin N. 25, 27, 29, 38, 40
Emley, Alan M. 131
Farnell, Kim xviii, 113, 114, 115, 153, 165, 167, 169, 172
Firmicus Maternus, Julius 8, 9, 11, 12, 17, 20, 22, 24, 47
Fomalhaut 235–37, 240, 242, 243
Gadbury, John 48, 49, 50
Gama, Marcel 270
Gauquelin, Françoise 95
Gauquelin, Michel 95, 98
Genty, P. 239, 270
George, Demetra 276, 277
George, Llewellyn 71–72, 124, 243–44, 246–47, 252
Glahn, A. Frank 87–89, 92, 93, 95
Goodman, Linda 117, 130
Grant, Russell 152
Green, H. S. 78, 80, 81, 83, 134, 143, 257
Gross, J. P. 247
Guichard, H. 274
Haly Abenragel. *See* Al-Rijāl
Hand, Robert 41
Hephaestio of Thebes 4, 22, 23, 24, 26
Herschel, William 182
Heydon, C., Jun., 184–85
Holden, James Herschel 3, 6, 46, 98, 228
Houlding, Deborah xvii, 10
Hugo of Santalla 24
Hunter, M. Kelley 275, 277
Ibn Ezra 36, 37
Indagine, Johannes ab (Johannes von Hagen) 114, 116

Jekhowsky, Benjamin 276
John of Seville 29, 30
Johnson, Margaret 113
Jones, Marc Edmund 134
Jung, C. G. 246, 253
Kepler, Johannes xviii, 63, 66–72, 74, 77–87, 91–93, 94, 97, 159, 209
Kirk, Eleanor 125, 126, 127, 145
Koch, Walter 68, 91, 92, 93, 94
Kotyk, Jeffrey 271
Krafft, Karl-Ernst 98
Lacey, Frederick 75, 76, 77, 78, 79, 80, 81, 230
Lang-Wescott, Martha 277
Latham, John 118
Lehman, J. Lee xvi, 82, 276, 277
Leo, Alan xiii, 3, 10, 50, 54, 75, 76, 78–83, 122, 123, 131, 135–40, 142–45, 230, 239, 257, 265, 266, 268
Leo, Bessie 248
Leopold of Austria 10, 28, 40, 43
Le Verrier, Urban 224
Lewi, Grant 122, 128, 131
Liber Hermetis 10, 24
Lilly, William 44, 46, 48, 50, 64–66, 68, 69, 71, 73, 75–77, 80, 118, 158, 211
Lowell, Percival 235, 238, 249
Lyndoe, Edward 128, 171, 172, 174, 175, 176
Lyon, Karleen S. 248
Macnaughton, Duncan 235
Manilius, Marcus 3, 4, 9, 10, 11, 12, 13, 17, 19, 21, 37
Masha'Allah 24, 25, 26, 37

McCaffery, Ellen 136, 137
McCann, Maurice xvii,
   65, 66, 78, 79
Merton, Holmes Whittier
   123
Michigan Astrological
   Papyrus 6, 17, 18, 19
Morin de Villefranche,
   Jean-Baptiste 10, 46,
   47, 48, 54
Morrison, Al. H. 276
Morrison, Richard 69, 72,
   73–76, 79, 81–83, 85, 90,
   204–11
Muir, Ada 128, 134
Naylor, R. H. xiii, 154,
   171–76
Nemo (pseud.) 229, 230,
   232
Néroman, Dom. *See*
   Rougié, Maurice
Nicollaud, Abbé.
   See Fomalhaut
North, J. D. 5
Old, Walter Gorn.
   See Sepharial
Omar of Tiberias 25
Orger, Thomas 187
Ormsby, Frank Earl 122–23
Ovason, David 136
Oxley, Thomas 203
Pagan, C. Hilda 128
Pagan, E. H. C. 249
Pagan, Isabelle M. 124,
   236, 237, 238, 249, 254
Parchment, S. R. 131
Parkes, David 212, 213, 214
Paulus Alexandrinus 12,
   13, 17, 20, 21, 23, 31, 47
Pearce, Alfred J. 80, 81, 82,
   83, 227, 232, 269
Placido de Titus 185
Porphyry 5, 19

Powley, P. (editor) 155,
   174, 228
Press, Nona Gwynn 277
Ptolemy 4, 15, 16, 22, 35, 63,
   64, 69, 181, 184, 193, 199,
   200, 228, 231, 232
Pynson, Richard 113
Raphael I. *See* Smith,
   Robert Cross
Raphael VI. *See* Cross,
   Robert T.
Rhetorius 10, 12, 13, 17, 22,
   23, 24, 27, 47
Ring, Thomas 93, 94
Rolt-Wheeler, Francis 241
Rougié, Maurice 271–75
Rudhyar, Dane xiii, 128,
   134, 154, 176
Ruyl, Beatrice Baxter 128
"Sagittarius" 230, 232
Sahl 27, 28, 31
Schöner, Johann 10, 41, 42
Sepharial 83, 84, 132, 133,
   134, 239, 248, 256–64,
   267–71
Shemaya, Ebn. *See* Parkes,
   David
Sibly, Ebenezer 184, 185
Sibly, Manoah 185
Sieggrün, Friedrich 88
Simmonite, W. J. 66, 85,
   92, 228
Smith, Robert Cross 75,
   115, 116, 194, 200–4, 225
Spadacine, Sinibal de 113
Stella, Rupertus 203
Swift, P. J. 187
Thierens, A. E. 238–39, 248
Thoresby, Frederick 247
Thrasyllus 5, 6, 7, 8, 12, 13,
   28, 47
Tompkins, Sue 98, 99
Tyl, Noel 94

Valens, Vettius 9, 12, 13, 15,
   16, 17, 20, 23, 24, 25, 28,
   34, 40, 47
Varley, John 210
Vehlow, Johannes 84
von Elmensberg, K. W. 88,
   89, 92, 93, 94, 95
Walker, Charlotte Abell
   127, 130
Wallace, James Clyde 167,
   168
Waltemath, Georges
   256–58, 260, 262–63,
   264, 266–67, 269–71
Wemyss, Maurice. *See*
   Macnaughton, Duncan
Weston, L. H. 242–44
White, Frederick 122
Whitehead, Willis F. 122
White, Thomas 187
Wiggins, E. Stone 265, 267
Wilde, George 82, 85–87,
   93, 97
Wilson, James 68, 69, 72,
   118, 158, 182, 192, 193, 201
Wilson, J. 261, 263, 264
Witte, Alfred 88
Worsdale Jr., John 185
Worsdale Sr., John 185
Wrey, A. M. 238, 239
Wynn 165–67, 169, 171,
   172, 175
Zadkiel 69, 72, 76, 79, 81,
   118, 137, 156, 204, 210,
   226. *See* Morrison,
   Richard
Zahel. *See* Sahl
Zain, C. C. *See*
   Benjamine, Elbert
Zoller, Robert 24

www.ingramcontent.com/pod-product-compliance
Lightning Source LLC
Chambersburg PA
CBHW030512080526
44586CB00011B/153